OKANAGAN

MW01224573

Vít Smetana

In the Shadow of Munich
British Policy towards Czechoslovakia
from the Endorsement to the Renunciation
of the Munich Agreement
(1938–1942)

VÍT SMETANA

IN THE SHADOW OF MUNICH
British Policy towards Czechoslovakia
from the Endorsement to the Renunciation
of the Munich Agreement
(1938–1942)

Charles University in Prague
Karolinum Press 2008

Reviewed by prof. JUDr. Jan Kuklík, DrSc.
PhDr. Petr Mareš, CSc.

ISBN 978-80-246-1373-4

CONTENTS

ACKNOWLEDGEMENTS

This book could never have been written without the kind help of many people and institutions. My greatest thanks go to the Open Society Institute in Prague and the Foreign and Commonwealth Office in London, as well as to the British government, which provided two generous scholarships to finance my studies and research in Oxford – the *OSI-FCO/Chevening Scholarship Scheme*, 1997-1998, and the *Scatcherd Scholarship*, 2000-2003. Equally important was the grant No. KJB8063405 of the Grant Agency of the Academy of Sciences of the Czech Republic 'Czechoslovak-British relations 1938-1948' that I held in the years 2004-2006.

At the University of Oxford I was lucky to be supervised by Dr. Anne Deighton to whom I owe much for her informal lectures in academic writing, her kind assistance in various other respects and willingness to help with virtually anything at any time. She also introduced me to Prof. R. A. C. Parker. Meeting this personality of British academic life was yet another good fortune of my stay in Oxford. I recall the numerous conversations that we had during our walks along the Thames and elsewhere or afternoons spent at the Parkers' marvellous house in Iffley whose hospitality was always there for me and for my wife. It was a real pleasure to spend four unforgettable days with the Parkers in Prague in October 1998 and to watch their sincere admiration for historical and cultural beauties of the Czech capital. Alastair Parker taught me much about British political life in the 1930s and 1940s and, indeed, about British history and culture in general. I was sincerely grieved to learn in the spring of 2001 that Alastair Parker had died. I will always treasure those four years of our friendship.

I am also grateful to both of my supervisors at the Institute of International Studies, Faculty of Social Sciences, Charles University in Prague, to Prof. Vladimír Nálevka, for his support and encouragement he has always had for me and to Dr. Petr Mareš. The latter influenced

(9)

me most of all in my gradually growing interest in modern history of international relations. I found his lectures that I was attending in the 1990s to be really first class. I also recognised in him a kind and witty man with whom I always enjoy speaking not only about history. The same applies to two other teachers of mine, Dr. Jiří Rak and Doc. Jan P. Kučera, who for years have been struggling to raise my cultural and cultural-historical horizons. In October 1998 Dr. Jaroslav Hrbek, another one of my favourite lecturers, invited me to join him in the newly set-up Department of the Second World War History at the Institute of Contemporary History, Academy of Sciences of the Czech Republic in Prague. I have always been grateful for his offer since in this institution directed by Dr. Oldřich Tůma I found many kind and highly educated people as well as a friendly atmosphere and generally ideal conditions for my work. I am happy to say that this remains so as I am writing these lines. I am indebted to both Dr. Jaroslav Hrbek and Dr. Stanislav Kokoška for respecting my professional interests and letting me do research and study, both at home and abroad, according to personal wishes and preferences.

I have always profited from discussing various aspects of modern history with several colleagues of mine. This applies especially to Doc. Jaroslav Kučera, Prof. Jan Kuklík Jr., Prof. Jiří Pešek, Dr. Michal Kopeček, Dr. Petr Hofman or Dr. Milan Drápala. With Dr. Jiří Ellinger I share a similar professional interest; his excellent doctoral thesis about Neville Chamberlain and British foreign policy served as a vitally important inspiration for me in the difficult stages of writing this book.

I am most grateful to Hana Velecká, my former colleague at the Institute of Contemporary History, for providing me with numerous photocopies of archival documents, especially from the 'Beneš Archive' deposited in the Archive of the T. G. Masaryk Institute in Prague. Dr. Pavel Šrámek was kind enough to send me photocopies of two important documents relating to the failed efforts to sell some Czechoslovak military material to Britain prior to 15 March 1939. Prof. Vilém Prečan lent me microfilms of the Foreign Office 371 series concerning Czechoslovakia in 1940 that he had bought in the Public Record Office in London from one of his grants. I would also like to thank many archivists in several archives in four countries for their help and advice.

Many other people deserve a mention here for helping me during my work. Lucia Faltin, Angus Thomson, Vladimír Bilčík, Larissa Douglass,

Jan Stráský Jr., Hana Bygraves, Anita Grmelová, Monika Studená, Meda Mládková, and Tomáš Kočiš with his wife Zuzana kindly offered me accommodation, at various stages of my research, in Cambridge, Oxford, London, Birmingham, Washington, D.C. and Moscow. On many occasions in their flat in Brussels Doc. Petr Luňák with his wife Karin provided a hospitable refuge and pleasant company for me and my family on our ways to and from Britain. I am equally grateful to my brother Martin and his wife Karolína who have for years been providing their flat in Jablonec nad Nisou as an ideal base-camp for our common exploring the beauties of north-Bohemian mountains and as a natural centre of various sport activities – an almost indispensable supplement to my research and writing.

Vladimír Bilčík deserves my thanks for struggling bravely with the peculiarities of my English. And I am very grateful to the publishing house Karolinum, headed by Dr. Jaroslav Jirsa, for the interest to publish this book in English.

At the end I would like to thank my wife Veronika whose support and understanding has always been of the greatest importance for me. Our three children, Julie, Prokop and Sára, on their part, have been reminding me every day that some aspects of human life are much more important than academic career.

And my loving memories go to my parents who, sadly and tragically, died too young to see much of not only my academic progress.

Aims and methodology

To these days very few topics in Czech history remain as sensitive as the events of September 1938. This book focuses on the processes that ensued and were intrinsically connected with Munich. Great Britain played a significant role in them. It can be said that never has the Czech or Czechoslovak history been so much entangled with the British one as in the period between Munich and the end of the Second World War. Indeed, for five years free Czechoslovakia found refuge in Britain. At the same time very few topics in Czech *historiography* have been so systematically distorted by most of the previous writing as British policy towards Czechoslovakia during the period. Numerous myths and stereotypes about British perfidy, built on the British part in Munich and alleged Great Powers' deal on the spheres of influence (in its extreme case reached at the Yalta Conference in February 1945[1]), are so deeply rooted that they often serve as an automatic explanation of every single step that the British made and that at the same time did not meet with a complete agreement on the Czechoslovak part. 'Munich policy' and 'spheres of influence' are thus until now the two principal terms labelling British policy during World War II in by no means a negligible part of Czech historiography. Although Western historians dealing with British foreign policy or Great Power diplomacy of the late 1930s and early 1940s are usually free from this sort of prejudices, they often approach the topic with just a limited knowledge of Czechoslovak realities, which again often results in a distorted picture of the relationship between Czechoslovakia on the one hand and Great Britain on the other hand.

1) On this topic see: Smetana, Vít, Sféry vlivu a Československo: oběť, nebo spoluarchitekt? [Spheres of influence and Czechoslovakia: victim or co-architect], In: *Československo na rozhraní dvou epoch nesvobody*, eds. Z. Kokošková – J. Kocian – S. Kokoška, Praha, Národní archiv – Ústav pro soudobé dějiny AV ČR 2005, pp. 58–65.

I have been researching British primary sources, both archival and edited ones, for more than a decade. First I focused on Anglo-Soviet relations in the period of the Nazi-Soviet co-operation, later on the Anglo-Czechoslovak relationship from Munich to the Communist takeover in 1948. This research has only rarely confirmed what I read before about the period in most of the Czech books. Thus, in my historical writing I have so far striven to dispel those frequent legends and stereotyping surrounding this era and have offered alternative explanations of several contentious events and episodes, whether it was the question of the Munich guarantee in 1938–1939, the 'Czech gold scandal' in the spring of 1939, the Anglo-German financial negotiations about the Czechoslovak deposits in London in the summer of that year, the repercussions of Munich in foreign policy negotiations during the Second World War, British help for the resistance movement in Czechoslovakia at the end of the war, or, more generally, the mutual relationship between Beneš and the British officials throughout the war.[2] This book is my first attempt to out-root hitherto prevailing stereotypes and pre-conceived views entirely in a larger text that systematically covers a longer period.

Both the chronological and the thematic span, however, have certain limits. My focus is restricted to the period from Munich to its renunciation by the British government in 1942. The reason is practical: the close and in some respects intimate nature of the Anglo-Czechoslovak relationship resulted, amongst other things, in an enormous quantity of

2) Smetana, Vít, Británie a československé zlato. 'Case study' britského appeasementu? [Great Britain and the Czechoslovak gold: A case study of British appeasement?], *Soudobé dějiny* [Contemporary history], Prague, Vol. 8, 2001, No. 4, pp. 621–658; Idem, Nevyřízené účty. Problém československých aktiv v britských bankách a snahy britské administrativy o jeho řešení po 15. březnu 1939 [Accounts to be dealt with. The problem of Czechoslovak assets in British banks and British Government's attempts at its settlement after 15 March 1939], *Český časopis historický* [Czech historical journal], Prague, Vol. 102, 2004, No. 3, pp. 521–551; Idem, Ozvěny Mnichova v zahraničněpolitických jednáních za 2. světové války [The echoes of Munich in foreign policy negotiations during World War II], In: *Mnichovská dohoda. Cesta k destrukci demokracie v Evropě* [Munich agreement. The way to destruction of democracy in Europe], ed. J. Němeček, Praha, Karolinum 2004, pp. 145–163; Idem, Mise Plukovníka Perkinse v kontextu britské politiky vůči Československu a pomoci jeho odbojovému hnutí na sklonku 2. světové války [Colonel Perkins' mission in the context of British policy towards Czechoslovakia and help for its resistance movement towards the end of the Second World War], *Historie a vojenství* [History and military], Prague, Vol. 50, 2001, No. 3, pp. 692–736; Idem, Beneš a Britové za druhé světové války [Beneš and the British during the Second World War], In: *Na pozvání Masarykova ústavu* [At the invitation of The Masaryk Institute], Prague, Masarykův ústav AV ČR 2004, pp. 73–86.

documentation on various important affairs. I decided to process and analyse the relevant material carefully and cover just a shorter period of time, rather than to produce a superficial essay based on a fragmentary documentation.

There are also several limitations with respect to the chosen topic. The book centres on political, economic and strategic issues present in the Anglo-Czechoslovak relationship. I did not for example follow in detail the ups and downs of the mutual military co-operation, though it also provides an important background. The common thread of the topics to which the book pays attention can be found in the consequences, repercussions and 'undoing' of Munich.

Although my interest lies in the Anglo-Czechoslovak relationship, the main focus of the book is on British policy. The reason is connected with the chosen methodology. This is a study in *international history*. Some authors point out – and I agree – that this discipline 'has superseded the old specialisation of diplomatic history by paying far more attention to the non-governmental forces which cross boundaries and in many respects shape the crucial domestic environment of foreign policy'.[3] Indeed, as long as 35 years ago John Lewis Gaddis postulated the assumption 'that foreign policy is the product of external and internal influences, as perceived by officials responsible for its formulation.[4] To achieve this, it is necessary to examine 'traditional' sources, as well as parliamentary debates and, at least to some degree, also contemporary press. Thus the domestic dimension of foreign policy, the influence of intellectuals and of public opinion, as well as of such phenomena as psychological prejudices or feelings of guilt or injustice (such as Munich in the case of my topic), offers much fuller picture of this subject.

The reason for focusing primarily on British policy is twofold. Firstly, one of the principal points of my interest is the process of change of British foreign policy in 1939 and the way it influenced British dealings with Czechoslovakia. At that time, however, there was no partner on the Czechoslovak side as the exile representation abroad only started to

3) Hill, Christopher, *Cabinet Decisions on Foreign Policy. The British Experience. October 1938 – June 1941*, Cambridge, Cambridge University Press 1991, p. 4. More specifically his study History and International Relations, In: Steve Smith (ed.), *International Relations: British and American Perspectives*, Oxford, Basil Blackwell 1985.
4) Gaddis, John Lewis, *The United States and the Origins of the Cold War 1941–1947*, 2nd edition (first published in 1972), New York, Columbia University Press 2000, Preface from May 1971 – p. xiv.

emerge in late summer of 1939. Secondly, I have not had the ambition to analyse the methods whereby Czechoslovak foreign policy was being enacted in particular stages between 1938 and 1942. It would demand a separate study to cover systematically the process of this dramatic change. However, it is clear that from 1940 onwards Edvard Beneš together with a small bunch of his collaborators dominated the foreign policy field, while the government and the State Council entered it merely occasionally. Nevertheless, the Czechoslovak role is certainly not neglected. On the contrary, I pay attention especially to the resonance of British policy amongst Czechoslovak politicians in exile.

Central to this book is to find out the impact of crucial Czechoslovak events upon important British decisions. More generally: to what extent did Czechoslovakia matter in British foreign policy throughout the period? And was there any 'policy' towards this country at all? According to all the evidence that I have gathered, the answer to the last question is in the affirmative. However, this policy was certainly influenced or even determined by far more important considerations and self-reflections, as was the case in British policy towards *all* minor Allies. Besides the apparently decisive framework of the prospect of war and that of the policy towards the other Great Powers, British foreign policy of the period was generally conditioned by imperial considerations and also by respect towards the position of the Dominions, which influenced the process of British foreign policy decision-making in the specific case of Czechoslovakia to a remarkable extent.

Any historian dealing with British policy towards Central Europe during World War II sooner or later finds out that Czechoslovakia from time to time emerged as a problem for British foreign policy, and then allegedly disappeared, at least from the agenda of top decision-making bodies. It was partly caused by the fact that His Majesty's Government was reactive rather than proactive in its policy towards Czechoslovakia throughout the period. Its policy of no definitive commitments before the end of war, as far as the post-war shape of Central Europe and its frontiers were concerned, naturally clashed with the detailed plans of Czechoslovak exile representatives, with Edvard Beneš at their head. However, the quantity and nature of problems connected with Czechoslovakia differed decisively from those associated with its northern Slavonic neighbour. Therefore the 'Czechoslovak story' serves as comparison with the case of Poles and their government in exile.

Various players dominated British policy towards Czechoslovakia during those 5 years, thus influencing and sometimes even changing the whole course of policy. It was, naturally, the Cabinet that adopted fundamental decisions on foreign policy. But its course was influenced by various governmental bodies, amongst which the Foreign Office (with the key position of its Central Department dealing with the Czechoslovak agenda – apart from eleven other countries including Poland and Germany) played the prominent role. Its officials were running everyday policy *vis-à-vis* Czechoslovakia at the time when no governmental directives were available or were already getting out of date and ministerial attention was focused elsewhere. These officials prepared materials for the Foreign Secretary and Cabinet, thus having crucial upward influence on governmental decisions. It is therefore essential to find out what drove officials to adopt the decisions they did, against what background, tendencies, experience or even prejudices these people operated. Was there not anything like a bureaucratic changelessness that influenced the process and quality of their decision-making? On the other hand, Foreign Office officials often proved to be much more circumspect in their foreign policy expectations than the 'foreign policy executive'[5] or other Cabinet ministers. But their ability to imprint their ideas in actual policy varied. From all this is clear that an insight into the Foreign Office workshop was inevitable. Likewise, I asses the influence of the other relevant governmental departments.

My specific focus is set into a broader framework. The most obvious one is the general context of British foreign policy during the period of change from appeasement to participation in the anti-Hitler coalition. I am trying to find out whether there were any threads of continuity in the conduct of British foreign policy during this period. The 'uneasy relationship between expediency and morality' in the case of the Baltic States and British policy towards the Soviet Union has already been identified.[6] Nonetheless, of all relations with the other Great Powers the policy towards the Soviet Union was naturally important with respect to the minor allies in Central and Eastern Europe and it deserves to be treated as such. As I have indicated, a comparison with British policy towards these countries (Poland above all) is indispensable. These as-

5) Foreign policy executive compounds of the Prime Minister and his Secretary of State for Foreign Affairs. See Hill, *Cabinet Decisions on Foreign Policy*, p. XVIII.
6) See Child, Victoria, *British Policy towards the Soviet Union 1939–42 with special reference to the Baltic States*, unpublished D.Phil Thesis, Oxford, Trinity Term 1994, p. 3.

pects are at least in some cases compared with the U.S. policy, the other important determinant of British foreign policy.

All this is necessarily described against two main settings. One is the Czechoslovak history of the period, especially the history of the exile representation in London and its activities. Firstly, the British themselves conditioned recognition of the Czechoslovak government in exile by settling internal disputes among various groups, by incorporating Slovak representatives, the Sudeten German ones, etc. Secondly, as time went by, the British merely responded to Beneš's initiatives and demands. The origins of and reasons for these initiatives form a part of this narrative. The interactive approach to the topic has been inevitable, and this is also true for my archival research. The second main setting consists of Czechoslovak relations with other countries, especially with Poland and the Soviet Union. Such a framework provided me with an opportunity to describe the role played by the British in the origins and beginnings of the gradual Czechoslovak drift into the Soviet orbit.

Many Czech historians still approach these topics with preconceptions and prejudices, often finding their 'guilty men'. Indeed, though many decades have passed, it is difficult to look at Munich and the ensuing events entirely neutrally, despite all rationalisations. It has been, of course, my intention to avoid any recriminations, to resist condemning those 'responsible' for the fatal failures of the period, unless such arguments are fully supported by documentary evidence. The principal aim of the book is to reconstruct events as well as it is feasible according to the available sources, and to describe the modalities and causes of their actors' deeds as objectively as possible.

Bibliographical essay
Secondary sources

To start with western historiography, the interest of British and most other historians in Czechoslovak matters usually ends with the occupation of Bohemia and Moravia on 15 March 1939.[7] From mid-1930s up to

---

7) Some leading historians are not even very much certain about the date. While Donald Cameron Watt writes about 'March 13, 1939', Anita Prażmowska points out 'the German occupation of Prague on 14 March and the creation of the German protectorate in Slovakia a few days later', which is a remarkable accumulation of mistakes in one single sentence. Cf. Watt, Donald Cameron, *How War Came*, p. 141; Prażmowska, Anita J., *Britain and Poland 1939–1943. The Betrayed Ally*, Cambridge, Cambridge University Press 1995, p. 31.

that date Czechoslovakia enters European history. Then the Czechoslovak story vanishes from books about the Great Powers' diplomacy, usually re-emerging just as an example of the communist perfidy and shrewdness in February 1948. This situation is completely different from that of Poland that represented one of major problems of wartime relations among the Big Three.[8]

There are only a few relevant secondary sources concerning this particular topic. The only scholarly attempt to cover the whole period from Munich to February 1948, written by Mark Cornwall, is just 21 pages long and starts the story of a 'special relationship' as early as in 1930. However, it is a well-thought-out essay contending that by 1939 Czechoslovakia secured 'a unique and sensitive place in evolution of British appeasement' while during the war the British link resumed a special significance for the Czechs and Slovaks. The author concludes that the 'special relationship' between Britain and Czechoslovakia was something of a 'brief encounter', conditioned by the international situation and geographical position of Czechoslovakia.[9]

Another historical work that has so far attempted to cover British policy towards Czechoslovakia is a book written by Martin David Brown.[10] His text is highly readable and comprehensive, but it also suffers from several liabilities. He sets the story of British dealings with the Czechoslovak democrats into the context of western historiography. Yet, I cannot agree with his labeling of many titles as 'Cold War' literature. By the same token, he did not get acquainted with a greater part of relevant Czech literature on the topic (although he included a number of largely irrelevant titles dealing with older periods into his bibliography). The very fact that as archival sources he used merely British documentation (mostly deposited in the Public Record Office – The National Archives) necessarily narrows his perspective. When reading his book at some points I regretted that he did not apply the

8) See e.g. the otherwise brilliant post-revisionist book by John Lewis Gaddis about the U.S. road to the Cold War where Czechoslovakia is mentioned just twice, in both cases in connection with the February coup, while Poland represents one of the key issues: Gaddis, *The United States and the Origins of the Cold War*.
9) Cornwall, Mark, The Rise and Fall of a 'Special Relationship'?: Britain and Czechoslovakia, 1930–1948, In: *What difference Did the War Make?*, eds. B. Brivati – H. Jones, Leicester, Leicester University Press 1993, pp. 130–150.
10) Brown, Martin David, *Dealing with Democrats. The British Foreign Office and the Czechoslovak Émigrés in Great Britain, 1939 to 1945*, Frankfurt am Main, Peter Lang 2006.

same critical approach to the Czech (published) sources and literature as he did in the case of British sources and historiography. This applies especially to the memoirs by Edvard Beneš. At the same time Brown either ignored or dismissed Czech and Russian sources that shed a peculiar light especially upon Beneš's policy towards the Soviet Union. All this resulted in the author's maximum tolerance and understanding when he writes about Czechoslovak foreign policy and its protagonists, quite in the contrast with some of his overcritical judgments on British foreign policy and the Foreign Office in particular. The relationship between its officials on the one hand and Eden with Churchill on the other hand was more complex and complicated than his often used term 'short-circuiting' seems to suggest. There are numerous factual mistakes in the text and, last but not least, some of Brown's footnotes are 'blind' or in fact do not match with the meaning or location of the actual sources.[11] In spite of all this, however, Brown really deserves a tribute for his attempt to cover this difficult and wide-ranging topic, as well as his important contribution to some subtopics, such as the military co-operation and the special operations to Czechoslovakia.

The remarkable book by Detlef Brandes covers British policy towards Poland, Czechoslovakia and Yugoslavia in 1939–1943.[12] It tackles only very briefly the period between Munich and the outbreak of war, although the subtitle of its Czech edition states something else.[13] However, as I have pointed out elsewhere,[14] the book slightly suffers from being overburdened with facts which are not always relevant to its central theme and sometimes appear at the expense of the author's analysis. Brandes has used enormous quantity of archival documents as well as published sources when working on his book. In comparison with the possibilities that Detlef Brandes had in the mid-1980s, we now have access to other important sets of documents, whether it is the SOE files in London, wide spectrum of Russian sources and, of course, archival

11) For further details see my book review in *Soudobé dějiny* [Contemporary history] – forthcoming.
12) Brandes, Detlef, *Großbritannien und seine osteuropäischen Alliierten 1939–1943. Die Regierungen Polens, der Tschechoslowakei und Jugoslawiens im Londoner Exil vom Kriegsausbruch bis zur Konferenz von Teheran*, München, R. Oldenbourg Verlag 1988.
13) *Exil v Londýně 1939–1943. Velká Británie a její spojenci Československo, Polsko a Jugoslávie mezi Mnichovem* [sic!] *a Teheránem*, Praha, Karolinum 2003.
14) Smetana, Vít, Kniha, o které se hovoří [A book which is being discussed], *Dějiny a současnost* [History and present], Vol. 26, 2004, No. 2, p. 57.

sources in Prague. Polish historian Radosław Żurawski vel Grajewski has also recently addressed certain stages of the British policy towards Czechoslovakia during World War II.[15] However, he chose a peculiar method of analysing this policy purely from Czech archival sources and ignored the British ones altogether. I really wonder about the reasons for such an approach, more than a decade after the fall of the communist regimes in East-Central Europe and with wide possibilities for doing research in British archives. It goes without saying that the absence of relevant sources only results in an unbalanced perspective of his articles.

Hana Velecká has dealt with the topic of British assistance to refugees from Czechoslovakia in 1939, as well as with British policy towards Czechoslovakia between March 15 and the outbreak of war.[16] David Blaazer, an Australian researcher, has also written an article about the transfer of the Czechoslovak gold to Germany in 1939.[17] However, the text distinguishes itself by its complete disregard for other than English-written historiography (no matter whether or not English summaries are available on the internet). Thus he has not added anything new to the discussion and his article is in itself an essay in discovering of what has already been discovered.

15) Żurawski vel Grajewski, Radosław, Starania dyplomacji czechosłowackiej o cofnięcie uznania rządu brytyjskiego dla umowy monachijskiej (sierpień 1941 – sierpień 1942 r.) [Efforts of the Czechoslovak diplomacy to undo the British consent with the Munich Agreement (August 1941 – August 1942)], In: *Czechosłowacja w stosunkach międzynarodowych w pierwszej połowie XX wieku* [Czechoslovakia in international relations in the first half of the 20th century], A. M. Brzeziński (ed.), Warszawa, Wydawnictwo Naukowe 2003, pp. 69–128. Żurawski vel Grajewski, Radosław, Z historii stosunków brytyjsko-czechosłowackich w okrsie II wojny światowej (lipiec 1940 – lipiec 1941) [From the history of British-Czechoslovak relations in the course of World War II (July 1940 – July 1941), In: *Z polityki zagranicznej Wielkiej Brytanii w I połowie XX wieku* [From British foreign policy in the first half of the 20th century], A. M. Brzeziński (ed.), Łódź, Wydawnictwo Uniwersytetu Łódzkiego 2002, pp. 102–127.
16) Velecká, Hana, Britská pomoc uprchlíkům z Československa od okupace do vypuknutí války v roce 1939 [British assistance to Czechoslovak refugees, from the German occupation till the outbreak of war in 1939], *Soudobé dějiny* [Contemporary history], Prague, Vol. 8, 2001, No. 4, pp. 659–691; Idem, Agónie appeasementu. Britská politika a rozbití Československa 15. 3.–31. 8. 1939 [The agony of appeasement. British policy and the break-up of Czechoslovakia 15. 3.–31. 8. 1939], *Český časopis historický* [Czech historical journal], Prague, Vol. 99, 2001, No. 4, pp. 788–822.
17) Blaazer, David, Finance and the End of Appeasement: The Bank of England, the National Government and the Czech Gold, *Journal of Contemporary History*, Vol. 40, 2005, No. 1, pp. 25–39.

We can find the account of the slow recognition of the Czechoslovak government by Britain in three authors' studies, written by Johann Bruegel, Michael Dockrill and Jan Kuklík.[18] Two more academics have dealt with British policy. Slovak historian Edita Ivaničková has outlined several aspects of the Slovak dimension of British policy.[19] Her Czech-American colleague Harry Hanak, known for his studies about Stafford Cripps' mission to Moscow,[20] has also written two general essays on British attitudes towards Czechoslovakia.[21]

Alan Brown has analysed the military aspects of the Anglo-Czecho-slovak relationship. However, in his effort to be as critical as possible both to the British military authorities on the one hand and to Beneš and his instrumental use of the Czechoslovak military forces for his political aspirations on the other hand, it is sometimes impossible to grasp where his argument actually lies. In some cases it even seems that he contradicts himself.[22]

18) Bruegel, Johann Wolfgang, The Recognition of the Czechoslovak Government in London, *Kosmos – Journal of Czechoslovak and Central European Studies*, Vol. 2, 1983, No. 1, pp. 1–13; Dockrill, Michael, The Foreign Office, Dr Eduard Benes and the Czechoslovak Government-in-Exile, 1939–41, *Diplomacy & Statecraft*, Vol. 6, 1995, No. 3, pp. 701–718; Kuklík, Jan, The Recognition of Czechoslovak Government in Exile and its International Status 1939–1941, *Prague Papers on History of International Relations*, Vol. 1, 1997, pp. 173–205.

19) Ivaničková, Edita, Československo-maďarské vzťahy v stredoeurópskej politike Veľkej Británie (1938–1945) [Czechoslovak-Hungarian relations and the 1938–1945 policy of Great Britain towards Central Europe], *Historický časopis* [Historical journal], Bratislava, Vol. 46, 1998, No. 2, pp. 250–260; Idem, Slovensko-český vzťah v mocenskom zápase v ČSR 1945–1948 z pohľadu britskej diplomacie [Slovak-Czech relations in the 1945–48 power struggle as seen by the British Foreign Office], *Soudobé dějiny* [Contemporary history], Prague, Vol. 5, 1998, No. 2–3, pp. 274–280; Idem, Zahraničnopolitická orientácia Slovenska v dokumentoch britskej Foreign Office (1939–1941) [Foreign policy orientation of Slovakia in documents of the British Foreign Office (1939–1941)], *Historický časopis*, Vol. 44, 1996, No. 2, pp. 207–220.

20) Hanak, Harry, Sir Stafford Cripps as British Ambassador in Moscow, May 1940 to June 1941, *English Historical Review*, Vol. 94, 1979, pp. 48–70; Idem, Hanak, Harry, Sir Stafford Cripps as British Ambassador in Moscow, June 1941 to January 1942, *English Historical Review*, Vol. 97, 1982, pp. 332–344.

21) Idem, Great Britain and Czechoslovakia, 1918–1948. An Outline of their Relations, In: *Czechoslovakia Past and Present*, Vol. I., ed. M. Rechcígl, The Hague, Czechoslovak Society of Arts and Sciences in America – Mouton 1968, pp. 770–800; Idem, Prezident Beneš, Britové a budoucnost Československa [President Beneš, the British and the future of Czechoslovakia], *Historie a vojenství*, Vol. 44, 1995, No. 1, pp. 13–39.

22) Brown, Alan, The Czechoslovak Armed Forces in Britain, 1940–1945, In: *Europe in Exile. European Exile Communities in Britain 1940–45*, eds. M. Conway and J. Gotowitch, New York – Oxford, Berghahn Books 2001. It is not for example clear which of the fol-

The Sudeten German issue is in itself a topic of the greatest importance and also significance in Czech historiography since 1989. Indeed, it already has its own historiography.[23] Two excellent books, written by Detlef Brandes and Francis Dostál Raška, have been devoted to the Sudeten German question in exile.[24] It is not my ambition to add much to the discussion on either the origins of the transfer of the Sudeten Germans or the position of the Sudeten German refugees and their political leaders in exile. The reason is simple: Although from the Czech perspective it looks like the central topic even in the Anglo-Czechoslovak relationship, this opinion was hardly held by the British foreign-policy--makers of the time.[25]

Much more attention than to the Anglo-Czechoslovak relationship has been paid to the analogous Polish topic. Besides Brandes, Anita Prażmowska has written an interesting and highly readable book setting Poland's place in British foreign policy. Despite the rather emotive title (*The Betrayed Ally*) she is also ready to see how over-ambitious the program of the Polish government in exile was, as well as the intrigues and quarrels amongst both the exile politicians, and the officers of the Polish exile army.[26] However, books about Poland between East and West started to appear as early as in 1947/1948 with the memoirs of Jan Ciechanowski, Stanisław Mikołajczyk, and Edward Raczyński,[27] and the flow of publica-

lowing statements is valid – either that both 'the War Office and the Air Ministry held the Czechoslovak soldier and airman in high regard' (p. 175), or whether 'all of the history of British-Czechoslovak military relations seems to be nothing but a catalogue of distrust and contempt' (p. 178) and 'the overall impression of the exiled Czechoslovak armed forces was, in the eyes of some senior British officers at least, one of a deeply flawed force riddled with intrigue, insubordination, dissatisfaction and dangerous politics' (p. 110).

23) Kopeček, Michal – Kunštát, Miroslav, „Sudetoněmecká otázka" v české akademické debatě po roce 1989 ['The Sudeten German issue' in Czech academic discussion after 1989], *Soudobé dějiny* [Contemporary history], Prague, Vol. 10, 2003, No. 3, pp. 293–318.

24) Brandes, Detlef, *Der Weg zur Vertreibung 1938–1945. Pläne und Entscheidungen zum 'Transfer' der Deutschen aus der Tschechoslowakei und aus Polen*, München, R. Oldenbourg 2000; Czech edition: Cesta k vyhnání 1938–1945. Plány a rozhodnutí o „transferu" Němců z Československa a z Polska, Praha, Prostor 2002; Raška, Francis Dostál, *The Czechoslovak Exile Government in London and the Sudeten German Issue*, Prague, The Karolinum Press 2002.

25) See esp. Chapter 6.

26) See Prażmowska, *Britain and Poland 1939–1943*, pp. ix, 10, 12 and elsewhere.

27) Ciechanowski, Jan, *Defeat in Victory*, London, Gollancz 1947; Mikolajczyk, Stanislaw, *The Rape of Poland: Pattern of Soviet Aggression*, New York, Whittlesey House 1948; Raczyński's revealing diary-memoirs were published in 1962: Raczynski, Edward, *In*

tions has continued ever since.[28] Indeed, the Polish question, unlike the Czechoslovak one, cannot escape attention of any historian interested in the Great Powers' diplomacy during World War II and the origins of the Cold War. Prażmowska, like her Polish colleague Anna Cienciala, and Simon Newman, all dealt in monographs specifically with the question of the British guarantee to Poland that had eventually brought Britain into the war.[29] This topic forms a part of virtually every book about the origins of the Second World War.

When writing about British foreign policy during and after World War II, one cannot escape from dealing with the vast literature on appeasement. This applies also to my topic that starts in the months after Munich. As N. J. Crowson puts it, the topic of appeasement 'has generated its own scholastic mini-industry'.[30] Thus the original 'guilty men' literature[31] was later replaced by books stressing economic and military weaknesses, as well as British public opinion, in assessments of British foreign policy under Chamberlain.[32] In 1993 R. A. C. Parker challenged

Allied London. The Wartime Diaries of the Polish Ambassador, London, Weidenfeld and Nicolson 1962.

28) I venture to mention just some of them: Lipski, Józef – Raczyński, Edward – Stroński, Stanislaw, *Trzy podróże gen. Sikorskiego do Ameryki* [Three journeys of gen. Sikorski to America], London 1949; Polonsky, Anthony, *The Great Powers and the Polish Question, 1941-1945. A Documentary Study in Cold War Origins*, London, LSE 1976; Lukas, Richard C., *The Strange Allies. The United States and Poland, 1941-1945*, Knoxville, University of Tennessee Press 1978; Kacewicz, George V., *Great Britain, the Soviet Union and the Polish Government in Exile (1939-1945)*, The Hague, Martinus Nijhoff 1979; Terry, Sarah M., *Poland's Place in Europe. General Sikorski and the Origin of the Oder-Neisse Line, 1939-1943*, Princeton, Princeton University Press 1983.

29) Prażmowska, Anita J., *Britain, Poland and the Eastern Front 1939*, Cambridge, Cambridge University Press 1987; Cienciala, Anna M., *Poland and the Western Powers 1938-1939. A Study in the Interdependence of Eastern and Western Europe*, London 1968; Newman, Simon, *March 1939. The Making of the British Guarantee to Poland*, Oxford, Clarendon Press 1976. See also Strang, Bruce, Once More unto the Breach. Britain's Guarantee to Poland, March 1939, *Journal of Contemporary History*, Vol. 31, 1996, pp. 721–752.

30) Crowson, N. J., *Facing Fascism. The Conservative Party and the European Dictators 1935-1940*, London and New York, Routledge 1997, p. 2.

31) 'Cato', *Guilty Men*, London, Gollancz 1940. In a more academic form: Wheeler-Bennett, Sir John, *Munich, Prologue to Tragedy*, London, Macmillan 1948; Gilbert, Martin – Gott, Richard, *The Appeasers*, London, Weidenfeld and Nicolson 1962.

32) See e.g.: Medlicott, W. N., *Contemporary England, 1914-1964*, London 1967; Kennedy, Paul, *The Realities Behind Diplomacy*, London, Fontana 1981, chapters 5 and 6. To a lesser degree the fundamental book on the origins of World War II written by D. C. Watt can also be considered as 'revisionist': Watt, Donald Cameron, *How War Came, the Immediate Origins of the Second World War, 1938-1939*, London, Heinemann 1989.

this school of thought in his persuasive 'counter-revisionist' analysis. He argues that in reality the Prime Minister and his colleagues made choices among alternative policies. The one that they followed before and after Munich, however, rested upon a wrong interpretation of the way the Third Reich worked. The conduct of this policy strengthened rather than weakened Hitler's ambitions and his domestic authority. After the occupation of Prague, Chamberlain did his best to hinder any effort to create an effective deterrent through an alliance with the Soviet Union.[33] However, if Chamberlain was cautious, Stalin was even more cautious. It is very unlikely, according to the available information, that the latter was willing to build Soviet security upon any co-operation with western powers as late as in the spring of 1939.[34]

As regards sources on the general conduct of British foreign policy during World War II, the official history in five volumes written by Sir Llewellyn Woodward is still indispensable.[35] It provides a lot of details and citations from the Foreign Office files, although it has also become a target of criticism.[36] Among other secondary sources for studies in British foreign policy, I am inclined to praise highly Churchill's official

33) Parker, R. A. C., *Chamberlain and Appeasement. British Policy and the Coming of the Second World War*, London, Macmillan Press 1993, esp. pp. 346–347. See also his other book on the topic: Parker, R. A. C., *Churchill and Appeasement*, Basingstoke and Oxford, Macmillan Press 2000.

34) There are, however, conflicting views on this topic. Most recently see the book by Geoffrey Roberts and the critical book-review by Jonathan Haslam. Roberts, Geoffrey, *The Soviet Union and the Origins of the Second World War: Russo-German Relations and the Road to War, 1933–1941*, New York, St. Martin's 1995; Haslam, Jonathan, Soviet-German Relations and the Origins of the Second World War: The Jury Is Still Out, *Journal of Modern History*, Vol. 69, 1997, No. 4, pp. 785–797. I was myself most sceptical in my account of Soviet policy in 1939, arguing that it was in fact Stalin with Molotov who did their best to break the negotiations with the British and French by escalating their conditions, though they may have been driven by perfectly understandable realist reasons. Smetana, Vít, *Enigma zahalená tajemstvím. Britská politika a Sovětský svaz v roce 1939* [Enigma Wrapped in a Mystery. British Policy and the Soviet Union in the Year 1939], Unpublished M.A. Thesis, Prague, Charles University 1997.

35) Woodward, Sir Llewellyn, *British Foreign Policy in the Second World War*, 5 Vols., H.M.S.O., London 1970–76.

36) See e.g. the comments by Warren Kimball in: *Churchill and Roosevelt, the Complete Correspondence*, 3 Vols., ed. W. F. Kimball, Princeton (NJ), Princeton University Press 1984, p. XXIX: 'Woodward is carefully uncritical of British policy...'; Ross, Graham, Foreign Office Attitudes to the Soviet Union 1941–1945, *Journal of Contemporary History*, Vol. 16, 1981, pp. 512–540, here p. 521: 'But limitations of space meant that he had to concentrate on the substance of British policy rather than thinking behind it and he tends in any case to be discreet about differences of view and emphasis between individuals.'

biography by Martin Gilbert.[37] Though the author failed to come up with any fascinating new theories or historical conceptions denying all conclusions undertaken so far,[38] he provided us with abundance of facts, this time relevant for his topic. This is an admirable piece of academic work together with the companion volumes and Churchill's war papers, though unfortunately so far available only up to Vol. III (1941).[39]

Much has been written about the British foreign policy 'axis', the relationship with the Soviet Union. Two contradictory scholarly accounts of the initial phase (1939–1942) of the strange relationship were written in the 1980s.[40] While Steven Meritt Miner contends that the search for British co-operation with the USSR was doomed to failure because of their differing worldviews, Gabriel Gorodetsky offers a revisionist view. He says that it was possible for the British to co-operate with the Soviet Union even before Barbarossa, but the Churchill government did not sincerely explore this chance. Graham Ross argues quite convincingly that throughout the war, and even as late as at the end of 1944, the Foreign Office was setting much store on developing co-operation with Russia, while having little faith in the United States as a post-war collaborator in Europe.[41] It could be argued that it was the Cabinet that played the key role in conducting the policy. However, in the war years the Cabinet's attention was often directed elsewhere, thus the actual foreign policy course was an inconsistent product of interplay between the Foreign Office and the Cabinet.[42] Martin Kitchen tended to see the

37) Gilbert, Martin, *Prophet of Truth. Winston S. Churchill 1922–1939*, London, Heinemann 1976; Idem, *Finest Hour. Winston S. Churchill 1939–1941*, London, Heinemann 1983; Idem, *Road to Victory. Winston S. Churchill 1941–1945*, London, Heinemann 1986.
38) As an example of such an attempt see e.g.: Charmley, John, *Churchill: The End of Glory*, London, Hodder and Stoughton 1993.
39) *Winston Churchill*, Companion Vol. V., *The Coming of War,* 1936–1939, ed. M. Gilbert, London, Heinemann 1975; *The Churchill War Papers*, Vol. I., *At the Admiralty, September 1939 – May 1940*, Vol. II., *Never Surrender, May 1940 – December 1940*, Vol. III., *The Ever Widening War, 1941*, ed. M. Gilbert, London, Heinemann 1993, 1994, 2000.
40) Gorodetsky, Gabriel, *Stafford Cripps' Mission to Moscow*, Cambridge, Cambridge University Press 1984; Miner, Steven Meritt, *Between Churchill and Stalin. The Soviet Union, Great Britain and the Origins of the Grand Alliance*, North Carolina, The North Carolina Press 1988.
41) Ross, Foreign Office Attitudes to the Soviet Union 1941–1945, p. 532. See also his important documentary edition: *The Foreign Office and the Kremlin. British Documents on Anglo-Soviet Relations, 1941–1945*, ed. G. Ross, Cambridge, Cambridge University Press 1984.
42) Cf. Child, *British Policy towards the Soviet Union 1939–42*, p. 26.

war-time history of British-Soviet relations quite fatalistically, arguing that the alliance was in fact enabled only by the common enemy, and that even then there was merely a minimal degree of co-operation between the two Allies. This peculiar friendship was bound to end once Germany was defeated.[43] Dealing with Soviet foreign policy during World War II and afterwards, no historian should overlook an important book written by Vojtěch Mastný.[44] We now also know much more about the specific Soviet policy towards Czechoslovakia in the war years, above all thanks to the numerous studies and articles written by Valentina Vladimirovna Mar'ina, based on her extensive research in the Russian archives.[45]

Finally, I would like to add just a few words about the Czech and Slovak historical writing on the topic of Czechoslovak exile in Britain. The quantity of books and articles written about Edvard Beneš's second exile or, broadly speaking, about Czechoslovak history 1938–1945 is enormous. However, their quality varies. The secondary sources worth mentioning might be divided into three groups: those published in the late 1960s when Czechoslovak historiography achieved a certain level

43) Kitchen Martin, *British Policy Towards the Soviet Union During the Second World War*, London, Macmillan 1986, p. 270; see also Idem, Winston Churchill and the Soviet Union during the Second World War, *Historical Journal*, Vol. 30, 1987, No. 2, pp. 415–436.

44) Mastny, Vojtech, *Russia's Road to the Cold War: Diplomacy, Warfare, and the Politics of Communism, 1941–1945*, New York, Columbia University Press 1975.

45) Marjina, Valentina V., Brána na Balkán. Slovensko v geopolitických plánech SSSR a Německa v letech 1939–1941 [The gate to the Balkans. Slovakia in the geopolitical plans of the USSR and Germany], *Soudobé dějiny* [Contemporary history], Prague, Vol. 1, 1993/1994, No. 6, pp. 827–846; Idem, K historii sovětsko-československých vztahů v letech 1938–1941. Nad deníkem Ivana M. Majského [Towards the history of the Soviet-Czechoslovak relations, 1938–1941. Reading the diary of Ivan M. Maisky], *Soudobé dejiny*, Vol. 6, 1999, No. 4. pp. 514–533; Idem, Nejen o Podkarpatské Rusi. Jednání Beneš-Molotov v Moskvě v březnu 1945 [Not only about the Sub-Carpathian Russia. The negotiations Beneš-Molotov in Moscow in March 1945], *Dějiny a současnost* [History and present], Prague, 1996, No. 4, pp. 48–51; Idem, Od důvěry k podezíravosti. Sovětští a českoslovenští komunisté v letech 1945–1948 [From trust to suspicion. The Soviet and Czechoslovak communists, 1945–1948], *Soudobé dějiny*, Vol. 4, 1997, No. 3–4, pp. 451–467; Idem, Politika SSSR po czechoslovackomu voprosu nakanune Velikoi Otechestvennoi voiny (sentiabr' 1940 – iiun' 1941 g.), *Mezhdunarodnye otnosheniia i strany Centralnoi i Yugo-Vostochnoi Evropy*, Moskva, Institut slavianovedenia i balkanistiki 1989, pp. 117–129; Idem, Sovetsko-germanskij pakt o nenapadenii i nachalo vtoroi mirovoi voiny v ocenke czeshskoi obshchestvennosti, In: *Politicheskii krizis 1939 g. i strany Centralnoi i Yugo-Vostochnoi Evropy*, Moskva, Institut slavianovedenia i balkanistiki 1989, pp. 117–129; Idem, SSSR i czechoslovackii vopros. 1939 god, In: *Mezhdunarodnye otnoshenia i strany Centralnoi i Yugo-Vostochnoi Evropy*, Moskva, Institut slavianovedenia i balkanistiki 1990, pp. 95–128.

of uncensored openness and hence also quality, those published in the exile, and the post-1989 writing. Amongst those from the first category two books on the Czechoslovak resistance abroad 1938–1940 by Jan Křen and another one on the history of Czechoslovak military units in the West by Toman Brod with Eduard Čejka are quite important and at least in some aspects still usable.[46]

Relevant books published in Czech in exile have mostly been re-published during the 1990s in Prague. Some fairly influential books were written in English, in particular those by Eduard Táborský and Josef Kalvoda.[47] The former worked as Beneš's private secretary during the war. However, he based his book not only on his private archive, but also on archival material from several countries including Britain. His outstanding book can be considered as academic work, despite the author's background. Rather surprisingly, he managed to be fairly critical of Beneš's diplomacy as well as of Beneš himself. Kalvoda is even more critical of the former President. The author worked extensively with U.S. archival documents, but also relied on other, hardly reliable sources, thus sometimes distorting the whole picture.

Amongst publications from the 1990s, those of Jan Kuklík, who also used British sources, deal with the initial phase of Beneš's exile in London.[48]

46) Unlike many other historians, Křen was 'lucky' enough to have an access to archival sources in the late 1950s and throughout the 1960s. Křen, Jan, *Do emigrace. Buržoazní zahraniční odboj 1938-1939* [Into the exile. The bourgeois resistance abroad 1938–1939], Praha, Naše vojsko 1963. However, Křen rewrote his book in the time of the Prague spring and it was published in 2nd edition with a changed title: *Do emigrace. Západní zahraniční odboj 1938-1939* [Into the exile. The western resistance abroad 1938–1939], Praha, Naše vojsko 1969; Idem, *V emigraci. Západní zahraniční odboj 1939-1940* [In the exile. The western resistance abroad 1939–1940], Praha, Naše vojsko 1969; Brod, Toman – Čejka, Eduard, *Na západní frontě. Historie československých vojenských jednotek na Západě v letech druhé světové války* [At the Western front. History of the Czechoslovak military units in the West in the years of the Second World War], Praha, Naše vojsko 1965.
47) Táborský, Eduard, *President E. Beneš Between East and West 1938-1948*, Stanford, Hoover Institution Press 1981; in the Czech version as: *Prezident Beneš mezi Západem a Východem*, Praha, Mladá fronta 1993; Kalvoda, Josef, *Czechoslovakia's Role in Soviet Strategy*, University Press of America 1978 (Czech edition: *Role Československa v sovětské strategii*, Kladno, Dílo 1999).
48) Kuklík, Jan, *Londýnský exil a obnova československého státu za druhé světové války* [The exile in London and the reconstruction of the Czechoslovak state during World War II], Praha, Karolinum 1998; Idem, *Vznik Československého národního výboru a prozatímního státního zřízení ČSR v emigraci* [The creation of the Czechoslovak National Committee and the provisional state regime of the Czechoslovak Republic in Exile], Praha, Karolinum 1996.

Together with Jan Němeček they wrote two excellent books dealing with the principal political conflicts in exile. The latter one contains also an important chapter on British attitudes towards the Czechoslovak anti--Beneš opposition in London.[49] Politically and legally the most fascinating issue – launching the resistance action in exile – attracted several Czech historians' attention.[50] Other authors conducted research concentrating on the Soviet dimension of the Czechoslovak foreign policy.[51] The recent book by Jan Němeček about Czechoslovak-Polish relations, setting this relationship into a broader international perspec-

49) Kuklík, Jan – Němeček, Jan, *Hodža versus Beneš*, Praha, Karolinum 1999; Idem, *Proti Benešovi! Česká a slovenská protibenešovská opozice v Londýně 1939-1945* [Against Beneš! The Czech and Slovak anti-Beneš opposition in London 1939-1945], Praha, Karolinum 2004.

50) See e.g.: Jožák, Jiří, K historii čs. zahraniční akce v USA (15. 3.–1. 9. 1939) [Towards the history of the Czechoslovak exile action in the USA (15 March – 1 September 1939)], *Historie a vojenství* [History and military], Prague, Vol. 40, 1991, No. 5, pp. 43-77; Klimek, Antonín, Edvard Beneš od abdikace z funkce presidenta ČSR (5. října 1938) do zkázy Československa (15. března 1939) [Edvard Beneš from his resignation the presidency of the Czechoslovak Republic (5th October 1938) to the destruction of Czechoslovakia (15th March 1939)], In: *Z druhé republiky. Sborník prací Historického ústavu armády České republiky* [Inside the Second Republic. Collection of studies, published by the Historical Institute of the Czech Army], Praha 1993, pp. 155-241; Hauner, Milan, Čekání na velkou válku 1939 /I.-II./. Edvard Beneš mezi Mnichovem, 15. březnem a porážkou Polska [Waiting for a great war. Edvard Beneš between Munich, March 15 and the defeat of Poland], *Dějiny a současnost* [History and present], Prague, Vol. 21, No. 4, pp. 12-15, No. 5, pp. 36-39 Kuklík, Jan – Němeček, Jan, K počátkům druhého exilu E. Beneše 1938-1939 [Towards the origins of E. Beneš's second exile, 1938-1939], *Český časopis historický* [Czech historical journal], Prague, Vol. 96, 1998, No. 4, pp. 803-823.

51) See e.g.: Brod, Toman, *Osudný omyl Edvarda Beneše* [Edvard Beneš's fateful mistake], Praha, Academia 2002; Němeček, Jan, Československá diplomatická mise v Moskvě (březen-prosinec 1939) [The Czechoslovak diplomatic legation in Moscow (March-December 1939)], *Moderní dějiny* [Modern history], Prague, Vol. 4, 1996, pp. 221-275; Idem, Edvard Beneš a Sovětský svaz 1939-1945 [Edvard Beneš and the Soviet Union], *Slovanský přehled* [Slavic survey], Prague, Vol. 87, 2001, No. 3, pp. 313-343; Idem, Československý zahraniční odboj a sovětsko-finská válka 1939-1940 [The Czechoslovak resistance abroad and the Soviet-Finnish war], *Moderní dějiny*, Vol. 3, 1995, pp. 139-157; Idem, Němeček, Jan, Edvard Beneš a Sovětský svaz 1939-1940 [Edvard Beneš and the Soviet Union 1939-1940], *Slovanské historické studie* [Slavonic historical studies], Prague, Vol. 23, 1997, pp. 179-193; Janáček, František, Pakt, válka a KSČ. První týdny po 23. srpnu a 1. září 1939 [The Pact, the war and the Communist Party of Czechoslovakia. First weeks after 23rd August and 1st September 1939] *Historie a vojenství* [History and military], Prague, 1969, pp. 425-457; Janáček, František – Němeček, Jan, Reality a iluze Benešovy 'ruské' politiky 1939-1945 [Realities and illusions of Beneš's 'Russian' policy, 1939-1945], In: *Edvard Beneš, československý a evropský politik* [Edvard Beneš, Czechoslovak and European politician], Praha 1994, pp. 71-95.

tive of the Second World War diplomacy, is certainly a remarkable achievement.[52]

Primary sources

Several diaries are indispensable for understanding the conduct of British foreign policy in the war years as well as the way the Foreign Office worked. This applies above all to the diaries of the Permanent Under-Secretary of State Sir Alexander Cadogan.[53] It is a fascinating reading written by a skillful Machiavellian diplomat, who changed his opinions lightheartedly, both on foreign policy matters and on the people inside that specific world. Professionally edited by David Dilks, this book is a 'must' read. The diaries of Oliver Harvey, the Private Secretary of Lord Halifax and Anthony Eden, also provide interesting insights into the Foreign Office and foreign policy conduct.[54] Amongst other diaries I should point out those of two more people connected with Czechoslovak matters – Harold Nicolson and Sir Robert Bruce Lockhart.[55] The former, a prominent journalist and also M.P., belonged to the 'Eden group' of opponents of appeasement in 1938–1939 and also had numerous Czech and Slovak friends. The latter spent much time in Prague during the inter-war period, was appointed a liaison officer to the Czechoslovak National Committee in 1939, and then in 1940–1941 served as the British representative to the Provisional Czechoslovak government. As such he really played principal role in the Anglo-Czechoslovak encounter of that time. From the diaries recorded by the Czechoslovak politicians and officials, those by Jan Opočenský, the President's archivist throughout the war, published in an excellent edition, are most revealing on various themes including the perceptions of Britain and her policy by the Czechoslovak exiles.[56] However, when dealing with diaries one

52) Němeček, Jan, *Od spojenectví k roztržce* [From alliance to quarrel], Praha, Academia 2003.
53) *The Diaries of Sir Alexander Cadogan, 1938–1945*, ed. D. Dilks, New York, G. P. Putnam's Sons 1972.
54) *The Diplomatic Diaries of Oliver Harvey 1937–1940*, ed. J. Harvey, New York, St. Martin's Press 1970; *The War Diaries of Oliver Harvey 1941–1945*, ed. J. Harvey, London, Collins 1978.
55) Nicolson, Sir Harold George, *Diaries and Letters*, Vol. I, *1930–1939*, Vol. II, *1939–1945*, Vol. III, *1945–1962*, ed. N. Nicolson, London, Collins 1966, 1967, 1971; *The Diaries of Sir Robert Bruce Lockhart*, Vol. I, *1915–1938*, Vol. II, *1939–1965*, ed. K. Young, London, Macmillan 1973, 1980.
56) *Válečné deníky Jana Opočenského* [Jan Opočenský's war-time diaries], eds. J. Čechurová – J. Kuklík – J. Čechura – J. Němeček, Praha, Karolinum 2001; see also Táborský,

(29)

should also bear in mind that these editions are usually selective and some important passages are often left out of the original diaries.[57]

I should also say a few words about perhaps the most problematic 'primary' source – the memoirs. Prominent British and American diplomats usually mention Czechoslovakia only occasionally.[58] Nonetheless, even these utterances have certain value, although one should be always cautious in taking them for granted, word for word. There were, however, several diplomats who had to deal with Czechoslovakia, but the quality of their memoirs varies. *Comes the Reckoning* by Sir Robert Bruce Lockhart, also translated into Czech soon after the war, is most informative about Czechoslovak matters, though the loyal Beneš's and Jan Masaryk's friend hardly offered a critical appraisal of Czechoslovak policy during the war.[59] The memoirs of the Soviet Ambassador in London Ivan Maisky on the contrary, though dealing quite extensively with the British and Czechoslovak affairs, belong to those recollections which one cannot really take fully seriously.[60]

Anthony Eden's memoirs contain several comments about the proposed Czechoslovak confederation with the Poles and the Soviet-Czechoslovak treaty.[61] The memoirs by Sir Frank K. Roberts, the key official in the Central Department of the Foreign Office during the war, can – besides numerous inaccuracies – in many cases serve as an example of projecting later thoughts into previous events.[62] Autobiographies of many British politicians are entered in the bibliography; all of them com-

Eduard, *Pravda zvítězila. Deník druhého zahraničního odboje*, [The truth has triumphed. The diary of the second resistance movement abroad], Praha, Fr. Borový 1947.

57) Out of the books I have mentioned, this applies especially to Lockhart's diaries and also Cadogan's diaries.

58) See e.g.: Kirkpatrick, Ivone, *The Inner Circle. Memoirs*, London, Macmillan 1959; Strang, William, *Home & Abroad*, London, A. Deutsch 1956; Bohlen, Charles E., *Witness to History 1929–1969*, New York, Norton & Company 1973; Harriman, W. Averell, and Abel, Eli, *Special Envoy to Churchill and Stalin 1941–1946*, London, Hutchinson 1976; Hull, Cordell, *The Memoirs of Cordell Hull*, 2 Vols., London, Hodder and Stoughton 1951; Kennan, George F., *Memoirs 1925–1950*, Boston-Toronto, Little, Brown and Company 1967.

59) Lockhart, Sir Robert Bruce, *Comes the Reckoning*, London, Putnam Comp. 1947; Czech edition: *Přichází zúčtování*, Praha, Fr. Borový 1948.

60) Maisky, Ivan, *Memoirs of a Soviet Ambassador, The War 1939–1943*, London, Hutchinson 1967.

61) Eden, Anthony (Lord Avon), *The Reckoning*, London, Cassell 1965, p. 533.

62) Roberts, Frank, *Dealing with Dictators. The Destruction and Revival of Europe 1930–1970*, London, Weidenfeld & Nicolson 1991. It was the name of Roberts' memoirs that Martin D. Brown paraphrased for the title of his own book.

menting on the course of British foreign policy during World War II. They bear several common signs: the authors usually stress their critical attitude towards the policy of appeasement and their worries and later regrets concerning the Sovietisation of Eastern Europe. Now, when so many archival documents uncovering British foreign policy in the 1930s and 1940s are accessible to research, memoirs are more useful for remembered 'tone', for understanding interpersonal or even interdepartmental relations – something where the official documents usually remain silent – than for descriptive accounts of policy.

Many Czechoslovak (ex)politicians put on the paper their recollections of the war years and sometimes also the post-war period. The general limitations, which I have outlined in the previous two paragraphs about memoirs of British politicians, apply here as well, and there are additional shortcomings. These naturally concern the autobiographies published in Czechoslovakia after 1948[63] but also those published in the exile. The urge to find the 'guilty men' who had marked the fate of the country, seemingly for the good, was sometimes irresistible. Beneš's memoirs are not very reliable, offering a big quantity of half-truths, and this applies even more to both volumes of Zdeněk Fierlinger's memoirs.[64] The voluminous memoirs by Prokop Drtina, Beneš's assistant in London, and later Minister of Justice, were smuggled out of communist Czechoslovakia and published in Canada in 1982.[65] The most revealing memoirs of Karel Ladislav Feierabend, the Minister of Finance in the Czechoslovak government in exile, were first published in the sixties in Washington and caused a real turmoil amongst Czechoslovak emigrants.[66] Wenzel

63) See e.g. Laštovička, Bohuslav, *V Londýně za války* [In London during the war], 3rd edition, Praha, Svoboda 1978.
64) Beneš, Edvard, *Paměti. Od Mnichova k nové válce a k novému vítězství*, Praha, Orbis 1947 (English edition: *Memoirs of Dr. Eduard Beneš. From Munich to a New War and a New Victory*, Boston, 1954); Fierlinger, Zdeněk, *Ve službách ČSR. Paměti z druhého zahraničního odboje* [In the services of the Czechoslovak Republic. Memoirs of the second resistance abroad], 2 Vols., Praha, Svoboda 1947 and 1951. Fierlinger served as Czechoslovak Minister to Moscow and then became the first post-war Czechoslovak Prime Minister. However, his relations with the Kremlin were far stronger than just diplomatic...
65) Drtina, Prokop, *Československo můj osud: kniha života českého demokrata 20. století* [Czechoslovakia – my fate: A book of life of a Czechoslovak democrat of the 20th century], 2 Vols., 2nd edition, Praha, Melantrich 1991–1992 (first published in Toronto, Sixty Eight Publishers, Corp. 1982).
66) Feierabend, Ladislav Karel, *Politické vzpomínky* [Political memoirs], 3 Vols., Brno, Atlantis 1994, 1996 (first published in 4 Volumes in Washington, D.C., at the author's own expense, in 1965–67).

Jaksch, the leader of the Sudeten German Social Democrats, published his memoirs – which can be also labeled as an anti-Beneš essay – 13 years after the war.[67]

The Czechoslovak exile representation, as well as the democratic Sudeten Germans or anti-Beneš Slovaks, produced innumerable pieces of propaganda, such as edited speeches, various pamphlets, etc. Some of them are entered in the bibliography. Several western intellectuals were also productive in this sense.[68]

The most important published primary sources are undoubtedly documentary editions. The official series of *Documents on British Foreign Policy* unfortunately end with the date of British entry into the Second World War.[69] But the more recent documents from the Foreign Office confidential print have compensated this disadvantage substantially; *British Documents on Foreign Affairs* represent perhaps the most important printed source for anyone dealing with the British foreign policy during the Second World War.[70] Warren Kimball's edition of the complete correspondence between Churchill and Roosevelt represents another important source, although Czechoslovakia is mentioned just once, and then only in connection with Poland.[71] But this is naturally not Kimball's fault, the fact rather reflects the importance or comparatively unproblematic nature of Czechoslovak affairs. I also drew extensively upon the *Hansards*, the verbatim records of parliamentary debates, a crucial source to research interconnections between foreign and domestic policies.[72]

---

67) Jaksch, Wenzel, *Europas Weg nach Potsdam. Schuld und Schicksal im Donauraum*, Stuttgart, Deutsche Verlags-Anstalt 1958 (English edition: *Europe's Road to Potsdam*, London, Thames and Hudson 1963; Czech edition: *Cesta Evropy do Postupimi*, Praha, ISE 2000).

68) See e.g.: Grant Duff, Shiela, *A German Protectorate. The Czechs under Nazi Rule*, London, Macmillan 1942; Wright, Quincy, The Munich Settlement and International Law, *American Journal of International Law*, 1939, No. 33.

69) *Documents on British Foreign Policy*, 1919–1939, 3rd series, 1938–1939, 9 Vols., London, H.M.S.O. 1949–57 (hereafter *DBFP*).

70) Most important for my particular topic are the following series: *British Documents on Foreign Affairs – reports and papers from the Foreign Office confidential print* (hereafter *BDFA*), Part III, *From 1940 through 1945*, Series A, *The Soviet Union and Finland*, 5 Vols., Bethesda (MD), University Publications of America 1998; Ibid., *From 1940 through 1945*, Series F, *Europe*, 26 Vols., Bethesda (MD), University Publications of America 1997.

71) *Churchill and Roosevelt, the Complete Correspondence*, Vol. II, Doc. No. C-533.

72) *Parliamentary Debates, House of Commons*, London, H.M.S.O., 5th Series, 1938–1942 (hereafter *H. C. Deb.*); *Parliamentary Debates, House of Lords*, London, H.M.S.O., 5th Series, 1938–1942 (hereafter *H. L. Deb.*).

On the Czech part, the edition based on papers of Beneš's chancellor Dr. Jaromír Smutný is still indispensable.[73] However, during the last 15 years the most substantial and remarkable research has been done on documentary editions. Some of them are now absolutely necessary for anybody who wants to tackle the problem of Czechoslovakia's place in Europe during World War II and after.[74] Although an edition focusing on Anglo-Czechoslovak relations has not been published, some of the cited editions reflect this theme too, though usually including only Czech archival sources.

This book is, however, based primarily on archival material. I have done most of my research in the *Public Record Office* in London (in 2003 it was renamed to *The National Archives,* but I rather decided to stick to its original and traditional name under which I did most of my research and which is less bound to be confused with the National Archives in Washington, D.C.), especially on the Foreign Office files, Cabinet papers, Premier series, War Office files and SOE files (HS). Especially the detailed nature of the Foreign Office records, including the 'minutes'

73) *Dokumenty z historie československé politiky 1939–1943* [Documents from the history of Czechoslovak politics 1939–1943], eds. L. Otáhalová a M. Červinková, Praha, Academia 1966 (hereafter *DHČSP*).
74) *Dokumenty československé zahraniční politiky. Československá zahraniční politika v roce 1938.* Svazek II (1. červenec – 5. říjen 1938) [Documents on Czechoslovak Foreign Policy. Czechoslovak Foreign Policy in 1938, Volume II (1 July – 5 October 1938)], Praha, ÚMV – UK – Karolinum – HÚ AV ČR 2001 (hereafter *DČSZP 1938*); *Dokumenty československé zahraniční politiky. Od rozpadu Česko-Slovenska do uznání československé prozatímní vlády 1939–1940 (16. březen 1939 – 16. červen 1940)* [From the break-up of Czecho-Slovakia until the recognition of the Czechoslovak provisional government (16 March 1939 – 16 June 1940)], Praha, ÚMV – UK – Karolinum – HÚ AV ČR 2002 (hereafter *DČSZP 1939–1940*); *Československo-sovětské vztahy v diplomatických jednáních 1939–1945*, Dokumenty 1–2 [Czechoslovak-Soviet relations in diplomatic negotiations 1939–1945. Documents I–II], Praha, Státní ústřední archiv v Praze [State Central Archive in Prague] 1998–1999 (hereafter *Dokumenty ČSR-SSSR*); *Czechoslovak-Polish Negotiations of the Establishment of Confederation and Alliance 1939–1944*, Prague, Publishing House Karolinum and the Institute of History, Academy of Sciences of the Czech Republic 1995; *Češi a sudetoněmecká otázka 1939–1945. Dokumenty* [The Czechs and the Sudeten German question. Documents], ed. J. Vondrová, Praha, Ústav mezinárodních vztahů 1994; Edvard Beneš v USA v roce 1943. Dokumenty [Edvard Beneš in the United States in 1943], eds. J. Němeček, H. Nováčková, I. Šťovíček, *Sborník archivních prací* [Reports of archival works], Prague, Vol. 49, 1999, No. 2, pp. 469–564; *Edvard Beneš: Vzkazy do vlasti* [Edvard Beneš: Messages home], ed. J. Šolc, Praha, Naše vojsko 1996; *Československo-francouzské vztahy v diplomatických jednáních 1940–1945* [Czechoslovak-French relations in diplomatic negotiations 1940–1945], eds. J. Němeček – H. Nováčková – I. Šťovíček – J. Kuklík, Praha, HÚ AV ČR – SÚA – UK – Karolinum 2005.

– comments written by particular officials upon every single diplomatic affair – provides the researcher with an amazing opportunity to trace the process of consensus-building inside the key governmental office dealing with foreign policy. It should be stressed that this habit of 'minuting' was something unique amongst other foreign ministries – including the U.S., Russian, French and Czechoslovak ones.[75]

I could supplement these public records with the private papers and diaries of numerous British politicians and diplomats, deposited in London, Cambridge, Oxford and Birmingham. Here I would like to point out at least the 'Czechoslovak' files in the *Bank of England Archive* and also the diaries of Sir Robert Bruce Lockhart located in the *House of Lords Record Office*. These include the hitherto unexplored 'Czechoslovak diary' of 1941 which was also entirely neglected by the editor of the published version of Lockhart's diaries and which throws an interesting light on how British policy towards Czechoslovakia was enacted.

As I have hinted before, the interactive approach is necessary. Therefore my research in the Czech archives, especially the *Foreign Ministry Archive* and the *National Archive* in Prague provided me with valuable material from the 'other side'. Thanks to Hana Velecká I could also make use of the fruits of her own research in the so-called 'Beneš Archive' at the *Archive of the T. G. Masaryk Institute*. Crucial for my topic were also collections of several Czechoslovak émigrés (Eduard Táborský, Ladislav Karel Feierabend, Ivo Ducháček) as well as a few Bruce Lockhart files deposited in the *Hoover Institution Archives* at Stanford University. My research in the *Archiv vneshnei politiki* (Foreign Policy Archive) in Moscow and in the *National Archives* in Washington, D.C., enabled me to view certain aspects of British foreign policy in comparison with the policies of the other two Great Powers.

Structure of the book

Any historian, when thinking about the structure of his text, has to make a decision whether to follow the sequence of events, or whether to divide the whole issue into particular subtopics and only within them follow the time-line. Each of the two approaches has its obvious disad-

---

75) Quite typically, Martin Brown who worked only in the British archives, and thus did not have the opportunity to compare the nature of the archival material produced by the Foreign Office with any other one, tends to stress only the weakneses of the Foreign Office minutes and memoranda. See Brown, *Dealing with Democrats*, pp. 34–40, esp. p. 37.

vantages. Roughly they may be described as the danger of unclearness due to abundance of facts relating to numerous unrelated topics versus an incoherent picture caused by following particular topics singled out of global picture. Therefore I decided to combine the two approaches: Generally, the text is structured along the time-line, but each chapter is divided into sub-chapters according to particular topics that I regard as most significant for the Anglo-Czechoslovak relationship in a given period. Nevertheless, several times I had to return back to the past to provide the historical background for explaining the problems which dominated the relationship only later. Certain overlaps were thus unavoidable (or at least I was unable to escape them).

Chapter 1 (*British foreign policy and Czechoslovakia before Munich 1938*) provides a historical introduction to the topic. It reveals British strategic doctrine and priorities and it assesses the origins, nature and course of the British engagement in the 'Sudeten crisis'.

Chapter 2 (*Britain and the crumbling of Czechoslovakia*) deals with the complex diplomacy of September 1938 to March 1939. It examines the ambiguities of the September 1938 Agreement and its impact on British politics. It reveals the lack of political will on the part of Chamberlain's cabinet to honour its hated guarantee of the Czechoslovak boundaries, which was undertaken in Munich. On the other hand, the financial support to the crippled state and its refugees was thought to assuage the growing feeling of guilt over the Munich settlement. The chapter further reveals that British intelligence failed to predict German intentions until very recently before the German occupation of Bohemia and Moravia and that British politicians agreed with the French that they should not interfere in the new crisis.

Chapter 3 (*Towards the outbreak of war*) covers British policy towards Czechoslovakia between 15 March and the outbreak of the war. It analyses the immediate reaction in Britain to the German destruction of Czechoslovakia and the impact of this event upon the whole course of British foreign policy. It further deals with the residual issues connected with Czechoslovakia, some of which virtually stirred British political scene, while others just testified to lack of political control, during the spring and summer of 1939, in what was considered as minor political issues.

Chapter 4 (*British attitudes towards the development of Czechoslovak political representation in exile*) analyses British policy towards Czechoslovak exiles

(35)

after the destruction of Czechoslovakia and in the initial phase of World War II. It briefly describes overall British assistance to Czechoslovak refugees, before focusing on the attitude to most prominent Czechoslovak politicians who left Czechoslovakia. It examines varying British attitudes to Edvard Beneš and to his attempts to establish a government in exile. It explains why in the autumn of 1939 his efforts fruited in recognition of a mere 'Czechoslovak National Committee'. It further suggests that British policy suddenly changed only after the fall of France and Churchill's accession to power.

Chapter 5 (*The other life of Munich and the 'unbearable lightness' of provisional status*) displays the increasingly important role that Munich played in Anglo-Czechoslovak relationship and the way it influenced the policy of Edvard Beneš and his collaborators on the one hand and Churchill, Eden and the officials at the Foreign Office on the other hand. It further accounts for several achievements of the Provisional government, before focusing on the difficult path to the full *de jure* recognition. It points out the crucial role of external factors in these negotiations, namely the influence of the Dominions upon British policy, and then the Soviet Union with its sudden foreign policy shift after 22 June 1941.

Chapter 6 (*Planning for the future while looking to the past*) shows how the experience of the inter-war years influenced the political planning of Britain and Czechoslovakia. The British clearly favoured federative solution of the problem of Central and South-Eastern Europe. Correspondingly, the Czechoslovak government earned much of its reputation by its advanced negotiations with their Polish counterparts on the establishment of a Confederation. Far more vigorously, however, the protagonists of Czechoslovak foreign policy strove to secure their major aims – reconstitution of Czechoslovakia in her pre-Munich borders and solution of the Sudeten German problem. By mid-1942 they reached the limits of what they could extract from the British, entrenched in their principle of non-commitment. This undoubtedly had its impact on further foreign policy orientation of Czechoslovakia, since Edvard Beneš and his collaborators could far more easily secure their principal aims by the way of close co-operation with the Soviets.

A few terminological comments are perhaps necessary at the end of this introduction: British politicians and officials often used 'the Czechs' when in the politically correct language there should be 'the Czechoslovaks' or rather 'the Czechs and Slovaks' or perhaps even 'the people of Czechoslovakia'. I respect the terminology of the day not only when quoting, but sometimes even when paraphrasing. The same, of course, applies to the pertaining adjectives, as well as to 'Russia', 'Russians' and 'Russian' for the – politically correct – 'Soviet Union', 'Soviets' and 'Soviet'. Similarly, 'Anglo-Czechoslovak' or, indeed, 'Anglo-Czech' should correctly read 'British-Czechoslovak'. However, such are settled terms and I see no point in correcting them. Knowing how sensitive some Czech historians are in these issues and how much they are able to read into it, especially when it comes to Czechoslovakia, I am rather stressing all this.

When I presented the results of my research at an international conference in Austrian Waidhofen an der Thaya,[76] the whole concept of my research and also this book was challenged from a rather unexpected corner: Slovak historian Beata Blehova wondered how I could speak of British policy towards *Czechoslovakia* in 1938–42 if that country had ceased to exist as early as on 14 March 1939. She further underpinned her argument by stressing the legal position of the Slovak government in Bratislava throughout the war as well as of the Soviet government in Moscow from December 1939 to June 1941. My answer to such reservations is – as it was already at the conference – that 'Czechoslovakia' remained at least a concept to which the hopes of most Czech and Slovak refugees, as well as vast majority of inhabitants in the Czech Lands and gradually also in Slovakia, aimed ever since 1939 onwards. Furthermore, none of the democratic powers ever recognised either the German occupation of the Czech Lands or the independent Slovakia *de jure*.[77] I am not willing to adjust the terminology of this book either to the opportunism of the Kremlin rulers or to the position held by father Tiso's government in Bratislava.

76) Conference *Rakousko-české historické dny na Waldviertel Akademie* [Austrian-Czech historical days at the Waldviertel Akademie] – Waidhofen an der Thaya (Austria), 20–21 October 2006. I presented there a paper called *Britská politika a československá otázka mezi Mnichovem a jeho oduznáním v roce 1942* [British policy and the Czechoslovak question between Munich and its renunciation in 1942].
77) However, the British, the French and the U.S. accepted the shift to the hyphenated name of the state since November 1939 – for further details see Chapter 2.

BRITISH FOREIGN POLICY
AND CZECHOSLOVAKIA BEFORE MUNICH 1938
(HISTORICAL INTRODUCTION)

British strategies in the inter-war period

British foreign policy of the inter-war period inherited much from its 19th century paradigm. Although the term 'splendid isolation' does not apply to the years 1918–1938 completely – by then the world became too interconnected by various economic, cultural and other ties – British foreign policy principles towards Continental Europe were similar to those that had served in previous centuries. Under the shadow of the Great War hecatombs British sentiment swung back towards isolation in Europe. Imperial concerns and efforts to promote free trade in the world again dominated the British foreign policy agenda. Britain's involvement in continental affairs remained limited to stability in the west. This was allegedly secured in Locarno in 1925 by the Rhine Pact. Although an alliance with France remained important for any British strategy and it was very unlikely that the Rhine Pact could ever function the other way round (that is to bring Great Britain to Germany's assistance against a French or even Belgian aggression), alliance with France, in A. J. P. Taylor's words, 'expressed a modified form of isolation. Great Britain, by pledging herself to defend France's frontier, would also show that she had no commitment beyond it.'[1] British renunciation by Stanley Baldwin's Cabinet (with Austen Chamberlain as foreign secretary in 1925) of the Geneva protocol that should have committed all signatory states to support any attacked state, only underlined Britain's reluctance to intervene mili-

---

1) Taylor, A. J. P., *The Origins of the Second World War*, London, Penguin Books 1991 [first published by Hamilton 1961], p. 60. Gábor Bátonyi has recently attempted to refute what he called the myth of British désintéressement upon events in Central and Eastern Europe in the 1920s and early 1930s. He derives his conclusion mainly from the huge quantity of British diplomatic papers dealing with the events in those particular countries. See Bátonyi, Gábor, *Britain and Central Europe, 1918–1933*, Oxford, Clarendon 1999. This correspondence, however, only very seldom went beyond monitoring of events or providing mere British recommendations. Apart from commercial exchange, Britain's strategic interest in that part of Europe was limited.

tarily in any territorial disputes beyond the Rhine. The more so, that the Conservative politicians in London did not think that the peaceful development of Europe was intrinsically connected with territorial status quo.

French strategic considerations went in a somewhat different direction. Exposed to the potential threat from Germany – the biggest European Power with a population of 65 million – France with only 40 million people had relied on the alliance with Russia during the last two pre-war decades. Such an alliance automatically halved the German military potential in the west. With the rise of the Bolsheviks in 1917 this alliance became impossible. Hence France focused on developing close ties with new East-Central European states created after the Great War, above all with Poland and Czechoslovakia. France especially supported Poland financially and sent military advisers to both countries. However, the mutual relationship between the two countries was hampered during the whole inter-war period by an unresolved dispute over the Těšín (Teschen) district, while certain animosity between the Poles and Czechs had its roots even deeper in history. Thus it was rather a myth than a reality that the intended alliance of 40 million French with 30 million Poles and 15 million Czechoslovaks would outweigh the 65 million Germans. But the most serious problem of these 'uneasy alliances' was French military doctrine, which under the gloomy impression of heavy casualties in the previous war gradually developed in a defensive way. The decision to erect a set of heavy fortifications along the German border, the notorious Maginot line, emphasised this tendency to divert French military strategy from the country's political strategy.[2] Or it rather indicated that France was ready to make use of alliances with minor allies, while in exchange she was willing to offer little more than an agreement to man her border fortresses. It is also fair to note that the economic reality spoke against political thoughts: while economic ties between France and Poland and Czechoslovakia remained negligible, Germany became a major trading partner for both Czechoslovakia and Poland. Generally speaking, the French alliance system of the inter-war period, which had been intended to prevent Germany from potential expansiveness, remained fragmentary. 'For its full implementation France had neither political flexibility, nor economic power', as noted by Robert Kvaček.[3]

2) See Kissinger, Henry Alfred, *Diplomacy*, New York, Simon & Schuster 1995, pp. 280, 302.
3) Kvaček, Robert, *Obtížné spojenectví. Politicko-diplomatické vztahy mezi Československo-*

The *Machtergreifung* of the Nazis in 1933 accelerated the decline of the European international system as established by the Paris Peace Settlement. The *'Sanacja'* regime in Poland, as it emerged from the coup d'état in May 1926, hastened to negotiate a non-aggression pact with Germany and found *Reichskanzler* Hitler willing to undertake such a vague commitment. Prague, on the contrary, followed Paris in signing a treaty with the Soviet Union only some three weeks after the signing of the French-Soviet alliance. All this was assisted by the Soviet move towards a policy of 'collective security' in Europe in the autumn of 1934. This divergence from foreign policy only fostered mutual suspicion between Warsaw and Prague. While France as a Great Power, though weakening, could afford an alliance with anybody, Czechoslovakia was immediately labelled as the 'aircraft-carrier of Bolshevism' in Europe – a picture colourfully developed above all by the Nazi propaganda. Although Article 2 of the Soviet-Czechoslovak treaty of 16 May 1935 conditioned mutual assistance by previous military support from France, there were numerous influential politicians even in Britain sensitive to this propaganda. Sir John Simon, the then Foreign Secretary and later Chancellor of the Exchequer at the time of Munich, was told, for example, by Hermann Göring in Berlin in April 1935 that there was an arrangement between Czechoslovakia and Soviet Russia by which Russian aeroplanes were to use Czech aerodromes, in the case of an attack against Germany. So much was the Foreign Secretary impressed by the General's 'revelation' that he could not resist four and a half years later, even after the outbreak of war, to ask Edvard Beneš, the then exiled Czechoslovak ex-President, whether Göring's statement had been true. Of course, Beneš's reply was in the negative.[4] However, it should be mentioned that Edvard Beneš himself (still as the Czechoslovak Foreign Minister) 'deserved', to a certain degree, the charge by which Czechoslovakia was branded as Stalin's spy and bastion of Communist International. Compared to Pierre Laval, the French Prime Minister and signatory of the treaty with the USSR, Beneš did not keep calm: after he returned from his visit to the Soviet Union in June 1935, he quite unnecessarily talked to western diplomats, including British

venskem a Francií 1937–38 [A Difficult Alliance. Political-diplomatic relations between Czechoslovakia and France 1937–38], I., Praha, Univerzita Karlova 1989, p. 327.
4) *Bodleian Library*, Oxford (hereafter *Bod. Lib.*), Simon Papers, No. 11, diary entry for 29 September 1939.

Minister Sir Joseph Addison, about the situation in the USSR in such words, with such an enthusiasm, that he soon earned a reputation for naïvety and receptivity towards Stalinist wooing.[5]

Sir John Simon's receptivity towards Göring's contentions can serve as a good example of numerous British self-delusions and misunderstandings in policy towards (Nazi) Germany. This was deeply rooted in the post-Versailles sobering. John Maynard Keynes condemned the Treaty of Versailles as a tool for impoverishing Germany or obstructing its development in the future.[6] Eagerness for revenge was soon replaced by forgiveness for the charge of causing the worst war in history. In certain Conservative circles the feeling that Germany had been deprived of her vital interests became especially widespread. This self-reflection was followed by a search for those who were responsible for agreeing to the 'impossible peace' in Versailles and who were now preventing it from being redrawn. The French became an easy target, no matter that their previous firmness, expressed most emphatically in 1923 by the occupation of the Ruhr district, gradually vanished. Conviction in Britain that something should be done about the unjust post-war settlement deepened with the increasing number of complaints coming from Germany itself about German grievances.

The year 1933 provided an opportunity for Britain to find new foreign policy priorities and to recognise new threats. Instead, however, the British continued to perceive the preservation of their world position as their major priority and therefore continued in their search for European settlement based upon four-power agreement.[7] Reports of Nazi cruelties and analyses of the real character of the new regime, voiced from Germany by British Ambassador Sir Horace Rumbold and other eye-witnesses from the early days since Hitler's rise, were barely heeded beyond the Foreign Office.[8] Yet, although the bulk of the Foreign Office headed by Sir Robert Vansittart realised the growing threat from Germany, it voiced no calls for firmness. As R. A. C. Parker has put it,

5) Lukes, Igor, *Czechoslovakia between Stalin and Hitler. The Diplomacy of Edvard Beneš in the 1930s*, Oxford, Oxford University Press 1996, pp. 52–58.
6) Keynes, John M., *The Economic Consequences of the Peace*, London, Macmillan 1919; see also Neville, Peter, *Hitler and Appeasement. The British Attempt to Prevent the Second World War*, London, Hambledon Continuum 2006, pp. 6–8.
7) See Newman, Michael, The Origins of Munich: British Policy in Danubian Europe, *The Historical Journal*, Vol. 21, 1978, No. 2, pp. 371–386.
8) Gilbert, Martin – Gott, Richard, *The Appeasers*, London, Weidenfeld & Nicolson 1967, pp. 26–27.

all memoranda about Germany from 1934–35 onwards 'set out gloomy forebodings about German intentions and growing German power and then went on to urge compromise and conciliation'.[9] Looking for Anglo-German friendship was perceived by numerous politicians as a necessary precondition for European peace and prosperity. The changing of frontiers – especially in the east of Europe, which was not covered by the Locarno treaties – was gradually viewed in Britain as a possible method for achieving this goal. This tendency reached its zenith in the inglorious visit of Lord Halifax, the then Lord President of the Council, to Hitler's Bavarian mountain residence refuge on Berghof in November 1937. There he told on his own initiative to the German Führer of 'the category of possible alterations in the European order which might be destined to come about with the passage of time'. As such examples he mentioned Danzig, Austria and Czechoslovakia and only made it clear that in Britain's view such 'alterations' should come 'through the course of peaceful evolution'.[10] It is true that amongst British politicians, intellectuals and officials there was a diversified spectrum of opinions as to how to treat Germany. For Eden and Vansittart for example, Halifax's message was a mistake.[11] The position of others slowly stiffened during the late 1930s. Nonetheless, there was also a small but influential band of Germanophiles who were prepared to go to almost any length to avoid another Anglo-German war.[12] And in 1936–38 such approaches were gradually gaining an upper hand.

Simultaneously the British 'National Government' viewed French entanglement in Eastern Europe with a growing feeling of distrust. The Franco-Soviet and Soviet-Czechoslovak treaties seemed to increase the risk of French, and therefore possibly British, involvement in the quarrels of Eastern Europe, and made more likely the division of Europe into rival groupings. Britain, on the contrary, strove to include Germany in negotiated agreements. The French government often seemed to the British Cabinet to be the origin of the continued disappointment. The victory of the Popular Front in the French elections of May 1936 under-

9) Parker, *Chamberlain and Appeasement*, p. 59.
10) Roberts, Andrew, *'The Holy Fox': a Biography of Lord Halifax*, London, Weidenfeld & Nicolson 1991, p. 71.
11) Colvin, Ian, *Vansittart in Office*, London, Victor Gollancz Ltd 1965, p. 165.
12) See Watt, Donald Cameron, Chamberlain's Ambassadors, In: *Diplomacy and World Power. Studies in British Foreign Policy 1890–1950*, eds. M. Dockrill and B. McKercher, Cambridge, Cambridge University Press 1996, p. 146, footnote no. 25.

pinned this feeling of distrust towards France in a British government dominated by the Conservatives. Léon Blum's government set up in June could not shield off the impression of France's weakness, so much highlighted by her lack of response to Hitler's remilitarisation of the Rhineland two months earlier. On the other hand, the composition of the left-wing French government, although only supported by the Communists, added to the instinctive fear of communism – one of the reasons for appeasing Germany. An exaggerated fear of domestic communism in Britain brought many Conservatives to support the rehabilitation of Germany, which was often considered the only real bulwark against Russian penetration westwards. As Paul Kennedy pointed out, this was 'a curious reversal of the pre-war *Realpolitik*, which had encouraged a strong Russia in order to check German expansionism'.[13] And with few exceptions within the Conservative party, this remained a Conservative prejudice until as late as the spring of 1939. Even Hitler's regime was, after all, openly anti-communist and seemed to be capable of preventing the spread of communism in Europe.[14]

The successful remilitarisation of the Rhineland that provoked virtually no Anglo-French reaction gave Hitler clear indication of the lack of western preparedness to defend the European status quo. He became more confident that he could assume even greater risks. Germany could only grow stronger and less vulnerable by fortifying its western border and continuing to rearm. 'Its position, it seemed, could only get better, its risks decrease, as the war France and Britain had been unwilling to chance when they were in a strong position would become more and more dangerous for them.'[15] Halifax's message in November 1937 only confirmed this Hitler's impression.

The 'Czechoslovak year': 1938

After the *Anschluss* of Austria in March 1938, another flagrant violation of the Versailles Treaty, which by then was gradually changing into a piece of historical writing, it became clear that Czechoslovakia was the next item on Hitler's list. Foreign policy experts inside the Foreign Office

---

13) Kennedy, *The Realities behind Diplomacy*, p. 246.
14) Gilbert – Gott, *The Appeasers*, pp. 24–25.
15) Weinberg, Gerhard L., *The Foreign Policy of Hitler's Germany*, Vol. I – *Diplomatic Revolution in Europe*, Chicago and London, The University of Chicago Press 1970, pp. 262–263.

had anticipated this, some of them even with hope and expectation. 'Germany needs Sudetenland, the fate of independent Czechoslovakia is uncertain... The Czechs will no doubt loose their political and economic independence,' a Foreign Office analyst and notable political scientist Edward H. Carr wrote in February 1934, four and a half years before Munich. He expected that the whole Danube basin would gradually be transformed into a zone dominated by German political and economic influence, and concluded that this would bring significant advantages for Great Britain since Central Europe would finally gain a political and economic stability.[16] This position was by no means exceptional within British governmental circles. The popular term of 'self-determination' (of Sudeten Germans) came to be used frequently in the following years in connection with Czechoslovakia. Thomas Inskip, Minister for the Co-ordination of Defence, referred to Czechoslovakia as 'an unstable unit in Central Europe' at the meeting of the Cabinet's Foreign Policy Committee on 18 March 1938, and 'he could see no reason why we should take any steps to maintain such a unit in being'.[17] Sir John Simon, possibly worried by a potential spread of communism via Czechoslovak aerodromes, was quick to call this country 'a modern and very artificial creation with no real roots in the past'.[18] Such a position of Cabinet ministers only mirrored the constant misinformation delivered by several envoys abroad in previous months and years. Among them Sir Joseph Addison, British Minister to Czechoslovakia in 1930–36, played a key role. His telegrams and reports sent from the Thun Palace in Prague were rife with prejudices against the Czechs, who were viewed as 'inferior Slavs', and Czechoslovakia, a nonviable 'artificial country'. He also longed for the reestablishment of the pre-1914 European borders.[19] Similarly Robert Hadow, Addison's trusted deputy, repeatedly depicted a distorted picture of the minority question in Czechoslovakia, relying

16) *Public Record* Office, London (hereafter *PRO*), Foreign Office (hereafter FO) 371/18351, R 2190/37/3, FO Memorandum by E. H. Carr, 26 February 1934.
17) Cited from: *Winston Churchill*, Companion Vol. V., *The Coming of War, 1936–1939*, pp. 948–949.
18) *Ibid.* This was by no means an isolated opinion within the British governmental circles. See Goldstein, Erich, Neville Chamberlain, the British Official Mind and the Munich Crisis, *Diplomacy and Statecraft*, Vol. 10, 1999, No. 2&3 – Special Issue on The Munich Crisis, 1938. Prelude to World War II, pp. 276–292, here p. 282.
19) Cornwall, The Rise and Fall of a 'Special Relationship'?: Britain and Czechoslovakia, 1930–1948, *op. cit.*, pp. 133–134.

primarily on information from Sudeten German leaders, amongst whom Konrad Henlein, the chairman of the semi-Nazi *Sudetendeutsche Partei* (SdP), had a prominent position. Thus Hadow frequently said that Czechoslovakia had ceased to be a democratic country.[20] He also stated that 'Austria and Czechoslovakia had no right to separate existence' and that German hegemony in south-eastern Europe was not only inevitable but desirable.[21] Also Sir Nevile Henderson, the British Ambassador in Berlin who has received much criticism in post-war historical writing,[22] often emphasised 'the highest moral principle', self-determination, in his despatches concerning the Sudeten question.[23] He also had a prejudiced view of the Czechs as a 'pig-headed race'[24] and in D. C. Watt's words thought of 'Czechoslovakia an artificial creation dominated by a people who were collectively not worth the candle and had exaggerated notions of their international status'.[25]

Chamberlain's approach to the crisis in 1938 was in part shaped by the fact that key diplomats and many other influential personalities viewed Czechoslovakia's German minority as morally in the right and the government in Prague in the wrong. The Prime Minister's policy was above all driven by the fear that something that he considered a minor territorial dispute might precipitate a German attack, which, again through the existence of international treaties (resembling the events of 24 years earlier), would draw France and then Russia into a military conflict with Germany. Then the dilemma what Britain should do would arise. On 21 March 1938, the Chiefs of Staff concluded in this regard that no pressure that Britain and her possible allies could bring to bear 'could prevent Germany from invading and over-running Bohemia and from inflicting a decisive defeat on the Czechoslovakian Army'. Thus Britain would be faced with a prolonged struggle with Germany to restore

20) Michie, Lindsay W., *Portrait of an Appeaser. Robert Hadow, First Secretary in the British Foreign Office*, 1931–1939, London 1996, pp. 29–37.
21) These words were reproduced in a telegram sent by George S. Messersmith from the U.S. Legation in Vienna to the Secretary of State in Washington on 4 June 1936. Cited from: Lukes, *Czechoslovakia between Stalin and Hitler*, p. 56.
22) See e.g. Gilbert, Felix, Two British Ambassadors: Perth and Henderson, In: *The Diplomats 1919–1939*, eds. G. A. Craig and F. Gilbert, Princeton, Princeton University Press 1981 [first published by Hamilton 1961], pp. 537–554.
23) Cornwall, The Rise and Fall of a 'Special Relationship'?, *op. cit.*, p. 132.
24) *DBFP*, Vol. II, No. 551, p. 11, letter from Sir N. Henderson to Viscount Halifax, July 26, 1938.
25) Watt, Chamberlain's Ambassadors, *op. cit.*, p. 151.

Czechoslovakia's lost integrity. In such a case both Japan and Italy would probably strive to further their own ends and Britain, in consequence, would envisage not a limited European war, but a world war. Such a world war Britain certainly did not have the resources to win – a warning that had been repeated in similar terms several times from autumn 1935 onwards. However, in this analysis the Chiefs of Staff operated with very doubtful figures. These included a significant underestimation of the strength of the Czechoslovak army (based on the estimates from 1935) and of its stage of readiness (above all the build-up of border fortifications), and dubious foreign policy considerations such as the inclusion of Russia among countries that would remain neutral in the case of European conflagration over Czechoslovakia.[26] In the midst of the crisis, on 14 September 1938, the Chiefs of Staff repeated their view. Although this time they upgraded the figures for the Czechoslovak armed forces, they nevertheless warned against a simultaneous war with Germany, Italy and Japan, which 'neither the present nor the projected strength of our defence forces is designed to meet, even if we were in alliance with France and Russia'.[27] An important incentive for these warnings was Britain's weakness in air defences, as the Air Staff believed that the war would start with an aerial bombardment of England. Correspondingly, and in line with visionary texts by numerous writers, politicians on both sides of the Channel expected Germany's indiscriminate bombing, merciless assaults with germ bombs, explosives and gas to be launched against western capitals immediately upon the outbreak of war. In reality, however, the *Luftwaffe* had neither strategy nor sufficient numbers of necessary heavy-bombers to carry out such 'knock-out-blow'.[28]

If Neville Chamberlain was well aware of how vulnerable the vast and rich British Empire was, the evasive position of the four Dominions, South Africa, Canada, Australia and New Zealand, did not add to Britain's determination to resist German expansion in Central Europe either. The Dominions were not willing to fight to uphold the 1919 treaties. As the key South-African politician Jan Smuts, the Deputy Prime

26) Hauner, Milan, Czechoslovakia as a Military Factor in British Considerations of 1938, *The Journal of Strategic Studies*, Vol. 1, 1978, No. 2, pp. 196–198.
27) *Ibid.*, p. 198.
28) Overy, Richard, *Why the Allies Won*, 2nd edition (first published in 1995), London, Pimlico 2006, pp. 128–131; Howard, Michael, *The Continental Commitment. The Dilemma of British Defence Policy in the Era of Two World Wars*, London, Penguin Books Ltd. 1974, p. 125.

Minister and later Prime Minister during World War II, stated in his letters to several British politicians in March–June 1938, the Dominions as a group would probably fight only in two scenarios: if Britain was in danger of being attacked, and if a member of the Commonwealth was actually attacked.[29]

The British newspapers, an influential catalyst of public opinion, were in the weeks following the *Anschluss* for the most part united that the Sudeten question should not become a *casus belli*, that the real solution lay in negotiation and that a certain pressure by the British government should be exerted upon Prague in this direction.[30] Some of them, such as Lord Beaverbrook's *Evening Standard* and also the appeasement voice, *The Times*, kept the line of seeking a peaceful solution at all costs and recommended British pressure upon the government in Prague, even after it had become clear that a negotiated solution between Hodža's government and representatives of the Sudeten Germans was impossible.

Considering all these factors and arguments the efforts of the British Cabinet until September 1938 went in the direction of preventing this crisis from becoming anything more than a local difficulty.[31] However, there was a certain difference between the British policy in the period before and after the *Anschluss*. While in the former phase the approach of Chamberlain's Cabinet characterised its determination to avoid an Anglo-German clash arising out of the German effort to change the status quo, in the post-Anschluss time Whitehall tried to 'manage' the crisis. Hence, it exerted pressure on the government in Prague to satisfy the grievances of Germans inside Czechoslovakia. If negotiations failed, the Czechs were to understand that Britain and France would not act in the case of German military action against Czechoslovakia. The French would be restrained from promises of armed support for Czechoslovakia against German aggression by the British refusal to promise aid to France. Simultaneously, German violence would be restrained by possible British involvement in a subsequent war. In R. A. C. Parker's

29) Fry, Michael Graham, Agents and Structures: The Dominions and the Czechoslovak Crisis, September 1938, *Diplomacy and Statecraft*, Vol. 10, 1999, No. 2&3 – Special Issue on The Munich Crisis, 1938. Prelude to World War II, pp. 291–341, here p. 296.
30) See Gannon, Franklin R., *The British Press and Nazi Germany 1936–1939*, Oxford, Clarendon Press 1971, pp. 164–165.
31) See Prażmowska, Anita J., *Eastern Europe and the Origins of the Second World War*, New York, St. Martin's Press 2000, p. 94.

words: 'The French and Czechs would be restrained by what the British might not do; the Germans by what the British might do.'[32] However, one important dimension of this policy was spoiled from the very beginning by personal factors, since Nevile Henderson, who frequently ignored instructions from the Foreign Office, was unable to play the warning and restraining role with his German contacts. Convinced that all attempts to deter Hitler would be self-defeating, he was inclined to water down the warnings he was supposed to transmit.[33] He rather decided to intimate to a German diplomat in August 1938 that 'Great Britain would not think of risking even one sailor or airman for Czechoslovakia'.[34] Thus all that remained of the British 'strategy' was pressure on the Czechoslovak government and calls for French restraint.

The story of British involvement in the 'Sudeten crisis' has been narrated many times.[35] Here I will limit myself to a few points:

British politicians, scarcely with any exception, failed to grasp the real substance of the Sudeten question and the position of Konrad Henlein and his associates. Henlein, the gymnastics teacher, succeeded in impressing even the most far-sighted diplomats and politicians in London. Vansittart was 'on very friendly terms' with him and had seen him during each of his three visits to London.[36] In his speeches to the

32) Parker, *Chamberlain and Appeasement*, p. 140.

33) Watt, Chamberlain's Ambassadors, *op. cit.*, p. 152.

34) *Documents on German Foreign Policy*, 1918–1945, Series D, Washington, United States Government Printing Office 1949–1964 (hereafter *DGFP*), Vol. II, No. 337, p. 536, Memorandum by an Official of Political Division I (Heyden-Rynch) for the Foreign Minister, 6 August 1938.

35) Out of uncountable books and studies I would mention just Telford Taylor's encyclopaedic, 1084 pages long, opus magnum: Taylor, Telford, *Munich. The Price of Peace*, London–Sydney–Auckland–Toronto, Hodder and Stoughton 1979. Jindřich Dejmek has recently attempted to provide a complex picture of British-Czechoslovak political and diplomatic relations in the inter-war period and he has also focused in detail on the role that the Sudeten German issue played in that relationship. Dejmek, Jindřich, *Nenaplněné naděje. Politické a diplomatické vztahy Československa a Velké Británie (1918–1938)* [Dashed hopes. Czechoslovak-British political and diplomatic relations (1918–1938)], Praha, Karolinum 2003, esp. pp. 311–450. His work, however, deserves criticism for focusing almost exclusively on diplomatic relations, for the way the author has dealt with both primary and secondary sources, and for his bias against British policy and its representatives. See Smetana, Vít, Dejmkovo velké dílo pod drobnohledem [Dejmek's magnum opus under the microscope], *Soudobé dějiny* [Contemporary history], Prague, Vol. 11, No. 4, pp. 97–116.

36) *Churchill College Archive*, Cambridge, Vansittart Papers, VNST II/17, Vansittart's Memorandum of 16 May 1938 about his lunch with Henlein. This memorandum was

Royal Institute of International Affairs, Henlein emphasised how the Soviet-Czechoslovak treaty of 1935 had turned Czechoslovakia into Russia's aircraft carrier and he stated that the Czechs were tainted with the bacillus of communism.[37] In mid-May 1938 Henlein visited Britain again and Halifax informed the Cabinet afterwards: 'Sir Robert Vansittart had formed two conclusions from his conversation, first that Dr Henlein had no instructions from Berlin, and second that Dr Beneš could get an agreement of a useful character if he would only act quickly.'[38] During his talk with many people of importance Henlein spread the impression that he was just struggling for local autonomy for Sudeten Germans and did not wish them to join Germany.[39] Even Churchill, who met Henlein together with Archibald Sinclair, the leader of the Liberals, 'was very much pleased with the result of the talk'.[40] Both Chamberlain and Halifax expressed their gratefulness for his efforts. Basil Newton, the British minister in Prague, was then informed by Halifax about Henlein's 'present disposition by which Vansittart was impressed', and he was instructed to urge the Czechoslovak government that it 'should make a sincere and thorough going offer at the earliest possible moment, since if the present opportunity is boldly seized a large offer of basis of negotiations made quickly may lay the foundation of an agreement'.[41] But all this was in vain; Henlein was just able to play his role of a moderate politician in London very successfully. As Vansittart's biographer Norman Rose says: 'With all the vast intelligence sources at his disposal, or perhaps because of them, Van[sittart] failed to penetrate beneath the surface of Henlein's masquerading.'[42] The same applied to his less provident and informed colleagues. As early as November 1937, Henlein sent a lengthy memorandum to *Führer*, where he stated that understanding between the Germans and Czechs in Czechoslovakia was practically impossible; the solution was attainable only by the Reich, and he asked

printed as an appendix in *DBFP*, 3rd Series, Vol. I, pp. 630–633. Rather interestingly, the following first sentence of the original memorandum was left out: 'I have been on very friendly terms with Herr Henlein for some years past and have seen him frequently during his visits to London.'

37) See Roberts, *'The Holy Fox'*, pp. 104–105.
38) Cited from: Parker, *Chamberlain and Appeasement*, p. 147.
39) See Nicolson, *Diaries and Letters*, 1930–1939, pp. 340–341.
40) *Winston Churchill*, Companion Vol. V., pp. 1024–1025.
41) *Ibid.*
42) Rose, Norman, *Vansittart, Study of a Diplomat*, London, Heinemann 1978, p. 224.

Hitler for political instructions.[43] On 28 March 1938, he was satisfied by his talk with Hitler in Berlin: '... demands should be made by the Sudeten German Party which are unacceptable to the Czech Government.' Hitler also asked him 'to continue to use his influence with a view to ensuring non-intervention by Britain'.[44] Henlein consented and in the last respect he did a good job two months later.

A week after Henlein's visit to London latent tension in Central Europe suddenly veered towards war. On the basis of intelligence reports of a concentration of German units in the border districts of Saxony, the government in Prague, fearing an incident in the borderland followed by German intervention during the forthcoming municipal elections in Czechoslovakia, early on 21 May decided to call up one class of reservists and several classes of military specialists. Soon the key report compiled by a German Social Democratic politician Willi Lange (agent D-14 in his code name for the 2nd intelligence department of the Czechoslovak General Staff) from messages of his many collaborators turned out to be wrong, but several reports also reached the British Intelligence Service and the Foreign Office.[45] In reality at that moment Hitler was not yet preparing to wage war against Czechoslovakia, but the Czechoslovak move added to his exasperation and on 30 May he signed the *Fall Grün* directive, which opened with the following words: 'It is my unalterable decision to smash Czechoslovakia by military action in the near future.'[46] The rumours, which reached both London and Prague, reflected the turbulent international atmosphere after the *Anschluss* of Austria, rather than any conspiracy instigated by German or even Soviet secret services.[47]

43) *DGFP*, Series D, Vol. II, No. 23, pp. 49–62, The Leader of the Sudeten German Party (Henlein) to the German Foreign Minister, 19 November 1937.
44) *Ibid.*, No. 107, pp. 197–198.
45) See Kokoška, Stanislav, Několik poznámek k československé částečné mobilizaci v květnu 1938 [Several notes on Czechoslovak partial mobilisation in May 1938], In: *Pocta profesoru Janu Kuklíkovi* [Essays in honour of professor Jan Kuklík], Praha, Karolinum 2000, p. 109; see also Parker, *Chamberlain and Appeasement*, p. 148.
46) *DGFP*, Series D, Vol. II, No. 221, p. 358, Directive for Operation 'Green' from the Führer to the Commanders in Chief, 30 May 1938.
47) Kokoška, Několik poznámek..., *op. cit.*, pp. 106–110. The author refuted persuasively Igor Lukeš's unfounded contention that the long report was in fact provocation of the Soviet intelligence service. See Lukeš, Igor, The Czechoslovak Partial mobilisation in May 1938: A Mystery (almost) Solved, *Journal of Contemporary History*, Vol. 31, 1996, pp. 699–720. From indirect evidence Kokoška also deduced that it was not an intelligence game of the German *Abwehr* either.

The British responded in the spirit of their balanced policy: Berlin was warned not to count upon Britain 'being able to stand aside if from any precipitate action there should start a European conflagration'. At the same time Paris was also warned – that it could not count on British assistance in defence of Czechoslovakia, and Halifax told Jan Masaryk, the Czechoslovak Minister in London and son of the first Czechoslovak President, that the least Prague 'could get away with' would be autonomy on 'the Swiss model' and neutrality in foreign policy (!).[48] A clear looser of the 'weekend crisis' was no doubt President Beneš, who was soon stigmatised as a warmonger, as a man of the past who – owing to his intransigence – almost pulled Europe into war just for his concern to keep the 'Versailles order'. However, this concern of his was understandable because the fate of Czechoslovakia was intrinsically connected with this order. On the other hand, the western Great Powers were more and more disposed to significant changes in the Versailles order – if only by peaceful methods.[49] Paradoxically, it was in fact Beneš himself who persuaded the Czechoslovak military commanders on 20 May that they should be content with the calling up of just one class of reservists.[50]

In the spring of 1938 the Sudeten question became an international matter that attracted the attention of the British press and public. Previous assurances of sympathy made to Henlein on his visits to London, although they had been made off the record, had their effect both on him and on his Nazi masters. Thus this attitude contributed to the internationalisation of the Sudeten problem, despite the fact that the Foreign Office was aware that vital British interests were not directly affected there.[51] This process reached its first climax in the summer of 1938. At Basil Newton's suggestion the British government decided to offer its support to the hitherto fruitless negotiations between the Czech government and the Sudeten Germans by sending an 'impartial' intermediary. President Beneš accepted this unusual proposal despite all its liabilities: such a decision was beyond his constitutional powers, it constituted a clear interference in Czechoslovak sovereignty, and it *de facto* ascribed to

48) Parker, *Chamberlain and Appeasement*, p. 149.
49) See Zeman, Zbyněk, with Klimek, Antonín, *The Life of Edvard Beneš 1884–1948. Czechoslovakia in Peace and War*, Oxford, Clarendon Press 1997, pp. 123–124.
50) Kokoška, Několik poznámek..., *op. cit.*, p. 104.
51) Cornwall, The Rise and Fall of a 'Special Relationship'?, *op. cit.*, pp. 136–137.

the government in Prague and the Sudeten Germans the same international status. However, in late July it still seemed that the British envoy would try to mediate a solution within the current Czechoslovak borders and Beneš wanted to show the world Prague's readiness for compromise and also to gain British support. Even Churchill, otherwise openly critical of the government's foreign policy, told his constituents: 'We are all in full agreement with the course our government have taken in sending Lord Runciman to Prague.'[52] Walter Runciman, the National Liberal ex-President of the Board of Trade, declared upon his arrival in Prague that he came 'as an independent person, acting with no instructions, and free from prejudice'. In fact all sides considered him a British official representative and Runciman was aware of Lord Halifax's opinion, that Britain would find it 'very embarrassing' if his mission ended by blaming the SdP for the lack of a settlement.[53] As it became likely towards the end of August that Runciman's effort, despite all his optimistic forecasts, would fail, and the Foreign Office obtained information that Hitler might solve the 'Sudeten problem' by force between the end of September and mid-October, the Prime Minister made a crucial decision to try to avert the growing danger of war by his own negotiations with Hitler. But Runciman's mission, which ended on 15 September after the outbreak and prompt suppression of a Sudeten German uprising by Czechoslovak police, was not useless from the British point of view. At least on 4 September Runciman helped to extract from Beneš his ultimate consent to almost all Sudeten German claims – the eight points of the 'Carlsbad programme' from April 1938. This was to give the Germans full autonomy to such a degree that it hardly made further existence of the common state of Czechs and Germans possible.

From this consent it was only one step towards the complete extinction of Czechoslovakia's Sudeten German territory. It is arguable that this last step, this time already under direct Prime Minister's control, would not have been possible without Lord Runciman's previous efforts.[54] However, his final report came out only at the end of September – it was 'drafted' before the Cabinet meeting held on 21 September and later still rewritten in the Foreign Office.[55] The final version, which was

52) Cited from: Parker, *Churchill and Appeasement*, p. 172.
53) Cornwall, The Rise and Fall of a 'Special Relationship'?, *op. cit.*, p. 137.
54) See Lukes, *Czechoslovakia between Stalin and Hitler*, p. 189.
55) Kvaček, Robert, Mise lorda Runcimana [Lord Runciman's Mission], In: *Osudové*

to condone the current course of British policy, concluded that parts of Czechoslovak territory should be transferred to Germany 'at once', 'promptly' and 'without procrastination'. The report blamed Henlein, his deputy and later German state minister for the *Protectorat Böhmen und Mähren* K. H. Frank, and other 'radical elements' in the *SdP* for the breakdown of negotiations. However, in complete disregard of the latest far-reaching concessions by Beneš, Runciman's report also criticised the Czechoslovak government for its unwillingness to remedy the grievances of the Sudeten Germans.[56]

In the fatal dilemma – how to respond to the frequently reported danger of Hitler's use of force against Czechoslovakia and the threat of a subsequent European war – Neville Chamberlain preferred placating the Berlin dictator rather than threatening him. Under Nevile Henderson's influence the Prime Minister was convinced that threats only added to Hitler's irritation and made him react irrationally. Offers to mediate a settlement of German grievances seemed to be a good prescription for averting the war. In fact Hitler was irritated by *any* British interference in Central European matters. Although amongst his ministers the feeling that Britain 'ought to show that we were thinking of the possibilities of using force' grew stronger and this attitude prevailed also in the Foreign Office, the Prime Minister, assisted by Simon and Samuel Hoare, the Home Secretary, still managed his Cabinet and had an upper hand over his foreign policy advisers.[57] On 7 September the *SdP* broke off the negotiations with the Prague government, under the pretext of an incident in Moravská Ostrava, but above all after Beneš had accepted all their demands. The situation in the border districts of Bohemia and Moravia escalated after Hitler's speech in *Sportpalast* in Nuremberg on 12 September. An uprising broke out, and the following day the government in Prague declared martial law in some parts of the *Sudetenland*. The British 'Inner Cabinet', composed of Chamberlain, Simon, Hoare and Halifax, together with Sir Alexander Cadogan, the Permanent Under-Secretary of State at the FO, then decided to launch the 'Z' plan: twice the Prime

osmičky. *Přelomové roky v českých dějinách* [The Fateful 'Eights'. Turning years in the Czech history], Praha, Nakladatelství Lidové noviny 1999, pp. 182–189. Most authors otherwise just quote the final report as it was published either in the *DBFP* or in *The Times* on 29 September 1938.

56) *DBFP*, 3rd series, Vol. II, Appendix II, pp. 675–679, Letter from Lord Runciman to President Benes, 21 September 1938.

57) Parker, *Chamberlain and Appeasement*, pp. 156–160.

Minister flew to negotiate with Hitler. On his first visit, at Hitler's 'Eagle's Nest' in Obersalzberg, the transfer of districts with German majority was approved in principle. Such a solution had been publicly proposed for the first time by the *Times* foreign policy correspondent Leo Kennedy on 9 September. Since that newspaper was by then considered a vehicle of Cabinet appeasement policy, the article was highly inconvenient as it limited Britain's negotiating position.[58]

The Prague government agreed with the 'Anglo-French' plan to hand over the districts with more than 50% of Germans only after British and French ministers Newton and de Lacroix exerted strong pressure upon Beneš in the early hours of 21 September. This pressure amounted to an ultimatum: in the case of Czechoslovak disapproval Britain would accept no responsibility for further development, whereas France could not fulfil her alliance commitment. On the other hand, the British were willing to join in an international guarantee of the new boundaries of the Czechoslovak state. The 'Inner executive' in London regarded this new commitment for Britain in the centre of the continent of Europe as 'a very grave matter indeed'.[59] Politicians in Prague, however, perceived this as a treacherous act, especially from the French, but also from the British. The roots of much misunderstanding and disappointment in Anglo-Czechoslovak relations in the years to come stemmed from the events of the last ten days of September 1938.

Then, shamefully, Hodža's government consented and decided not to summon the Parliament. Having committed an unconstitutional act, of renouncing the territory without the parliamentary approval, the government resigned the following day. But its decision remained valid. Thus, after Chamberlain's second meeting with Hitler, at Bad Godesberg on 22 September, had failed and French and British governments could not 'continue to take responsibility of advising them [the Czechs] not to mobilise,'[60] a rather peculiar mobilisation started. Men enlisted, quite enthusiastically, to defend their republic in its current borders, while the new government headed by Jan Syrový, hero of the Czechoslovak Legions' performance in the Eastern Front in 1917–1918, with his one eye permanently covered with a black patch so much reminiscent of the

58) Nicolson, *Diaries and Letters*, 1930–1939, pp. 358–359.
59) *Bod. Lib.*, Oxford, Simon Papers, No. 10, diary entry for 29 September 1938.
60) *DBFP*, 3rd series, Vol. II, No. 1027, p. 461, Halifax to Newton, 22 September 1938.

legendary and invincible Hussite military commander of the early 15th century Jan Žižka, discussed what this 50% threshold for districts populated by the Germans actually meant and which disputed areas could be rescued for the future.[61] In several communications to Paris and to London the Czechoslovak government confirmed its general commitment to give up the borderlands inhabited by German population.[62] Munich, a week later, came as a shock to the Czechoslovak government, because the ministers in Prague were not consulted at all and were not able to rescue anything.

If there was any shock for those British politicians who were determined to 'appease' Germany, it came at the meeting in Bad Godesberg. A growing number of ministers in London perceived as blackmail Hitler's further territorial claims and his resolution to get the territory right now, by 28 September. Nothing like an international supervision of handing over of the territory or the intended plebiscites in disputed areas would then be possible. The noble concern of self-reflection, hitherto underlying willingness to bow to German pressure, was suddenly replaced by a feeling that agreement to such blackmail was impossible and that British honour was at stake. 'I *know* we and they [the French] are in no condition to fight,' Cadogan wrote in his diary, 'but I'd rather be beat than dishonoured.'[63] In the following days the Prime Minister was confronted by strong opposition against any further concessions to Germany. Amongst these 'dissidents' were several key ministers including Oliver Stanley, President of the Board of Trade, and Halifax himself, who was apparently under the growing influence of Cadogan. Chamberlain could not withstand their possible resignation.[64] Yet, through Nevile Henderson's co-operation and another mediation in Berlin by Chamberlain's closest ally and personal envoy, Horace Wilson, he eventually avoided showing of resolution and secured a rather 'dishonoured' peace. He felt that he had public opinion behind him in his policy towards Germany. 'How horrible, fantastic, incredible it is that we should be digging trenches and trying on gas-masks here because of a quarrel in a far-away country between people of whom we know nothing,' he said in his broadcast to

61) See Tesař, Jan, *Mnichovský komplex* [The Munich complex], Praha, Prostor 2000, pp. 18–23.
62) Dejmek, *Nenaplněné naděje*, pp. 330–333.
63) *Cadogan Diary*, diary entry for 24 September 1938, p. 104.
64) See Parker, *Chamberlain and Appeasement*, pp. 171–177.

the nation in the evening of 27 September.[65] These words are until these days perceived as an embarrassment in Britain.[66] For decades they have been used by many as a symbol of short-sightedness and even cowardice. But there was, above all, a good deal of common sense in this sentence. The distribution of gas-masks and digging of trenches in St. James's Park and elsewhere in the last days of September 1938 came as a great shock to the British public and remained in its memory for years.[67] War, again! Just twenty years after the horrors of the Great War, in which more than nine hundred thousand British soldiers had died and one generation of the British upper class had been almost entirely exterminated! When the next day Chamberlain suddenly announced Hitler's invitation to Munich at the very end of his speech in the House of Commons, after a couple of days of the greatest war scare since 1918, the feeling of relief was universal. Leaders of all opposition political parties hurried to express their support to Prime Minister's policy. Only the sole Communist deputy, William Gallacher, publicly refused to be a party to the dismemberment of Czechoslovakia.[68] Even Churchill approached Chamberlain and wished him 'God-speed' in his mission. However, his press statement suggests that he rather wished that the ensuing conference failed.[69] Jan Masaryk was in the Foreign Office soon after the Parliament adjourned and was told that public opinion would not tolerate a disruption of the conference over the issue of Czechoslovak representation.[70]

65) *Documents on International Affairs*, Royal Institute of International Affairs, London, OUP 1943, p. 270.

66) See e.g. my interview with R.A.C. Parker, 'Nejen o appeasementu' ['Not only about appeasement'], *Dějiny a současnost* [History and present], Prague, Vol. 21, 1999, No. 1, pp. 44–47, here p. 47.

67) See Hennessy, Peter, *Never Again. Britain 1945–1951*, London, Vintage 1993, pp. 6–7.

68) *H. C. Deb.*, 5th Series, Vol. 339, 28 September 1939, Cols. 26–28.

69) *Winston Churchill*, Companion Vol. V., pp. 1184–1185.

70) See Taylor, *Munich*, p. 11.

The implementation of Munich
and its immediate impact upon British politics

It is not the objective of this chapter to describe, like so many have before,[1] the course of the Munich conference and its results for Czechoslovakia. Rather, I would like to focus on the impact of Czechoslovak problems upon British policy in the aftermath of Munich.

In the evening of 30 September, after his arrival from Heston airport to Westminster, 'amid scenes of indescribable enthusiasm'[2] and proclamation of 'peace for our time' and 'peace with honour', the Prime Minister was greeted at a special meeting of the Cabinet by Simon who expressed 'on behalf of the whole Cabinet, their profound admiration for the unparalleled efforts the Prime Minister had made and for the success that he had achieved'. The Chancellor emphasised 'how proud they were to be associated with the Prime Minister as his colleagues at this time'.[3] The Prime Minister was able to persuade them that he had achieved most satisfactory results, 'he had done his best for Czechoslovakia in the absence of a Czech Government representative' and that the Munich terms differed substantially from those of Godesberg. He stressed that the Munich settlement was similar to the original Anglo-French plan, the evacuation of ceded areas would last longer and conditions for transfers of property ('existing installations') would be more liberal, all disputed areas would be delimited by plebiscites and before these have taken place, supervised by international troops.[4]

The following days and weeks were to show how wrong the Prime Minister was. An international commission, where Czechoslovakia was

1) See e.g. Mosley, Leonard, *On Borrowed Time*, London, Weidenfeld and Nicolson 1969, pp. 63–68; Kee, Robert, *Munich: The Eleventh Hour*, London, Hamish Hamilton 1988, pp. 198–204.
2) Duff Cooper, Alfred, *Old Men Forget,* New York, Dutton 1954, p. 242.
3) *Bod. Lib.*, microfilm of Public Record Office files (hereafter microfilm), CAB 23/95, Cab 47(38), 30 September 1938.
4) *Ibid.*

to have a representative, besides four others representing the Munich Powers, was established to settle all disputed matters. But the two Czechoslovak delegates, Arnošt Heidrich and Eduard Machatý, adhered in the following weeks to a new foreign policy doctrine of post-Munich Czechoslovakia. The protagonists of co-operation with the West disappeared after the Munich fiasco: Foreign Minister Kamil Krofta resigned on 4 October, President Beneš the following day. The new Foreign Minister František Chvalkovský, convinced of future long-term German supremacy in Europe, embarked on a policy of submitting to numerous German demands as a way of securing national existence.[5] The international commission achieved most of its decisions in accordance with several German-Czechoslovak 'agreements', in which neither the French, nor the British representative (Nevile Henderson) interfered in principle. Henderson's position during the negotiations in Berlin was 'that the Czechs should now come to the Germans and say: "We abandon the Benes policy and we wish to live in peace with Germany both politically and economically. Let us delimitate our own frontiers and settle our outstanding questions between ourselves."'[6] Accordingly, a crucial decision was reached to dispense with plebiscites, which, as Halifax noted, 'incidentally, relieved us of the responsibility for sending out the British Legion to police the plebiscite areas'. The final frontier between Germany and Czechoslovakia was to be settled by representatives of the two governments.[7] When it was finally agreed on 20 November, Chamberlain described the result as 'a compromise in which Czechoslovakia had conceded everything and gained nothing' and referred to a further 30,000 Czechs and 6,000 Germans who had passed under German rule. 'The result was to be deplored but there was nothing that we could do in regard to the matter,' the Prime Minister concluded at a Cabinet meeting.[8]

Similarly, the treaty signed by the Czechoslovak-German Commission on 20 November 1938, effectively denied the Germans domiciled

5) See Dejmek, Jindřich, Československá diplomacie v době druhé republiky (říjen 1938 – březen 1939) [Czechoslovak diplomacy in the time of the Second Republic (October 1938 – March 1939)], In: *Pocta profesoru Janu Kuklíkovi* [Essays in honour of professor Jan Kuklík], Praha, Karolinum 2000, pp. 9–26.
6) *DBFP*, 3rd series, Vol. III, Appendix I, p. 615, Letter from Henderson to Halifax, 6 October 1938.
7) *Bod. Lib.*, microfilm, CAB 23/96, Cab 49(38), 19 October 1938.
8) *Ibid.*, Cab 56(38), 23 November 1938.

in the Sudeten German territories the right to opt for Czechoslovakia. The discriminatory clause was introduced by the Czechoslovak government which after the recent experience did not wish to receive any more Germans on its territory and the German government readily gave in.[9] Growing anxiety in Parliament about the fate of German Jews, socialists and other democrats,[10] however, forced Chamberlain in February 1939 to inquire this matter of the German Ambassador during their common dinner at the German Embassy. After having consulted the Wilhelmstrasse, Herbert von Dirksen stated that the Munich Agreement had not indicated which persons should have the right of option, and he referred to the treaty which based the decision 'on the principle of parity' whereby the right of option applied only to the Germans in Czechoslovakia and non-Germans in the Sudetenland. He further stated that the anxieties of the Opposition were 'unfounded' because 'almost all those Germans who [had] feared to be brought to justice for former offences', no less than 13,000, had moved into Czechoslovakia before the German troops had occupied the Sudeten districts. 'I should think this is very likely,' Chamberlain commented and decided to thank the German Ambassador 'and leave it at that'.[11] Cadogan, on the other hand, called the refusal of the right to opt 'a breach of the spirit, if not of the letter, of the Munich agreement',[12] but no official protest followed.

For the purpose of public statements, however, the position was clear. As late as on 2 February 1939, the Parliamentary Under-Secretary of State for Foreign Affairs, Richard A. Butler, replied on behalf of the Prime Minister with a simple affirmative to a parliamentary question whether he was satisfied that the conditions of the Munich Agreement had been, or were being, carried out.[13] 'It would be hard to maintain that the spirit of the Munich Agreement had been observed,' Frank Roberts of the Central Department of the Foreign Office noted, 'but it is, I think possible to maintain that technically the conditions of the Munich Agreement have been carried out.'[14]

9) *PRO*, FO 371/22995, C 3555/19/18, Makins' minute, 20 February 1939.
10) *H. C. Deb.*, 5th Series Vol. 343, 13 February 1939, Cols. 1350–1351.
11) *PRO*, FO 371/22995, C 3555/19/18, Dirksen to Chamberlain, 23 February 1939, 3 undated Chamberlain's comments.
12) *Ibid.*, Cadogan's minute, 16 February 1939.
13) *H. C. Deb.*, 5th Series, Vol. 343, 2 February 1939, Col. 384.
14) *PRO*, FO 371/22991, C 1484/17/18, Roberts' minute, 1 February 1939.

The feeling of relief and enthusiasm was by no means universal after Chamberlain's return from Munich. On 1 October Churchill adjured the Czechoslovak Government not to hand vital fortifications at least for the next 48 hours. According to Masaryk's report he was convinced that 'a great reaction against the betrayal committed on us' occurred and grew in Britain.[15] Masaryk evidently toned down Churchill's assertion; Chamberlain immediately complained to his sister about Churchill-Masaryk conspiracy: 'I had constant information of their doings and sayings which for the nth time demonstrated how completely Winston can deceive himself when he wants to and how utterly credulous a foreigner can be when he is told the thing he wants to hear. In this case the thing was that "Chamberlain's fall was imminent"!'[16] Apparently, Churchill could not imagine that his telephone talks might be intercepted; when in May 1939 Masaryk worried – in one of his telegrams sent from the United States – lest the information contained got 'to some Munichites', Churchill placated him: 'Have no fear about our telegrams being under surveillance by the Government. We have not got to that yet here.'[17] Obviously this was 'the nth + 1' case that Winston Churchill deceived himself...

Nonetheless, the situation became really serious for Chamberlain in the days after Munich. First Lord of the Admiralty Duff Cooper resigned in protest against Munich and received some four thousand letters in the following days, about 90% of them congratulatory.[18] Harry Crookshank, the Secretary for Mines and a person highly influential in the Conservative Party, also delivered his resignation to the Prime Minister and changed his mind only after an intervention from the Chief Whip and after Chamberlain himself had spent with him 'a hectic half hour'.[19] Another important minister who came close to resignation over Munich was Oliver Stanley, the President of the Board of Trade. He considered the Agreement an uneasy truce and in a letter from 3 October he warned the Prime Minister that he would express publicly his scepticism as to Nazi promises and his real opinion of Nazi policy in response to any

---

15) *DČSZP 1938*, II, No. 788, p. 471, Masaryk to Foreign Ministry, 1 October 1938.
16) *Birmingham University Library*, Chamberlain Papers, NC 18/1/1071, Neville Chamberlain's letter to his sister Ida, 9 October 1938.
17) *Winston Churchill*, Companion Vol. V., pp. 1503–1504.
18) Duff Cooper, *Old Men Forget*, p. 245.
19) *Birmingham University Library*, Chamberlain Papers, NC 18/1/1071, Neville Chamberlain's letter to his sister Ida, 9 October 1938.

possible attempt to lull public opinion.[20] Con O'Neill, 3rd Secretary of the British Embassy in Berlin, expressed his disagreement with Munich in a letter to William Strang, the head of the Central Department, and resigned from the diplomatic service. Halifax himself read the 31 pages long letter 'with much interest'.[21] Chamberlain temporarily gave up further negotiations with the dictators for fear that it would set off additional resignations from the government.[22] This continued later on; as late as in December Chamberlain complained to both of his sisters of crisis mood in the Cabinet and constant threats of resignations.[23]

It is easy to find numerous records of disappointment and worries scattered in diaries of many politicians and diplomats.[24] Foreign Office civil servants, debating options for the future course of British foreign policy, did not hesitate to call Munich a *'debacle'* and all stressed the necessity of adopting a substantial rearmament programme.[25] Indeed, the government found themselves in a quandary. In Harold Nicolson's words, it was difficult to say: 'This is the greatest diplomatic achievement in history: therefore we must redouble our armaments in order never again to be exposed to such humiliation.'[26] But this was almost exactly what happened. Recent research suggested that Chamberlain returned from Munich genuinely convinced that it was possible to remodel

20) See Watt, *How War Came,* p. 80.

21) *Churchill College Archive,* Cambridge, Strang Papers, STRN 4/2, O'Neal to Strang, 29 November 1938, Halifax's minute, 16 December 1938.

22) *Birmingham University Library,* Chamberlain Papers, NC 18/1/1071, Neville Chamberlain's letter to his sister Ida, 9 October 1938.

23) *Ibid.,* NC 18/1/1079, Neville Chamberlain's letter to his sister Hilda, 11 December 1938; NC 18/1/1080, Neville Chamberlain's letter to his sister Ida, 17 December 1938.

24) Nicolson, *Diaries and Letters 1930–1939,* diary entry for 30 September 1938, p. 372: 'Still this great acclamation of Chamberlain, but in it a note of uncertainty beginning to come through.'; Amery, Leo, *The Empire at Bay. The Leo Amery Diaries 1929–45,* ed. J. Barnes and D. Nicholson, London, Hutchinson 1988, diary entry for 4 October 1938, p. 526: 'Meanwhile the situation in unhappy Czechoslovakia looks like sliding from bad to worse every minute. The worse it gets the greater I fear will be the growing disappointment and alarm of the British public.'; *The Diplomatic Diaries of Oliver Harvey 1937–1940,* diary entry for 30 September 1938, p. 203: 'Vast crowds in the streets – hysterical cheers and enthusiasm. P. M. on balcony at Buckingham Palace. But many feel it to be a great humiliation.'; *The Diaries of Sir Robert Bruce Lockhart 1915–1938,* diary entry for 2 October 1938, p. 399: '... there was much cheering of Chamberlain but also a few shouts of 'What is your peace worth?' and 'How long'.'

25) Lammers, Donald, From Whitehall after Munich: The Foreign Office and the Future Course of British Policy, *The Historical Journal,* Vol. 16, 1973, No. 4, pp. 831–856.

26) Nicolson, *Diaries and Letters 1930–1939,* p. 374.

Europe in a peaceful and just manner and did not consider Munich as a *'borrowed time'* for the stiffening of Britain's armament programme.[27] However, in the House of Commons he was confronted with a severe criticism from members of all parties.

Winston Churchill, evaluating the situation from strategic position, spoke of 'a total and unmitigated defeat'. He expected the growth of the German army in the following year and regretted the loss of 'that fine army of ancient Bohemia' that would have required not fewer than 30 German divisions for its destruction. 'Many people, no doubt, honestly believe that they are only giving away the interests of Czechoslovakia, whereas I fear we shall find that we have deeply compromised, and perhaps fatally endangered, the safety and even the independence of Great Britain and France.' Churchill predicted prophetically that 'in a period of time which may be measured by years, but may be measured only by months, Czechoslovakia will be engulfed in the Nazi régime' and pointed out the apparent alienation of the whole region of East-Central Europe.[28] Besides members of 'Churchill and Eden groups' strong criticism of Chamberlain's 'Munich' policy came from Archibald Sinclair's Liberals and also from the Labour Party (Arthur Greenwood in particular[29]) – but only several years after Labour politicians had criticised (until 1937) virtually every penny assigned to armament. 'All the world seemed to be full of my praises except the House of Commons,' Chamberlain bitterly complained to his sister.[30] At the end of the 'Munich debate', which lasted four days, the Prime Minister was compelled to dismiss any idea of disarmament, 'until we can induce others to disarm too' and pledged to a 'thorough inquiry' of previous military and civil preparations with the aim to find out 'what further steps may be necessary to make good our deficiencies in the shortest possible time'.[31] 'We have avoided the greatest catastrophe,' he wrote in a letter to his sister Hilda on 15 October, 'but we are very little nearer the time when we can put all thoughts of war out of our minds.'[32] He found the conciliation part of the policy and the rearm-

27) Parker, *Chamberlain and Appeasement*, pp. 180–181.
28) *H. C. Deb.*, 5th Series, Vol. 339, 5 October 1938, Cols. 360–374.
29) *Ibid.*, Cols. 351–359.
30) *Birmingham University Library*, Chamberlain Papers, NC 18/1/1071, Neville Chamberlain's letter to his sister Ida, 9 October 1938.
31) *H. C. Deb.*, 5th Series, Vol. 339, 6 October 1938, Col. 551.
32) *Birmingham University Library*, Chamberlain Papers, NC 18/1/1072, Neville Chamberlain's letter to his sister Hilda, 15 October 1938.

ing equally important. Although he did not give up his hopes for general disarmament, the records of follow-up Cabinet meetings show that at least in one case it was Chamberlain himself who called for further intensification of Britain's rearmament effort and production of anti-aircraft guns in particular.[33] The Cabinet launched the production of heavy bombers, while at the same time manufacture of fighters and searchlights were accelerated. Leslie Hore-Belisha, the War Minister, argued successfully for an increase in the Expeditionary Force and by early 1939 he managed to persuade his colleagues that if there were war in Europe, Britain would have to send a considerable army to the Continent. Its 'strength' of just two divisions had weakened Britain's position vis-à-vis France significantly in the recent crisis.[34] Chamberlain was also determined to do something to encourage Daladier 'to put France's defences in order'.[35]

The ecstasy of Munich gradually vanished and was replaced by painful sobering. In Piers Brendon's words: 'What had seemed a brave bid for peace in September appeared, as autumn progressed, to be a fatal act of cowardice in the face of alien might.'[36] It became clear that the new settlement was catastrophic for Czechoslovakia even in comparison to Hitler's demands in Godesberg.[37] Hostile utterances about Britain and her politicians in several of Hitler's speeches did not seem promising for future European peaceful coexistence, while dark barbarism of the *Kristallnacht* shocked British public and its political elite.

33) At a December Cabinet meeting he proposed to 'adopt a somewhat bolder course' than suggested by the Minister for Co-ordination of Defence, Sir Thomas Inskip, and to build a new factory with a larger output than 300 guns a year. *Bod. Lib.*, microfilm, CAB 23/96, Cab 60(38), 21 December 1938.

34) See Watt, *How War Came*, pp. 93–94, 165.

35) *Birmingham University Library*, Chamberlain Papers, NC 18/1/1075, Neville Chamberlain's letter to his sister Hilda, 6 November 1938.

36) Brendon, Piers, *The Dark Valley. A Panorama of the 1930s*, London, Pimlico 2001, p. 534.

37) Czechoslovakia lost vast territories as a result of Munich and the delimitation of the border with Germany, Polish occupation of the Teschen district and the Vienna Award, which meant cession of southern Slovakia to Hungary. Out of pre-Munich 140 530 km^2 only 102 530 km^2 remained. Thus almost 5 million inhabitants were transferred to bordering states, including 1,1 million of Czechs and Slovaks. Czechoslovakia lost about 70% of coal deposits. Also 70% of iron industry got lost, losses of glass and textile industry exceeded 80%. The key railways and roads were cut and it became necessary to cross German territory when travelling from Bohemia to Moravia and from Moravia to Slovakia. Main source of electricity for the capital was transferred to the Reich and many big cities were now dependent on supplies of potable water from abroad. Feierabend, *Politické vzpomínky*, Vol. I, p. 51.

None of the eight Parliamentary by-elections in autumn 1938 signalled enormous gratitude to Chamberlain for ensuring 'peace for our time'. Indeed, the Conservatives lost two seats. The initial idea to make use of Prime Minister's popularity for running a General Election was soon abandoned.[38] Two by-elections attracted most attention: In Oxford Conservative candidate Quintin Hogg, who supported Chamberlain, eventually headed the poll, but the result was by no means satisfactory to the government as the Conservative majority dropped by half compared to General Election of 1935.[39] In Bridgwater Vernon Bartlett, the independent candidate and well-known journalist and broadcaster supported by the Liberals, easily destroyed what seemed a safe Conservative majority.[40]

Besides intensification of Britain's rearmament (though insufficient compared to Germany), the results of the Czechoslovak crisis brought along a fresh wave of support for an alternative anti-Chamberlain government. But the time was not yet ripe for any radical changes. Despite some consultations among several Labour and National Liberal MPs together with members of the Eden and Churchill groups, these initiatives led up to nothing. The Labour Party was not ready to compromise its independence unless there was a big breakaway in the Conservative Party. This, however, did not happen.[41] Indeed, the major advocate of such a *volte-face* of the Labour policy, Sir Stafford Cripps, along with his associates, was excluded from the party as late as in the spring of 1939, precisely for his stubborn public calls for the Popular Front.[42]

The question of the Munich guarantee

British as well as French diplomacy played a peculiar role with respect to the guarantees for Czechoslovakia given in Munich, or even before it – as a reward for succumbing to the Anglo-French 'timetable' of 19 September 1938 for handing over the Czechoslovak borderlands. The

38) Parker, *Chamberlain and Appeasement*, p. 189.
39) Macmillan, Harold, *Winds of Change 1914–1939*, London, Macmillan 1966, p. 584.
40) Parker, *Churchill and Appeasement*, pp. 198–199.
41) Dalton, Baron Hugh, *The Fateful Years: Memoirs 1941–1945*, London, F. Muller 1957, pp. 198–207.
42) Bryant, Chris, *Stafford Cripps. The First Modern Chancellor*, London, Hodder & Stoughton 1997, pp. 169–182; Clarke, Peter, *The Cripps Version. The Life of Sir Stafford Cripps*, London, Allen Lane 2002, pp. 80–83; Dalton, *The Fateful Years*, pp. 209–221.

annex to the Munich Agreement of 29 September 1938 stated that the British and French governments had 'entered into the above agreement on the basis that they stand by the offer, contained in paragraph 6 of the Anglo-French proposals of 19 September relating to an international guarantee of the new boundaries of the Czechoslovak State against unprovoked aggression'. Germany and Italy undertook to give their guarantees 'when the question of the Polish and Hungarian minorities in Czechoslovakia has been settled'.[43]

Historiography has so far paid little attention to the long drawn-out negotiations between October 1938 and February 1939 over the promised guarantee, or to the role that this topic played in the relations among the four Munich Powers.[44] The focus is traditionally upon the Prime Minister's words in the House of Commons of 15 March 1939 that the Slovak proclamation of independence the day before had made the British guarantee of Czechoslovakia meaningless.[45] This limited interest of most historians is all the more surprising because, unlike in September 1938, this time Britain was bound by a written international commitment and thus her failure to stand up to the German aggression hardly added to Britain's international reputation, and, above all, appeared to vindicate the already enormous suspicion of Stalin. The actual deliberations over the guarantee in the Foreign Office and the painful search for a way out of this unwelcome commitment have so far not been sufficiently analysed.

Chamberlain said to his Cabinet immediately after his return from Munich that 'the guarantee of France and Great Britain entered into operation at once', while guarantees of Germany and Italy depended on the settlement of the Hungarian and Polish minority questions.[46]

43) *DBFP*, Vol. II, No. 1224, pp. 628–629, United Kingdom Delegation (Munich) to Halifax, 30 September 1938.
44) Exceptions are: Bystrický, Valerián, Otázka garancie hraníc Československa po mníchovskoj konferencii [The question of the guarantee of the Czechoslovak frontiers after the Munich conference], *Slovanský přehled* [Slavic survey], Prague, 1990, No. 2, pp. 115–125; Procházka, Theodore, *The Second Republic: The Disintegration of Post-Munich Czechoslovakia (October 1938 – March 1939)*, New York, Columbia University Press 1981, pp. 76–83; Adamthwaite, Anthony, *France and the Coming of the Second World War, 1936–1939*, London, Totowa 1977, pp. 269, 278–279; Taylor, *Munich*, pp. 918–922. None of these authors, however, worked with British archival documents.
45) *H. C. Deb.*, 5th Series, Vol. 345, Cols. 437–442. See e.g. Watt, *How War Came*, pp. 87, 166–7; Parker, *Chamberlain and Appeasement*, pp. 200–201.
46) *Bod. Lib.*, microfilm, CAB 23/95, Cab 47(38), 30 September 1938.

During the 'Munich debate' Home Secretary Hoare expressed his be-lief 'that the international guarantee in which we have taken part will more than compensate for the loss of the strategic frontier'. Even more binding was the declaration made by the Minister for Co-ordination of Defence, Sir Thomas Inskip, that his government felt 'under a moral obligation to Czechoslovakia to treat the guarantee as being now in force. In the event, therefore of an act of unprovoked aggression against Czechoslovakia, His Majesty's Government would certainly feel bound to take all steps in their power to see that the integrity of Czechoslovakia is preserved.'[47]

However, real political steps in the subsequent weeks aimed at Britain's practical withdrawal from this commitment. The more Czecho-slovakia was pulled into the German orbit, the stronger was this British tendency to withdraw. In Halifax's words, it was desirable that Britain should avoid taking action 'with France and Russia against Germany and Italy on behalf of a State which we were unable effectively to de-fend'.[48] French diplomats had suggested that the guarantee should be 'joint and several'. However, this was not acceptable to the British. In a Cabinet Paper dated 12 November the Foreign Office wished virtu-ally everyone to join in a guarantee to the crippled country: the four Munich Powers, Poland, Rumania, Yugoslavia – even the Soviet Union, although 'considerable difficulties in the way of securing her inclusion' were to be seen, given Hitler's objective of excluding Russia from Central Europe, and Poland's categorical refusal to allow the transit of Russian troops across her territory. However, in spite of these deficien-cies the paper argued that the British 'should endeavour to arrange that Russia should be a guarantor' unless it became apparent that German or Italian objections to this would cause the entire scheme to break down. The memorandum further suggested that the minimum number of guarantors should be four out of the six Great Powers (Great Britain, France, Germany, Italy, Poland 'and perhaps Russia'). It was obvious that a strictly joint guarantee, which would only become operative if all the guarantors agreed to act, would, 'from the point of view of Czechoslovakia, not be worth the paper it was written on'. On the other hand, the Foreign Office wanted to avoid the possibility of stand-ing together with France against Germany and Italy: 'For instance, on

47) *H. C. Deb.*, 5th Series, Vol. 339, 4 October 1938, Col. 303.
48) *Bod. Lib.*, microfilm, CAB 23/96, Cab 57(38), 30 November 1938.

geographical and strategic grounds and in view of Germany's military superiority in the air and on land, a guarantee limited to, say, France and Great Britain could probably not be effectively implemented in the present circumstances, and for this reason would not act as a deterrent,' especially if Italy and Czechoslovakia's neighbours were to support Germany.[49]

During Anglo-French conversations at the Quai d'Orsay on 24 November, Halifax and Chamberlain then proposed that the guarantee would only come into force as a result of a decision to act by *three* of the four *Munich* Powers. French Foreign Minister Georges Bonnet argued that although such a guarantee was not 'out of conformity with the letter' of the Anglo-French plan of 19 September, 'it was hardly in conformity with the spirit'. However, despite initial protests that such a guarantee could, in fact, be worth less than one made by any of the four Powers alone, the French eventually – as so many times before and after[50] – gave in. Halifax warned against 'a repetition' of the September crisis, 'for, in the future, France and Great Britain would be in a far worse position'. The two delegations concurred that 'the working of the guarantee in the event of unprovoked aggression by Germany or her satellites against Czechoslovakia could not, in fact, help the latter country'. It was decided to ascertain the views of the Czech government on the proposed joint guarantee and to handle the problem through Prague,[51] although the German influence there was increasing every day.

Although the Czechs had intimated in October that they wanted the guarantee as soon as possible, this eagerness started to disappear after Chvalkovský was confronted with Hitler's blackmail and open threats during his visit to Berlin on 13–14 October. Hitler, hating *any* British interference in Continental affairs,[52] discounted hopes of Western guarantees and argued that the only guarantee, which mattered, was the German one. However, he made it conditional by insisting on internal changes

---

49) *Bod. Lib.*, microfilm, CAB 24/280, C. P. 258(38), British Guarantee for Czechoslovakia, 12 November 1938.

50) This growing French dependence on British foreign policy proved itself for example in Munich, as well as in the guarantees given to Poland where Paris again only followed British initiative.

51) *DBFP*, 3rd Series, Vol. III, No. 325, pp. 300–306, Record of Anglo-French Conversations held at the Quai d'Orsay on 24 November 1938.

52) See e.g. Kershaw, Ian, *Hitler 1936–1945. Nemesis*, London, The Penguin Press 2000, pp. 123, 178.

in Czechoslovakia. After this experience Chvalkovský decided 'not to believe in chimeras and phantasms' any more, and to do everything to extract the desired guarantee from Berlin.[53] The British and French were, of course, aware of growing Czechoslovak dependence on Germany. Indeed, as early as mid-October, Halifax had thought that the Czechoslovak government would have to come to terms with Germany on both economic and political matters.[54] Basil Newton reported signs of growing authoritarianism and Czecho-Slovak[55] dependence on Germany. On 5 December he concluded – quite correctly – that 'while at bottom feelings of the Czechs have probably altered but little towards Germany as a result of the crisis, and while they would like to preserve their economic independence as far as possible, no Czechoslovak Government today has any option but to submit to German dictation whether in political or economic field'.[56] After reading one of Newton's despatches Sir Orme Sargent, Deputy Under-Secretary of State in the Foreign Office, began 'to wonder what purpose will be served by our guaranteeing the vassal state – and for whose benefit we shall be giving our guarantee and against whom it is likely to be invoked. It is as though Germany were to guarantee Egypt!'[57] Sir Robert Vansittart, perhaps the starkest opponent of the policy of appeasing Germany who had been correspondingly sidelined to the newly created position of the Chief Diplomatic Adviser of the government, disagreed. Although he admitted that Czechoslovakia was now a 'vassal state', he reminded his FO colleagues that the British were 'at least partly responsible for that'. Though there was nothing left to guarantee, he thought that the argument that Britain should now renege from her promise did not 'lie well in *our* mouths. It would come better from the enslaved.'[58]

---

53) Dejmek, Československá diplomacie..., *op. cit.*, p. 13.
54) *Bod. Lib.*, microfilm, CAB 23/96, Cab 49(38), 19 October 1938.
55) On 22 November 1938, two constitutional laws granting autonomous status to Slovakia and Ruthenia (Sub-Carpathian Russia) came into force. These changes established also the new – hyphenated – name of the state. British diplomats stuck strictly to this name at least until the outbreak of war and in some cases even as late as in 1940. Since this hyphenated version was valid only from 22 November 1938 till 14 March 1939, I am using it only when quoting or interpreting diplomatic correspondence where it was used.
56) *DBFP*, 3rd Series, Vol. III, Nos. 245, 398, 413, pp. 213–217, 380–381, 407–414, Newton to Halifax, 1 November, 5 December, 8 December 1938.
57) *PRO*, FO 371/21580, C 15338/2475/12, Sargent's minute, 16 December 1938.
58) *Ibid.*, Vansittart's minute, 23 December 1938.

The Foreign and War Offices were sensitive to the strategic aspects of the influence exercised by Germany and followed movements of German troops across Czecho-Slovak territory with growing misgivings, well aware that Britain could hardly change these geo-strategic realities.[59] Much attention, even in Parliament, was paid to the agreement to use Czechoslovak railways for German military purposes and the construction of a German highway from Breslau to Vienna, which was to be available for the free passage of German troops.[60] This autobahn, 210 miles long and due to be completed by 1940, was to be fenced in and considered German territory, thus facilitating potential concentrations of troops against Poland or against Yugoslavia and confirming the defencelessness of Prague. As a War Office 'appreciation paper' pointed out, 'the Germans, by building a main line of communications through Czechoslovakia have clearly created a position which in fact, if not in name, reduces that country to the status of a dependency of the Reich'. It was also expected that future Czechoslovak communications would be developed in accordance with the requirements of Germany's plans for an eastward advance.[61] Similarly, the Military Attaché in Prague Major G.A.C. Macnab viewed the capabilities of the post-Munich Czechoslovak army with realistic pessimism: 'The present shape of Czechoslovakia, combined with its lack of fortifications, render it a virtual impossibility for the Czechoslovak army in its reorganised state to defend the country against future German aggression.'[62] Indeed, 'Czechoslovakia as an independent State economically and militarily exists today only on sufferance,' Military Intelligence concluded in mid-December; the state could 'put no reliance in France and ourselves as guarantors of the frontier since we are not in a position to render effective assistance'.[63]

59) *PRO*, FO 22992, C 1385/19/18, Troutbeck to Foreign Office, No. 44, 30 January 1939, C 2200/19/18, Foreign Office to Troutbeck, No. 5 Saving, 22 February 1939; FO 371/22958, C 2099/13/18, Troutbeck to Foreign Office, No. 38 Saving, 16 February 1939.
60) *PRO*, FO 371/22992, C 1164, C 1192, C 1385, C 1609, C 2491/19/18; *H. C. Deb.*, 5th Series, Vol. 342, 21 December 1938, Col. 2853; Vol. 343, 6 February 1939, Col. 623.
61) *PRO*, WO 190/741, Communication Developments in Czechoslovakia, January 1939.
62) *DBFP*, 3rd series, Vol. III, Enclosure in No. 414, pp. 416–417, Memorandum respecting Military Aspects of the Proposed Breslau-Vienna Autostrada, 1 December 1938.
63) *PRO*, WO 190/731, Note on Value of Czechoslovakia as an independent State since Munich, 13 December 1938.

Jan Masaryk was well aware of how the British were interpreting events on the ground in Czechoslovakia, and on 5 December, in the last report before his resignation, informed his Foreign Ministry that the British now viewed Czechoslovakia as a German satellite.[64] The more obvious this became, the less the Western Powers were prepared to guarantee its independence and frontiers. However, the same applied the other way round: The greater this lack of will in London and Paris, the more hazardous and futile it was for the new Czechoslovak political representatives to rely on Anglo-French support.

When Newton was informed about the conclusions of the Anglo-French conversations of mid-November, he was reminded that the British government was not prepared 'to consider a guarantee which might oblige them, alone or with France, to come to the assistance of Czechoslovakia in circumstances in which effective help could not be rendered'. That would be the case if either Germany or Italy were the aggressor and the other declined to fulfil the guarantee. He was also warned that Czechoslovakia, counting upon French and British help, 'might be tempted to adopt an attitude towards Germany which would only create the trouble we all wish to avoid'. This was an odd warning, considering the hopeless position of post-Munich Czechoslovakia, deprived of her fortifications, strategic resources and having her railways and roads cut in pieces. Newton was further told that any prospective guarantee by other states should not influence the general position. The only exception was Russia. If she were brought in as guarantor, Newton was warned, it was probable that Germany and Italy would refuse to join in the guarantee. The British 'should, if matter came to one of clear choice between Germany and Russia, prefer the former at the price of exclusion of the latter'. Newton was then asked to enquire of the Czechs 'what sort of guarantee they had in mind'.[65]

Before executing the instructions from London, Newton offered his observations on existing situation in Czecho-Slovakia. He thought that this might alter the whole basis upon which the British government made their statement on 4 October regarding a guarantee against unprovoked aggression. He concluded that Germany now held a predominant

64) *Jan Masaryk. Depeše z Londýna* [Despatches from London], ed. V. Olivová, Praha, Společnost Edvarda Beneše 1996, pp. 111–114.
65) *DBFP*, 3rd eries, Vol. III, No. 408, pp. 398–399, Halifax to Newton, 8 December 1938.

position in Czecho-Slovakia and 'could impose her will upon it in any direction she cared'. He also drew attention to the disintegrating tendencies arising 'from the discord between the Czechs and Slovaks'. He pointed out two new factors which arose since the signature of the Munich Agreement and which had not been foreseen at the time. These were the planned construction of the Autobahn Vienna-Breslau, which presented 'a further nail to the coffin of the independence', and the meaning of the Minorities Declaration adopted by the Czecho-Slovak government according to which the German government obtained the legal right to look after the interests of the German minority in Czechoslovakia. Newton also added three other developments that would affect the territorial integrity of Czecho-Slovakia: a possible customs union with Germany; a takeover of Ruthenia by Hungary or its merger in a new Ukrainian State; and a breaking away of Slovakia. Out of these three possibilities he found the Slovak question most important and added a gloomy foreboding: 'A new situation would definitely arise were it to break away, for in that case the Czechoslovak State would have ceased to exist.' All these facts added arguments in favour of Britain's withdrawal from the Munich guarantee. Newton further pointed out Czechoslovakia's reluctance to invoke British assistance, and the fact that there had been no appeal to the British guarantee when Czechoslovakia had been faced with fresh territorial demands, 'based upon no principle of justice', from Germany, Poland and Hungary. Ironically, he ended with the same conclusion as Adolf Hitler two months earlier when he had been shouting at Chvalkovský: '... the only Power physically capable of guaranteeing it is Germany herself.'[66]

Newton's talk with Chvalkovský two days later only supported British circumspection and added further arguments for finding a way out of the guarantee. Newton found the Minister 'very guarded and reluctant to express opinions'. After lunch, which somehow helped the conversation, Chvalkovský said that the Czechoslovak government had done its part in the full and prompt execution of the Munich Agreement, and now looked to the four signatory Powers to do theirs. If possible, he wished all four Munich Powers to act in agreement, but showed that his government realised the major importance of German guarantee. He admitted 'indirectly and unofficially' that 'the German guarantee was what mattered and that our [i.e. the British] guarantee was more of the

66) *Ibid.*, Nos. 413, 414, pp. 407–414, 414–416, all Newton to Halifax, 8 December 1938.

nature of a confirmatory and reassuring gesture'. He intimated his own worries that a Soviet guarantee might be 'a cause of embarrassment or be other than helpful'.[67] According to the Czech record the British Minister said bluntly that 'the English are not prepared to give a guarantee which they could not keep in operation' and that the only thinkable guarantee for British diplomacy was 'if at least three of four would act in favour of Czechoslovakia'.[68]

Meanwhile the French were apparently playing for time. Bonnet found German Foreign Minister Ribbentrop highly reticent about the guarantee during their conversations in Paris, which concluded with the notorious Franco-German declaration of 6 December 1938,[69] an analogy of the Anglo-German one signed by Chamberlain and Hitler on 30 September 1938. Ribbentrop objected that 'Czechoslovakia might some day be hostile again to Germany and might even be governed by another Benes' and described the establishment of friendly relations between Czechoslovakia and Germany as 'the best and most effective guarantee of Czechoslovakia'.[70] While Alexis Léger, Secretary General for Foreign Affairs, laid great stress on the four-Power guarantee, Bonnet, according to the German record, 'confined himself to saying that it was actually more by force of circumstances that France had come to envisage undertaking a guarantee herself'.[71] However, Léger informed the British Ambassador, Sir Eric Phipps, about Ribbentrop's worries of Czechoslovakia's relapse into an anti-German Beneš policy, and pointed out that this abandonment of the guarantee would create a very bad impression in France.[72] Sir Ogilvie-Forbes, Chargé d'Affaires in Berlin (who had been deputising for the terminally ill Nevile Henderson since October and thus had an opportunity, until Henderson's return in the middle of February 1939, to provide London with a completely different and much more fearful interpretation of real German aims and

67) *Ibid.*, No. 423, pp. 423–424, Newton to Halifax, 10 December 1938.
68) Cited from: Dejmek, Československá diplomacie..., *op. cit.*, p. 15.
69) *DGFP*, Vol. IV, No. 369, p. 470, Franco-German Declaration of 6 December 1938.
70) *PRO*, FO 371/22991, C 659/17/18, Extract from record of conversations between Prime Minister and Secretary of State and French Ministers in Paris on 20 January 1939; *DGFP*, Series D, Vol. IV, No. 370, p. 474, Conversation between von Ribbentrop and Bonnet on 6 December 1938.
71) *Ibid.*, pp. 474–475.
72) *PRO*, FO 371/22991, C 646/17/18, FO memorandum: Guarantee of Czechoslovakia, 9 January 1939.

intentions,[73]) considered that the German government regarded Czecho-Slovakia as their own preserve and intended to choose their own time and conditions for the guarantee. According to Sir Ogilvie-Forbes the German government in its present anti-British temper would not at all be likely to be forthcoming in discussing a joint guarantee. Similarly French Ambassador in Berlin Robert Coulondre informed Ogilvie-Forbes that he had found German State Secretary Ernst von Weizsäcker unwilling to discuss the matter.[74]

French diplomacy did not 'handle the problem through Prague' but through the Czechoslovak Minister in Paris, Štefan Osuský. Replying to British enquiries the French indicated that it had proved impossible to elicit any definite views on the subject from the Czechoslovak government.[75] Indeed, to Halifax's direct question conveyed by Phipps on 22 December the Quai d'Orsay did not answer with their findings until 18 January.[76] However, on 9 January Bonnet told the British Ambassador that French government would prefer a joint guarantee of Czechoslovakia by four Munich Powers.[77] This was understood in the Foreign Office to mean that the guarantee would only operate if all the guarantors acted, so that if one of them was the aggressor it would not operate at all. William Strang pointed out that the French went from one extreme to another: after having objected to the British proposal that three of the four Munich Powers had to agree, as a condition for the obligation to come into effect, they now suggested a guarantee which was, in fact, quite meaningless. Strang saw the explanation as the consequence of a possible French decision 'to pull out of Central and Eastern Europe altogether'. He described further the growing obscurity of these discussions: 'We are, however, coming to think that the question of the Czechoslovak guarantee is becoming an academic one. Czechoslovakia has become in a large degree a vassal State...' He underpinned his statement by citing

73) Strang, Bruce, Two Unequal Tempers: Sir Ogilvie-Forbes, Sir Nevile Henderson and British Foreign Policy, 1938–39, *Diplomacy and Statecraft*, Vol. 5, 1994, No. 1, pp. 107–137.
74) *DBFP*, 3rd Series, Vol. III, No. 444, p. 446, Ogilvie-Forbes to Halifax, 22 December 1938.
75) *Ibid.*, No. 441, pp. 444–445, letter from Sargent to Phipps, 21 December 1938.
76) *Ibid.*, No. 439, pp. 440–441, Halifax to Phipps, 21 December 1938; No. 446, p. 447, Phipps to Halifax, 23 December 1938; No. 553, pp. 606–608, Phipps to Halifax, 19 January, 1939.
77) *PRO*, FO 371/22991, C 320/17/18, Phipps to Halifax, No. 11, 9 January 1939.

a newspaper report that Germany wished to conclude a special military convention with Czechoslovakia, by which Czechoslovakia would act in common with Germany in the event of war. Thus 'the whole basis upon which the guarantee was originally proposed would disappear'.[78] Sir Orme Sargent ended successive deliberations as to whether or not the joint guarantee would be acceptable to the House of Commons. He stressed that Parliament had hitherto shown itself strongly opposed to any British commitment in Central Europe and hence he did not expect much criticism of a joint guarantee 'merely because it did not commit Great Britain far enough'.[79]

On 10 January Chamberlain and Halifax met French ministers in Paris again. Both parties now preferred a joint guarantee of Czechoslovakia by the four Munich Powers, but one that would only come into play if three of the four guaranteeing Powers were in agreement. As both parties still felt bound by their guarantee of Czechoslovakia, whilst Germany and Italy were quite free, it was agreed not only that the question should be raised by the British and French representatives in Berlin, but also by Chamberlain and Halifax during their forthcoming visit in Rome.[80]

British politicians departed for their negotiations in Rome with a Foreign Office note drafted by Strang, which pointed out, damningly, that Czechoslovakia had already 'alienated her independence to such a degree that any guarantee from other States would be futile'. The agreement for Germany's construction and administration of the motorway across Czech territory seemed to be inconsistent with the 'neutralisation' of Czechoslovakia and it was one of the reasons why the British 'did not wish to go very far in our proposed approach to Berlin and Rome'.[81] On 12 January, after having seen a gymnastic display by fourteen to eighteen years old youths and girls and a few small eight years old boys upwards with their miniature rifles at Foro Mussolini, a militaristic *passo romano* which the whole British delegation found 'quite ridiculous',[82] negotiations between Chamberlain and Halifax with Mussolini and

78) *Ibid.*, Strang's minute, 9 January 1939.
79) *Ibid.*, Sargent's minute, 11 January 1939.
80) *Ibid.*, C 659/17/18, Extract from record of conversations between Prime Minister and Secretary of State and French Ministers in Paris on 20 January 1939.
81) *Ibid.*, C 646/17/18, Guarantee for Czechoslovakia. Note for the Rome conversation, 9 January 1939.
82) *The Diplomatic Diaries of Oliver Harvey 1937–1940*, p. 240.

Count Ciano came to the question of the guarantee. However, the British tandem was confronted with highly evasive replies on the Duce's part. Having listened to the British proposal (for the guarantee to become operative as a result of a decision of three out of four Powers), he explained at great length that virtually no country intended to attack on Czechoslovakia. In reply to Chamberlain's question whether it was desirable to leave this question of the guarantee open for the present, he argued that any consideration of a guarantee had to be preceded by the settlement of three questions: the internal constitution of Czechoslovakia; the establishment of her neutrality; and the actual demarcation of her frontiers on the ground, 'for hitherto they had only been shown on maps'. Afterwards 'a guarantee might be considered but, in the meantime, owing to the actions of Germany and Italy it was considered that Central Europe would remain quiet'.[83]

The approach in Berlin was even less satisfactory. The exact wording of the telegram ordering the British Chargé d'Affaires in Berlin to work with his French colleague, and to enquire of the attitude of the German government while also informing them of the line taken by Mussolini, became a matter of interference from the highest places. This also caused further delays. Halifax thought on 16 January, that the drafts should be seen by the Prime Minister before issue: 'I think we are bound by arrangement with French to put question to Berlin – but I fear we shall not get much result.' However, the Prime Minister was increasingly finding himself in disagreement with the Foreign Office as well as with Halifax himself. As he wrote: 'I was under the impression that the Foreign Secretary had agreed with me that it was best to let this matter alone for the present and that there was a chance that if not cleared up the guarantee might fade out.' He further misinformed his colleagues that in Paris the British and French delegations had agreed to take no final decision until after the Rome visit, and he rather fancied 'it w[oul]d be best to leave the matter alone for the present'.[84] However, the Prime Minister was no longer able to get his own way unconditionally. A telegram was sent to Berlin on 26 January, containing a reference to one of previous telegrams to Berlin, which had pressed for elucidation of the German

83) *PRO*, FO 371/22991, C 659/17/18, Extract from record of conversation, which the Prime Minister and the Secretary of State had with Signor Mussolini and Count Ciano at Rome on January 12, 1939.
84) *Ibid.*, Halifax's minute, 16 January, Chamberlain's minute, 20 January 1939.

position, despite the Prime Minister's suggestion to omit this reference – 'thus leaving the position more open'.[85]

Ogilvie-Forbes met his French colleague the following evening and left with him a draft of a communication to the German government. Coulondre had no instructions from Paris, but he made a comment relating to Mussolini's second preliminary question, namely the establishment of neutrality of Czecho-Slovakia: he thought that this would relate to the Franco-Czechoslovak Pact on which the Soviet-Czechoslovak Pact was dependent. Ogilvie-Forbes argued that the Munich Agreement had superseded the Franco-Czechoslovak Pact. Coulondre agreed that it did so psychologically, but not juridically and 'he thought the guarantee would have to contain a statement to the effect that this pact automatically lapsed'.[86] Apparently the last ties between Czechoslovakia and its major inter-war protector were disappearing. It was not until 8 February that both missions in Berlin simultaneously sent their notes to the Wilhelmstrasse, indicating that the four Munich Powers should now implement the guarantee. The British government repeated that Mussolini's conditions had to be settled before a guarantee could be considered and then asked about 'the views of the German Government at Munich in regard to the guarantee of Czecho-Slovakia'.[87] The French proposal was perhaps less defensive.[88] Nonetheless, the Germans did not hurry to reply.

Meanwhile the Czechoslovak government took a surprising initiative in its effort to secure the desired guarantee. Indeed, it was to be the last foreign policy initiative taken by Czechoslovak politicians from Czechoslovak territory for the next six years. The British found it most unexpected, as the Foreign Office thought that the subject of the guarantee had not even been discussed during the visit of Dr. Chvalkovský to Berlin on 21 January. However, as Frank Roberts admitted, the British accounts of these interviews were incomplete.[89] True, Chvalkovský was exposed to numerous reproaches from both Hitler and Ribbentrop concerning the internal situation in Czechoslovakia and to criticism of influence of the Jews and the old Beneš civil servants allegedly leading

85) *Ibid.*, O.S.C.'s minute, 26 January 1939. The telegram in question was No. 447, Halifax to Phipps, 21 December 1938, see *DBFP*, 3rd Series, Vol. III, No. 439, pp. 440–441.
86) *DBFP*, 3rd Series, Vol. IV, No. 42, p. 41, Ogilvie-Forbes to Halifax, 28 January 1939.
87) *Ibid.*, Nos. 90–91, pp. 86–87, Ogilvie-Forbes to Halifax, 8 February 1939.
88) *Ibid.*, No. 95, pp. 91–92, Ogilvie-Forbes to Halifax, 9 February 1939.
89) See *PRO*, FO 371/22991, C 1485/17/18, Roberts' minute, 30 January 1939.

'almost everywhere to a stiffening of the Czechoslovak attitude toward Germany', and he also listened to gloomy warnings of 'catastrophic consequences for Czechoslovakia' if the development did not change. However, when he was asked by Ribbentrop about reducing the Army, which both Nazi leaders found essential for their 'judgement of the situation', Chvalkovský dared to remind him of the frontier guarantee: 'If the frontier of Czechoslovakia were guaranteed, she could consider herself a neutral state and could do with a very small army.' Ribbentrop, not surprisingly, refused to see any connection between the two questions and for the rest he repeated his exhortation to eliminate the influence of the Jews.[90]

Although well aware of the impending danger of Germany's liquidation of Czechoslovak independence, Chvalkovský decided to launch his last initiative precisely one month after his journey to Berlin. On 21 February he instructed the legations in Berlin, Rome, Paris and London to remind the four governments that all the conditions for the international guarantee had already been accomplished. The Czecho-Slovak government was ready to make a declaration of neutrality in the context of the promised guarantee. However, the wording of this note written in French was not clear enough, so that Cadogan in the Foreign Office did not know whether Prague was going to make the neutrality declaration in any case, or merely in exchange for the offer of a suitable guarantee. Since Czecho-Slovak Chargé d'Affaires Karel Lisický had received no further instructions, he could not enlighten Cadogan on that point.[91] The Czecho-Slovak Chargé d'Affaires in Berlin, Ladislav Szathmáry, when handing his *démarche* to the State Secretary met with astonishment that, in such a matter, the Czechoslovak government was approaching all four Munich Powers simultaneously, without first having entered into an exchange of views with Germany alone.[92]

Chvalkovský himself had already talked about his idea of Czecho-slovak neutrality to Sir John Troutbeck, the British Chargé d'Affaires in Prague who was deputising for Newton, though this was in rather vague terms, making comparison with the position of Belgium. Chval-

90) *DGFP*, Series D, Vol. IV, Nos. 158–159, pp. 190–202, Conversations between the Führer and Chvalkovsky and Ribbentrop and Chvalkovsky, 21 January 1939.
91) *DBFP*, 3rd Series, Vol. IV, No. 138, p. 141, Note by Sir A. Cadogan, 22 February 1939.
92) *DGFP*, Series D, Vol. IV, No. 171, p. 215–216, Memorandum by the State Secretary, 22 February 1939.

kovský's Chef de Cabinet, Hubert Masařík, explained the idea more fully to Troutbeck: The guarantee was apparently in cold storage, so the idea of declaration was meant as an initiative to dispel German doubts as to Czechoslovak loyalties. Troutbeck was not authorised and thus refrained from telling the Czechs that the Prime Minister had replied to Mussolini's demand for Czechoslovakia's neutrality as a condition for granting the guarantee, that this had always been the idea of the British government. The British Chargé d'Affaires discussed the idea with his French colleague who, however, expressed his feeling that Germany had, since Munich, extended her tentacles so far over Czecho-Slovakia 'that it could not any longer be a properly neutral State'. De Lacroix mentioned the arrangements reached whereby German troops and war material could be transported across Czecho-Slovakia, and said that it would be the reverse of neutrality if Czecho-Slovakia allowed Germany to back up the Italians in a possible joint war against Great Britain and France, as she would no doubt be made to do.[93] Foreign Office legal experts pointed out in their internal minutes that Czecho-Slovakia could hardly act unilaterally and make a declaration of 'neutrality' until she freed herself from obligations incompatible with the status of a neutralised state. These were treaties of alliance with France and Russia, her membership in the Little Entente and, to a lesser degree, membership in the League of Nations. The same applied to the recent agreements concluded with Germany in regard to the autobahn and the passage of the troops. However, it was decided not to act as legal advisers to the Czechs and deter them from their plan for legal objections, and not even to answer the Czecho-Slovak note – in the light of further development with respect to the guarantee.[94]

Neither Czechoslovak nor Anglo-French initiatives that aimed to secure German approval of the international guarantee were welcomed in Berlin, as it had already been decided that Czechoslovakia would be occupied. As early as in mid-October Hitler ordered preparations for liquidation of the *rest-Tschechei* and on 17 December 1938, the O.K.W. Chef Wilhelm Keitel signed the pertinent military directive.[95] By Feb-

93) *DBFP*, 3rd Series, Vol. IV, No. 126, p. 129–131, Letter from Mr. Troutbeck (Prague) to Mr. Strang, 20 February 1939.
94) *PRO*, FO 371/22992, C 2340/19/18, Makin's minute, 28 February, Kirkpatrick's minute, 1 March, Malkin's minute, 2 March, Sargent's minute, 6 March 1939.
95) Brandes, Detlef, *Češi pod německým protektorátem. Okupační politika, kolaborace a odboj 1939–1945* [Czechs under the German Protectorate. Occupation policy, collabo-

ruary 1939 the Headquarters of the Wehrmacht were already finalising their military preparations. No wonder that the long expected German answer to the Anglo-French note, dated 28 February and delivered to the British and French Ambassadors in Berlin on 2 March, was not only evasive, but hostile. The German government saw, in 'an extension of this guarantee obligation to the Western Powers not only no factor for the appeasement', but rather 'a further element likely to strengthen wild tendencies, as has been the case in the past'. The development in this part of Europe was in the German view 'primarily within the sphere of the most important interests of the German Reich, not only from the historical point of view, but in the light of geographical and above all economic necessity'. The German government intended first 'to await a clarification of the internal development of Czecho-Slovakia' and improvement of her relations with surrounding countries before making 'any further statement of its attitude'.[96] 'Translated from diplomatic language', French Ambassador Coulondre commented, it said that the Western Powers had 'no longer any right to interest themselves in central European affairs.'[97]

For Chvalkovský in Prague, who had been informed by his Minister in Berlin Vojtěch Mastný of the nature of German reply, the condition that all the other neighbouring states must be prepared to assume a similar obligation was a new one, and he bitterly complained to Newton that the Germans had specifically mentioned Poland and Hungary without mentioning Rumania, which would doubtless be willing to give a guarantee. He assured Newton that relations between Czecho-Slovakia on the one hand and Poland and Hungary on the other hand continued to improve and that frontier had now been agreed.[98]

The Foreign Office also found the German arguments disingenuous. They seemed 'to be mere pretexts to enable Germany to get out of her offer to guarantee Czechoslovakia'. Moreover, as Sargent pointed out on 6 March, they were 'somewhat ominous when we take into account the recent rumours which have reached us regarding Germany's intentions as regards Czechoslovakia', referring specifically to Germany's instigation

ration and resistance, 1939–1945], Praha, Prostor 1999, p. 21; Dejmek, Československá diplomacie..., *op. cit.*, p. 23.
96) *DBFP*, 3rd Series, Vol. IV, No. 171, p. 171–173, Henderson to Halifax, 3 March 1939.
97) Cited from: Adamthwaite, *France and the Coming...*, p. 269. See also Procházka, *The Second Republic*, pp. 76–83.
98) *DBFP*, 3rd Series, Vol. IV, No. 188, p. 204, Newton to Halifax, 8 March 1939.

of Slovakia to assert her independence against the Central Government at Prague. He did not find it useful to argue with the Germans concerning their reasons for not proceeding with the guarantee, especially as the Italians would probably give the same answer. 'But in that case there seems nothing for it but for us tacitly to allow the whole question of the guarantee to lapse until and unless some fresh development enables us to raise it again under new conditions.' Sargent recommended working with the French, and did not find it necessary to approach the Czech Government, unless there was a Czech initiative.

However, one trouble was that the British were still bound by Sir Thomas Inskip's October declaration in Parliament. The government and the Foreign Office always hoped that this moral obligation would be eventually replaced by a new multilateral guarantee 'hedged round by very definite conditions. It now looks as though this method of escape is going to be denied us, and, failing that expedient, it is difficult to see how we are to rid ourselves of this dangerous commitment. All we can do is to assume that in the altered circumstances it is already a dead letter.' But it was clearly impossible to say this in Parliament without arousing an unpleasant and unprofitable controversy. This was all the more so, since the government was frequently questioned about the fate of Munich guarantee in the House of Commons and the members of the executive always provided answers in the sense that negotiations were in progress.[99] 'I am inclined to think', Sargent concluded, 'that there is nothing for it but tacitly to allow the present unsatisfactory situation to continue, in the hope that nothing will occur which might give occasion to the Czech Government to invoke this pledge and to call upon us to fulfil it.'[100] Other senior officials at the Foreign Office agreed. Cadogan provided the following reasoning: 'I am afraid one probably has to be cynical about this, and to recognise that, with the passage of time, the question of the guarantee loses more and more of whatever it had of actuality. If in Sept.-Oct. last we couldn't save Czechoslovakia from what was then done to her, it is plain that we shall not be able to save her from further consequences.'[101]

99) *H. C. Deb.*, 5th Series, Vol. 341, 14 November 1938, Cols. 476–477; Vol. 342, 28 November 1938, Col. 22, 12 December 1938, Col. 1587; Vol. 343, 31 January 1939, Col. 26, 2 February 1939, Col. 384; Vol. 344, 20 February 1939, Cols. 15–16, 21 February 1939, Col. 224, 27 February 1939, Col. 883.
100) *PRO*, FO 371/22992, C 2340/19/18, Sargent's minute, 6 March 1939.
101) *Ibid.*, Cadogan's minute, 6 March 1939.

The Central Department was considering a reply to the German statement, but by 11 March Strang feared 'that events may overtake us within next few days'.[102] Three days later the Foreign Office was expecting a German intervention in Slovakia, and Halifax himself reviewed a draft of telegram to Paris dealing with the question of the guarantee. In view of subsequent events which accelerated in the next day or two, it was decided not to send the telegram. However, the telegram draft remains in the archives, and records reasoning that the British government would have used for not fulfilling their pledge, had the Germans directly attacked Czecho-Slovakia and regardless of Slovakia's declaration of independence of 14 March 1939. The British government felt that there was nothing that they could do and they presumed that the French government found itself in the same situation. Despite the government's earlier readiness to join in an international guarantee of the Czechoslovak frontiers, Halifax stressed that it 'was never their intention to give any individual guarantee or indeed a guarantee with France alone'. Inskip's October statement on behalf of the government in the House of Commons had been 'made in reply to a question as to what the situation was, pending agreement on the form of the guarantee' and had been 'designed to cover a transition period pending the negotiation of an agreement. That agreement has now been found to be impossible and in changed circumstances H.M.G. are not accordingly prepared to hold themselves bound indefinitely by what they were prepared to accept as transitory obligation.'[103] However, the events in Slovakia that day provided Halifax and Chamberlain with a possibility to leave this spurious explanation aside and to find a much more sophisticated justification of Britain's inaction vis-à-vis the German occupation of Prague on 15 March.

Thus, similarly as in the pre-Munich Anglo-French negotiations from April 1938 onwards,[104] the British succeeded in influencing France towards withdrawal from her Central European commitment, which would not involve Italian or/and German participation. And in spite of numerous French objections during all mutual consultations it seems that, at the end of the day, the French were quite grateful for this inducement. As

102) *PRO*, FO 371/22991, C 2657/17/18, Strang's minute, 11 March 1939.
103) *PRO*, FO 371/22992, C 3532/17/18, draft of a telegram to Paris, 14 March 1939, revised by Halifax.
104) *DBFP*, 3rd series, Vol. I, No. 164, pp. 198–235, Record of Anglo-French Conversations, held at No. 10 Downing Street, on April 28 and 29, 1938.

the 'Czecho-Slovak crisis' of March 1939 was reaching its climax, Foreign Minister Georges Bonnet and President of Foreign Affairs Committee of the Senate Henry Berenger remarked, while talking to the British Ambassador, that the British and French 'nearly went to war last Autumn to boost up a State that was not viable'.[105] It is also arguable that the French themselves recognised 'tacitly' German predominance in Central Europe soon after Munich.[106] But they did not move away hastily; on the contrary, they strove to reassert economic influence. The objective of this double-track policy was to bargain French respecting of Germany's domination in the East for German moderating influence in Rome. In the autumn of 1938 Italy's threats to French positions in the Mediterranean were perceived as very dangerous and the Franco-German declaration of 6 December was intended and later used *inter alia* to show France's understanding for 'vital German interests' in exchange for extracting some 'reciprocity' from Wilhelmstrasse.[107]

The British never got as far as giving Germany a free hand in the East. Although such ideas had been accepted by former Prime Minister Baldwin and sometimes by John Simon as well, Chamberlain himself preferred to use British influence to facilitate the reshaping of the Continent in a peaceful and just manner, in order to satisfy what he (in some cases at least) considered to be the legitimate demands of Hitler and Mussolini.[108] The promise of an international guarantee that was contained in the Anglo-French plan of 19 September 1938, and then again in Inskip's parliamentary declaration of 4 October, although considered 'a very grave matter indeed',[109] confirmed the belief in a possible attainment of some new European settlement. With the passage of time and further German aggressive and hostile actions, this turned out to be a mere illusion. The growing Czechoslovak dependence on and loyalty to Germany made the whole concept of a viable guarantee ever more hypothetical. From late January British diplomacy and military planning were also facing an allegedly impending threat of an attack by Hitler against Switzerland, Netherlands or even Britain herself.[110] In such cir-

105) *PRO*, FO 371/22897, C 3051/7/12, Phipps to Halifax, No. 104, 14 March 1939.
106) Adamthwaite, *France and the Coming...*, p. 278.
107) *Ibid.*, p. 279.
108) See e.g. Parker, Nejen o appeasementu, *op. cit.*, pp. 45, 47; Idem, *Chamberlain and Appeasement*, p. 180.
109) *Bod. Lib.*, Oxford, Simon Papers, No. 10, diary entry for 29 September 1938.
110) See Watt, *How War Came*, pp. 99–108.

cumstances the commitment towards a country which was apparently already in the German orbit, was considered an unrealistic, as well as unbearable burden. However, subsequent events in Slovakia, instigated from Berlin, provided the British with an opportunity to rationalise away from the promised guarantee. Yet, the Foreign Office documents show clearly that it was considered a 'dead letter' well before the final break-up of Czecho-Slovakia and German occupation of its western part – once it became clear that both Italy and Germany had no intention to take part in a multilateral form of the guarantee.

Britain's policy towards Central Europe between Munich and 15 March 1939

Chamberlain's Cabinet after Munich focused in its general policy course both on rearmament and on attempts to achieve conciliation with Germany. Chamberlain was determined to do maximum to take up contacts with Hitler and Mussolini. On 11 October 1938 George F. Steward, Chamberlain's close assistant at No. 10 Downing Street, had a long conversation with Dr. Hesse, representative of *Deutsches Nachrichtenbüro* and the *Dienststelle Ribbentrop*, as well as assistant to the press attaché in London. Steward said that in the recent crisis the Prime Minister had made decisions entirely alone with his two intimate advisers and had no longer consulted his Cabinet, not even Lord Halifax. The Foreign Office was hostile towards Germany and Sir Nevile Henderson, too, was unreliable. Therefore all major questions in future should be dealt with directly, thus bypassing the Foreign Office and Henderson. German press in the future should refrain from attacks on opposition groups comprising Eden, Churchill, Duff Cooper, Attlee, Sinclair, etc., as this would only provide a sort of gratuitous advertisement for them. Chamberlain should be trusted. His attitude in the Czech conflict 'had never been dictated by a consciousness of military weakness but exclusively by the religious idea that Germany must have justice and that the injustice of Versailles must be made good'.[111] Steward further asked for some declarations and speeches preaching peace between Britain and Germany, and also for restraint in public references to the colonial question, which could only be solved parallel with the disarmament question. The impact of this approach was limited, as Weizsäcker, playing his own anti-Hitler game,

111) *DGFP*, Series D, Vol. IV, No. 251, pp. 305–308, Dirksen to Weizsäcker, 12 October 1938, Enclosure 2 – Memorandum by Dr. Fritz Hesse of 11 October 1938.

refused to pass the message on to Ribbentrop.[112] However, a report about it reached the Foreign Office from MI5 at the end of November and caused much indignation. Chamberlain himself rather denied any knowledge of this contact.[113] Similarly at October weekends Samuel Hoare and Leslie Burgin, Minister of Transport, talked to Ambassador Herbert von Dirksen, about possibilities of an Anglo-German *rapprochement*, which was for Chamberlain 'simultaneously dictated by the head and by the heart'. Questions of rearmament and humanising of air warfare were supposed to be the main issues, while after further *rapprochement* between the four European Great Powers, 'the acceptance of certain defence obligations, or even a guarantee by them against Soviet Russia, was conceivable in the event of an attack by Soviet Russia'. From other 'friendly persons' Dirksen also knew about readiness of Chamberlain and other members of the Cabinet to discuss the colonial question.[114]

All this was in vain. The only reply Chamberlain got from the German side was strengthened anti-British press propaganda, inspired directly by Ribbentrop,[115] and several Hitler's speeches hostile to Britain. The atrocities of the *Kristallnacht* on 10 November, together with German press attacks on Churchill, Duff Cooper and Attlee as the alleged instigators of the Jewish student Grynzspan whose murder of the Third Secretary at German Embassy in Paris three days earlier served the Nazis as a pretext for the horrible wave of anti-Semitic barbarism, made impossible Chamberlain's further approaches to Germany at least for a few months.

After all direct approaches to Berlin had failed, Chamberlain decided to use an alternative course to achieve reconciliation with Germany – via Rome. Besides clearing up 'some misunderstanding', the major purpose of the visit in the middle of January 1939 was, in Prime Minister's words, 'securing Signor Mussolini's good offices in Berlin' where for some time it had been impossible for Britain 'to take any useful action'. Chamberlain hoped, however, 'that Signor Mussolini could be persuaded to prevent Herr Hitler from carrying out some "mad dog" act'.[116] After his return, Chamberlain referred about his visit to the Cabinet quite

112) *Ibid.*, No. 254, p. 312, Weizsäcker to Dirksen, 17 October 1938.
113) *Cadogan Diary*, p. 127.
114) *DGFP*, Series D, Vol. IV, No. 260, pp. 319–323, Dirksen to Weizsäcker, 31 October 1938.
115) *Ibid.*, No. 253, pp. 311–312, Weizsäcker to Dirksen, 17 October 1938.
116) *Bod. Lib.*, microfilm, CAB 23/96, Cab 60(38), 21 December 1938.

enthusiastically and was rewarded by congratulation from his ministers. However, it all concerned moods, feelings and expressions of friendliness at most. In its major objective, to find a direction to Anglo-German conciliation, the visit did not bring any result. Indeed, on 18 January, the day the Cabinet discussed the visit to Rome, Halifax for the first time revealed to his colleagues disquieting reports as to possible German intentions against Holland and asked the Chiefs of Staff to bear them in mind.[117] Even vis-à-vis Italy defensive precautions began: Military planners started discussing a pre-emptive strike against Italy in the event of war against both totalitarian Powers, anti-aircraft defences at Malta were reinforced and fortifications started on the road from Libya to Egypt at Sidi Barrani and Mersa Matrûh.[118]

'We must cut our losses in central and eastern Europe – let Germany, if she can, find there her "lebensraum", and establish herself, if she can, as a powerful economic unit.'[119] These are words written by Cadogan after Munich and they are often quoted as a comment of Britain's *désintéressement* about events in Central and Eastern Europe and respect of German sphere of influence in that part of the world. In fact these words only reflected the already established reality of German economic preponderance in that region, which was followed by growing political influence. And Cadogan, as a realist, in his analysis depicted current state of affairs before he started looking for possibilities of British foreign policy, however limited they were. He described the state when Germany would elaborate clearing up or barter systems with countries that produced what Germany wanted (food and raw materials in cases of Hungary, Yugoslavia and Rumania) and for which Germany paid in goods (generally, now, munitions): 'This system, if developed, will enlarge the German economic sphere and develop and complete her "autarky".' All this occurred in a situation that the League system was if not dead, then in a state of suspended animation, and the British and French were on the defensive. Cadogan proposed to solidify the defences, to maintain British influence in Western Europe and the Mediterranean, to foster trade with other parts of the world and with the Empire and to facilitate commercial exchange with the United States. He reminded that in early 1936 he had suggested a conference, which should have

117) *Bod. Lib.*, microfilm, CAB 23/97, Cab 1(39), 18 January 1939.
118) See Watt, *How War Came*, p. 97.
119) *Cadogan Diary*, p. 119.

reviewed the Peace settlement and put it right. 'However, it is probably too late for that now, and we should look to our defences, to retain what we may and in the hope that all Hitler's grandiose plans may not work out quite so easily as he expects.'[120]

An Inter-Departmental Committee on Central and South-Eastern Europe, set up in accordance with decisions of the Cabinet Committee on Foreign Policy in June 1938 and headed by Chief Economic Adviser to the Government Sir Frederick William Leith-Ross, was dealing with possibilities of promoting British political influence in South-Eastern Europe by economic measures. On 26 October 1938, after five meetings the Committee produced an interim report of the situation. It outlined a gloomy picture where the required increase of export of these countries (Greece, Rumania, Yugoslavia, Bulgaria, Hungary, while Czechoslovakia was excluded after Munich) to the United Kingdom market was spoiled by financial and monetary policies in conjunction with heavy German buying, which had allowed their internal prices to rise. The Committee proposed four possibilities that could improve the situation: modifications of UK tariffs, quotas and preferences; direct purchases either by the Government or by some organisation with Government backing; increased purchases by great trade interests in such commodities as wheat, oil, and particularly tobacco; the grant of credits either on a frankly non-commercial or on speculative basis. Although each of these suggestions presented 'great and obvious difficulties', the Committee stressed that unless the government was prepared to adopt some of these measures, it would not be possible to maintain any substantial volume of British trade with these countries, 'or keep up our influence in that part of Europe so far as this depends on commercial as opposed to military and political factors'.[121]

On 16 November Halifax, armed with a lengthy memorandum and the above mentioned interim report, confronted his governmental colleagues on the UK policy towards Central and South-Eastern Europe after the 'Anschluss' and the incorporation of the Sudeten districts of Czechoslovakia by Germany. The memorandum rejected power politics as a method to stop Germany from realising the greater part of her ambitions in this area, i.e. alliances, military conventions, close under-

120) *Ibid.*, pp. 118–119.
121) *Bod. Lib.*, microfilm, CAB 24/280, Interim report of the Inter-departmental Committee on Central and South-Eastern Europe.

standings etc., 'which necessarily involve, and are often based upon, large scale armaments credits and agreements. This is a possible policy but it almost certainly leads directly to war, will be unpopular in this country and is uncertain in its operation.' Instead, the memorandum strongly recommended using Britain's exceptional financial and economic power and consuming capacity. By using methods, which hitherto had been regarded as unorthodox, Britain could strengthen her 'political influence in at least some of these countries by the judicious encouragement of trade, industry and capital investment'. As a method to increase Britain's trade with these countries Halifax recommended modifying such tariffs, quotas and preferences that restricted United Kingdom imports; and alternatively also encouraging private business interests to set up an organisation to foster trade with South-Eastern Europe along the same lines as Germany. Principal companies in Britain were to be persuaded to increase their purchases of such commodities as oil and wheat (this concerned especially Rumania) and tobacco. Britain's trade credits, especially to Greece and Yugoslavia, should further reduce Germany's influence. Another method was helping the Balkan countries build up their armed forces. Halifax concluded that promoting Britain's political influence by economic measures in South-Eastern Europe could be in a long run essential to Britain's ultimate security.[122] The memorandum with Halifax's comment won a sympathetic hearing at the Cabinet meeting.[123]

Britain's interest, quite naturally, concerned Greece in the first place, but Rumania, the barrier against any German or Italian pressure on Turkey, came second. King Carol visited Britain in mid-November and secured a trade mission and a British undertaking for purchase of 200,000 tons of wheat with an option on 400,000 more at prices above the world market level. What he did not get was a loan of £ 30 million, for which he had hoped. The House of Commons agreed with just £ 10 million for all political credits, out of which only £ 3 million were earmarked for the Balkans – £ 2 million for Greece and £ 1 million for Rumania. The legislative process took until February to pass.[124] When Halifax suggested, with direct reference to Rumania and Greece, that the figure of £ 10 million

122) *Ibid.*, C.P. 257(38), Memorandum by the Secretary of State for Foreign Affairs: Central and South-Eastern Europe, 10 November 1939.
123) *Bod. Lib.*, microfilm, CAB 23/96, Cab 55(38), 16 November 1938.
124) See Watt, *How War Came*, p. 90.

allocated to political credits in Export Credits Guarantee Bill, which was before Parliament, should be increased, Simon refused.[125]

In this context it is interesting to compare the measure and promptness of Britain's financial and economic assistance to countries of South-Eastern Europe with that provided to post-Munich Czechoslovakia. Immediately after Munich Jan Masaryk asked the British government to guarantee a loan of £ 30 million for two purposes: 1) to deal with the problem of refugees from the areas ceded to Germany (some 1 million of refugees was expected) and 2) to buttress the country's economic life, which would be upset by the cession of districts containing many industrial establishments. At the Cabinet meeting held on Monday, 3 October, Chamberlain doubted the estimated figures and expressed his belief that the German government was doing their best to prevent incidents and that 'many of those who were now leaving the territories to be ceded would before long return to the homes from which they were flying in such a haste'. He, however, thought that public opinion in Britain would feel that it was 'in accordance with our best traditions that this request should meet with a sympathetic response'.[126] A discussion then developed, whether the assistance should have a form of a free grant or a guaranteed loan. Chancellor Simon emphasised that Czechoslovakia had no legitimate grievance against Britain: 'On the contrary, the position was that a world war had been averted and thereby Czechoslovakia was saved.' Also Governor of the Bank of England Montagu Norman had been anxious lest the announcement of a gift would be taken as implying some consciousness of moral guilt. It was decided to arrange for an advance of £ 10 million to be made immediately available to the Czechoslovak government for their instant needs. The term 'advance' was considered as consistent with either a gift or a first instalment of guaranteed loan. Further examination of the whole position was necessary for a final decision.[127] Later in the afternoon the Prime Minister said in the House of Commons that Czechoslovakia, which had 'earned our admiration and respect for her restraint, for her dignity, for her magnificent discipline in face of such a trial as few nations have ever been called upon to meet,' had been put in a position where she had got to reconstruct her whole economy, and in doing so would not

125) *Bod. Lib.*, microfilm, CAB 23/97, Cab 3(39), 1 February 1939.
126) *Bod. Lib.*, microfilm, CAB 23/95, Cab 48(38), 3 October 1938.
127) *Ibid.*

be able to solve all difficulties alone. Referring to Masaryk's approach he expressed his belief 'that the House will feel with the Government that that is an appeal which should meet with a sympathetic and even a generous response'. Pointing at the proverb 'He who gives quickly gives twice', Chamberlain said that the Chancellor of the Exchequer had addressed a letter to the Bank of England requesting the Bank to provide the necessary credit of £ 10 million and that when the House resumed in November it would be asked to pass necessary legislation to reimburse the Bank of England.[128]

However, the 'expert examination' and following negotiations of the precise amount of the gift and loan were by no means smooth and quick. As early as 13 October, in reply to a previous enquiry by the Foreign Office whether the German government were disturbed by the decision to afford financial assistance to Czechoslovak government, Henderson answered from Berlin in the negative, but added a sentence, which marked the process of British doubts and hesitations about the whole financial assistance: 'If Czechoslovakia, as seems likely, falls into the German economic orbit, financial assistance may prove very useful and welcome to Germany.'[129] A Czechoslovak delegation arrived in London in mid-October to negotiate the exact terms of assistance and presented that Czechoslovakia would have very large capital expenditure to face, in particular on the score of the reconstruction of communications and other public works as well as the refugees and immediate general expenses. It also promised to regard the British credit as available to provide sterling to enable refugees leaving the country to take with them a moderate amount of capital. The British representatives stressed that refugees from the Sudeten districts (especially Jews) were not to be expelled back into now German areas.[130] The Chairman of the delegation, director of *Pražská městská spořitelna* (Prague City Savings Bank) Dr. Vilém Pospíšil, referred to the government in Prague about the first round of negotiations and their expected outcome most optimistically.[131]

128) *H. C. Deb.*, 5th Series, Vol. 339, 3 October 1938, Cols. 46–47.
129) *DBFP*, 3rd Series, Vol. III, Appendix IV, iv, p. 630, Henderson to Halifax, 13 October 1938.
130) *PRO*, T 160/1324, F 13577/05/1, 'Note of a meeting between the Czecho-Slovak Financial Mission and representatives of HM Treasury, held on Saturday, 15th October 1938'; FO 371/22903, C 1720/1720/12, Annual Report, 1938, p. 29, Newton to Halifax, 14 January 1939.
131) Feierabend, *Politické vzpomínky*, Vol. I, p. 82.

Meanwhile Robert J. Stopford of the Treasury was sent to Prague as a liaison officer to keep the government informed of the progress of the expenditure of the financial assistance granted and also to keep in touch with the programmes drawn up by the Czecho-Slovak government for the relief and re-settlement of refugees. As late as in mid-November the British government was yet prepared to treat £ 5 million of the advance as a gift, while the French government, who had been approached by the British in this matter in early October,[132] did not offer any money and were only willing, on certain conditions, to cancel the existing loan of 700 million francs from 1932, which was due in 1937-42. A loan of another £ 10 million raised on the London market was to be guaranteed, while 50 per cent of any money required to implement the guarantee were to be found by each government. Several ministers, however, expressed their worries lest the help would involve a certain measure of reflex benefit to Germany.[133]

In early December the situation changed. By then the British had already been disturbed by Czechoslovakia's growing dependence on Germany and also by certain anti-Semitic tendencies. The Treasury officials worried that the Czechs were only waiting to get the British funds before launching anti-Jewish measures.[134] Some members of the Parliament expressed their anxiety about the actual use of this public money, which had been dispensed without any authority of the House of Commons and now could be used for example for the build-up of the German military motor road across the territory of Moravia. Although Simon assured the House that this would not be the fate of the advance,[135] the government was growing increasingly cautious. The matter was discussed by the Foreign Policy Committee on 6 December and it recommended reducing the gift from £ 5 million to just £ 4 million, which would correspond to the French measure of 'help', and also to limit the loan guaranteed by the British and French governments from £ 10 million to just £ 6 million. The Chancellor of the Exchequer said the following day to his colleagues that he was satisfied that 'there was no case for giving assistance to Czechoslovakia on the more liberal

---

132) *DBFP*, 3rd Series, Vol. III, Appendix IV, i + ii, pp. 629–630, Halifax to Phipps, 3 October 1938, Phipps to Halifax, 7 October 1938.

133) *Bod. Lib.*, microfilm, CAB 23/96, Cab 55(38), 16 November 1938.

134) *PRO*, FO 371/21576, Waley to Makins, 23 November 1938.

135) *H. C. Deb.*, 5th Series, Vol. 342, 29 November 1938, Cols. 243–244.

scale', pointing at possible difficulties in meeting other claims on the Exchequer if the original proposal remained unaltered.[136] The next round of negotiations between a Czecho-Slovak financial delegation and British and French representatives took place in London shortly afterwards. The Czecho-Slovak delegation was informed that no fresh money beyond the £ 10 million already paid over could be made available and was provided with the already approved exact terms of British and French assistance. Both western delegations emphasised that the loan should be used primarily for refugee purposes and reference was made to disquieting indications of anti-Semitic tendencies in Czecho-Slovakia. The Czecho-Slovak delegation, headed again by Pospíšil, did not conceal their disappointment and returned to Prague to consult with their government.[137]

At the turn of the year, however, the Treasury initiated to increase the already provided advance by another £ 2 million. The reason for this was to achieve 1) that the money would be actually used for the support of refugees and 2) that nobody in Czecho-Slovakia would be persecuted on behalf of his creed. The Foreign Office strongly opposed this suggestion. 'I should not attach much value to Czech pledges,' Cadogan minuted, 'simply because they will not be in a position to carry them out. I should certainly not estimate their value as high as £ 2,000,000.'[138] In Prague Dr. Krno, chief of the Political section of the Czecho-Slovak Foreign Ministry, complained to Newton on the New Year's day about the British treatment of the financial aid and he remarked 'a little bitterly' that it was hoped that Britain's government would show their interest and practical sympathy not only for the Jews and the Social Democrat Germans but also for the Czechs and Slovaks. He said that instead of accusing Czecho-Slovakia of having lost her independence she should be helped to maintain it. However, Krno complained even more about the attitude of the French government, which at the time of Munich had promised any financial and economic help for the reconstruction of the country and this promise weighed considerably in taking the hard decision. In fact the French had not as

136) *Bod. Lib.*, microfilm, CAB 23/96, Cab 58(38), 7 December 1938.
137) *PRO*, FO 371/22903, C 1720/1720/12, Annual Report, 1938, p. 29, Newton to Halifax, 14 January 1939.
138) *PRO*, FO 371/22893, C 95/3/12, Waley (Treasury) to Strang, 2 January 1939, Cadogan's minute, 5 January 1939.

yet provided any fresh money at all. Newton, in his own comment sent to the Foreign Office, referred to a general impression, which he had personally shared, that when the British government had announced the intention of providing ten million pounds there had been an underlying suggestion that there would be a further instalment. He added a few words about Britain's prestige and reputation involved and concluded with the following prophetic foreboding: 'In the future Great Britain will doubtless need all her money but may be in even greater need of all her friends and this reputation may be of special value to us in a world which is so full of menace and uncertainty.'[139] These arguments persuaded Halifax that there was a reason to give the Czechs further money if acceptable treatment of refugees and their emigration were to be achieved. The offer of fresh money should be related to the needs for financing emigration.[140] Members of the staff of the Czecho-Slovak Legation urged further money at the Treasury on 6 January, while Pospíšil, talking to Leith-Ross five days later, asked on behalf of the Czecho-Slovak government for £ 15 million, apart from any free grant allocated to refugees. He skilfully conditioned using any money for the support of refugees by obtaining at least £ 10 million for general reconstruction. In further talks with Treasury officials he referred to the public opinion, 'mentally' anti-German, which would be gravely disturbed if no further help were forthcoming and 'would accuse the Western Powers of having again let them down'. All this pressure eventually brought some fruits. Leith-Ross thought that it would be possible to meet the Czecho-Slovak request half way and to agree upon £ 8 million as a guaranteed loan.[141] After some diplomatic effort the British also succeeded in persuading the French, who were irritated by the governmental sale of their shares in one of the biggest ammunition factories in Europe, Škoda Pilsen, about the sense of such increase.[142] Thus the total assistance available

139) DBFP, 3rd Series, Vol. III, Appendix IV, xii, pp. 633–634, Newton to Halifax, 2 January 1939.
140) PRO, FO 371/22893, C 180/3/12, Makins' minute, 9 January 1939.
141) Ibid., C 466/3/12, Stopford (Treasury) communicated, 6 January 1939, C 543/3/12, Treasury communicated, 11 January 1939, C 545/3/12, Leith-Ross (Treasury) to Foreign Office, 12 January 1939, C 702/3/12, Stopford (Treasury) communicated, 14 January 1939.
142) Ibid., C 614/3/12, UK Delegation (Geneva), 16 January 1939, C 838/3/12, Phipps to Halifax, 20 January 1939, C 847/3/12, Phipps to Halifax, 19 January 1939, C 862/3/12, Phipps to Halifax, 22 January 1939, C 928/3/12, Phipps to Halifax, 23 January 1939.

by way of British free gift (£ 4 million) and of the joint Anglo-French guaranteed loan (£ 8 million) was increased to £ 12 million. Together with the French 'gift' it was a total of £ 16 million overall. After these long protracted negotiations the treaty was signed by Halifax, Ambassador Corbin and Pospíšil on 27 January 1939.[143] Simon drew attention of his colleagues to the arrangement made whereby Britain's free gift of £ 4 million would be paid into a special account and used for refugees.[144] However, the legislative process took until 28 February to pass the bill.[145] Due to the ensuing events the loan was never to be raised on the London market...

Even after the final increase the quantity of Britain's financial assistance to Czecho-Slovakia was much below the expectations of politicians in Prague. On the other hand, measured by British standards and possibilities, it was surprisingly high. It much exceeded the loans provided to any other country in that period and the amount of British part of gift and loan granted to Czecho-Slovakia almost reached the total amount of sterling provided as political credits for the rest of the world. The figure of £ 8 million of British support seems similarly impressive in another comparison: with the measure of mutual commercial exchange. Exports of UK goods consigned to Czecho-Slovakia in 1938 were valued at £ 2,287,000.[146] Whether it was for public opinion and for defusing of deputies in opposition benches or whether the driving force for financial support was real gratitude for Czechoslovakia's sacrifice in the interest of continuing European truce combined with at least subconscious feeling of guilt, the British government was willing to provide the 'far--away country' with a substantial financial support in spite of the highly reserved attitude of the Foreign Office. With the exception of Basil Newton, British diplomats and FO officials viewed any increase in financial assistance to Prague as a useless and dangerous waste of money, which could be and should be used above all for improving Britain's defences. Financial assistance to the government in Prague was, with the passage of time and Czecho-Slovakia's increasing submission to Germany's

143) *Ibid.*, C 1408/3/12, Waley to Foreign Office, 27 January 1939.

144) *Bod. Lib.*, microfilm, CAB 23/97, Cab 3(39), 1 February 1939.

145) *Treaty Series No. 9, Financial Assistance to Czecho-Slovakia*, London, H.M.S.O. 1939; *H. C. Deb*, 5th Series, Vol. 344, 28 February 1939, Cols. 1090, 1154.

146) See the statement by the President of the Board of Trade, Sir Oliver Stanley, in the House of Commons on 21 March 1939: *H. C. Deb*, 5th Series, Vol. 345, 21 March 1939, Col. 1113.

demands, perceived by officials from Cadogan downwards as a pure assistance to Germany.

It is not therefore surprising that the Foreign Office, aware of geo-strategic realities, tended to avoid any British commitments to the future of the crippled state, beyond those adopted in Munich and the already publicly announced loan and help for refugees. Both British and French ministers strongly recommended to the government in Prague that it should ask for arbitrage in the matter of Czechoslovak-Hungarian frontier only in Berlin and Rome.[147] The 'Vienna Award' of 2 November resulted in further loss of vast territories, this time in southern parts of Slovakia and Sub-Carpathian Ruthenia. Around 20% of inhabitants of these regions were Slovaks. According to the Munich Agreement it was only in the event of not settling the problems of Polish and Hungarian minorities with the respective governments within three months that these would have formed the subject of another meeting of the Munich Powers. 'Agreement was, in fact, reached between the Czechoslovak and Hungarian Governments when they agreed to accept as final the arbitral award of the German and Italian Governments,' Chamberlain explained in the House, 'and in consequence no question of action by His Majesty's Government arises.' Sinclair immediately asked whether the moral guarantee previously mentioned by Inskip was now in operation 'in regard to these frontiers'. 'Yes, Sir,' confirmed Chamberlain[148] – an astonishing statement that was later entirely forgotten by the government and neglected by historiography. Quite to the contrary, Britain's absence in this settlement later enabled the Foreign Office to regard the Vienna Award as 'a German-Italian diktat' with which Britain 'was in no sense associated'.[149]

Nor did London strive to intensify mutual commercial relations. At the end of November, in reply to a question by Geoffrey Mander, a Liberal MP who for many years had been doggedly confronting governmental foreign policy, Oliver Stanley said that there were no trade negotiations with Czechoslovakia. When reminded by Mander that it would be a method how to help the country, Stanley provided the following answer: 'If it had been likely that we could have come to a special treaty with Czechoslovakia, no doubt we should have entered into

147) See e.g. Feierabend, *Politické vzpomínky*, Vol. I, pp. 48–49.
148) *H. C. Deb.*, 5th Series, Vol. 341, 14 November 1938, Col. 477.
149) *PRO*, FO 371/24290, C 13413/2/12, Roberts' minute, 16 December 1940.

negotiations some time ago, as we have done with many other countries, but I do not think there is any basis for a special treaty.'[150]

What is even more surprising, however, is the fact that British military authorities failed to purchase something of the huge military surpluses of the Czechoslovak army, which suddenly remained uselessly over-armed after Munich. Those Czechoslovak representatives who realised the potential danger and contacted French and British diplomats to negotiate sales of Czechoslovak arms, met with a complete disinterest. This confirms that Munich was hardly a mere tactical manoeuvre, forced by the state of British and French armaments, as part of Western historiography tends to claim.[151] Two British military experts reached Prague as late as in early March of 1939 and they found incredible possibilities to buy huge quantities of war and air material for more than reasonable prices, but their mission did not lead to immediate results; before anything could have been agreed, the Germans entered the *rest-Tschechei*.[152] Similarly, Colonel Heliodor Píka of the Czecho-Slovak General Staff visited London in early March to dispose of surplus stocks of armaments available in Czecho-Slovakia. It was already at the time when German military and technical men were inspecting factories all over Czecho-Slovakia. This conveyed to Morton of I.I.C. 'the impression that they were assessing the capacity of the country to manufacture war stores in emergency in the same fashion as they did in Austria some time before Anschluss'.[153] Probably as an encouragement Píka submitted a list of heavy armaments, which had been offered to the French and British in October 1938. This offer received no response and the armaments were later sold to the Germans.[154] But not even this led to any immediate and prompt decisions on the British side. Rather fatalistically, the Foreign Office saw the signs of growing German control of the armaments industry in Czechoslovakia

150) *H. C. Deb.*, 5th Series, Vol. 341, 22 November 1938, Col. 1509.

151) See Kvaček, Robert – Chalupa, Aleš – Hejduk, Miloš, *Československý rok 1938* [The Czechoslovak year 1938], Praha, Panorama 1988, p. 304; Tesař, *Mnichovský komplex*, p. 105. For Western historiography see e.g. Dilks, David, 'We must hope for the best and prepare for the worst.' The Prime Minister, the Cabinet and Hitler's Germany 1937–9, *Proceedings of the British Academy*, London, Vol. 73, 1987, pp. 309–352.

152) *PRO*, FO 371/22995, C 3710/19/18, 'Industrial Survey – 2nd March to 9th – by Thomas G. Jones'.

153) *PRO*, FO 371/22901, C 2817/44/12, Morton to Foreign Office, 8 March 1939.

154) *Národní archiv* [National Archive], Praha (hereafter *NA Praha*), fund Národní soud [National Court], box 77, No. 1290; *Archiv ministerstva vnitra* [Archive of the Ministry of Interior], Praha, 300-8-3, 8 March 1946. Courtesy Pavel Šrámek.

as 'inevitable'. A former plan to create a British holding company that would control the Vítkovice steel works in Northern Moravia, one of the largest steel factories in Europe, was abandoned.[155]

Fortunately, not all attempts in this field failed: The London representative of the arms factory Zbrojovka Brno, František Slabý, in co-operation with the British Ministry of Supply (MOS) succeeded in preventing the royalties from the manufacture in Britain of the BREN gun, the light machine gun designed by Czechoslovak engineers, from going to Germany. Slabý, together with his young assistant Jan David, further inspired the action which led to the systematic escape during the ensuing months of several hundred Czechoslovak armament engineers and technical personnel, mostly through the Balkans for eventual employment on small arms production in India, and also for the delivery, to neutral Turkey and under the nose of the Germans, of a consignment of most valuable precision instruments, which were also sent to India. The program was financed from the assets of the Bren Gun Co., released by the MOS, and assisted by the diplomatic personnel and SIS agents in the Balkans. No matter that the relations between Slabý and the MOS later deteriorated, the crucial help of the Czechoslovak engineers to produce this weapon was to become perhaps the most valuable Czechoslovak contribution to the Allied war effort.[156]

Towards the March ides

Besides negotiations of the loan and four-Power guarantee of Czechoslovakia, the British interest in Czechoslovak affairs in the winter of 1939 hardly went beyond observations of what the Foreign Office called the 'Slovak crisis'. At midnight from 9 to 10 March new President Emil Hácha, the old lawyer who was considered 'an excellent choice in all the circ[umstance]s.' by the British Foreign Office,[157] published a decree

155) *PRO*, FO 371/22901, C 2435/44/12, Ashton Gwatkin's minute, 3 March, Sargent's minute, 6 March 1939. However, although taken over by the Germans in mid-March, the factory continued to sell armour plate to the British Admiralty until the outbreak of war. FO 371/24291, C 6409/6409/12, Brig.-Gen. Spears to Butler, April 30, 1939.
156) *PRO*, FO 371/56034, N 293/293/12, Gibson to Nichols, 19 December 1945; Brown, *Dealing with Democrats*, p. 77.
157) *PRO*, FO 371/21580, C 14771/2475/12, Roberts' minute, 2 December 1938. In this assessment the Foreign Office coincided with those democratic politicians who still remained in Czechoslovakia. See e.g. Drtina, *Československo můj osud: kniha života českého demokrata 20. století*, Vol. 1, book 1, p. 289. Hácha was elected by the Parliament on 30 November 1938.

dissolving the Slovak autonomous Cabinet. Simultaneously the Czecho-slovak police in Bratislava occupied the Slovak government offices and arrested several radical Slovak politicians. This vigorous dealing with the eastern province, which had only recently received an autonomous status but had already made use of it to model its political life upon that of the Germans – including one-party system, oppression of the Jews and domination of streets in Bratislava by para-military troops called the Hlinka Guards – stemmed from numerous cases of propaganda for complete independence and from reports that a Slovak declaration of independence was imminent. Politicians in Prague did not know, however, that the Slovak separatism was supported from Berlin, that Hitler had already made a decision to end the Czechoslovak existence and that Walter Schellenberg of the *Sicherheitsdienst* had been charged with an internal break-up.[158] The German press wrote about Prague ter-rorising Slovakia, which was soon to be replaced by passionate stories about alleged sufferings of the German minority at the hands of the brutal Czechs. Father Tiso, the deposed Slovak Prime Minister, was summoned to Berlin, where on 13 March Hitler confronted him with an ultimatum: either Slovakia declares independence immediately and then Germany would guarantee her security, or she will find herself at the mercy of the Hungarians and Poles. The next day the Slovak Assembly unanimously voted for a declaration of independence and Tiso was entrusted with creating the first government of independent Slovakia.[159] The same day, following German advice, the Hungarian forces invaded Ruthenia.

Disturbed by the German attitude towards the events in Slovakia, Chvalkovský arranged for President's visit to Berlin. The train with the two statesmen arrived in Berlin at 9 p.m. on 14 March. However, it was not until 1.15 a.m. that Hitler received the old and ill President and informed him in one of his pathetic outbursts that the German army would march at 6 o'clock in the morning. Hácha was given four hours to arrange things so that there would be no Czech resistance. Exposed to colourful threats from Ribbentrop and especially Göring of immediate aerial bombing of Prague and after having suffered a minor heart attack,

158) See Watt, *How War Came*, pp. 145–146.
159) See Kamenec, Ivan, *Slovenský stát* [The Slovak State], Praha, Anomal 1992, pp. 22–24; Gebhart, Jan – Kuklík, Jan, *Druhá republika 1938–1939* [The Second republic 1938–1939], Praha–Litomyšl, Paseka 2004, pp. 236–238.

Hácha telephoned to Prague to urge that there should be no resistance and at 4 o'clock in the morning he signed a document stating that he 'confidently placed the destinies of the Czech people and country' into Hitler's hands.[160] The first German columns, which had begun to move towards the Czechoslovak frontier in the evening of 11 March, crossed the border before night and reached Prague at about 9 o'clock in the morning of 15 March.

D. C. Watt states that the Secret Intelligence Service had given 'very precise warning of Hitler's intentions' concerning Czechoslovakia 'at least a fortnight earlier'.[161] However, he doesn't support his statement by any archival reference.[162] There is no specific information in the official history of British intelligence for that period either.[163] As the SIS files are still unavailable for historical research, we can only find out how these prospective intelligence warnings resonated in British political circles and in the Foreign Office. Judged from the available evidence it seems, however, that warnings were coming only from Vansittart's secret sources, and were correspondingly discounted by Chamberlain, Halifax and Cadogan. British secret services provided their first specific information only on 11 March.[164]

Vansittart, when commenting on 8 March on Frank Ashton-Gwatkin's report of his visit to Germany in late February – a mission which sought an economic rapprochement between the two countries but which he himself had vehemently opposed – pointed out that the Germans had practically told Ashton-Gwatkin what he, Vansittart, had foretold Halifax 'some weeks ago, i.e. that they are going to destroy the remains of Czechoslovakia'. The reference pointed to Ribbentrop's hint of 'some adjustment in a part of Europe where England has no business to in-

160) Pasák, Tomáš, *JUDr. Emil Hácha (1938–1945)*, Praha, Horizont 1997, pp. 44–51.
161) Watt, *How War Came*, p. 166.
162) The same applies to D. C. Watt's 'British Intelligence and the Coming of the Second World War in Europe', In: *Knowing One's Enemies: Intelligence Assessment between the Two World Wars*, ed. Ernest R. May, Princeton, Princeton University Press 1984, p. 249. Christopher Hill also points out this discrepancy. See Hill, *Cabinet Decisions on Foreign Policy. The British Experience. October 1938 – June 1941*, p. 269.
163) Hinsley, Francis Harry, *British Intelligence in the Second World War*, Vol. 1, London, H.M.S.O. 1979, pp. 58, 83.
164) Christopher Andrew reached a similar tentative conclusion. See Andrew, Christopher, *Secret Service: The Making of the British Intelligence Community*, London, Sceptre/Heinemann 1986, pp. 584–586.

tervene'. Vansittart further thought that Ashton-Gwatkin should have responded that if the Germans 'meant any further outrage in regard to Czechoslovakia, there would be goodbye to any chance of Anglo-German understanding in view of the indignation that it would raise'.[165] Ashton-Gwatkin, however, asked Prince Max von Hohenlohe of the meaning of Ribbentrop's hint. Hohenlohe was sure (from his recent talk with Hitler) 'that this referred to Czechoslovakia, and to nowhere else – not Hungary or Roumania'. He expected 'a further extension of German influence over the Czech State', including a 'German Resident in Prague who would direct policy'. On 28 February Roberts commented that this bore out 'recent suggestions that Germany's next design may now be the complete absorption of Czechoslovakia'.[166] Neither Halifax, nor Cadogan, however, read Hohenlohe's correct predictions. Similarly on 9 March, Vansittart delivered to the Foreign Office a memorandum, compiled by a German officer, containing the main points in a secret lecture by Ribbentrop before a circle of senior officers from about mid-February. It forecasted a German 'cleaning up operation in Central Europe', following very probable Hitler's ultimatum to Prague. Ribbentrop compared recent Chvalkovský's visit to that of Austrian Chancellor Schuschnigg last year, and he emphasised, quite rightly, that the Western Powers would not be able to persuade their own people that 'they must now suddenly fight for the more or less doubtful sovereignty of the Czechoslovak State'. Therefore 'the Führer was absolutely convinced that he could execute his plan without war'. However, nobody of the senior FO officials read this report and the only departmental minute attached to this very precise information is by Frank Roberts and is dated 17 March![167]

This was not the only case of ignored warning of the imminent German aggression: On 7 March the Air Attaché in Prague, A. H. H. MacDonald, reported with the information from the head of the 2^{ieme} Bureau: the Germans were withdrawing numbers of police from all over the country, similarly as they had done before the occupation of Austria and Sudetenland, and a number of indications appeared to show

165) *PRO*, FO 371/22951, C 3938/8/18, Vansittart to Secretary of State, 8 March 1939.
166) *PRO*, FO 371/22950, C 2345-6/8/18, Holman (Berlin Embassy) to Strang, 23 February; Roberts' minute, 28 February 1939.
167) *PRO*, FO 371/22966, C 3096-7/15/18, FO Minute (Sir R. Vansittart), 9 March, Roberts' minute, 17 March 1939.

that the Germans were preparing for some offensive around 15 March. The first departmental minute came again from Roberts, and again too late, on 16 March: 'Now of historical interest. But the information was very correct.'[168] Both these cases could happen by chance. Nonetheless, another congestion of vital information inside the Foreign Office was to occur in mid-August 1939: then a Washington telegram passing on most important U.S. information about the imminent Soviet-German deal was held up for four critical days in the Communication Department. This was done by Francis Herbert King, a Soviet spy in the Foreign Office, who had been providing the Soviet Embassy with top secret British correspondence from early 1939 onwards.[169]

Already on 20 February, when assessing possibilities of Hitler's further expansive plans, Vansittart predicted that the German dictator was now 'thinking of annexing the remainder of Czechoslovakia in April or May'.[170] On 9 March he retorted Cadogan's hope that the German Government did not presage active German mischief in Czecho-Slovakia: 'They certainly do.'[171] Four days later Vansittart complained to the Secretary of State that he had had no opportunity to interview Halifax on his recent information, which only confirmed what he had been foretelling about German intentions for Czechoslovakia. Vansittart had wanted the government to take action that would have deterred Hitler from a step bringing 'a further humiliation for the Western Powers'. Nevertheless, even on 13 March Vansittart, with the 'personal secret service' at his disposal, was not sure whether the Germans wanted to occupy Prague or 'bully the Czechs into any further disintegration or serfdom'.[172]

Similarly the Foreign Office only presumed that the Germans had their hand in the crisis in Slovakia, but gathered it predominantly from the pro-Slovak propaganda of the German press.[173] While the Prague

168) *PRO*, FO 371/22958, C 2837/13/18, Newton to Foreign Office, 7 March 1939, Roberts' minute, 16 March 1939.
169) Watt, Donald Cameron, Francis Herbert King. A Soviet Source in the Foreign Office, *Intelligence and National Security*, 1988, No. 3/4, pp. 78–79.
170) *PRO*, FO 371/22958, C 1822/13/18, Vansittart's minute, 20 February 1939.
171) *PRO*, FO 371/22992, C 2319/19/18, Cadogan's minute, 7 March, Vansittart's minute, 9 March 1939.
172) *PRO*, FO 371/22966, C 3234/15/18, Vansittart to Secretary of State, 13 March 1939.
173) *PRO*, FO 371/22896, C 3046/7/12, Roberts' minute, 13 March 1939.

government 'faithfully carried out all the provisions of the Slovak autonomy law', the Slovak leaders never ceased to attack the Czechs 'and generally to behave as if they were the leaders of an independent rather than autonomous state'. But the Foreign Office did not know to which measure they were supported from Berlin in their attitudes, and the estimations of the agenda dealt with during several Slovaks' visits to Berlin did not go beyond what had been published in *The Times*. 'We know very little about the developments since the beginning of this month,' Robert Speaight of the Central Department admitted on 10 March.[174] A memorandum of 14 March found it only 'probable', not certain, that the declaration of Slovak independence was passed at the instigation of Germany.[175] Paradoxically, at the same time, or even a day earlier, some MPs had no doubts about the German inspirations of the Slovak demands.[176]

Who completely failed to forecast German intentions in relation to Czechoslovakia was the Embassy in Berlin and in particular Nevile Henderson, who had in mid-February returned to Berlin. On 18 February he assured London of his 'definite impression... that Herr Hitler does not contemplate any adventures at the moment and that ill stories and rumours to the contrary are completely without real foundation'.[177] This misleading report was apparently one of the factors that on 9 March prompted Chamberlain to issue to the members of the British press responsible for parliamentary reporting a *note d'ordre* to the effect that the international position could now be viewed with confidence and optimism.[178] Of course, this evidently inspired (as it appeared in all the press) assessment of the international situation became an easy target for parliamentary criticism, once it proved entirely wrong.[179] In his effort to

174) *Ibid.*, C 2774/7/12, Speaight's minute, 10 March 1939.
175) *Ibid.*, C 3249/7/12, Makins' memorandum, 14 March 1939.
176) See e.g. Nicolson, *Diaries and Letters 1930–1939*, diary entry for 13 March 1939, p. 392.
177) *DBFP*, 3rd Series, Vol. IV, No. 118, p. 121, Henderson to Halifax, 18 February 1939.
178) *PRO*, FO 371/22896, C 2914/7/12, Sargent's minute, 16 March 1939; see also *Cadogan Diary*, pp. 154–155.
179) Commander Bower wondered about this 'astounding pronouncement ... that everything in the garden was lovely and that we were well on the way to an agreement for arms limitation. I do not know where that came from. I cannot believe that it emanated from the Foreign Office. It seems to me that the Government must have been singularly out of touch with affairs in Europe if they expected that anyone was going to believe that pronouncement.' *H. C. Deb.*, 5th Series, Vol. 345, 15 March 1939, Col. 489.

eliminate everything that could be harmful 'to good relations between England and Germany', Henderson even attempted to dissuade the Consulate-General in Munich from also sending copies of their 'alarming' reports to the Foreign Office. Some of these reports were of 'sensational character' and might in his view 'be misunderstood by the Foreign Office and given more importance' than they actually deserved. 'This requires a firm reply,' Roberts commented in the Foreign Office, thus setting the tone of a tough letter to the Berlin Chancery.[180]

On 10 March Henderson sent the first, though only conditional, hint that matters might develop unsatisfactorily: 'If Herr Hitler seeks adventure the most obvious form which it would be likely to take would be some coup in Czecho-Slovakia.'[181] But the next day he doubted whether Hitler had yet taken any decision and he recommended that nothing should be said or published during the weekend, which would 'excite him to precipitate action'. This was clearly impossible as the Czechoslovak question had by then become a front-page issue. The following day Henderson wrote to London: 'Up to the present I have no evidence that the German Government intend to exploit the present unrest in Czecho-Slovakia.' 'Sir N. Henderson is always convinced that Hitler has not made up his mind!' Sargent commented sarcastically.[182] On 13 March Henderson finally admitted that German government was contemplating 'some form of intervention either by force or by ultimatum under armed menace', but he trusted, quite incredibly, the German propaganda that 'the threatening attitude of the German Government is due at least in part to the belief that M. Beneš's party is contemplating a coup with a view to provoking international complications'.[183]

MI5 provided its first really solid information of the impending German attack on Czechoslovakia probably as late as 11 March when its head, Major-General Sir Vernon Kell, caused Cadogan's hair to rise 'with tales of German going into Czechoslovakia in next 48 hours'. Cadogan immediately informed both Halifax and Chamberlain. More precise information later in the day talked about 14 March as the 'D-day'.[184] Most

180) *PRO*, FO 371/22958, C 2882, C 2885/13/18, Henderson to Foreign Office, No. 296, 8 March 1939, Roberts' minute, 15 March, Strang to Holman, 21 March 1939.
181) *PRO*, FO 371/22896, C 2914/7/12, Henderson to Halifax, No. 84, 10 March 1939.
182) *Ibid.*, C 2925/7/12, Henderson to Halifax, No. 85, 11 March, Sargent's minute, 13 March 1939, C 2927/9/12, Henderson to Halifax, No. 87, 12 March 1939.
183) *Ibid.*, C 2999/7/12, Henderson to Halifax, No. 91, 13 March 1939.
184) *Cadogan Diary*, diary entry for 11 March 1939, p. 155.

probably it came from Prague where Major Strankmüller of Czechoslovak intelligence had just informed the local resident of British Military Intelligence, Major Harold Gibson, of the German attack planned for the night of 14/15 March. Gibson telegraphed to London at once, and later that day he received a reply from his superiors, expressing extreme interest of the SIS in continuation of co-operation with the Czechoslovak intelligence even after the German occupation and offering to Czechoslovak intelligence officers British hospitality and good conditions for further work. Eleven of them led by Colonel František Moravec, and equipped with necessary intelligence files etc., left Prague for Britain via Rotterdam in a British civilian plane in the afternoon of 14 March. Later that night they landed in Croydon, where they were welcomed, due to a leakage of information, by a group of journalists and photographers. Articles about a mysterious flight of some important Czech nationals on the eve of German occupation thus appeared in newspapers throughout Europe in the following days.[185] Nonetheless, this episode started six years of fruitful co-operation between the two intelligence services.

On Monday, 13 March, Cadogan showed to the Prime Minister further information from SIS of German readiness to walk into *Slovakia*, however, he was unable to say whether the Germans *would* actually put their plan into operation.[186] As late as at 5 p.m. on 13 March a War Office summary of information predicted rather inconclusively that the German

185) Kokoška, Jaroslav – Kokoška, Stanislav, *Spor o agenta A-54* [The dispute over the agent A-54], Praha, Naše vojsko 1994, pp. 118–130. The Czechoslovak intelligence had at their disposal various pieces of information, some of them from French sources. The key report, however, came on 11 March from the alleged intelligence 'ace', agent A-54, in reality a double agent of the German *Abwehr* Paul Thümmel, who above all needed money from all possible sources for his profligate way of life. This time, however, he warned his Czech 'donors' to make sure that they would liquidate all traces of his former activity before the Germans would come. The legend about an agent who had known almost everything about German intentions and had until 1942 supplied the Czechoslovaks and British with first class material on German strategic planning, was in 1975 strongly underpinned by Moravec's memoirs, a misleading book completed after the Colonel's death by his daughter, and it later penetrated even into the official history of British intelligence and, indeed, Oxford history of World War II. Moravec, František, *Master of Spies*, London, Bodley Head 1975; Hinsley, *British Intelligence in the Second World War*, Vol. 1, p. 58; *The Oxford Companion to the Second World War*, eds. I. C. B. Dear and M. R. D. Foot, Oxford – New York, Oxford University Press 1995, p. 1108.
186) *Cadogan Diary*, diary entry for 13 March 1939, p. 156.

government was 'preparing for the possible necessity of intervening in Czecho-Slovakia' that would 'probably take the form of active intervention by occupying Slovakia by paramilitary and police formations'. 24 hours later the summary no. 2 concluded: 'Germany probably intends actively to intervene in Czecho-Slovakia by occupying Slovakia and possibly Bohemia with para-military formations. Troops will only be used in the event of Czech resistance.'[187] It looks that unlike French intelligence which had accurately forecasted the German blow as far back as 6 March,[188] British secret services failed to do so until as late as 11 March, and even then they were not clear about the actual aim and timing of the forthcoming German military action in Central Europe.

Even if British secret services actually did provide their alarming warnings 'at least a fortnight earlier', which seems very unlikely according to available evidence, the information had no impact upon the government. A month later Churchill wondered about this failure and about another one in the case of Italian seizure of Albania when holiday routine was observed despite the fact that Italian concentration and preparations were repeatedly reported in the press. Churchill, assuming that the British Secret Service was the best in the world, criticised the instructions to the press and also the notorious Samuel Hoare's optimistic speech, delivered, oddly, on 10 March: 'How was it that on the eve of the Bohemian outrage Ministers were indulging in what was called 'sunshine talk', the golden age prospects? ... I wonder whether there is not some hand which intervenes and filters down or withholds intelligence from Ministers. ... It seems to me that Ministers run the most tremendous risk if they allow the information collected by the Intelligence Department, and sent to them I am sure in good time, to be sifted and coloured and reduced in consequence and importance, and if they ever get themselves into a mood of attaching importance only to those pieces of information which accord with their earnest and honourable desire that the peace of the world shall remain unbroken.'[189]

Whatever was the available information about the forthcoming German adventure, the diplomats both in the Foreign Office and abroad

---

187) *PRO*, WO 190/757, Summary of information No. 1, 13 March 1939; WO 190/758, Summary of information No. 2, 14 March 1939.
188) Young, Robert J., French military intelligence and Nazi Germany, 1938–1939, In: *Knowing One's Enemies*, p. 285. See also Adamthwaite, *France and the Coming...*, p. 300.
189) *H. C. Deb.*, 5th Series, Vol. 346, 13 April 1939, Cols. 33–34.

concurred that the government could do no more for the present than 'watch the situation carefully'.[190] 'For God's sake don't let's do anything about it,' Cadogan advised Halifax about the 'Slovak crisis'.[191] On 14 March, when the Foreign Office already knew that the German troops were on the march towards the Czech frontiers and would move in the following night,[192] it was agreed at a meeting in Halifax's room that Britain must make 'no empty threats' since she was not going to fight for Czechoslovakia any more than for Danzig, while any attack against Switzerland, Belgium, Holland or Tunis would be considered a *casus belli*. It was preliminarily decided to stop the visit of Oliver Stanley, President of the Board of Trade, to Berlin, which was due to start the following day. Vansittart further pressed for recalling Henderson to London 'for consultations', but so far with no success.[193]

The major concern of British foreign-policy-makers in these critical days was to show that Britain did not regard herself as in any way guaranteeing Czechoslovakia. Frank Roberts, in a memorandum written on 13 March, attempted to bring evidence that British government had 'no *locus standi* for taking any initiative in this matter', as Hitler would never admit that the Slovak dispute was a question concerning Great Britain or France, on the lines of the declarations of 30 September or 6 December 1938, respectively. Nor were the British prepared to take any action regarding the annex to the Munich Agreement stating that both Western governments felt bound by the offer of 19 September 1938, to join in an international guarantee of the new *boundaries* of the Czechoslovak state, as any effective action was conditioned by a parallel French action which, however, seemed very unlikely. This memorandum was almost acclaimed by senior officials in the Foreign Office, who – most ironically – in search of additional arguments, stated that the *boundaries* of Czecho-Slovakia were not threatened, it was the independence and integrity which were in danger.[194] In a conversation with the French

190) *PRO*, FO 371/22896, C 3052/7/12, Halifax to Kennard, No. 29, 14 March 1939, C 3065/7/12, Phipps to Halifax, 14 March 1939.
191) *Cadogan Diary*, diary entry for 11 March 1939, p. 155.
192) This information came from the French General Staff, from the French Consul in Dresden, and it was confirmed by Colonel Mason-MacFarlane, the British military attaché in Berlin. *PRO*, FO 371/22896, C 3117/7/12, Speaight's minute, 14 March 1939.
193) *The Diplomatic Diaries of Oliver Harvey 1937–1940*, diary entry for 14 March 1939, p. 261; *Cadogan Diary*, diary entry for 14 March 1939, p. 156.
194) *DBFP*, 3rd Series, Vol. IV, No. 230, pp. 238–241, Foreign Office Memorandum on the

Ambassador in the afternoon of 14 March, Cadogan refused any formal enquiry of the German government as to their intentions, which the Germans would doubtless retort that the British had no interest in Czecho-Slovakia whatsoever. He also refused Corbin's reminder that the British were under 'some obligation in view of their promise of guarantee', stating that they had been 'released from it by the fact that they had tried to negotiate an international guarantee of Czecho-Slovakia but had failed through no fault of their own'.[195] Similarly in reply to the question of the Leader of the opposition what action the government had taken in view of the guarantee, the Prime Minister answered the same day that the question of any action had not yet arisen. When further pressed by Attlee, Chamberlain complained: 'I am not sure what the right hon. Gentleman thinks we should do. I might remind him that the proposed guarantee is one against unprovoked aggression on Czecho-Slovakia. No such aggression has yet taken place.'[196] However, under the impression of the general atmosphere in the House Halifax instructed Cadogan to draft a telegram to Berlin deploring any action in Central Europe that would cause a setback to a relaxation of tension and to the growth of general confidence. Then, rather surprisingly, he slightly stiffened its wording. Still, it said almost apologetically at the beginning that the British government had 'no desire to interfere unnecessarily in matters in which other governments may be more directly concerned'.[197] Henderson was to carry out this démarché the following morning when, however, the situation was entirely different and thus he simply sent the written communication to Ribbentrop.[198] This was, on Cadogan's instruction, soon followed by a message stating that in view of the present situation the visit of the President of the Board of Trade and Robert Hudson, the Secretary to the Department of Overseas Trade, would be 'inopportune'.[199]

Position of His Majesty's Government in connexion with possible Developments of the Slovak Crisis, 13 March 1939; *PRO*, FO 371/22896, C 3381/7/12, Makins' and Sargent's minutes, 13 March 1939.

195) *DBFP*, 3rd Series, Vol. IV, No. 277, pp. 266–268, Halifax to Phipps, 15 March 1939; *Cadogan Diary*, diary entry for 14 March 1939, p. 156.

196) *PRO*, FO 371/22896, C 3117/7/12, Parliamentary Question (Mr. Attlee), 14 March 1939.

197) *PRO*, FO 371/22966, C 3090/15/18, Cadogan's draft of tel. No. 49 with Halifax's corrections, 14 March 1939.

198) *DBFP*, 3rd Series, Vol. IV, No. 264, p. 259, Henderson to Halifax, 15 March 1939.

199) *Ibid.*, No. 266, pp. 260–261, Minute by Mr. Strang, 15 March 1939.

At the Cabinet meeting on 15 March, Chamberlain surpassed Halifax's reasoning of Britain's inaction based on previous discussions in the Foreign Office and argued that Czechoslovakia had fallen apart before any German action took place: 'It might, no doubt, be true that the disruption of Czechoslovakia had been largely engineered by Germany, but our guarantee was not a guarantee against the exercise of moral pressure.'[200] Later that day in the House, though pointing out the fact that the German government for the first time effected a military occupation 'of territory inhabited by people with whom they have no racial connection' and admitting that these 'events cannot fail to be a cause of disturbance of the international situation,' he refused any British obligation to Czecho-Slovakia, as the state had finished its existence by an internal break-up. Then he added a few words exceeding Cadogan's draft: although the Prime Minister 'should bitterly regret what has now occurred,' he refused to be 'deflected of our course,' reminding the hopes of the peoples of the world of peace and stressing that 'the object that we have in mind is of too great significance to the happiness of mankind for us lightly to give it up or set it on one side'.[201] The loss of liberty of just an eight-million-nation was clearly not seen by the Prime Minister as a topic big enough to give up the bigger nations' hopes in peaceful coexistence.

By orchestrating the Slovak declaration of independence before their own aggression against Bohemia and Moravia the Germans managed to provide Britain with a welcomed pretext for withdrawing from her hated commitment. For a little while it seemed that the Czechoslovak fate had been sealed with hardly more than a very weak protest on the British side and that the outward aggression and first annexation of a territory inhabited almost purely by non-Germans would not have any major impact upon the general course of British foreign policy.

200) *Bod. Lib.*, microfilm, CAB 23/98, Cab 11(39), 15 March 1939.
201) *H. C. Deb.*, 5th Series, Vol. 345, March 15, 1939, Cols. 437–442; *Cadogan Diary*, diary entry for 15 March 1939, p. 157.

The immediate repercussions
of the March ides in British politics

After 15 March events in the Czech lands had a crucial impact upon the general course of British foreign policy. It was clearly not Chamberlain himself who initialised the changes, which came from growing pressure from all corners including his own party and some ministers. Leslie Hore-Belisha, the Minister of War, challenged the Prime Minister's words about an internal break-up of Czechoslovakia with his view that the German move meant the beginning of a process of eastern expansion and colonisation.[1] Practically all newspapers, including Lord Beaverbrook's widely read *Daily Express*, deplored the German aggression.[2] Cadogan viewed Chamberlain's parliamentary supplement to his own draft – that the government would go on with its policy – as 'fatal'.[3] Harold Nicolson noted in his diary: 'The feeling in the lobbies is that Chamberlain will either have to go or completely reverse his policy.'[4]

Indeed, in the debate that followed Chamberlain's statement and that lasted eight hours, the Prime Minister was exposed to hitherto unparalleled criticism: David Grenfell of the Labour Party opened the discussion, wondered about the Prime Minister's 'remarkable state of detachment' and called 15 March 'a day of humiliation and shame for us'. He stressed that appeasement only added impetus to the 'steady and

1) *Bod. Lib.*, microfilm, CAB 23/98, Cab 11(39) 2, 15 March 1939.
2) See Gannon, *The British Press and Nazi Germany*, pp. 235–261. On 14 October 1938, however, Beaverbrook had himself criticised the British guarantee given to rump Czechoslovakia in Munich when he wrote in *The Daily Express*: 'Remember always that the British Empire is a Treasure House. ... And do not get caught up in quarrels over foreign boundaries that do not concern you.' Taylor, A. J. P., *A Biography of Beaverbrook*, New York, Simon and Schuster 1972, p. 384.
3) *Cadogan Diary*, diary entry for 15 March 1939, p. 157.
4) Nicolson, *Diaries and Letters*, 1930–1939, diary entry for 17 March 1939, p. 393.

violent disintegration of the European system'. He found it incredible that Chamberlain still believed that what had been done in Munich had been done in good faith. The Munich Agreement had been in fact destroyed long before, since the plebiscites in the disputed territories had been repudiated, a right of option into and out of the transferred territories forgotten, and nothing remained of the guarantees to the new frontier. Grenfell was first in a long row of MPs calling on the government to make a 'firm gesture signifying that we stand by all those who defend liberty and freedom for the people in any land'. Archibald Sinclair, the Leader of the Liberals, called the Prime Minister's policy 'disastrously misconceived', as appeasement was 'nothing but following the line of least resistance, regardless both of moral principle and of the consequences of handing powerful positions and great resources' to the aggressive powers.

Anthony Eden, in an elegant speech, sought broad parliamentary support for his carefully worded message to the Prime Minister, and urged him to stiffen the country's foreign policy. First he postulated that everyone in the House viewed the German action as a flagrant and unprovoked aggression that was probably also 'in direct contrast not only to the hopes but to the convictions which many held in the autumn last year'. He did not forget to attribute 'a sense of deep feeling as to the new situation' in the Prime Minister's statement. After Munich there were two views (on the one hand of those who saw in the Agreement the beginning of better things, and on the other hand of those who saw in it nothing but a brief respite), 'but surely today after recent events no two views are possible,' and nobody could think that Britain had more than another brief respite before further demands were made and another victim arraigned. 'I am convinced,' he urgently warned the House, 'that if the present methods in Europe are to be allowed to continue unchecked we are heading straight for anarchy, for a universal tragedy which is going to involve us all.' He called on Parliament 'to convince the world of the strength and the unity of this nation' and argued that Britain should 'consult all those nations who are like minded with us' and 'to make with them at once the military plans to give effect to our decisions'.[5] The former Foreign Secretary was apparently preparing the field for the abortive motion which he and about thirty other Conserva-

5) *H. C. Deb.*, 5th Series, Vol. 345, 15 March 1939, Cols. 443–464.

tives presented later that month – calling for a national government 'on the widest possible basis'.[6]

Some Conservatives (Somerville, De Chair, Donner, Southby), however, still believed that continuation in the policy of appeasement would secure permanent peace for Britain and, indeed, Europe. Donner even stated that 'the frontiers of Czecho-Slovakia ... bore as little relation to justice as the act of the German Government now under consideration'. However, such odd arguments did not draw a wider appeal even amongst Conservatives. The loyalist voices were outnumbered by those Conservative backbenchers who in their majority supported Eden's appeal for national unity and immediate consultations with other nations. Besides France, Poland, Rumania, Greece, Turkey, Yugoslavia, and above all the United States and the USSR were several times mentioned. The leadership was severely criticised at a meeting of their Foreign Affairs Committee and the impression that Chamberlain's speech had not been 'very convincing' prevailed.[7]

Labour MPs, however, though otherwise appreciating Eden's speech, refused to unite behind the current Prime Minister. Hugh Dalton, the former Parliamentary Under-Secretary of State at the Foreign Office, in particular subjected Neville Chamberlain and his 'personal policy' to a devastating criticism and stated that he (Chamberlain) 'should disappear from the office'. Dalton pointed out bluntly that the declaration of independence of Slovakia, 'paid for by German money and ... organised by German agents', had furnished the Prime Minister with 'a convenient legal get-out of the guarantee'. Probably in response to the denigration from several Conservatives he called Czechoslovakia 'once free and happy model democracy in Central Europe' and dismissed their incredulity with a reminder that none of them had ever been to that country, unlike he and many others in the House. He further stressed the 'rapidly increasing danger' to Britain, supported Eden's proposal to build a strong collective force, and appealed to the government that it at least drew a barrier saying to the totalitarian states: 'Thus far, but no further.'

It remained to Simon to conclude the debate on behalf of the government. When supporting 'the obvious point', that the guarantee to Czecho-Slovakia did not apply any longer, he did not hesitate to quote

6) Parker, *Churchill and Appeasement*, pp. 214–215.
7) Crowson, *Facing Fascism*, p. 115.

Joseph Goebbels' press statement in the sense that the state of Czecho-Slovakia had ceased to exist. Although Simon joined 'in deploring these recent events,' he refused to join in any condemnation of Chamberlain's policy and assured the House that the Prime Minister 'intends to pursue that policy and so do his colleagues'. The Chancellor correspondingly argued against entering 'into extensive, indefinite commitments with the result that the control of our own action ... will depend not on this country ... but upon a whole lot of foreign countries'. He, however, provoked several hostile interjections and his defence of appeasement was not convincing.[8]

The next day Chamberlain's isolation became even more evident. Indeed, in the first two days after the German aggression, the Prime Minister seemed to be unable to understand the dramatic change in public opinion since the time of his Munich triumph. He retorted to a parliamentary question – whether he would indicate to the German government that any attempt to attack the lives or liberties of the Czech leaders would in Britain intensify the indignation at the German aggression – with the following words: 'I think it wrong to assume that the German Government have any such intention.' He was immediately reminded by two MPs of the press reports of first people arrested in Prague by the Germans. Even Viscountess Astor, who five months ago interrupted Churchill's gloomy evaluation of Munich ('a total, unmitigated defeat') with an emphatic interjection ('Nonsense!'), now asked whether the Prime Minister would 'lose no time in letting the German Government know with what horror the whole of this country regards Germany's action'.[9]

If Chamberlain's government was to survive, something had to be done. The first changes of British policy originated partly in the Foreign Office and partly abroad. According to the FO's suggestion on 15 March the government approved and announced in Parliament that the previously planned ministerial visits of Oliver Stanley and Robert Hudson to Berlin would be postponed.[10] In the afternoon of 15 March Halifax expressed to the German Ambassador, Herbert von Dirksen, his govern-

8) *H. C. Deb.*, 5th Series, Vol. 345, 15 March 1939, Cols. 464–566. D. C. Watt describes the outcome of Simon's effort as a 'crashing failure'. Watt, *How War Came*, p. 167.
9) *Ibid.*, 16 March 1939, Cols. 614–615.
10) *Bod. Lib.*, microfilm, CAB 23/98, Cab 11(39) 2, 15 March 1939; *H. C. Deb.*, 5th Series, Vol. 345, 15 March 1939, Cols. 440, 550. It is typical that Hudson did not want to relinquish his journey to Berlin. See *Cadogan Diary*, diary entry for 14 March 1939, pp. 156–157.

ment's sense of outrage at the German aggression and reminded him of Hitler's post-Munich public statement that he had no more territorial ambitions. The immediate result of his present action was that 'nobody felt the assurances of the German Government to be worth very much'. Halifax 'could well understand Herr Hitler's taste for bloodless victories, but one of these days he would find himself up against something that would not be bloodless'. The conclusion would be drawn that the German Government 'were seeking to establish a position in which they could by force dominate Europe and, if possible, the world' and people inevitably asked what the next German objective would be. To this Dirksen with an incredible sincerity responded that the only danger spots of which he was aware were Memel and Danzig.[11]

Immediately after Dirksen, Halifax saw his French colleague who for the first time mentioned the idea of a protesting *démarche* in Berlin. When they were discussing the last German action, however, Halifax mentioned 'the one compensating advantage ... that it had brought to a natural end the somewhat embarrassing commitment of a guarantee', in which both countries had been involved.[12] The next morning Corbin called on Cadogan to inform him that the French Government felt that it was its duty to make a formal protest against 'Germany's forcible gesture, which had destroyed the first attempt at an agreement between the four Munich Powers'. The Foreign Office, as Sargent recorded, was 'inclined to doubt of such a gesture'.[13] Corbin, however, later rang up again to say that the French would protest, whether the British acted similarly or not. On this Cadogan drafted a protest, from which Halifax (probably after having discussed the issue with Chamberlain[14]) crossed out the key sentence stating that the government was 'unable to recognise the legality of the changes effected in Czechoslovakia'. Instead, the government just protested against these changes, which were 'in their view devoid of any basis of legality'. The following reminder to Hitler was also left out by the Foreign Secretary: 'The subjugation of nearly 8,000,000 Czechs is not only a denial of the right of self-determination but a repudiation by the German Chancellor of the racial principle which he has himself

11) *DBFP*, 3rd Series, Vol. IV, No. 279, pp. 270–272, Halifax to Henderson, 15 March 1939. Memel was seized on 23 March, Danzig in September 1939.
12) *Ibid.*, No. 280, pp. 272–273, Halifax to Phipps, 15 March 1939.
13) *PRO*, FO 371/22966, C 3102/15/18, Sargent's minute, 17 March 1939.
14) *Ibid.*, Cadogan's minute, 17 March 1939.

enunciated.'[15] Henderson delivered this protest against 'a complete repudiation of the Munich agreement' to the Wilhelmstrasse on 18 March and according to the FO instructions he immediately left Berlin 'to report'.[16] His French colleague made similar steps. Weizsäcker tried to dissuade both diplomats from presenting their notes, but finally accepted them, most unwillingly, 'as if they had been sent by post'.[17]

The British did not similarly protest against the Hungarian seizure of Ruthenia, although they knew about the collusion between Germany and Hungary that had given the latter a free hand in Ruthenia.[18] Chamberlain's written answer to a parliamentary question about British position towards the future status of Ruthenia declared that it was 'apparently being settled directly between the Ruthenian authorities and the Hungarian Government. I do not think that any useful purpose would be served by intervention on the part of His Majesty's Government.'[19] Britain was not bound by the terms of the Vienna Award and her inaction was further motivated by an effort to prevent Hungary from falling into the German camp – a line to be followed at least for another year.[20] The British as well as the French hoped that Hungary's long-desired and finally reached frontier with Poland 'would constitute a barrier of some sort against the German expansion eastward'.[21] Thus, from the strategic viewpoint this territorial change was perceived as advantageous: Hore-Belisha thought that the incorporation of Ruthenia into Hungary was in the British interest, even before it actually occurred.[22]

On 16 March Halifax talked to Chamberlain before his long-arranged meeting with Birmingham Conservatives.[23] As a result the Prime Minister delivered a speech that marked a significant shift in British

15) *PRO*, FO 371/22994, C 3318/19/18, Cadogan's minute + draft, 17 March 1939.
16) *DBFP*, 3rd Series, Vol. IV, No. 308, p. 291, Halifax to Henderson, 17 March 1939, Note 1.
17) *Survey of International Affairs, 1939–1946: The Eve of the War 1939*, Royal Institute of International Affairs, Oxford, Oxford University Press 1958, pp. 63–64.
18) *PRO*, FO 371/22966, C 3136/15/18, Makins' minute, 16 March 1939; FO 371/22994, C 3453/19/18, Kennard to Halifax, No. 55, 17 March 1939.
19) *H. C. Deb.*, 5th Series, Vol. 345, 16 March 1939, Col. 632.
20) See Ivaničková, Československo-maďarské vzťahy v stredoeurópskej politike Veľkej Británie (1938–1945), *op. cit.*, pp. 250–260.
21) *DBFP*, 3rd Series, Vol. IV, No. 277, p. 268, Halifax to Phipps, 15 March 1939.
22) *Bod. Lib.*, microfilm, CAB 23/98, Cab 11(39), 15 March 1939.
23) *PRO*, FO 371/22993, C 3313/19/18, Cadogan's minute, 16 March 1939. See also *The Diplomatic Diaries of Oliver Harvey 1937–1940*, diary emtry for 16 March 1939, p. 262.

foreign policy towards deterring aggression. Although the first half of the speech consisted of defending his previous policy, the second half implied a clear challenge to further German aggression. For the first time Chamberlain spoke of war as an evil, but an evil that was preferable to surrender. 'Is this the last attack upon a small State, or is it to be followed by others? Is this, in fact, a step in the direction of an attempt to dominate the world by force?' He talked about national security as a primary purpose of British national life. He spoke about liberty. He said that Britain was not disinterested in what went on in South-Eastern Europe.[24] It is clear that, even for Chamberlain, Hitler's action ended once and for all any further reliance on German good faith.[25] In letters to his sisters he described Hitler as a fanatic who could do anything and with whom he could not feel safe. 'I saw that it was impossible to deal with Hitler after he had thrown all his own assurances to the winds,' was how Chamberlain recorded the impact that the last Hitler's action had had upon him.[26] After 'Prague' Chamberlain's previous scepticism towards 'rumours' about further German aggressions also vanished. Even R.A.C. Parker, otherwise Chamberlain's sharp critic, admits that he now 'became more ready to warn Hitler', although 'he remained anxious not to provoke him'.[27]

Nomination of certain politicians into the government might have represented such a 'provocative' warning. Popularity of two Conservative politicians grew rapidly during the spring of 1939: that of Anthony Eden and of Winston Churchill. When on 14 March Churchill, in his constituency in Waltham Abbey, defended himself against constant attacks from the local party officials against his Munich speech, he was able to say: '... never did I make a truer statement to the House. Practically everything that I said has already proved true.' He analysed the gloomy strategic position, saying that Britain was to promise to send nineteen divisions to the Continent as a result of the destruction

24) *Documentary Background of World War II, 1931–1941*, ed. W. Gantenbein, New York, Columbia University Press 1948, Address by Neville Chamberlain, Prime Minister, at Birmingham, 17 March 1939, pp. 385–390.
25) See Overy, Richard, with Wheatcroft, Andrew, *The Road to War*, London, Macmillan 1989, p. 96.
26) *Birmingham University Library*, Chamberlain Papers, NC 18/1/1090, Neville Chamberlain's letter to his sister Hilda, 19 March 1938; NC 18/1/1091, Neville Chamberlain's letter to his sister Ida, 26 March 1938.
27) Parker, *Chamberlain and Appeasement*, p. 205.

of Czechoslovakia, by which the entire balance of Europe had been deranged and the German Army became free to turn in any direction. He reminded the listeners of his statement from last October that the guarantees to Czechoslovakia had not been 'worth the paper they were written on, or the breath that uttered them. What is the position now? The Czechoslovak Republic is being broken up before our eyes.' He did not doubt that the disturbances in Slovakia had been fomented at Hitler's instigation and he added another two incredibly precise prophecies: 'Their gold is to be stolen by the Nazis. ... They [the Czechs] are being completely absorbed, and not until the Nazi power has passed away from Europe will they emerge again in freedom.'[28] Next day in the House of Commons Thomas M. Sexton reminded his colleagues of the veracity of Churchill's October forecasts.[29] However, though both Eden and Churchill apparently wanted to rejoin the government and had the growing support of the press and public opinion for this, Chamberlain wanted neither of them. He had probably two motives for his obstinacy: the first one was personal, as any of these two politicians would have significantly limited his domination of the Cabinet; the other reason was especially Churchill's reputation as a warrior and staunch opponent of Nazism, which would have definitively excluded Chamberlain's last hopes of reconciliation with Germany. Nonetheless, after his Birmingham speech Chamberlain tried to convince his colleagues in the Cabinet and Parliament that his policy was 'Churchillian' enough, so that bringing Churchill into the government was unnecessary.[30]

British international efforts between 15 March and the outbreak of the war

Numerous alarming reports of an impending danger of a German attack upon Rumania or Poland in the second half of March,[31] i.e.

28) *Winston Churchill*, Companion Vol. V., pp. 1389–1390.
29) *H. C. Deb.*, 5th Series, Vol. 345, 15 March 1939, Cols. 507–508.
30) See Parker, *Churchill and Appeasement*, pp. 221–223, 229–245; see also *The Diplomatic Diaries of Oliver Harvey 1937–1940*, pp. 209, 280–281, 289–291.
31) See e.g. *DBFP*, 3rd Series, Vol. IV, Nos. 270, 275, 297–298, p. 263, 265, 283–285; *PRO*, FO 371/22966, C 3136/15/18, Speaight's minute, 16 March 1939; also *Cadogan Diary*, pp. 160–167; Watt, *How War Came*, p. On the impact of Virgil Tilea's false warnings of 'an almost immediate' German thrust against Rumania see most recently: Aster, Sidney, Viorel Virgil Tilea and the Origins of the Second World War: An Essay in Closure, *Diplomacy & Statecraft*, Vol. 13, 2002, No. 3, pp. 153–174. An SIS report of 18 March pointed out that virtually all the German specifically offensive troops were concentrated in the East and

immediately after the German invasion of the Czech lands, prompted radical change of British policy towards large commitments in Central and South-Eastern Europe. Indeed, by then even Nevile Henderson was outraged by the 'utter cynicism and immorality' of the annexation of Bohemia and Moravia, which was 'entirely contrary to right of self-determination and utterly immoral'. After all his assurances of Hitler's good will and an alarming failure to predict the German aggression, Henderson now, most ironically, called upon his government to 'consider what attitude to adopt towards a Government which ... is apparently set on domination by force of the whole of the Danube basin.' Even Henderson was capable of making prophetic statements: 'Nazism has definitely crossed the Rubicon of purity of race and German unity and answer to this form of Pan-Germanism can only in the end be Pan-Slavism.'[32] The Military Attaché in Berlin, Col. Mason MacFarlane, also demanded action: 'We must make it clear that any further aggression on Germany's part ... will immediately entail armed intervention by France and ourselves.'[33]

A Foreign Office memorandum of 29 March 1939 assessed the situation after the absorption of Czecho-Slovakia by Hitler's Germany and suggested future possibilities for British policy. It was based on the assumption that the absorption of Czecho-Slovakia had revealed Germany's intentions, a departure from the Nazi racial theory under which the Reich would only include Germans within its boundaries, and it found 'every reason to suppose that the treatment applied to Czecho-Slovakia will be extended to other countries in Europe, notably Roumania and Poland'.[34] On 31 March, after two weeks of frenetic diplomatic activity in London, the Prime Minister announced the British guarantee to Poland in the House of Commons.[35] It was 'greeted with cheers from every side'.[36] Similar guarantees to Greece and Rumania followed soon.[37] The subsequent debate on European situation prompted Attlee to say: 'The

concluded that Germany might 'be preparing for a drive through Hungary to Rumania'. FO 371/22958, C 3565/13/18, FO Minute (Mr. Jebb), 18 March 1939.
32) DBFP, 3rd Series, Vol. IV, No. 288, pp. 278–279, Henderson to Halifax, 16 March 1939.
33) PRO, FO 371/22958, Ogilvie Forbes to Mr. Strang, Enclosure, 29 March 1939.
34) PRO, FO 371/22966, C 4319/15/18, FO Memorandum, 29 March 1939.
35) H. C. Deb., 5th Series, Vol. 345, 31 March 1939, Col. 2415.
36) Nicolson, Diaries and Letters, 1930–1939, 31 March 1939, pp. 393–394.
37) H. C. Deb., 5th Series, Vol. 346, 13 April 1939, Col. 13.

policy that has been pursued, against all the advice of experienced men on that side as well as this side of the House, is all in ruins. Czecho-Slovakia and Albania mark the end of the policy of unilateral appeasement, the end of the attempt to make peace by disregarding moral issues.' Indeed, after the Italian invasion of Albania the general atmosphere was best described by the Leader of the opposition: 'Everyone is asking who is to be the next victim – upon whom next will the quarrel be fixed?'[38] Throughout the whole of spring and summer of 1939, the fate of Czechoslovakia remained one of major tools used by the opposition and also by the dissent within the Conservative Party to put pressure upon the government to intensify its policy of building an international coalition against aggression and by no means to be derailed from the current foreign policy course.

New commitments came only after previous British attempts either 1) to agree upon consultation about joint resistance with France, Poland and the USSR to action threatening the independence of any European state or 2) to secure a commitment of mutual support with Poland and Rumania and between those two countries. Insistence by two important ministers (Stanley and Hoare) that the USSR should somehow be brought in, accompanied by the Chiefs of Staff's warnings about the military importance of that country, were appeased by Chamberlain and Halifax with a promise that Russia would be approached at a later date.[39] However, already in March there appeared two themes which eventually turned out to be critical for the British and French attempts to build an international coalition against aggression: the reluctance of the Polish Government to join the USSR in an anti-German coalition and the mistrust of British policy shown by the Soviet Government.[40]

The guarantee to Poland – a crucial moment in British foreign policy as within 6 months this specific commitment brought Britain to war – has been criticised by many authors who have for various reasons concluded that it was a 'bad policy, badly made'.[41] Simon Newman views the guarantee as a pure continuation of the previous policy of continental balance, but with the reservation that the Cabinet allied itself

38) *Ibid.*, Cols. 18–20.
39) See Hill, *Cabinet Decisions on Foreign Policy*, pp. 44–47.
40) See Parker, *Chamberlain and Appeasement*, p. 207.
41) Hill, *Cabinet Decisions on Foreign Policy*, p. 246.

'to continental war'.[42] Other authors condemn it as a continuation of appeasement since it left room open for possible territorial changes,[43] or a new wave of appeasement as the Cabinet in their view sought to avoid a real defence of Polish independence.[44] Anita Prażmowska points out that the guarantee could function only as a deterrent, as it lacked any political or military backing.[45] Similarly Andrew Roberts calls it a 'deterrent with no inherent power to deter'.[46] Maurice Cowling stresses the *Primat der Innenpolitik*, when he argues that the guarantee represented the only means by which Halifax could resist the growing power of the Labour Party.[47] D. C. Watt criticises that the guarantee left no option whatever to the British. The crucial decision on war or peace 'had been voluntarily surrendered by Chamberlain and his Cabinet into the nervous hands of Colonel Beck and his junta comrades-in-arms'.[48] R.A.C. Parker suggests that by agreeing with the guarantee to Poland Chamberlain sought to avoid co-operation with the Soviet Union and, moreover, did not accept the commitment wholeheartedly, when he congratulated himself, in a letter to his sister, 'on the limits on the scope of the commitment he put into the statement'.[49]

I agree with an evaluation perhaps not so academically brilliant, but more balanced and defensible, which has been provided by G. Bruce Strang, who argues that the guarantee represented 'a marked emphasis on resistance over appeasement'. It was not 'an example of brilliance in policy-making, but it was a coherent and rational response to a set

42) Newman, Simon, *March 1939. The Making of the British Guarantee to Poland*, Oxford, Oxford University Press 1976, pp. 5–6, 172.
43) Cienciala, Anna, *Poland and the Western Powers 1938–1939. A Study in the Interdependence of Eastern and Western Europe*, London, Routledge & K. Paul 1968, p. 223; Foster, Alan J., An Unequivocal Guarantee? Fleet Street and the British Guarantee to Poland, *Journal of Contemporary History*, Vol. 26, 1993, No. I, p. 46.
44) Gilbert – Gott, *The Appeasers*, pp. 241–242.
45) Prażmowska, Anita J., *Britain, Poland and the Eastern Front 1939*, Cambridge, Cambridge University Press 1987, p. 57; Idem, War over Danzig? The Dilemma of Anglo-Polish Relations in the Months Preceding the Outbreak of the Second World War, *Historical Journal*, Vol. 26, 1983, No. I, pp. 177–178.
46) Roberts, Andrew, *'The Holy Fox': a Biography of Lord Halifax*, London, Weidenfeld & Nicolson 1991, p. 149.
47) Cowling, Maurice, *The Impact of Hitler: British Politics and British Policy 1933–1939*, Cambridge, Cambridge University Press 1975, p. 9.
48) Watt, *How War Came*, pp. 185–186.
49) Parker, *Chamberlain and Appeasement*, p. 216–219; Idem, *Churchill and Appeasement*, p. 215.

of impossible conditions, and its authors deserve at least that it should be understood on those terms'.[50] The guarantee did not work, however, as planned, due to two flaws which undermined the Cabinet's policy: 1) the irrationality of Hitler who at the end of the day did not hesitate to fight a two-front war;[51] and perhaps even more importantly 2) Stalin's failure to recognise Hitler's aim to destroy the Soviet Union. Since the guarantee indirectly committed Britain to defend the Soviet Union, the Cabinet gave Stalin greater freedom to explore his negotiations with the Germans.

The British failure to consult intensively with the Russians upon the intended pledge to Poland may have added to Stalin's suspicions. However, the guarantee was an expression of improvisation, it was adopted within a very short period of time and in view of several reports of an imminent German attack on Poland.[52] And after all, Soviet Ambassador Ivan Maisky had been informed twice about the British intentions before the announcement of the guarantee – first by Cadogan on 29 March and then by Halifax two days later.[53] Historians, having only an old edition of Soviet documents at their disposal,[54] have so far thought that Maisky deliberately failed to inform his Soviet masters about his talk with Cadogan and British abandonment of the four-power declaration.[55] Recently released Soviet documents show, however, that he actually did inform Moscow, but added his personal comment expressing disbelief in any British commitment to the East.[56] Here, as well as during later negotiations, the Soviet diplomatic machinery showed an incredible tendency to delusion and self-deception. Soviet diplomats in

50) Strang, Bruce, Once More unto the Breach. Britain's Guarantee to Poland, March 1939, *Journal of Contemporary History*, Vol. 31, 1996, pp. 744–745.
51) This was, however, pointed out already by D. C. Watt. See his *How War Came*, p. 186.
52) See e.g. *Cadogan Diary*, pp. 164–167.
53) See Watt, *How War Came*, pp. 215–216.
54) *Soviet Peace Efforts on the Eve of World War II (September 1938–August 1939)*, ed. V. Falin et al., Moscow, Novosti Press Agency Publishing House 1973 (hereafter *SPE*), Vol. I.
55) See Watt, *How War Came*, pp. 215–216.
56) Either Litvinov or his deputy Potemkin even marked with a blue pencil that passage in Maisky's telegram which dealt with Poland's and Rumania's refusal to join in any combination with the USSR. *Archiv vneshnei politiki*, Moscow (hereafter *AVP*), fund Litvinov's Secretariat, 23/1/66 – 1939, Maisky to Litvinov, 29. 3. 1939. See also *Dokumenty vneshnei politiki*, Moskva, Mezhdunarodnye otnosheniia 1992–1998 (hereafter *DVP*), Vol. XXII (1939) – 1, No. 187, pp. 238–240, Maisky's record of his talk with Cadogan, 29. 3. 1939.

general were inclined to send to Moscow such comments and analyses which they expected to be appreciated by their masters. Therefore, as the above shows, their reports were usually full of general suspicion of the western world and tended to draw western intentions in the darkest colours. Maisky, who had almost miraculously survived Stalin's purges of the 1930s, was not an exception. Moreover, he was by his conviction too suspicious of what he saw as the 'conservative bourgeoisie', which ruled Britain. Thus, instead of cultivating his relations with cabinet ministers and trying to disperse their own suspicions about the real Soviet military strength and determination to resist Hitler, he rather tended to 'leak' to left-wing journalists, to agitate amongst trade unions and to organise political pressure against the government.[57] Then he complained about the lack of political confidence and tended to discount British concessions in the negotiations which had started in April and ended with the abortive mission of Anglo-French military experts to Moscow in mid-August 1939.[58] This way of reporting only added to already enormous suspicions of the Western Powers on the side of the Moscow leaders, demurred and isolated in the Kremlin.

Britain's road to an alliance with Russia, however, was anything but smooth. The Prime Minister, and to a lesser degree the Foreign Secretary, were hesitant to commit Britain closely to the East. 'I must confess to the most profound distrust of Russia,' Chamberlain wrote to his sister in late March. He had no belief in Russia's military strength and distrusted her motives, which seemed to him 'to have little connection with our ideas of liberty'. Moreover, Russia was hated by Poland, Rumania and Finland; thereby an association with the USSR might cost Britain 'the sympathy of those who would much more effectively help us if we can get them on our side'.[59] The government, however, could not ignore the growing pressure in the House for intense co-operation with the Soviet Union,[60] as well as a similar desire of the public opinion: 87 per

57) See Watt, *How War Came*, pp. 217–218.
58) See e.g. *DVP*, Vol. XXII (1939) – 1, No. 193, 212, 290, 422, pp. 245–246, 266–267, 348–349, 535–537, all: Maisky to NKID, 1, 11, 13 April, 5 May, 10 July 1939.
59) *Birmingham University Library*, Chamberlain Papers, NC 18/1/1091, Neville Chamberlain's letter to his sister Ida, 26 March 1938.
60) Only in the debate on European situation on 13 April a closer co-operation with Russia was demanded by Attlee, Sinclair, Churchill, Eden, Dalton and six other speakers. The practical proposals, however, varied even within the Labour Party – from 'a declaration of solidarity' between the three Powers 'of their general interests in the peace of

cent of respondents wanted 'a military alliance between Great Britain, France and Russia'.[61] Twice did the British propose that the Soviet Union should make a declaration of support to the potential victims of German aggression, similar to the British one, and twice it was refused by two Soviet Foreign Ministers (on 3 May Molotov replaced Litvinov). As an alternative, Moscow offered a triple alliance. The British finally agreed on 24 May 1939, after the process of change had taken place in the Foreign Policy Committee where Chamberlain's and partly also Halifax's objections had after several meetings been overridden by a majority opinion.[62] However, parliamentary pressure, public opinion, as well as the growing anxiety of the Chiefs of Staff, also played an important role in this process.[63]

Historians mostly agree that the subsequent negotiations consisted largely of a series of British progressive concessions and regular, if reluctant, decisions to acquiesce in extra demands made by the Soviet Union,[64] although Parker adds that it was Chamberlain who probably destroyed any hope of a military alliance between Great Britain, France and the USSR.[65] True, Michael Jabara Carley argued that the Grand Alliance did not materialise due to the inherent anti-Bolshevism of the British.[66] Keith Neilson, however, pointed out Stalin's belief that all of the Western powers, and in particular Britain, had as their primary motivation the destruction of the workers' paradise. Thus it is possible to turn Carley's argument on its head and say that the failure of the Anglo-Soviet negotiations in 1939 was due to Soviet, rather than Brit-

the world' (Attlee) to 'a triple alliance' (Dalton). *H. C. Deb.*, 5th Series, Vol. 346, 13 April 1939, Cols. 15–140.
61) *The Gallup International Public Opinion Polls. Great Britain 1937–75*, ed. G. H. Gallup, Vol. I, New York, Random House 1976, Gallup Poll, April 1939, p. 16.
62) See Hill, *Cabinet Decisions on Foreign Policy*, p. 83. For more details see also Manne, Robert, The British decision for alliance with Russia, May 1939, *Journal of Contemporary History*, Vol. 9, 1974, No. 1, pp. 3–26.
63) See Pozdeeva, L. V., *London – Moskva. Britanskoe obshchestvennoe mnenie i SSSR 1939–1945*, Moskva, Institut vseobshchei istorii RAN 2000, pp. 54–55.
64) Hill, *Cabinet Decisions on Foreign Policy*, p. 76. See also Parker, *Chamberlain and Appeasement*, pp. 236, 241. For more details see: Manne, Robert, The Foreign Office and the Failure of Anglo-Soviet Rapprochement, *Journal of Contemporary History*, Vol. 16, 1981, No. 4, pp. 725–755.
65) Parker, *Chamberlain and Appeasement*, p. 245.
66) Carley, Michael Jabara, *1939. The Alliance That Never Was and the Coming of World War II*, Chicago, Ivan R. Dee 1999.

ish, ideological antipathy.[67] It can be argued that Moscow was actually bringing new conditions (usually put as a *conditio sine qua non*) into negotiations with the Western Powers at the same time as a rapprochement with Berlin became more promising, and that from early 1939 Moscow viewed the prospect of a deal with Germany as a plausible option. Some of the British and French concessions in the negotiations with the USSR were unprecedented, such as the acceptance of military negotiations without any corresponding political treaty.[68] On the other hand, to agree to the Soviet definition of indirect aggression, which would have given Moscow a free hand to invade Poland virtually at any time, would have been unconscionable for the British and a repudiation of all that was best in British policy.[69] Stalin was hardly unaware of this fact. His August directive to Voroshilov, People's Commissar for Defence, for the negotiations with the western military missions can only be interpreted as an instruction to find a pretext for break-up of negotiations.[70] The simple mathematics, counting the days during which the ball was on the western side as opposed to the limited sum of days when Moscow was due to reply to western proposals or concessions, such as A. J. P. Taylor has done,[71] has in my view a zero explanatory value, considering the differences in the decision-making process in a communist system on the one hand and in two democracies combined on the other hand.

Christopher Hill is probably right when he says that 'by the time the decision was taken to go for an alliance with Moscow, developments in German-Soviet relations had already rendered it nugatory'.[72] Geoffrey Roberts argues that Stalin resorted to the alliance with Hitler only in the late summer of 1939 and purely because of the lack of interest by

67) Neilson, Keith, Stalin's Moustache: The Soviet Union and the Coming of War (review article), *Diplomacy & Statecraft*, Vol. 12, 2001, No. 2, p. 206.

68) Smetana, Vít, *Enigma zahalená tajemstvím. Britská politika a Sovětský svaz v roce 1939, op. cit.* See also Idem, Vítězství geopolitiky nad ideologií. Sovětsko-německý pakt 1939 [The victory of geopolitics over ideology. The Soviet-German pact 1939], *Dějiny a současnost* [History and present], Prague, Vol. 21, 1999, No. 4, pp. 24–29.

69) See Neilson, Stalin's Moustache, *op. cit.*, p. 201.

70) *DVP*, Vol. XXII (1939) – 1, No. 453, p. 584, Instruction to Voroshilov, 7 August 1939.

71) Taylor, *The Origins of the Second World War*, p. 282–283.

72) Hill, *Cabinet Decisions on Foreign Policy*, p. 84.

the British and French to meet the moderate Soviet claims.[73] He says that 'from Moscow's point of view the story of Soviet-German relations between May and August 1939 is one of persistent wooing by Berlin' and that until July 1939 Moscow did not even respond to German overtures and remained sceptical towards this effort to 'drive a wedge between the USSR and the Western Powers'.[74] However, Jonathan Haslam persuasively refuted this bold claim, which in confrontation with available evidence is hardly sustainable.[75] The British writing has a natural tendency to prioritise British policy, sometimes at the expense of a broader international interpretation.

It is arguable that a chance to build up the Grand Coalition had probably faded away soon after Munich and Britain's repudiation of her Munich commitment towards Czechoslovakia only diminished that chance. By then Chamberlain was considered by the Soviet diplomats and probably also by Stalin a highly untrustworthy partner. Hitler, on the other hand, had much more to offer: territorial expansion and avoidance of war, at least for some time.[76]

R.A.C. Parker suggests that 'Churchill's entry into the government could justify Russian acceptance of an alliance with Britain; his continued exclusion pointed to a British deal with Hitler.' However, later he hedges his bets slightly when he points out that Gabriel Gorodetsky has effectively shown, what deep mistrust Stalin felt about Churchill even on the eve of German invasion into the USSR.[77]

Chamberlain's secret overtures towards Germany through certain semi-official channels, in his hope to extract from Hitler some gesture of good will that would have made in his view a reconciliation with Germany possible, had undoubtedly the worst effect everywhere once they leaked to the press.[78] In Berlin they served as evidence that the

73) Roberts, Geoffrey, The Soviet Decision for a Pact with Nazi Germany, *Soviet Studies*, Vol. 44, No. 1, 1992, pp. 57–78.

74) Idem, *The Soviet Union and the Origins of the Second World War: Russo-German Relations and the Road to War, 1933–1941*, p. 73.

75) Haslam, Soviet-German Relations and the Origins of the Second World War: The Jury Is Still Out, *op. cit.*

76) For a similar view see: Strang, William, *Home & Abroad*, London, A. Deutsch 1956, p. 198.

77) Parker, *Churchill and Appeasement*, pp. 145, 259; Gorodetsky, Gabriel, *Grand Delusion: Stalin and the German invasion of Russia*, New Haven–London, Yale University Press 1999, pp. 155–178, 221, 246, 270.

78) See Watt, *How War Came*, s. 396–403.

new policy of guarantees was not something to be taken fully seriously, whereas in Moscow they only strengthened the already incredible suspicions about the real intentions of the Western Powers. Paradoxically, these contacts had in fact no chance to succeed; even if Berlin had responded sympathetically, the government could have hardly returned to its previous policy of appeasement. It is arguable that after 15 March an attempt for another Munich would have cost Chamberlain his position as the Prime Minister. Such 'nuances' of the democratic system, however, were hardly understandable to any of the dictators, including Stalin.

Some of these overtures have perhaps earned more attention amongst historians than they actually deserved. Probably the most important contact was Göring's adviser (and Vansittart's informant) Helmuth Wohlthat, ostensibly the leader of the German delegation to the International Whaling Conference during his crucial visit of London in mid-July. The fact that a file concerning this conference was to be closed for an exceptional period of 75 years has so far caused historians to speculate what it contains.[79] However, the file has been fully available to researchers since 1995 and the most sensitive information in it is about Norwegian support to the Japanese position in relation to whaling quotas which caused some FO officials to speculate that perhaps Norway was getting some trade concessions from Japan...[80] Nonetheless, Wohlthat at the same time played an important role in dealing with Czechoslovak affairs.

Military and economic implications
of the German subjugation of Czechoslovakia

Economic experts, when assessing various aspects of Germany's subjugation of Bohemia and Moravia, were inclined, rather oddly, to emphasise potential problems resulting for the German economy, rather than to point out the remarkable gains. Thus for example some found it unlikely that Germany's existing labour shortage would be substantially relieved, while at the same time mentioning the 148,000 unemployed and some

79) While Sidney Aster thought that it might have something to do with Wohlthat's surprising selection as a delegate for the conference, D. C. Watt is inclined to think that the file contains some information about Wohlthat's contacts with Vansittart and his warnings about the Soviet-German contacts. Aster, Sidney, *1939. The Making of the Second World War*, London, History Book Club 1973, s. 244; Watt, *How War Came*, s. 396.
80) *PRO*, FO 371/23661. See also Smetana, Nevyřízené účty, *op. cit.*, p. 539.

150,000 disbanded Czech troops.[81] It was generally considered that the Reich had secured yet another strongly industrialised region without the necessary raw materials to feed its industries. The former Czechoslovakia's industrial stability had depended on her export of manufactured goods, which was now to become more difficult as the products would be classified as German and would become subject to the same obstacles, for example in the United States. On the other hand, Germany was to shoulder new burdens of raw materials, including coal, metals of various kinds, and petrol.[82] 'It is uncertain whether the new territories will bring any economic gain to Germany,' the UK Embassy in Berlin stated. In order to prevent needless internal competition within the German customs union, the Embassy expected a far-reaching reorganisation of the new provinces, in the form of de-industrialisation and more intensive development of primary production, notably mining, forestry and agriculture.[83]

Financial, as well as military gains for Germany were, however, indisputable. A conservative estimate talked about 35–40 million pounds of gold and foreign exchange gained by the German Government from Czechoslovakia. However, a large part of the Czech National Bank's holdings was deposited abroad.[84]

It was generally known that in Czechoslovakia, Germany had obtained a large quantity of armaments. Already on 15 March, several MPs reminded the government of the '35 splendidly-equipped divisions' (at the time Britain only planned to build a territorial army of 19 divisions), ca. 1,000 aeroplanes, the fourth greatest armament industry in the world including 'the famous Skoda works' where 'the Bren gun was made'.[85] In addition to war stores of modern manufacture sufficient to equip some 30 to 40 divisions, the Industrial Intelligence Centre at the Department of Overseas Trade warned that Germany acquired good modern anti-aircraft artillery, which might be transferred westwards. The War Office estimated that the Germans obtained equipment for 38 divisions and 8 mobile divisions, *inter alia* 26,000 machine guns, 800 mortars, 1,800 anti-tank guns, almost 2,500 field guns and howitzers, 330 heavy guns, 420 tanks, etc. The Air Ministry provided a figure from the previous

81) *PRO*, FO 22996, C 3856/19/18, FO Memorandum, 17 March 1939; FO 22994, C 3507/ /19/18, M.Y.W., 17 March 1939.
82) *Ibid*; FO 371/22997, C 6002/19/18, ICF/1163, 1 April 1939.
83) *PRO*, CAB 21/589, Ogilvie Forbes to Halifax, No. 392, 28 March 1939.
84) *PRO*, FO 22996, C 3856/19/18, FO Memorandum, 17 March 1939.
85) *H. C. Deb.*, 5th Series, Vol. 345, 15 March 1939, Cols. 455, 534.

June: 636 planes.[86] Most of these figures were underrated, some of them by one half.[87]

Even more serious, perhaps, was the loss of industrial capacity for the manufacture of land armaments and aircraft, together with skilled labour. In the Škoda, in Vítkovice and in Brno, Germany acquired three of the principal armament manufacturing concerns in Europe; there were, however, other smaller armament factories and the British knew from Colonel Píka that every factory in Bohemia and Moravia capable of the effort had recently been supplied with additional plant and machinery to enable it to turn over to the manufacture of war stores if acquired. The Board of Trade expected that the Czechs had no chance to dismantle this additional capacity, which had been surveyed in the last few weeks before the invasion by German officers touring the country with the ostensible purpose of placing orders for goods. It is rather shameful, however, that no attempt to destroy either some of the huge arsenals or industrial plants to produce them occurred on the Czech side. The British were also aware that Yugoslavia and Rumania, and in a certain measure also Poland, whose own industry was 'quite inadequate to maintain their Forces in the Field,' would now be unable to obtain adequate armaments from the Czech factories in war, unless they fought on Germany's side.[88] The Rumanian Minister in London, Virgil Tilea, bitterly complained at the Foreign Office on 16 March that his government had recently concluded a contract with the Czechs whereby 'they were to lock, stock and barrel, the whole equipment of 4 divisions' and most of this material remained in Czecho-Slovakia.[89] The Industrial Intelligence Centre concluded that the armament stocks and plants acquired in Czecho-Slovakia might 'in a short time exceed Germany's own requirements even though she were to mobilise the maximum available manpower of the Reich'. Thus it became a real possibility that Germany would be able to arm, equip and

86) *PRO*, FO 371/22958, C 3495/13/18, WO to Speaight, 17 March 1939, C 3638/13/18, Speaight's minute, 18 March 1939.

87) D. C. Watt provides following estimates based on German sources: 2,000 anti-tank guns, 800 tanks, 2,000 pieces of artillery, 57,000 machine guns, 750,000 rifles, and 1,200 aircraft. Watt, *How War Came*, p. 195.

88) *PRO*, FO 371/22958, C 3638/13/18, Speaight's minute, 18 March 1939; WO 190/762, M.I.3.b., 17 March 1939; FO 371/22966, C 3368/15/18, Department of Overseas Trade (I.I.C.) to Foreign Office, 16 March 1939.

89) *DBFP*, 3rd Series, Vol. IV, No. 298, pp. 284–285, Minute by Sir O. Sargent, 16 March 1939.

maintain a large number of Italian divisions.[90] The Military Attaché in Berlin expected, quite paradoxically, that, although the ultimate military benefits for Germany of the inclusion of Bohemia and Moravia were great, for the next few months difficulties stemming from the formation of forces to take advantage 'of the windfall in armament' secured from Czecho-Slovakia would 'have a most adverse effect on the Army's ability to deal with a major war'.[91]

The War Office thought that the annexation of Bohemia and Moravia had been probably dictated primarily by strategic considerations: Germany acquired excellent railway facilities and a network of useful military roads, all usable in any future advance against Poland or towards the southeast. However, in general the WO doubted whether the subjugation of the Czechs would add to the strength of the Reich: 'The Czechs are bitterly opposed to the Germans and the history of their race makes it probable that in any future war they would be a thorn in the side of Germany, as they were in Austria-Hungary in the Great War.'[92] The future six years were to show how optimistic and wishful were both this expectation and the emphasis on economic liabilities connected with the German annexation. The Czech lands soon became a vital armoury of the Third Reich. It is also interesting that none of the governmental analyses pointed out that all the wealth that might have been used for the allied cause, had been in fact lost as early as in the end of September 1938.

'The Czech gold scandal'

Unlike in the case of Austria, the British government took prompt steps to prevent Czechoslovak deposits in London banks from being handed over to the Germans. On 15 March Chancellor Simon notified the Bank of England that no further transfers should be made from the two accounts where the unexpended parts of the free gift and of the loan to Czechoslovakia were deposited. Two days later he extended his request to all Czechoslovak balances in the Bank of England and asked the Governor to notify all British financial institutions in this respect. This order also effectively blocked the 26,793 kg of gold deposited in the Bank

90) *PRO*, FO 371/22966, C 3368/15/18, Department of Overseas Trade (I.I.C.) to Foreign Office, 16 March 1939.
91) *PRO*, FO 371/22994, C 3473/19/18, Ogilvie Forbes to Halifax, No. 343, Enclosure, 19 March 1939.
92) *PRO*, WO 190/797, The Annexation of Bohemia and Moravia, April 1939.

of England with the account of the National Bank of Czechoslovakia (NBČS). Within a week the Chancellor introduced pertinent legislation which blocked all Czechoslovak balances in British banks. The only exception from this law entitled the Treasury to release blocked balances of refugees from the Protectorate. The bill met with a general consent in Parliament and both chambers passed it by 27 March, twelve days after the German occupation had started.[93]

Communist historiography, as well as some British authors eager to make use of every opportunity to criticise Chamberlain and his colleagues, have tended to claim that the government showed a new 'wave' of appeasement, again at the expense of Czechoslovakia, as early as the end of March 1939, when consent was allegedly granted for the transfer to the German *Reichsbank* of another amount of Czechoslovak gold (23,087 kg) deposited in the Bank of England under the name of Bank for International Settlements (BIS).[94] Available documentation shows, however, that this criticism of the government is mostly unfounded. For the revisionist historians, who sought rational and economic explanations of Chamberlain's policy, this complicated matter lost an argumentative meaning and it correspondingly faded away from historiography of appeasement.[95] However, this omission in books dealing

93) *H. C. Deb.*, Vol. 345, 22, 23, 27 March 1939, Cols. 1299–1330, 1481–1488.
94) For communist historiography see: Křen, *Do emigrace*, p. 434; Nekrič, Aleksandr M., *Politika anglijskogo imperialisma v Jevropě: oktiabr 1938 – sentiabr 1939*, Moskva, Izdatelstvo Akademii nauk SSSR 1955, p. 334–336. See also the memoirs and diaries of Beneš's secretary, as well as his nephew: Táborský, *Prezident Beneš mezi Západem a Východem*, p. 60; Idem, *Pravda zvítězila* [The truth has triumphed], Praha, Družstevní práce 1947, diary entry for May 22, 1939, p. 169; Beneš, Bohuš, *Amerika šla s námi* [America went with us], 2nd edition, Zürich, Konfrontace 1977, p. 145. For British 'anti-appeasement' literature see: Einzig, Paul: *Appeasement Before, During and After the War*, London, Macmillan 1942, p. 122–135; Idem, *In the Centre of Things. The Autobiography of Paul Einzig*, London, Hutchinson 1960, p. 186–194; Gilbert – Gott, *The Appeasers*, pp. 208–211.
95) See e.g.: Medlicott, W. N., *British Foreign Policy since Versailles, 1919–1963*, 2nd edition, London, Methuen 1968; Crowson, *Facing Fascism. The Conservative Party and the European Dictators, 1935–1940*; Kennedy, *The Realities Behind Diplomacy*; Charmley, John, *Chamberlain and the Lost Peace*, London, Papermac 1991; Watt, *How War Came*; Aster, *1939. The Making of the Second World War*. R. A. C. Parker did not mention the episode in his 'anti-revisionist' book *Chamberlain and Appeasement* either. He did so, however, upon my notice, in his later book about Churchill: he quoted part of Churchill's speech on the topic in the House of Commons and suggested that Churchill 'deployed one of his Parliamentary techniques: that of courteous, gently supercilious patronage of a senior minister, this time Sir John Simon'. Parker, *Churchill and Appeasement*, pp. 226–227.

with Britain's politics before the outbreak of war verges on distortion of historical picture, as for two month the 'Czech gold scandal' became an issue of primary importance in Parliament and it attracted constant attention of British press.[96]

Two directors of the NBČS, Peroutka and Malík, were forced by the Germans to request a transfer of 23 tons of gold from a NBČS account to a *Reichsbank* account. The gold was, however, deposited in the Bank of England in the name of BIS. In Basel the Dutch President of the BIS, Johan W. Beyen, had been warned from Paris that the request from Prague was to be expected.[97] However, after a consultation with his legal adviser and having been assured both from *Banque de France* and from the Bank of England that neither of the two Governors, Pierre Fournier and Montagu Norman, wanted to call for a special meeting of the Board of Directors, the only body that could block the transfer, Beyen complied with the request from Prague and asked the Bank of England to transfer the gold from one BIS account (No. 2) to another (No. 17). This transfer occurred on 21 and 22 March.[98] In a series of clearing operations during the next few days other banks (especially *De Nederlandsche Bank* and *Banque de Belgique*) were credited with this gold, partly it was sold in London. Its real value of 5,512 million pounds eventually reached the *Reichsbank*; by 31 March the BIS account no. 17 was empty.[99]

The key question concerning British policy is, of course, whether the government or some of its members approved the transfer. Paul Einzig, an editor of *Financial News*, who had constantly criticised the government's economic policy in the 1930s, claims in his memoirs that it was so and he points the finger at Chancellor Simon.[100] However, his assertion is based on two later personal testimonies, none of them verifiable: one is attributed to 'official British circles sometimes in 1944', the

96) For further details see Smetana, Británie a československé zlato. 'Case study' britského appeasementu?, *op. cit.*

97) The Governor of Banque de France had probably been informed from Quai d'Orsay. One of the two Czech directors had warned the French Embassy. It seems, however, that the British Embassy was warned by Peroutka only on 24 March. The same day nBasil Newton sent a warning to the Foreign Office. PRO, FO 371/22895, C 4262/3/12, Newton from Stopford to Waley, 24 March 1939; C 4023/3/12, Newton to FO, 24 March 1939.

98) Smetana, Británie a československé zlato, *op. cit.*, pp. 631–634.

99) *Bank of England Archive* (hereafter *BEA*), C 43/374, Czecho-Slovakia – Memorandum, 24 March 1939.

100) Einzig, *In the Centre of Things*, p. 192.

other to Norman's successor Lord Catto in 1946, during the debate on nationalisation of the Bank of England. Catto, however, had died a year before Einzig's rather egocentric and not always reliable memoirs were published. No written document confirming Einzig's bold statement probably exists, while the available documentation seems to show to the contrary. The management of the Bank of England considered the transfer a technical operation, all the more so as it had only unofficial information about the real owner of the gold, and was generally reluctant to allow political considerations to interfere in banking operations concerning the BIS. Moreover, neither Norman nor Otto Niemeyer, the Executive Director of the Bank of England and the President of the Board of Directors of the BIS, wished to discourage Germany from further payments for her debt to the BIS which had originated in the bank's enormous investments in that country in early 1930s. Thus in a letter to Niemeyer to Basel on 1 April, Norman displayed his opinion about a recent French intervention to stop the transfer: 'In any case you will see that Fournier was simply playing politics! (perhaps had to) I can't imagine any step more improper than to bring the Gov[ernmen]ts into the current banking affairs of the B.I.S. I guess it w[oul]d mean ruins. I imagine the Germans w[ould]d never have paid any more interest to the B.I.S. and at the Board we should likely have found the Germans, Italians and Japs standing together! A nice kettle of fish for future smooth banking.'[101]

Having failed at the Bank of England, Paul Reynaud, the French Minister of Finance, arranged for several political interventions at the Foreign Office and Treasury.[102] Halifax thought that the decision rested with the Treasury, while the Foreign Office could only define its position on the political question. 'We should I think wish to ... prevent the gold, in present circumstances, from falling in the German hands,' he

---

101) *BEA*, 4/101, Norman's letter to Niemeyer, 1 April 1939. The bankers' efforts were successful; during World War II the *Reichsbank* paid 7.8 tons of gold to the Bank for International Settlements as interests for the pre-war investments in Germany. CLEMENT, Piet: The Bank for International Settlements during the Second World War. In: *Nazi gold: The London Conference, 2–4 December 1997*, London, Stationery Office 1998, p. 49.
102) *Documents Diplomatiques Français 1932–1939* (hereafter *DDF*), 2e Série (1936–1939), Tome XV (16 Mars – Avril 1939), Paris, Imprimerie Nationale 1981, No. 229, Note 2.

wrote. 'And I should hope that no ordinary routine objections should be permitted to interfere with the achievement of the object.'[103] Although Treasury officials tended to stress technical aspects of the operation and the independence of the BIS, on 3 April Chancellor Simon conveyed to the French Embassy via Strang his own hope that it might turn out differently: 'The B.I.S. will not pay over (unless it has done so already) if they are advised that the disappearance of the Cz. state invalidates the mandate [of the Czechoslovak National Bank]. I hope it may be so.'[104] The next day, however, a Treasury official was informed confidentially by the Director of the Bank of England, Cameron Cobbold, 'that the bird had already flown'.[105]

On 19 May information about the transfer leaked to the press[106] and it immediately caused a storm of parliamentary criticism including one debate on adjournment, in which Churchill delivered one of his magnificent speeches: 'Here we are going about urging our people to enlist, urging them to accept new forms of military compulsion; here we are paying taxes on a gigantic scale in order to protect ourselves. If at the same time our mechanism of government is so butter-fingered that this £ 6,000,000 of gold can be transferred to the Nazi Government of Germany, which only wishes to use it, and is only using it, as it does all its foreign exchange, for the purpose of increasing its armaments, if this money is to be transferred out of our hands, to come back in certain circumstances even quicker than it went, it stultifies altogether the efforts our people are making in every class and in every party to secure National Defence and rally the whole forces of the country.'[107] Numerous MPs called for a governmental intervention (it was not officially known whether the order had already been obeyed, and the Bank of England refused to provide the Chancellor with an official information about its client's account) and criticised the lack of political control of the Bank of England. Some even called for its nationalisation or for cancellation of British participation

103) *PRO*, FO 371/22895, C 4543/3/12, Halifax's minute, 1 April 1939.
104) *PRO*, T 160/1417, Simon's minute, 3 April 1939; *DDF*, 2e Série (1936–1939), Tome XV (16 Mars – Avril 1939), No. 244.
105) *PRO*, T 160/1417, Waley's minute, undated.
106) *Financial News*, 19 May 1939; *Daily Telegraph*, 19 May 1939.
107) *H. C. Deb.*, 5th Series, Vol. 347, May 26, Cols. 2759–2760. Churchill's biographer Martin Gilbert thinks, wrongly, that as a result of Churchill's and other MPs' pressure, the gold eventually remained in London. *Winston Churchill*, Companion Vol. V., p. 1508.

on the BIS.[108] The Chancellor insisted on governmental non-interference and on honouring international treaties establishing immunities of the BIS, in particular the convention respecting the BIS signed in the Hague in January 1930, the Constituent Charter granted by the Swiss Government and the Brussels Protocol of 1936. With respect to the Bank of England's decision he added a plausible warning: 'London will not remain the banking centre of the world for long if banks do not obey the cheques and orders of their customers.'[109] A month later, however, he called the transfer a 'deplorable event' and expressed his 'regret that this [had] happened', but did not see any way how to bring the existing immunities of the BIS to an end.[110] 'Hence, in spite of Sir John's deep regrets,' *Manchester Guardian* commented sarcastically, 'we look like being saddled with the B.I.S. and its curious ways for long time to come.'[111]

At least one of Simon's internal minutes in the Treasury shows that he felt great uneasiness about his role: 'The situation of having to defend in Parliament a position in which I have no responsibility and no possibility of control is naturally rather troublesome and, however right H.M.G. may be in all the elaborate explanations I have had to give, I do not think the Government is strengthened by having to give such explanations. The vulgar view is that H.M.G. by refusing to interfere and disclaiming responsibility has been handing Czech gold to Germany, and this is the actual result.'[112]

It is clear that 'the Czech gold scandal' contributed significantly to the process of growing parliamentary control of the foreign policy of Chamberlain's Cabinet in the spring and the summer of 1939. This was soon demonstrated by other 'Czechoslovak issues': the question of further dealing with the balances sequestrated in London and that of possible recognition of the German annexation.

108) *H. C. Deb.*,5ᵗʰ Series, Vol. 347, 19 May 1939, Cols. 1813, 22 May, Cols. 1917–1920, 23 May, Cols. 2079–2082, 24 May, Cols. 2269–2278, 25 May, Cols. 2531–2532, 26 May, Cols. 2703–2760; Vol. 348, 5 June, Cols. 35–41, 12 June, Cols. 880–881, 13 June, Cols. 1098–1103, 20 June, Cols. 2005–2012; Vol. 349, 27 June, Cols. 208–213; *H. L. Deb.*, Vol. 114, 11 July, 1939, Cols. 50–61.
109) *Ibid.*, Vol. 347, 23 May 1939, Cols. 2079–2082.
110) *Ibid.*, Vol. 348, 20 June 1939, Cols. 2010–2011.
111) *Manchester Guardian Commercial*, 23 June 1939.
112) *PRO*, T 160/1417, Simon's minute, 9 June 1939.

British policy towards the newly created state was rather ambivalent. On the one hand the British knew that the declaration of Slovak independence had been engineered by Germany after a ruthless blackmail, as well as they were aware of the limited Slovak sovereignty when the Germans were allowed by the means of a treaty of 23 March 1939 to build military bases in the western part of Slovakia.[113] The Foreign Office did not even acknowledge a letter from the new Slovak Foreign Minister, Ferdinand Ďurčanský, in which he informed London about the creation of the new state.[114] On the other hand, however, two experts on Czecho-Slovakia, Frank Roberts and E. H. Carr, agreed on 17 March 1939 that the British had always been inclined to under-rate the division between the Czechs and the Slovaks and that the very fact that the Slovak appeal for independence was of an artificial nature should not make the government to put the Slovak question in the forefront of its criticism of German aggression.[115] The British knew about political reprisals unleashed in Slovakia shortly after 15 March, including the establishment of the first concentration camp.[116] Nonetheless, for practical reasons the Central Department pleaded in mid-April to regularise the status of the Consulate in Bratislava and to instruct current Consul Pares to apply for an *exequatur* from the Slovak Government. Roger Makins pointed out that Pares' position was irregular, thus the Communication Department denied him of cyphers and he was obliged to stick to instructions for Consuls in a territory not recognised by Britain – to avoid contacts with ministers and to deal with officials only as far as necessary. The author also added rather peculiar argument that the new state had already been recognised by Germany, Italy and Poland. 'There is nothing but disadvantages in letting the present undefined position continue indefinitely...' All senior officials agreed that a Chargé d'Affaires should be appointed in Bratislava, once the Legation in Prague had been closed and the Protectorate recognised *de facto* – as was already planned.[117] This,

113) *PRO*, FO 371/22897, C 3925/7/12, Newton to Halifax, No. 129, 21 March 1939; FO 371/22898, C 6534/7/12, FO Memorandum (Makins), 12 April 1939.
114) *Ibid.*, C 3561/7/12, Slovak Minister for Foreign Affairs to Halifax, 14 March 1939.
115) *PRO*, FO 371/22995, C 3647/19/18, Roberts' minute, 17 March 1939.
116) *PRO*, FO 371/22897, C 5201/7/12, Pares to Halifax, No. 20, 11 April 1939.
117) *PRO*, FO 371/22898, C 6534/7/12, FO Memorandum (Makins), 12 April, Strang's minute, 4 April, Makins' minute, 17 April, Oliphant's minute, 19 April, Halifax's minute, 21 April, Butler's minute, 21 April 1939.

however, never materialised. In each case Butler, anticipating parliamentary opposition, wished to act with the French or at least to let them know. Other officials decided, however, not to wait for the French. The instructions to Paris were sent at the same time as those to Bratislava.[118] The French Government thought that the status of Slovakia might be changed towards further dependence on Germany, and feared that the position of French and British diplomatic representatives in Bohemia and Moravia might be affected. Therefore they wished to wait. It was already too late.[119] On 4 May British Consul Pares sought and obtained from the Slovak Government recognition as British Consul in Slovakia. Pares observed that the Slovak politicians were 'extremely pleased' and the recognition was accordingly used by Slovak propaganda.[120] The French granted *de facto* recognition to independent Slovakia only in mid-July, and then only under Slovak threat that their Consulate in Bratislava would be closed down.[121]

On 15 May Butler stressed in the House of Commons that the Slovak government had been informed that this step amounted to *de facto* recognition. Later he informed the House that the French government had been approached earlier, but its approval was not obtained. He also admitted that while the Czecho-Slovak Legation in London had neither been consulted beforehand, nor informed afterwards, the German government 'got to know' about this step. Although some MPs apparently had doubts about real Slovak independence, this recognition aroused comparatively less criticism than the later *de facto* recognition of the German annexation of Bohemia and Moravia.[122] Afterwards an appointment of British Chargé d'Affaires in Bratislava was mentioned only once in the Foreign Office files: in mid-July it was not thought that the British needed to 'be in any great hurry about that'.[123] Meanwhile the newly appointed Slovak Consul General, Milan Harminc, arrived to London.

118) *Ibid.*, C 6535/7/12, Halifax to Phipps, No. 188, 2 May, Halifax to Gainer (Vienna), No. 8, 2 May 1939.
119) *Ibid.*, C 6701/7/12, Phipps to Halifax, 6 May 1939.
120) *Ibid.*, C 6589, C6590/7/12, Pares to Halifax, 4 May 1939, C 7036/7/12, Pares to Halifax, 9 May 1939.
121) *Ibid.*, C 9567/7/12, Pares to Halifax, 8 August 1939, C 10158/7/12, Pares to Halifax, 15 August 1939.
122) *H. C. Deb.*, 5th Series, Vol. 347, 15 May, Cols. 961–962, 26 May 1939, Cols. 2686–2687.
123) *PRO*, FO 371/22898, C 9567/7/12, Troutbeck's minute, 12 July 1939.

This time also the Czecho-Slovak legation 'got to know'. Although the Foreign Office had felt bound to agree with his appointment, he was treated with great suspicion and his plea to be admitted by Halifax was politely turned down.[124]

After 15 March the British thought that they had for decades under-estimated the Slovak thirst for independence. For practical reasons they also wished to secure their immediate interests and consular agenda in the independent Slovakia as soon as possible – regardless of the symbolic meaning of granting *de facto* recognition to the new state. In this respect the British policy differed from the French. Nevertheless, the Foreign Office had no illusion about the real nature of this in-dependence and Slovakia was considered at best a puppet state of Germany.

Britain's de facto recognition of German annexation and the question of the Czechoslovak balances (a study of interdependence of foreign policy and economic interests)

On 16 March the German Embassy, upon instructions from Berlin, at-tempted to take over the Czecho-Slovak Legation in London. Chargé d'Affaires Karel Lisický immediately called on Cadogan who 'said any-how that he and his staff could stay' in Britain.[125] Then, having been in constant telephone contact with the Czechoslovak Legation in Paris, whose chief Štefan Osuský took the lead in the revolt of the key diplo-matic posts against German orders from Prague, Lisický resisted further German pressure for the rest of the day. On the next day, he stayed at home, 'as the exhausting negotiations of the previous evening had over-taxed' his strength. He, however, sent Jan Gerke, the First Secretary of the Legation, to the Foreign Office with a peculiar note declaring that he would 'hand over the archives and the property of the Legation' to the British authorities 'as soon as His Majesty's Government will *de jure* recognise the new state of affairs and as soon as I shall receive notification that the legal status of this Legation is no longer recognised in this coun-

---

124) *PRO*, FO 371/22904, C 8203/2875/12, Malkin's minute, 16 June, FO to Pares, 30 June 1939, C 10109/2875/12, Harminc to Halifax, 18 July, Kirkpatrick to Harminc, 25 July 1939.
125) *Cadogan Diary*, diary entry for 16 March 1939, p. 157; *PRO*, FO 371/22897, C 3281/7/12, Cadogan's minute, 16 March 1939.

try'.[126] Sargent understood clearly: the British government was asked to take the responsibility for deciding whether to hand over the Legation to the Germans.[127] On 20 March Lisický came himself and repeated to Strang that he placed himself in the hands of the British government and promised to refrain from seeing any journalists and from engaging in any political activity.[128]

Berlin, however, did not give up: Ambassador Dirksen came to inform the Foreign Office that persons of 'Czechoslovak race' in Britain would now 'be under the care of the German Embassy'. Since, however, Cadogan thought that the British government 'would not be able to recognise the legality of the change of status of Czechoslovakia,' this raised 'rather a difficult point'. Cadogan then dismissed the Ambassador's reference to Hácha's declaration that everything had been done with his agreement: '…such agreements were extracted in rather peculiar circumstances,' hence the government 'would be unable to attach much weight to that utterance.'[129] However, in future weeks and months this principled position faded away. Various 'law experts', as well as officials of other ministries anxious to continue in their 'smooth working' and generally inclined to ignore foreign policy aspects entailed, played an important role in the ensuing gradual change.

With respect to the Czechoslovak Legation, Sargent proposed that the British should, in concert with the French, decide to take over the Legation, the gold, etc., themselves and then inform the Germans about it. But the British could do this, as Cadogan noted, only if Lisický was ready to hand over to them. He, however, had made this conditional upon Britain's *de jure* recognition of the new state of affairs. On this the FO legal expert, Sir William Malkin, wrote that it would 'be unwise if the natural indignation which we all feel led us to committing ourselves never to recognise a state of affairs which exists in fact'. He referred to the experience with Ethiopia and Austria, which showed that it was impossible to maintain such an attitude permanently, and he suggested that this would be the case here. In each case, there was always the distinction to be made between *de facto* and *de jure*, 'though in practice

126) PRO, FO 371/22995, C 3628/19/18, Aide Memoire, 20 March 1939; *DČSZP 1939–1940*, No. 3, pp. 53–54, Lisický's note, 17 March 1939.
127) *PRO*, FO 371/22897, C 3548/7/12, Sargent's minute, 17 March 1939.
128) *PRO*, FO 371/22995, C 3628/19/18, Strang's minute, 20 March 1939.
129) *Ibid.*, C 3573/19/18, Cadogan's minute, 17 March 1939.

the distinction is not very great'.[130] In another paper, however, he recommended the following: if it was at some stage ('perhaps fairly soon') found impossible not to recognise the new state of affairs, 'to make one bite at the cherry as we [the British] did in the case of Austria, and not to draw the distinction between de facto and de jure recognition'. Nonetheless, he could understand that it might 'be desirable, if not necessary, for political reasons, to make the distinction'.[131] The Foreign Office, including the Foreign Secretary, was in general agreement that Britain should not be in a hurry to give any measure of recognition to the new status of Bohemia and Moravia, while at the same time it was seen as unwise to tie one's hands and 'to adopt an attitude which would commit us to refusing to recognise the fait accompli indefinitely'. The precedents of Manchukuo, Abyssinia and Austria were often mentioned.[132] Thus for some time the House of Commons was just to be given temporising answers on these issues: 'for the time being' the position of the Czecho-Slovak Charge d'Affaires, the diplomatic members of his staff, and Czecho-Slovak consular officials in Britain was to remain as before, as 'no decision has yet been reached about the future of the British Legation at Prague'.[133]

Makins first pointed out that Britain would no doubt recognise it indirectly in due course by converting of the Legation in Prague into a Consulate General.[134] A meeting of FO and Treasury officials on 23 March discussed various questions arising from the German annexation, including the future of the British Legation in Prague. It decided to call Newton back to London as 'his continued presence there served no useful purpose'. Cadogan stressed in a statement to the press that Newton had to return to take charge of the Legation in Baghdad. Otherwise the meeting was inconclusive with respect to the two possibilities: either 1) to carry on the Legation with John Troutbeck as Chargé d'Affaires until the German authorities requested its removal or otherwise made its existence impossible, or 2) to withdraw the Legation forthwith and request the German Government to grant an *exequatur* for a Consul-General. The first

130) *PRO*, FO 371/22897, C 3548/7/12, Malkin's minute, 20 March 1939.
131) *PRO*, FO 371/22995, C 3707/19/18, Malkin's minute, undated.
132) *Ibid.*, C 3841/19/18, Makins' minute, 18 March, Kirkpatrick's minute, 18 March 1939; FO 371/22996, C 3943/19/18, Sargent's minute, 21 March 1939.
133) *H. C. Deb.*, 5th Series, Vol. 345, 29 March, Cols. 1045–1046, 3 April 1939, Col. 2426.
134) *PRO*, FO 371/22995, C 3841/19/18, Makins' minute, 18 March 1939.

option would put all fault on the Germans, but it would entail the danger of a deliberate affront from the German authorities, including the refusal of cypher and bag facilities or forcible entry of the Legation to arrest refugees seeking asylum there.[135] The second option was seen as more practical and in no way equal to condoning what Germany had done, but the general public might not appreciate this distinction. The FO officials (especially Sargent and Makins) were in favour of early closure of the Legation, appointment of a Consul General and *de facto* recognition.[136] Also Halifax thought that it would be necessary to close the Legation soon and did not want 'to keep up a difficult fiction too long', but also thought that a decision in the matter should be postponed for the time being.[137] One of the reasons was the opinion of Robert Stopford who in Prague was negotiating with the Germans about conditions under which Czechs could emigrate, and viewed closing of the Legation as fatal for these negotiations.[138]

This discussion was further prompted by the German offer to start negotiating on mutual compensation for financial debts and capital payments – with a possible handing over of Czechoslovak assets blocked in Britain immediately after 15 March.[139] Sargent agreed and again suggested that Troutbeck should be withdrawn and London should ask for an *exequatur* for a Consul-General. Cadogan proposed to withhold *de jure* recognition by the simple expedient of keeping the Charge d'Affaires name on the British Diplomatic list, although he himself would hardly be able to say 'whom or what he represents. ... If and when the time comes, let us sign a Trade and Payment Agreement. And then people, if they want, will interpret that as de jure. We sh[oul]d. then be in the same position as the Soviets, who some years ago signed an agreement with Japan and Manchukuo concerning the Chinese Eastern Railway – about which nobody bothered overmuch.'[140]

135) On the issue of British support to the refugees from Czechoslovakia see Chapter 4.
136) *PRO*, FO 371/23081, C 4204/3955/18, FO minutes, 23 March, FO to Newton, No. 92, 25 March 1939.
137) *Ibid.*, C 4275/3955/18, Strang's minute, 12 April 1939.
138) *Ibid.*, C 4613/3955/18, Newton to Halifax, No. 186, 1 April 1939.
139) For further details see Smetana, Nevyřízené účty. Problém československých aktiv v britských bankách a snahy britské administrativy o jeho řešení po 15. březnu 1939, *op. cit.*, pp. 521–551.
140) *PRO*, FO 371/22951, C 4687/8/18, Sargent's minute, 4 April 1939, Cadogan's minute, 6 April 1939.

Halifax agreed both that the discussions must take place and that the Legation had to be closed. He, however, wished 'to hold off this matter for a bit, the events may make such decision both more obvious and less open to criticism'. The Treasury was authorised to start discussions with the German financial experts, but with the reservation that these – presumably complicated – negotiations would not be brought to any final conclusion until a decision on the point of Consul-General had been taken.[141]

Newton himself – together with Gibson, the local resident of Military Intelligence with his staff – left Prague on 3 April, about the same time as his French and US colleagues.[142] Meanwhile the Embassy was, under instructions from London, already burning the cyphers and destroying political archives.[143] Troutbeck expressed anxiety about uncertain status of him and his staff in the time when the general situation in Europe was deteriorating daily. Upon this Sargent minuted: 'I sympathise with Mr. Troutbeck and the Prague Staff. ... Their position is highly anomalous and they are doing no good – except the negative good of proving by their continued presence that His Majesty's Government has not recognised in any way Germany's annexation of Bohemia.'[144] Troutbeck later informed about signs of stiffening attitude by the German authorities towards the Legation.[145]

Henderson's return to Berlin on 24 April, one day after the Prime Minister had announced in the House of Commons Britain's intention to adopt conscription, brought about another occasion for the Central Department's call to cancel the Legation. By then all the refugees had left and the Foreign Office had decided to grant *de facto* recognition to Slovakia. Thus the anomalous position merely caused Britain, as Halifax underlined, 'increasing inconvenience and embarrassment without putting the Germans to any corresponding disadvantages'. Halifax, Cadogan and Butler agreed that the case for *de facto* recognition was strong enough, although they were aware that it would 'add fuel to parliamentary flames'. Cadogan, however, doubted 'if that really matters: they

---

141) *Ibid.*, Halifax's minute, 7 April, Strang to Waley, 12 April 1939.
142) *Ibid.*, C 4404/3955/18, Newton to Halifax, No. 179, 30 March 1939.
143) *Ibid.*, C 4757/3955/18, Makins' minute, 6 April 1939.
144) *Ibid.*, C 5129/3955/18, Troutbeck to Harvey, 1 April, Sargent's minute, 4 April 1939.
145) *PRO*, FO 371/23082, C 6858/3955/18, Troutbeck to Halifax, No. 95, 3 May 1939.

die down pretty quickly'.[146] Vansittart hated *any* form of recognition, on moral grounds, but his opinions did not matter much any more.[147] The French, however, did not like even British recognition of Slovakia, not to speak about Bohemia and Moravia. Phipps asked the Foreign Office for additional arguments, but he could not, on his part, understand, why in the case of Albania he had said to the French, upon instructions from London, that there was no material practical difference between *de facto* and *de jure* recognition. 'It would of course be simpler to grant de jure recognition in all these cases,' Strang argued, 'the objections to doing so in some of them are political.'[148] Although tempted to seek expedient solutions of most diplomatic problems, the FO officials had to take care of the political sensitivity of any dealing with Czechoslovak affairs after Munich and especially 15 March.

The Germans interrupted these deliberations with a note of 9 May informing the governments, which still held diplomatic representatives in Prague, that their exterritorial privileges would not be recognised after 25 May. Further, the consular offices were to be closed down by 20 June, unless the governments asked for a new *exequatur* by that date. This note caused real panic in the Foreign Office. Cadogan, for example, observed 'the futility of the doctrine of "non-recognition". Let us remember, in case such a question arises again, that unless we can hope, within a reasonable period, to reverse the "fait accompli", the best thing to do – as we did in the case of Austria – is to swallow it at once.'[149] Cadogan's lamentation, however, is hardly understandable, as there still remained more than a week to withdraw the Legation (and had the Berlin Embassy telegraphed a summary of the German ultimatum, there would have even been some five days more). It seems that some officials, for practical reasons, considered these annoying problems with a small state – that had gone down anyway – uselessly time-consuming.

146) *Ibid.*, C 6955/3955/18, Speaight's minute, 25 April, Cadogan's minute, 2 May, Halifax's minute, 2 May, Butler's minute, 2 May 1939.
147) *Ibid.*, C 6956/3955/18, Vansittart's minute, 5 May, Halifax to Chamberlain, 5 May 1939.
148) *Ibid.*, C 6992/3955/18, Phipps to Halifax, No. 276, 11 May, Strang's minute, 15 May 1939.
149) *Ibid.*, C 7075/3955/18, Henderson to Halifax, No. 550, 11 May, Speaight's minute, 16 May, Cadogan's minute, 18 May 1939.

Troutbeck left Prague with his staff on 25 May, at the same time as the French, and from then on only an inexperienced Vice-Consul remained in Prague.[150] There was now general agreement in the Foreign Office that Britain should apply for an *exequatur* and recognise the Protectorate *de facto*. However, the House of Commons made this virtually impossible. On 22 May Butler declared that the withdrawal of the Legation did not affect the government's position towards the annexation of Bohemia and Moravia. As a reply to Duncan Sandys' question the same day, the Financial Secretary to the Treasury, Captain Crookshank, admitted that informal conversations were taking place between the Treasury and representatives of the German Ministry of Economy in regard to the assets blocked by the Act of 27 March and that the object of these conversations was to see whether a basis existed 'for more formal discussion which would be held next month'. This again added fuel to parliamentary flames which did not seem to 'die pretty quickly'. In next two days numerous MPs asked for assurances that these negotiations did not imply recognition of the new status of Bohemia and Moravia, that the balances blocked in Britain would not be paid over to Germany without the previous consent of the House, and that no *de facto* recognition would be given at all. In the first two matters Simon and Chamberlain partly consoled the House, but statement that 'the question of the *de facto* recognition ... was being considered in connection with the future representation ... at Prague' was found unsatisfactory by the Opposition and Attlee notified the government that he would raise the matter on the Adjournment two days later. At the same time 'the Czech gold scandal' was to be debated.[151] On Chamberlain's suggestion and with Halifax's approval, the application for an *exequatur* was to be deferred – at least until other governments had done the same. Chamberlain, ironically, did not want Britain to act on her own ahead of everyone else.[152] During the debate on adjournment several more MPs protested against any sort of recognition. Simon tried to explain the necessity to have an officially recognised Consul in Prague who could serve not only British interests but also refugees. *De*

150) *Ibid.*, C 7404/3955/18, Troutbeck to Halifax, No. 254, 21 May 1939, C 8583/3955/18, Troutbeck to Halifax, No. 183, 25 May 1939.
151) *H. C. Deb.*, 5th Series, Vol. 347, 22 May, Cols. 1891–1892, 1917–1920, 23 May, Col. 2079–2082, 24 May 1939, Cols. 2269–2278.
152) *PRO*, FO 371/23082, C 7797/3955/18, Makins' minute, Mallett's minute, Loxley's minute, all 24 May 1939.

jure recognition was not contemplated, Simon declared, but an *exequatur* for Consul might be called *de facto* recognition. The Chancellor assured the House that no relevant action would be taken on the matter until the House resumed.[153]

Eventually the government waited even longer – until France, the United States and Poland also asked for their *exequatur*. It was not, however, possible to use this fact as a further argument in the House, as none of the states wished publicity in this matter. Only on 15 June Chamberlain authorised Henderson to ask for an *exequatur* for a new Consul-General; and only if the Germans raised the point he was to say that it was regarded as *de facto*. Henderson managed to avoid this reference.[154] Four days later, however, Butler in the House of Commons had to mention that the step amounted to *de facto* recognition, as two questions inquired about the nature of future British representation in Prague. Quite surprisingly, at that stage the announcement did not provoke much further criticism.[155]

A place where this reference aroused a negative reaction, however, was apparently Berlin itself. In a 'Note Verbale' of 30 June, after another British reminder, Berlin rejected the British request and conditioned its approval by British recognition of German sovereignty over the province in question. The Foreign Office was not prepared to 'submit to this German blackmail'. 'Recognition de jure at this moment,' Roberts argued, 'could only have a most deplorable effect by casting doubts upon our firmness in the face of general German policy. It might also seriously discourage the Czechs from any further resistance to German domination. Whatever our ultimate policy may be in regard to Bohemia and Moravia, I take it that we should not wish to make the German task there any easier at this critical juncture.' Troutbeck, who had just returned from Prague, found it wrong 'to grant de jure recognition now. I should hate to see it done at any time in view of the increasingly oppressive conditions under which the Czechs are having to live…' He reminded that opinion in the House would not allow recognition in any case.[156]

153) *H. C. Deb.*, 5th Series, Vol. 347, 26 May 1939, Cols. 2755–2757.
154) *PRO*, FO 371/23082, C 8466/3955/18, Makins' minute, 15 June, Halifax to Henderson, No. 187, 14 June, No. 190, 15 June 1939; C 8594/3955/18, Henderson to Halifax, No. 251, 16 June 1939.
155) *H. C. Deb.*, 5th Series, Vol. 347, 19 June 1939, Cols. 1786–1787.
156) *PRO*, FO 371/23083, C 9392/3955/18, Holman (Berlin) to Halifax, 1 July 1939,

Indeed, Archibald Sinclair regretted that the government had exposed itself to this rebuff, against which the Liberals had warned, and he wondered whether it would not have been very much better not to have asked for this *exequatur* at all, thereby according *de facto* recognition to German rule in Prague. The more so that the British interest in the refugees carried on. Butler repeatedly stated that the appointment of a Consul-General would have been preferable, but he failed to provide any argument in support of this statement. Nonetheless, Sinclair expressed his pleasure that the government stood firm and had not yielded to the German demands to recognise the annexation *de jure*.[157]

The Foreign Office decided to instruct the Vice-Consul to destroy all cyphers and secret papers, but to keep him and the Passport Control Officer in Prague until the Germans would ask them to leave. Kirkpatrick further proposed to inform the Germans that in view of their attitude Britain would not be prepared to discuss the question of the Czecho-Slovak assets blocked in Britain, but might pass legislation impounding them. Henderson, bravely and on his own initiative, made a similar veiled threat in his talk with Weizsäcker on 14 July.[158] Halifax, however, authorised a more moderate instruction to the Treasury: once the negotiations begin, the Germans should be warned that no progress could be expected unless Berlin changed its position with respect to the *exequatur*. He, however, declined to reply to the German proposal of 19 June to start negotiations.[159] Both the Treasury and Foreign Office preferred to solve the problem by negotiations rather than by internal legislation, as only co-operation with the 'de facto authorities' in the Protectorate made it possible to verify financial claims of British citizens against former Czechoslovakia. On the other hand, any idea to negotiate with the Germans was highly unpopular in Parliament. Already the preliminary talks between the Treasury and a delegation of German experts in the second half of May 1939, which had been immediately unveiled by the press, had been called 'the most squalid form

C 9349/3955/18, Henderson to Halifax, No. 757, 3 July, Roberts' minute, 6 July, Troutbeck's minute, 6 July, Kirkpatrick's minute, 7 July 1939.

157) *H. C. Deb.*, 5th Series, Vol. 350, 31 July 1939, Cols. 1932–1933, 1998.

158) *PRO*, FO 371/23083, C 9349/3955/18, Foreign Office to Mr. Pettitt (Prague), Kirkpatrick's minute, 7 July 1939, C 10065/3955/18, Henderson to Halifax, No. 814, 14 July 1939, Roberts' minute, 19 July 1939.

159) *PRO*, FO 371/23088, C 9183/5606/18, Kirkpatrick to Simon, 15 July 1939.

of appeasement'.[160] Simon thought that any further negotiations would 'be the B.I.S. over again multiplied by ten'. Moreover, the preliminary contacts had shown that the Germans sought to get additional foreign exchange by negotiation. Simon did not see how such a result could be agreed by the British government and expected that negotiations would break down anyway. 'However, I suppose there is something to be gained in postponement,' Simon ended his letter to Halifax.[161] Next day, on 12 July, at the Cabinet meeting Halifax explained that a plain rejection to negotiate could further weaken those moderates in the Nazi government, in whose existence and influence the Foreign Secretary persistently believed.[162] He also did not want to complicate the situation of those who in Prague were providing assistance to refugees. A memorandum from the Treasury preferred negotiations over legislation, but Simon, in Cabinet, mentioned a danger of which he had been reminded a day before in Parliament by an opposition MP: negotiations entailed a danger of disclosure to the Germans of those Czechs' names whose accounts were blocked in London which might result in their persecution.[163] The result was inconclusive. On 13 July the Chancellor promised to submit to the House, after the summer recess, a scheme for using the blocked assets as an offset against British claims. The total sum of British claims amounted to approximately £ 16 million, including £ 6 million of the advance to the Czecho-Slovak Government and £ 3.25 million of the unexpended balance of the free gift. Simon pointed out 'practical advantages in the detailed ad-

---

160) These were Brendan Bracken's words. *H. C. Deb.*, 5th Series, Vol. 347, 24 May, Cols. 2733–34. Both in Parliament and in the press these talks were intermingled with 'the Czech gold scandal'. Although this was incorrect and Simon, Chamberlain and Butler repeatedly strove to refute this rumour, the Czechoslovak politicians in exile drew a conclusion that the governmental consent for the transfer of the Czechoslovak gold was granted during these talks – as another sign of appeasement. Then this wrong information got to Czech historiography. Táborský, *Pravda zvítězila*, 19, 22 May 1939, pp. 165, 168–169; Čejka, *Československý odboj na Západě (1939–1945)*, pp. 53–54.

161) *PRO*, FO 371/23088, C 9911/5606/18, Simon to Halifax, 11 July 1939.

162) One of the very few valuable pieces of information from Helmuth Wohlthat during his visits to London was the one from 7 June 1939, when he said to Frank Ashton-Gwatkin that the British 'greatly exaggerated the influence which other people have over Hitler, and that as a matter of fact, nobody has any influence over him at all'. *PRO*, FO 371/22952, C 8306/8/18, FO Minute (F. Ashton-Gwatkin). However, this warning obviously met with no response in British governmental circles.

163) *Bod. Lib.*, microfilm, CAB 24/288, C. P. 152(39), Czech balances; CAB 23/100, Cab. Concl. 37(39), 12 July 1939.

ministrative arrangements (more particularly as regards handling the refugee problem) being worked out in conjunction with the Central Bank and the Refugee Institute at Prague, and this matter will be taken up with the German Government. It is not at present possible to say whether further legislation will be required, but in any event the arrangements will, as I have stated, be subject to confirmation by this House before they are operative.'[164]

Helmuth Wohlthat's mysterious 'whaling' journey to London in mid-July[165] provided further opportunity to inform the Germans that the negotiations about the blocked Czecho-Slovak assets were conditioned by granting the *exequatur* for the Consul-General in Prague. On 18 July Sigismund Waley of the Treasury further informed Wohlthat that representatives of the National Bank should take part in the negotiations and these should be started about on 31 July. Wohlthat expressed his conviction that the whole thing was a misunderstanding and he promised to inform Berlin immediately.[166] By the end of July, however, no reply had arrived; the Treasury suggested another reminder in Berlin. The Foreign Office refused: 'We feel that it would be a mistake to run after Germans just now, and that we had better things simmer for another few weeks.'[167] However, the Treasury insisted on having the negotiations launched before 4 September if the scheme was to be submitted to the House of Commons soon after the recess.[168] Thus Troutbeck, with Cadogan's approval, twice – on 14 and 21 August – met officials of the German Embassy, but their talks only revealed that Wohlthat had misinformed Berlin in the sense that London had allegedly asked for an *exequatur* upon *completion* of the negotiations. Dr. Weber, on the German part, proposed a compromise that granting of the *exequatur* should be parallel to beginning the negotiations. However, in the last week of August 1939 Troutbeck could no longer find any senior official who would have time to authorise this 'achievement'. Thus on 29 August he at least sent a report to the Treasury. Upon this, Waley, in a desperate effort to break what already seemed a deadlock, addressed a letter to the Berlin Embassy. This was not, however, sent because

164) *H. C. Deb.*, 5th Series, Vol. 349, 13 July 1939, Col. 2434.
165) See p. 124; see also Watt, *How War Came*, p. 399–403.
166) *PRO*, FO 371/23088, C 10175/5606/18, Waley to Troutbeck, 19 July 1939.
167) *PRO*, T 160/876, F 15959/07, Waley to Troutbeck, 27 July 1939, Troutbeck to Waley, 1 August 1939.
168) *Ibid.*, Waley to Troutbeck, 2 August 1939.

by then the bag post had been cancelled. Incredibly enough, the letter was thereafter sent, probably by somebody in the Communication Department to the German Embassy in London (!) which, however, returned it without comment. This obscure exchange probably took place already in the time when German planes were bombing Warsaw.[169]

The terms of the prompt blocking of the Czechoslovak assets in London, approved by all sides of the House, eventually turned out to be counter-productive: although they effectively prevented a large amount of money from being handed to the Germans, at the same time they made it complicated to use the unexpended part of the gift (less than £ 3.25 million in the Bank of England, plus over £ 400,000 that had been earmarked for Jewish refuge to Palestina and transferred to Lloyds Bank) for its original purpose. In order to enable the work for the Czech refugees to be carried on without interruption, the government had to seek further resources in an extremely strained budget.[170]

Eventually, British claimants were compensated for their properties and bonds blocked in Czechoslovakia by another Act of Parliament of 31 January 1940, the draft of which had been previously consulted with the Czechoslovak Legation.[171] The necessary financial means were drawn from the unspent part of the loan (£ 3.5 million) to post-Munich Czechoslovakia, while over £ 3.5 million remaining of the gift was to be used for the support of refugees. The government excluded any possibility to use for the purpose of indemnification that part of the Czechoslovak gold, which had been deposited in the account of the National Bank of Czechoslovakia and blocked immediately after 15 March 1939: 'If, later on, we recognised the existence of a properly constituted Czechoslovak Government, we might have to consider whether the gold should be handed over to that Government.'[172] It was to happen, under modified conditions, a year later.[173]

169) *PRO*, FO 371/23088, C 10842/5606/18, Cadogan's minute, 10 August, Troutbeck to Waley, 17 August 1939; FO 371/23089, C 12045/5606/18, FO minute (Mr. Troutbeck), 21 August 1939, Troutbeck's minutes, 21 & 24 August 1939, C 12842/5606/18, Communication Department minute, 9 September 1939.

170) *H. C. Deb.*, 5th Series, Vol. 349, 13 July 1939, Col. 2434.

171) *PRO*, FO 371/23089, C 20058/5606/18, Waley to Strang, 9 December 1939.

172) *PRO*, FO 371/23089, C 20206/5606/18, Cabinet Conclusions 111(39), 13 December 1939; *H. C. Deb.*, 5th Series, Vol. 356, 23, 24, 31 January 1940, Cols. 440–473, 613–629, 1159, 1174.

173) *BEA*, C 43/374. For further details see Chapter 5; also see Smetana, Nevyřízené účty, *op. cit.*, pp. 544–546.

The problem
of the Czechoslovak Legation in London

If the desire of some British departments to negotiate with the Germans about the blocked Czechoslovak balances can be explained by a need to achieve an expedient scheme for a fair indemnification of British investors and bondholders for their lost properties in the Czech lands, one cannot but wonder about the Foreign Office's effort to get rid of the Czechoslovak Legation in London as early as in the spring of 1939. The more so, that the available documentary evidence shows that this option was never used as a bribe for achieving German accommodation in other matters (such as getting the *exequatur* for a Consul in Prague), as some Czech writers have tended to claim.[174] On the contrary, once it became clear that the German attitude in other matters stiffened, the plan for closure of the Legation was postponed and later abandoned.

As early as on 30 March FO legal expert Malkin was considering the possibility of closing the Czechoslovak Legation in London, though without *de jure* recognition of the new state of affairs. Unlike in the case of Abyssinia there was no government in exile and no *de jure* head of the state, Malkin pointed out, thus Mr. Lisický represented nobody.[175] The German ultimatum of 9 May brought about another inducement to reconsider this matter. It was Sargent who again took up this matter, including 'the question of whether the Czech Legation house should be handed over to the German Gov[ernmen]t. or not,' though he conceded that there was 'no immediate hurry'. 'It will obviously be difficult to find a justification for continuing to recognise the Czechoslovak Legation in London,' Malkin disagreed, 'after we have recognised the existing situation in Bohemia de facto, especially as we have already done so in the case of Slovakia.'[176] However, it was a minor practical problem that prompted the real plan to close the Legation and to remove the Czechoslovak Chargé d'Affaires from the Diplomatic List – the question whether he should be invited to three summer Courts. Halifax thought that 'no more invitations should be issued' and asked Butler whether a

---

174) President Beneš's Secretary during his 'second exile', Eduard Táborský, claims that Wohlthat conditioned granting of the exequatur by closing of the Czech Legation. See Táborský, *Prezident Beneš mezi Západem a Východem*, p. 61; Idem, *Pravda zvítězila*, p. 255.
175) *PRO*, FO 371/23081, C 4686/3955/18, Malkin's minute, 30 March 1939.
176) *PRO*, FO 371/23082, C 7054/3955/18, Sargent's minute, 17 May, Malkin's minute, 18 May 1939.

parliamentary question could be planted justifying 'this action on the ground that, as we had recognised, Czechoslovakia had in fact ceased to exist as an independent state and that Mr. Lisicky accordingly represented nobody'. Sargent, however, mentioned the question of the future fate of the Legation building at Grosvenor Place. While Malkin took this as an order to start arranging for handing it over to the Germans and possibly Slovaks, Sargent asked whether it was desirable that the Germans should have another exterritorial house as Nazi headquarters in London. He further thought that a decision to change Lisický's status should be communicated to the Chargé directly and not indicated by merely withholding an invitation to Court. Further arguments to issue the invitations were mentioned by Sargent and Butler: the House of Commons knew that the French treated the Czechoslovak Minister as if his state still existed; and the fact that the German refused to grant an *exequatur* for the Consul in Prague. Halifax reluctantly agreed to invite Lisický to the three remaining functions, but it was assumed that his position should be cleared up as soon as possible so that 'the question of inviting him to any Court functions in the autumn' would not arise. At the same time the War Office was advised not to issue any invitations to the Military Attaché, Colonel Kalla, for September, and for the immediate future to restrict its dealings with 'that officer ... to the minimum compatible with courtesy'.[177]

Once the three Courts were over, Troutbeck, in accordance with previous Sargent's instructions, immediately informed Lisický that the Foreign Office was considering to remove his name from the Diplomatic List and asked him to provide details about property rights for the Legation. It seems that this haste was Troutbeck's personal initiative; he probably found it only logical that when 'his' Legation in Prague had been closed down, the same should happen with the Czechoslovak one in London. (Roberts at the same time tended to interpret the previous decision so that the position of the Legation should be reconsidered only in autumn.[178]) Unlike in Prague, however, in London the British intended to close the Legation completely, including the Consular agenda.

177) *PRO*, FO 371/23082, C 8918/3955/18, FO Minute (Mr. Mallet), 21 June, Sargent's minute, 22 June, Malkin's minute, 23 June, Mallet to Halifax, 5 July, Halifax's minute, 5 July, Butler's minute, 6 July 1939, C 9006/3955/18, War Office to Foreign Office, 26 June, Mallet's minute, 7 July, Sargent's minute, 8 July 1939.
178) *Ibid.*, C 9006/3955/18, Roberts' minute, 6 July 1939, C 9349/3955/18, Roberts' minute, 6 July 1939.

Thus Lisický, clearly shaken by these news, worried about ten thousand Czechs and Slovaks who possessed only Czechoslovak passports and also about the position of his staff and himself after the diplomatic immunities had been withdrawn.[179] The Home Office was prepared to mark Czechoslovak passports with the stamps 'stateless person' and it was generally thought that the people could continue to reside in Britain.[180] Meanwhile the Treasury came up with an effective proposal how to deal with the Legation building: A Coal Mining Association was interested in a purchase. The Central Department saw this as 'a very convenient solution' of British difficulties because it would not be taken over by the German or Slovak authorities. The building was, however, held on a lease, which was not to expire until 1956, and there were two proprietors: Tomáš Garrigue Masaryk, who had died two years ago, and - Edvard Beneš. Although the Foreign Office was considering extensively what to do if the Germans or Slovaks raised difficulties against the purchase, there is not a single note in the Foreign Office files considering whether Beneš actually wanted to sell the building. Of course, he did not. On the contrary, Beneš, who had by then returned to London from the United States,[181] sent a personal letter to Halifax in which he tried to dissuade the government from the idea 'to discontinue their present recognition of the legal status of the Legation'. Indeed, he did not refer to 'closing' of the Legation, as he knew that nobody could rightfully take it away from him. 'Such a decision would be a tremendous blow to our people at home,' Beneš argued, 'as they would all interpret it as a recognition *de jure* of the Protectorate. The Germans, on their part, would not fail to make the utmost use of such a step for their propaganda purposes among our oppressed people. I need hardly emphasise the pernicious effect, which this would have on the morale of our people, who represent one of the potential factors of resistance on the peace front.' Three days later he received a courteous reply, stating that his considerations would be taken into account by the government, whatever the decision might be.[182]

---

179) *PRO*, FO 371/23083, C 10294/3955/18, FO Minute (Mr. Troutbeck), 21 July 1939.
180) *Ibid.*, C 11349/3955/18, Jones (HO) to Troutbeck, 2 August, Roberts' minute, 27 July 1939.
181) On the beginnings of Beneš's exile see Chapter 4.
182) *School of Slavonic and East European Studies, University of London* (hereafter *SSEES*), Karel Lisický Collection, 3/1/11, Beneš to Halifax, 28 July, Halifax to Beneš, 31 July 1939 (also *PRO*, FO 371/22898, C 10874/7/12).

By then, however, the Foreign Office started to change its position. It was above all German obstinacy in other matters that eventually rescued the Czechoslovak Legation in London. 'There is no reason why we should go out of our way,' Roberts wrote on 28 July, 'to give the Germans satisfaction by liquidating the Czech Legation here until they show some readiness to meet us regarding our representation at Prague.' The Central Department was also anxious about the repercussions in France and the U.S.A. of British closing down 'the Czech Legation', especially as Legations still existed in both countries. (No plans to alter that state are known in the case of either of these two Powers.) Troutbeck mentioned the 'effect in Czechoslovakia itself, which would be of importance in the event of war,' if the Legation was shut down, and he pleaded to wait for 'the results of the crisis expected in August and September'.[183] On 11 August Cadogan agreed with his subordinates that this was not the moment to withdraw recognition, 'even if it were right,' and he proposed to bring it up again in a month.[184] The whole idea was definitively abandoned with the outbreak of war.[185] Ironically, the only non-Axis Great Power that eventually closed the Czechoslovak Legation and recognised the Slovak state *de jure*, was the Soviet Union in December 1939.[186] However, this step did not prevent that Power from making another U-turn in its policy towards Czechoslovakia in July 1941.

Conclusion

There is little doubt that Hitler's blatant aggression in Czechoslovakia caused a radical change of British foreign policy towards deterrence. The sad fate of Czechoslovakia so soon after the western concessions to Germany in Munich provided a psychological and mental underpinning for the stiffening of British policy. However, many authors have described certain aspects of British policy towards the remnants of former Czechoslovakia as endurance or even 'new waves' of appease-

183) *PRO*, FO 371/23083, C 11349/3955/18, Roberts' minute, 28 July, Troutbeck's minute, 28 July 1939.
184) *PRO*, FO 371/23083, C 11349/3955/18, Roberts' minute, 28 July, Troutbeck's minute, 28 July 1939.
185) *PRO*, FO 371/22898, C 13131/7/12, Sargent's minute, 4 September 1939. This document was reprinted in: Firt, Julius, Cestou k únoru: Počátky byly v Londýně [On the way to February. The origins were in London], *Svědectví*, Vol. 12, 1973, No. 46, pp. 212–267.
186) *Dokumenty ČSR-SSSR*, Vol. I, No. 39, pp. 107–108, Fierlinger to Beneš, 14 December 1939.

ment.[187] Archival material shows clearly that – rather than that – the signs of British policy towards Czechoslovakia that appeared to be a continuation of appeasement were driven by an effort of particular ministries and institutions to secure British interests and smooth solution of practical problems. Bank of England representatives wished to keep banking operations free from any political interference. The Treasury defended British financial and economic interests. The Foreign Office (unlike the Quai d'Orsay) wished to obtain efficient and reliable consular and possibly even diplomatic representation in both parts of former Czechoslovakia as soon as possible. These questions were not regarded as major issues of British foreign policy and their symbolic meaning hardly mattered for the pragmatic bureaucrats. Nor did the negative impact of such changes upon the morale both of Czechoslovak exiles and people in the Protectorate.

Britain's policy towards Czechoslovakia during the spring and summer of 1939 deserves criticism for lack of political leadership, rather than for resemblance to previous appeasement of Germany. The more clearly it reveals a classical conflict between expediency and morality. Ministry officials held the expedient position, whereas the moral standpoint was frequently defended in the House of Commons. Its members were most sensitive towards British dealings with Czechoslovak affairs, the more so as the previous fate of Czechoslovakia became a major tool of the opposition's criticism of British foreign policy. They effectively blocked some of the inventive proposals suggested by the Foreign Office and other ministries. Most paradoxically, such expedient proposals were at this stage often slowed down or even refused by major protagonists of appeasement – Butler or Simon – because they had to shoulder all the parliamentary criticism. On the other hand those officials, who were, by late 1938, already critical of appeasement, who had further major influence upon Britain's turn towards the policy of deterrence, and who during the spring of 1939 were suspicious of the 10 Downing Street's real intentions[188] – most prominently Cadogan and Sargent – advocated at the same time this practical approach to Czechoslovak affairs. It is perhaps

187) See e.g. Velecká, Agónie appeasementu. Britská politika a rozbití Československa 15. 3. – 31. 8. 1939, *op. cit.*, pp. 788–822; Kuklík, Jan, *Londýnský exil a obnova československého státu za druhé světové války* [The exile in London and the reconstruction of the Czechoslovak state during World War II], Praha, Karolinum 1998, p. 46.
188) *Cadogan Diary*, diary entry for 3 May 1939, p. 178.

most striking in the case of Orme Sargent, who was to be considered a friend of Czechoslovakia amongst Czechoslovak exiles during the war.[189] In one of his minutes he provided the following defense of expediency: 'A great deal of our trouble arises from the widespread delusion that we appoint Ambassadors, Ministers and Consuls abroad as a compliment to the foreign countries concerned, and the withdrawal or with-holding of these officials is therefore our very way of showing our disapproval of these countries. The truth, of course, is just the opposite. We appoint Ambassadors, Ministers and Consuls abroad because it is in our own interests to do so; and if we withdraw them or with-hold them, it is not the foreign country concerned which suffers, but we ourselves, since our interests in the country in question must cease to enjoy consular protection.'[190]

It was the growing international crisis in July and August that caused the political aspects relating to former Czechoslovakia to prevail in the Foreign Office. Some of the former plans were postponed, and then abandoned upon the outbreak of war. In the case of the Treasury, however, such change occurred only in September 1939. The same applies to other ministries: as late as the end of July, the Foreign Office had to resist a proposal by the Department of the Board of Trade to broaden the scope of the planned negotiations with the Germans on the payment difficulties, so as to cover the overall questions of future trade with the territory of former Czechoslovakia.[191] Apparently the lack of political leadership was the most remarkable sign of British dealing with Czechoslovak affairs in the months immediately preceding the outbreak of war.

The role played by the Czechoslovak Chargé d'Affaires in London, along with a previous instruction from Masaryk, was also inglorious and soon became a target of other émigrés' criticism.[192] True, he had refused, unlike most of his colleagues in other capitals, to hand over the Legation to the Germans.[193] It is hard to agree, however, that Lisický's ensuing

189) Feierabend, *Politické vzpomínky*, II, p. 117.
190) *PRO*, FO 371/23082, C 7797/3955/18, Sargent's minute, 24 May 1939.
191) *PRO*, FO 371/23088, C 10543/5606/18, Wills to Waley, 26 July, Troutbeck's minute, 3 August 1939.
192) See Čejka, *Československý odboj na Západě*, p. 55.
193) Only the following Czechoslovak Legations continued in their official activity after 15 March: Paris (Š. Osuský), London (K. Lisický), Moscow (Z. Fierlinger), Washington (V. Hurban), Warsaw (J. Slávik), Cairo (B. Szalatnay-Stachó). Apart from these twelve

tactics – of not drawing too much attention to the Czechoslovak Legation by public speeches etc. – was 'very effective'.[194] When his counterpart in Paris, Štefan Osuský, launched his noisy resistance action, claiming that he was the only holder of Czechoslovak national authority and that 'in the eyes of all Czechs and of all Slovaks the Czechoslovak Legation would be the torch of their national hope, the concrete expression of the immortality of the nation,' one of the officials in the Foreign Office, Robert Speaight, noted that 'M. Lisický's quieter line is more to be recommended'. He, however, drew this conclusion from the following consideration: 'M. Osusky spoke gallantly, but the French may well find his attitude embarrassing i f & w h e n they eventually recognise the new state of affairs.'[195]

Had Lisický behaved as Osuský did in Paris, he might have drawn even more parliamentary attention to the Czechoslovak cause, whereas his silence and inactivity only paved way to what must be considered as the most inopportune and short-sighted solution proposed by the Foreign Office – the closing of the Czechoslovak Legation which was evidently now perceived as nothing more than a hangover from the past. This approach, however, went clearly against Czechoslovak interests. Only in mid-summer 1939 did British diplomats start to reflect on the symbolic meaning that the Legations abroad had both for the Czechoslovak exiles and people in the Protectorate. Then, the outbreak of war ended this ill-considered proposal to close the Legation, the very existence of which made future co-operation between the British on the one hand and Czechoslovak exiles on the other hand much easier.

General Consulates and Consulates were rescued for future resistance action, including all five in North America. The Legations in Dublin, Belgrade, Lisbon and Santiago de Chile continued unofficially. Němeček, Jan, Československá diplomacie po 15. březnu 1939, In: *DČSZP 1939-1940*, p. 21–24. For further details see Idem, Likvidace československé zahraniční služby po 15. březnu 1939 [Liquidation of the Czechoslovak foreign service after March 15, 1939], *Acta Universitatis Carolinae – Philosophica et Historica* 1, *Studia Historica* XLVIII, Prague 1998, pp. 143–158.
194) Němeček, Československá diplomacie po 15. březnu 1939, *op. cit.*, p. 14.
195) *PRO*, FO 371/23081, C 4702/3955/18, Phipps to Halifax, No. 400, 3 April, Speaight's minute, 5 April 1939.

BRITISH ATTITUDES TOWARDS THE DEVELOPMENT
OF CZECHOSLOVAK POLITICAL REPRESENTATION
IN EXILE (OCTOBER 1938 – JULY 1940)

Britain's assistance to refugees
from Czechoslovakia, 1938–1939

When on 15 March 1939 Chancellor Simon announced for the first time to the House of Commons the Treasury's decision to block major Czecho-Slovak accounts in London banks, he assured the MPs that the government did not wish to abandon its efforts to assist refugees. He presented the figure of 5,500 refugees who had emigrated from Czecho-Slovakia by mid-February.[1] Some 1200 refugees were in Britain in mid-March and they were looked after by voluntary organisations.[2] The British Legation in Prague provided asylum for some prominent Czech and German refugees immediately after the German invasion. A number of further requests, however, were refused, save for most exceptional cases, as British Minister in Prague Basil Newton thought that taking all of them in 'might seem provocative'[3].

Newton's hesitancy reflected the overall tension in British dealing with the refugee question: although Britain strove to help more than any other country, she was not able or willing to oblige every claimant, not to speak of providing asylum to all. Similarly the House of Commons was divided in its criticism of governmental refugee policy: while some members (T. E. Harvey, E. Rathbone) called for more liberal policy in granting visas, and also found the sum of £ 4 million for the support of refugees as absolutely insufficient, others (Major Stourton, Wing-Commander James) were anxious about the burden on British taxpayers resulting from an influx of refugees from Central Europe and urged the government to accelerate their departure to other countries.[4]

1) *H. C. Deb.*, 5th Series, Vol. 345, 15 March 1939, Cols. 550–551.
2) *PRO*, FO 371/22895, C 3804/3/12, Waley (Treasury) to Foreign Office, 23 March 1939.
3) *PRO*, FO 371/22897, C 3217, C 3295/7/12, all Newton to Halifax, No. 100, 109, all 16 March 1939.
4) *H. C. Deb.*, 5th Series, Vol. 349, Cols. 2442–4, 13 July 1939; Vol. 350, Cols. 1691–2, 27 July 1939, Cols. 1920–1, 31 July 1939.

In the post-Munich period the British government organised a humanitarian system, which classified potential refugees according to the extent they were endangered, and sought to provide new homes for them in Britain, Palestine, Canada, etc. Refugees and potential refugees, around 40,000 in total, fell into three major categories: the Sudeten Germans, refugees from Germany and Austria, and the Jews from Sudetenland. The last category, though most numerous of all, was also the least preferred one; the Jews were, tragically, regarded as economic or 'racial', but by no means political refugees. This attitude deepened after the German seizure of the Czech lands: some 300,000 Jews were now potentially threatened, but both financial means for their assistance and political will in Britain and other countries for their admission was lacking.[5]

In the months immediately after Munich several voluntary organisations looked after the refugees in Czechoslovakia,[6] but the growing demand for refuge abroad led to the formation of the British Committee for Refugees from Czechoslovakia (BCRC). It was originally privately funded, but after 15 March it was increasingly supported directly by the Treasury. The money was to be repaid later from an unexpended part of the free gift, which, however, did not happen until 1940.[7] In July 1939 the Czech Refugee Trust Fund (CRTF), set up by the Home Office, took over the BCRC's functions. Correspondingly with the growing governmental spending the Whitehall was also imprinting its policy into the principal organisations assisting refugees – the BCRC and later the CRTF. With respect to the Jews the Home Office adopted the policy of blocking the Jewish exodus, desired by the Gestapo, and ensuring careful selection of Jewish entrants judged by their political activity.[8] Meanwhile the Home Office created escape routes for people whom, on the contrary, the Germans wished to prevent from leaving: German anti-Nazis and also Czech democrats. Organised transports of registered refugees went through Poland, while numerous refugees,

---

5) London, Louise, *Whitehall and the Jews 1933–1948. British Immigration Policy, Jewish Refugees and the Holocaust*, Cambridge, Cambridge University Press 2000, pp. 142–168.
6) Several private funds were created and run by the *Manchester Guardian*, the *News Chronicle* and, most importantly, by the Lord Mayor of London – Sir Harry Twyford. The last one collected about £ 400,000 in less than a month. Brown, *Dealing with Democrats*, p. 73.
7) See Chapter 3.
8) See London, *Whitehall and the Jews...*, pp. 159–160.

particularly volunteers who were determined to fight Nazism abroad, crossed the border illegally. Under Robert Stopford's influence British organisations were gradually also taking care of these 'illegals', which further complicated their position in Prague and the already difficult negotiations with the Germans about facilitating registered emigration from the country.[9] Estimations regarding the total number of refugees who left Czechoslovakia before the outbreak of war differ. One reliable Czech source, based on the statistics of the Czech Refugee Institute in Prague (not to be confused with the CRTF), provides the figure of 12,319 persons who were legally registered as refugees and left Czechoslovakia between 17 November 1938 and 14 September 1939. The largest part of them settled in Britain (2462), others in Palestine (2240), the USA (1621), Canada (626), South America, Scandinavia and elsewhere.[10] However, this figure does not involve 'illegal' emigrants, including several thousands of Czechoslovak soldiers. The Home Office registered some 14,000 people from Czechoslovakia who reached Britain by mid-May 1939, around 7,000 of them supported by the BCRC.[11] As of 27 August 1939, the CRTF in Britain was supporting 6660 Czechoslovak citizens, including Sudeten Germans (1770) and former Germans and Austrians (1185).[12] But there were numerous Czechoslovaks who did not ask for any help. And the immigration continued, reaching another height with the fall of France in 1940.

British assistance to refugees from Czechoslovakia before the war exceeded support from any other country. This applied both to private initiatives and to the state's assistance. Louis London is probably right when he says that such approach 'assuaged British guilt over the Munich settlement'.[13] Eleanor Rathbone in her parliamentary struggle for increase of governmental funds for the support of refugees pointed at British responsibility in the case of refugees from Czecho-Slovakia: 'No one is surely going to deny our responsibility. Indeed, nobody did dur-

9) For further details see Velecká, Britská pomoc uprchlíkům z Československa od okupace do vypuknutí války v roce 1939, op. cit.
10) Heumos, Petr, Die Emigration aus der Tschechoslowakei nach Westeuropa und den Nahen Osten 1938–1945: politisch-soziale Struktur, Organisation und Asylbedingungen der tschechischen, jüdischen, deutschen und slowakischen, Flüchtlinge während des Nationalsozialismus, München, Oldenbourg 1989, p. 58.
11) PRO, Home Office (hereafter HO) 294/44, Stopford's memorandum, 19 May 1939.
12) Velecká, Britská pomoc uprchlíkům z Československa..., op. cit., p. 690.
13) London, Whitehall and the Jews..., pp. 145.

ing the debate.'[14] Even in internal governmental correspondence the gift was called a 'conscience money'.[15] This factor obviously did not work in the case of other countries; for example to support refugees from Spain the British government offered just £ 100,000.[16] However, due to a combination of factors the British support fell short of the real possibilities to help. Only about £ 600,000 was spent on refugees, while more than £ 3.5 million that had been earmarked for this purpose, remained blocked in the Bank of England and Lloyds Bank, and was not released until January 1940.[17] The most tragic was the fate of the Jews, who were not regarded as the most endangered group, although – judged by events that had by then already happened in Germany, namely the *Kristallnacht* and the implementation of the Nuremberg Laws – they deserved a preferential treatment. Many of them were thus denied vital financial support or necessary British visas. For most of them such decision was to become fatal.

Britain's attitudes to the formation of Czechoslovak political representation abroad before the outbreak of war

Whether British support to Czechoslovak refugees was sufficient or not, the British had inhibitions to support Czechoslovak political representation abroad. Before the outbreak of war, such support was virtually out of the question, whereas from September 1939 onwards this attitude changed only reluctantly; many key officials at the Foreign Office were much more inclined to point out the weaknesses of the Czechoslovak action abroad, rather than to look for a credible partner representing the Czech and Slovak nations. This policy seems to have had deep historical roots. Apart from British geo-strategic ideas about the future of Central Europe, these attitudes were intrinsically connected with the personality

---

14) *H. C. Deb.*, 5th Series, Vol. 350, 4 August 1939, Cols. 2892–2906.
15) *PRO*, FO 371/24289, C 8466/2/12, Latham's minute, 23 July, Makins' minute, 1 August 1940.
16) *H. C. Deb.*, 5th Series, 4 August 1939, Vol. 350, Col. 2890.
17) *Ibid.*, Vol. 356, Cols. 437–444, 23 January 1940. The CRTF continued to support refugees from Czechoslovakia throughout the war. But the fact, that the Czechoslovak government in exile after it was recognised in July 1940 did not have any say in the distribution of support and also that high portion of those assisted were Sudeten Germans, became a source of Anglo-Czechoslovak quarrels. See Brown, *Dealing with Democrats*, pp. 84, 260.

of Edvard Beneš, as it was he around whom the major stream of political action against the destruction of Czechoslovakia started to coalesce as early as in the spring and summer of 1939.

After Munich there was a widespread aversion towards Edvard Beneš among British politicians and officials. He was often considered the man primarily responsible for the bad fortunes of his country: some blamed him for his alleged intransigence in dealing with the Sudeten issue,[18] others for lack of belligerence.[19] Cadogan felt 'sorry for the Czechs', but at the same time he was 'rather critical of Beneš'.[20] *The Times* linked his failure with the entire collapse of the artificial and misconceived 'French' post-war system in Europe, of which he was considered one of principal architects – along with Clemenceau, Poincaré, Austen Chamberlain and Barthou.[21] The irony of these controversial assessments reached its zenith when perhaps the greatest British warrior, Winston Churchill, in a letter to the Nobel Prize Committee in November supported Beneš's candidature for the Nobel Peace Prize.[22]

Beneš's physical presence in Czechoslovakia became uneasy for the post-Munich political elite soon after his resignation from presidency. He himself followed the advice of his friends in Britain (both Czech and English) voiced by his nephew Bohuš and a 'mysterious Englishman' (whose identity has never been revealed) that in the interest of his own safety he should leave the country.[23] On 22 October 1938, he flew (for the first time in his life) to London, to start his second exile. His somewhat improvised escape came as a surprise even to the

18) Lord Runciman, for example, blamed 'Benes' for being too clever and for procrastination. *Bod. Lib.*, Simon Papers, No. 85, Runciman to Simon, 6 October 1938.
19) This was for example Robert Boothby's opinion. See Rhodes James, Robert, *Bob Boothby*, London, Hodder & Stoughton 1991, p. 183.
20) *The Diaries of Sir Robert Bruce Lockhart 1915–1938*, 21 October 1938, p. 404.
21) *The Times*, 5 October 1938. See also Klimek, Antonín, Edvard Beneš od abdikace z funkce presidenta ČSR (5. října 1938) do zkázy Československa (15. března 1939) [Edvard Beneš from resigning the presidency of the Czechoslovak Republic (5th October 1938) to the destruction of Czechoslovakia (15th March 1939)], In: *Z druhé republiky. Sborník prací Historického ústavu armády České republiky* [Inside the Second Republic. Collection of studies, published by the Historical Institute of the Czech Army], Praha 1993, p. 172. Indeed, Klimek points out that Beneš did not appear in a bad company.
22) *Winston Churchill*, Companion Vol. V., pp. 1264–1265, Churchill to Nobel Prize Committee, 10 November 1938. The Nobel Prize, however, was not awarded between 1939 and 1943.
23) Drtina, *Československo můj osud*, Vol. I, book 1, pp. 264–265.

Czech Legation. Only on 28 October, the day of 20th anniversary of the proclamation of Czechoslovak independence, Masaryk hastened to the Foreign Office after he had found out that the British authorities had not been officially notified about the former President's arrival. Of course, he was most apologetic and pointed out the former President's acute illness that demanded long treatment.[24] He further stressed Beneš's wish to assure the British government that he would 'live here as an absolutely private individual, make no public or political contacts, grant no interviews and in no way make difficulties'. Lancelot Oliphant, the Deputy Under-Secretary of State, said that the apology was unnecessary and assured Masaryk that Halifax 'would be deeply distressed to hear of monsieur Benes's illness'. The Foreign and Home Offices soon agreed that they should have no objection to Beneš settling in Britain. Samuel Hoare even stated that 'personally he would do all he could to help', while Halifax sent a friendly letter to Beneš, drafted by Oliphant.[25] A bold statement of some Czech historians, apparently based on Beneš's memoirs, that upon his arrival the British authorities 'emphatically stressed' to him that he should refrain from any political activity and should not misuse British hospitality,[26] does not seem to be corroborated by archival evidence. Another statement about alleged Hoare's complaint to the German Ambassador (!) about Beneš's activities in London is based only on a third hand utterance.[27] The promise to remain silent came from the exhausted and broken Beneš himself, even though the Foreign Office probably welcomed it. Beneš stuck to his promise in the following weeks, at least with respect to the British government. He refused a house that Viscount Cranborne had offered to give him at his disposal and settled in a small house in Putney rented by his nephew Bohuš. He also turned down several offers for writing well paid articles and kept in touch only with several friends – journalist

24) For years Beneš had suffered from *Ménièr disease* that only exacerbated during the nerves shattering 'Munich period'.
25) *PRO*, FO 371/21588, C 13246, C 13548/13246/12, Oliphant's minute, 28 October 1938, Caccia's minute, 3 November 1938.
26) See Kuklík, Jan – Němeček, Jan, K počátkům druhého exilu E. Beneše 1938–1939, [Towards the beginning of E. Beneš's second exile, 1938–1939], *Český časopis historický* [Czech historical journal], Prague, Vol. 96, 1998, No. 4, pp. 805–806; Beneš, Edvard, *Paměti. Od Mnichova k nové válce a k novému vítězství*, Praha, Orbis 1947, p. 123.
27) Kuklík – Němeček, K počátkům druhého exilu…, *op. cit.*, p. 806; Idem, *Hodža versus Beneš*, Praha, Karolinum 1999, p. 30.

Henry Wickham Steed, historian Robert W. Seton-Watson, writer Herbert G. Wells or economist Walter Layton.[28]

During this London period Beneš sent several important messages home. These had wide circulation and serve as an evidence that in this post-Munich period Beneš reached several conclusions which later significantly influenced his policy during the war and afterwards. He expected a war in a near future, which would also provide a springboard for his political action aiming at reestablishment of free and independent Czechoslovakia. Its security he intended to base on co-operation and common border with the Soviet Union, while the internal system was to undergo radical changes from liberal democracy towards more socialism and state interventionism in the economic sphere. Beneš also assessed the events of last months and in a letter to Wickham Steed he reached the following conclusion: whatever were his own faults and those of the Czechoslovak government, they were negligible in comparison with those of French and British policy.[29] But here came a significant distinction: While he thought that France's role as a European power was now over for years if not decades, in the case of Britain he only blamed the 'appeasers' and was convinced that the practical and pragmatic British would soon recognise the real threats in the cruel world and would be able to replace Chamberlain's government by another one, which would finally defend British interests and also democracy against Nazi expansionism.[30]

On 2 February 1939, Beneš sailed from Portsmouth to the United States. There he was to teach for half a year at the University of Chicago, which was then still called the second largest 'Czechoslovak' city, after Prague, because of the number of people with Czechoslovak background. On 16 March 1939, he launched from the U.S. his struggle for reestablishment of independent Czechoslovakia by sending letters

28) Kuklík – Němeček, K počátkům druhého exilu..., *op. cit.*, pp. 805–806; Beneš, *Paměti*, p. 123.

29) See Klimek, Edvard Beneš od abdikace..., *op. cit.*, pp. 183–190, 213–222; Hauner, Milan, Čekání na velkou válku 1939 /I.–II./. Edvard Beneš mezi Mnichovem, 15. březnem a porážkou Polska [Waiting for a great war. Edvard Beneš between Munich, March 15 and the defeat of Poland], *Dějiny a současnost* [History and present], Prague, Vol. 21, 1999, No. 4, pp. 12–15, No. 5, pp. 36–39.

30) *Formování československého zahraničního odboje v letech 1938–1939 ve světle svědectví Jana Opočenského* [Forming of the Czechoslovak resistance abroad in the light of Jan Opočenský's testimony], ed. M. Hauner, Praha, Archiv akademie věd 2000, No. 11, Beneš to Rašín, undated [24 November 1938?], pp. 143–155.

to Chamberlain, Roosevelt, Daladier, Litvinov and one day later also to Joseph Avenol, the Secretary General of the League of Nations, in which he protested against the German aggression. Unlike Daladier, Chamberlain at least bothered to send a short reply, stating that he had defined the British position in his Birmingham speech.[31] Otherwise, however, the British government had little sympathy for Beneš's action. Indeed, the Foreign Office watched suspiciously his political activities in the United States and the growing support from Czechs and Slovaks there. Two days after the Nazi aggression against Czechoslovakia, Masaryk delivered one of his eloquent speeches, to 5,000 people in the Shrine Auditorium in Los Angeles, in which he stated that last September Czechoslovakia had been betrayed by France and England. Ambassador Ronald Lindsay called this 'a very direct and abusive attack upon the policies of British and French Governments'. While Frank Roberts of the Foreign Office Central Department found this 'unfortunate outburst excusable ... in all the circumstances', Makins retorted: 'I don't think it was excusable.'[32] Masaryk's personal popularity amongst British politicians and diplomats[33] hardly mattered in this case. Makins referred to 'ominous reports' of a 'nationalist' and 'irredentist' organisation under Beneš's leadership being formed in the U.S.A.,[34] and in the months to come he strove to slow down any process of recognition of Czechoslovak political representation abroad. When Lindsay reported that Beneš's leadership united most Czech and Slovak elements in the United States, another official, Robert Speaight, commented sceptically: 'Dr. Beneš is becoming very active, and, as was to be expected, the U.S. authorities are making no effort to discourage him.'[35] The British attitude to Beneš and his efforts remained cold during the spring and summer of 1939. Some officials at least considered him a man of the past, who had made numerous mistakes and should rather retire from public life.[36] However, that was never Beneš's intention, and even less so after March 15.

31) *DČSZP 1939-1940*, No. 1, pp. 51–52, Beneš's declaration, 16 March 1939.
32) *PRO*, FO 371/22903, C 5074/1840/12, Lindsay to Halifax, No. 135, 24 March 1939, Roberts' minute, 14 April, Makins' minute, 15 April 1939.
33) See e.g. *The Diaries of Sir Robert Bruce Lockhart 1915–1938*, 23 December 1938, p. 414.
34) *PRO*, FO 371/23081, C 4465/3955/18, Makins' minute, 1 April 1939.
35) *PRO*, FO 371/22898, C 6789/7/12, Speaight's minute, 15 May 1939.
36) See *PRO*, FO 371/23081, C 4465/3955/18, Rendel (Sofia) to Strang, 27 March 1939.

Beneš addressed numerous meetings of Czechoslovak compatriots all over the United States. At a rally of the Czech National Union in Chicago in mid-April, he was called on to become the head of the movement for Czechoslovakia's restoration. His activity led to the formation of a central organisation, the Czechoslovak National Council, representing vast majority of local groups of Czechs, Slovaks and Ruthenians in the United States (over 1 million people). On 28 May Roosevelt received him in Hyde Park for a private talk. According to Beneš's record FDR assured him that he still considered him to be the President and promised to grant recognition of Czechoslovak government in the case of war.[37] In a telegram to the Czechoslovak legations in Washington, Paris, London, Moscow and Warsaw Beneš stated that Roosevelt 'sharply condemned the policy of France and England, and especially that of Chamberlain, and he regarded the whole policy of appeasement as a fundamental mistake'.[38] U.S. record of the talk, typically for Roosevelt's negotiations, does not exist. In late June Beneš spoke with State Secretary Hull, his deputy Welles and Secretary of Interior Ickes.[39] On 8 June, at a meeting in Chicago, Beneš for the first time presented his theory of continuous existence of pre-Munich Czechoslovakia, based on the invalidity of the Munich Agreement from the very beginning, as that treaty had been imposed upon Czechoslovakia under threat of force and it had never been ratified by the Czechoslovak parliament. This juridical construction, which further implied continuity of Beneš's presidential function, was not acceptable to FO legal experts, and his former proclamation of 5 October 1938, that he had 'reached his decision to resign the Presidency freely and as a result of his personal conviction', was to be often quoted in FO's internal materials.[40]

37) Beneš, *Paměti*, pp. 121–122. The U.S. government, however, accorded its recognition to the Czechoslovak provisional government only on 30 July 1941, a year after Britain, and the full recognition on 26 October 1942. See *Formování československého zahraničního odboje...*, p. 44.
38) Cited from: Zeman, Zbyněk, with Klimek, Antonín, *The Life of Edvard Beneš 1884–1948. Czechoslovakia in Peace and War*, Oxford, Clarendon Press 1997, p. 148.
39) See e.g. Beneš, *Amerika šla s námi*, passim; Beneš, *Paměti.* p. 92–122; Táborský, *Prezident Beneš mezi Západem a Východem*, pp. 73–74.
40) *PRO*, FO 371/21579, C 12026/2475/12, Newton to Halifax, 7 October 1938. For the repercussions see e.g. FO 371/26394, C 4078/1320/12, Warr's minute, Roberts' minute, 29 April 1941; FO 371/26394, C 5339/1320/12, Roberts' minute, 4 May 1941; FO 371/30834, C 845/326/12, Makins to Nichols, 4 February 1942.

In mid-May, before a meeting of the Council of the League of Nations, Beneš sent another telegram to Avenol, Bonnet, Molotov and Halifax, this time protesting not only against German aggression, but also against the Hungarian occupation of Ruthenia (Sub-Carpathian Russia). 'I do not think we need acknowledge this,' Speaight expressed FO's scorn.[41] At the Council's meeting in Geneva Halifax supported Avenol in his ruling that Beneš's telegram should not be read. The former major protagonist of the League, President of its Assembly and of the Council was now considered a private person and to read his communication was in Halifax's view 'not ... in accordance with the Council's rules of procedure' and 'might cause serious difficulties'.[42] The President of the Council, Soviet delegate Ivan Maisky, had to back down, although he protested against stressing such formal aspects in view of open aggression. A week later, Beneš's telegram was officially presented to the members of the League on behalf of the Soviet government. In this context Halifax's legal purism seemed very odd, considering that other delegates had nothing against the telegram to be read at the meeting while the New Zealand's representative, William Jordan, even called for more information.[43] Of course, Beneš remembered such attitudes when he was later making his crucial foreign policy decisions.

When he returned to London on 19 July, the Foreign Office notified the Czechoslovak Embassy that it was 'confidently expected' that Dr. Beneš would not abuse Britain's hospitality.[44] This fact has often been repeated in Czech historiography as an example of British appeasement

41) *PRO*, FO 371/22898, C 7058/7/12, Beneš to Halifax, 15 May 1939, Speaight's minute, 15 May 1939.
42) *Ibid.*, C 7519/7/12, UK Delegation, Geneva, to Foreign Office, 22 May 1939.
43) It is not quite clear, what George Bonnet's attitude was. Czechoslovak representative Jaromír Kopecký, who however was not present to the session, states that Bonnet, unlike Halifax, did not take part in the debate and did not protest against Maisky's intention to read the telegram. Němeček, Jan, Okupace českých zemí 1939 a Společnost národů [Occupation of the Czech lands and the League of Nations], *Moderní dějiny* [Modern history], Prague, Vol. 5, 1997, pp. 149–161. Maisky himself, on the other hand, says in his diary that both Halifax and Bonnet had objections against his proposal, whereas other members 'were sitting like statues, noses sunk in their bumf'. Marjina, Valentina V., K historii sovětsko-československých vztahů v letech 1938–1941. Nad deníkem Ivana M. Majského [Towards the history of the Soviet-Czechoslovak relations, 1938–1941. Reading the diary of Ivan M. Maisky], *Soudobé dějiny* [Contemporary history], Prague, Vol. 6, 1999, No. 4. p. 526.
44) *PRO*, FO 371/22898., C 10944/7/12, Troutbeck's minute, 31 July 1939.

after 15 March 1939.[45] It is therefore interesting to compare Beneš's case with that of another prominent refugee from Czechoslovakia, leader of the Sudeten German Social Democrats Wenzel Jaksch who had facilitated Robert Stopford's efforts of helping refugees from the occupied districts prior to March 15 and later himself found refuge at the British Embassy when the Germans occupied Prague. After a few days he succeeded to escape unnoticed – dressed as a plumber – from the building, as well as from the country shortly afterwards. When, upon a German notice, Makins, careful to avoid 'trouble with the Germans', asked the Home Office in mid-May to hint to Jaksch that the duration of his stay in Britain might depend on his willingness to abstain from political activities, the Home Office replied that it must be left to his good sense: 'The Home Office has laid it down as a general principle, that foreigners while in this country should have the freedom which is allowed by our laws to all persons within their jurisdiction and it would only be in exceptional cases, in which special considerations might make it necessary, that certain restrictions would be imposed.'[46]

Why then this double standard in the cases of Jaksch and Beneš? Was the latter considered as such an 'exceptional case'? Possibly, yes. However, when we look further into the documentary evidence, we find that it was again a Czechoslovak representative who first came up with the topic of Beneš's activities in Britain. Charge d'Affaires Lisický asked the Foreign Office a month before Beneš's arrival whether it was expected that he would refrain from any political activity in Britain. The Home Office washed their hands when it emphasised that the responsibility whether to limit his activities or not rested entirely with the Foreign Office, though it suggested that the British 'should wish to make it clear' that they 'expected him [Beneš] not to abuse our hospitality'.[47] It took the Foreign Office more than a month to answer the initial enquiry in the above sense. Incredibly enough, Beneš did not leave it at that: towards the end of July he sent Lisický to ask the Foreign Office if they could not be a little more specific. He asked whether for example his recent 'entirely private' luncheon with Churchill and other politicians or his forthcom-

45) See e.g. Táborský, *Prezident Beneš mezi Západem a Východem*, pp. 61–62; Velecká, Agónie appeasementu..., *op. cit.*, pp. 817–818.
46) *PRO*, FO 371/22904, C 5152/5152/12, Makins to Cooper, 16 May 1939, C 8042/5152//12, Cooper to Makins, 6 June 1939.
47) *PRO*, FO 371/21579, C 9152/7/12, Sargent's minute, 28 June 1939.

ing lecture at Cambridge were considered as an abuse of hospitality. Quite naturally, the Foreign Office felt that it was not: 'There would be an outcry in any case if we tried to stop him.'[48] On 3 August Troutbeck repeated to Lisický the original fuzzy directive. Only after Lisický had insisted to hear an instruction in those two model examples, Troutbeck said that it was expected that Beneš would not speak in his lectures about current political topics and Czechoslovakia.[49]

In confrontation with archival sources the whole matter seems as an example of Czechoslovak diplomacy done more for historical record (to show the extent of Czechoslovak suffering from the cruel and perfidious Great Powers), rather than for achieving real political goals. Jaksch did not ask for any permission and no limitations were set for his activities, however the Foreign Office was for some time considering asking a non-governmental organisation (the BCRC) to intimate such limitations to him.[50] It is therefore unlikely that if the matter had never been raised by the Czechoslovak Legation, the British would have dared, in the summer of 1939, to set any limits to Beneš's activities.

It is arguable that the pre-war political strategy of Czechoslovak exiles in Britain, consisting of keeping silent and not irritating the British government, was entirely misconceived. Ironically, it followed assessments and recommendations by Masaryk,[51] who had served as a Minister to Britain for fourteen years. Although under his chairmanship in mid-April a Czechoslovak committee in Britain was set up, its major effort focused on securing visas for refugees.[52] An information bureau was established in early July,[53] but it also failed to draw further parliamentary or public attention to the Czechoslovak cause. Thus a chance to make use of the growing parliamentary opposition to anything that could remind of appeasement was missed. On the contrary, such passivity only facilitated the main objective of various British departments and ministries – to continue, even after 15 March, in their 'smooth working'.[54]

48) *Ibid.*, C 10944/7/12, Troutbeck's minute, 31 July 1939.
49) *SSEES*, Lisický Collection, box 9, 3/1/11, Lisický's record of his talk with Troutbeck at the FO on 3 August 1939.
50) *PRO*, FO 371/22904, C 8042/5152/12, Makins' minute, Randall's minute, 7 June 1939.
51) See Velecká, *Agónie appeasementu...*, *op. cit.*, p. 810.
52) See Křen, *Do emigrace*, p. 440.
53) Táborský, *Pravda zvítězila*, diary entry for 6 July 1939, p. 230.
54) See Chapter 3.

The 'entirely private' luncheon with Churchill et al. brought real encouragement and the only satisfaction for Beneš in this period of his London exile. The invitation came from a society called 'Focus for the Defence of Freedom and Peace'. On 27 July 1939, Beneš with his wife and Masaryk lunched with some forty opponents of governmental foreign policy and sympathisers with the cause of Czechoslovakia, including Churchill, Eden, Archibald Sinclair, Arthur Greenwood, Arthur Henderson, Lord Robert Cecil, Lord Lytton, Harold Nicolson, Violet Bonham-Carter, Megan Lloyd George, Edward L. Spears, Basil Liddell-Hart and Robert Seton-Watson. Of all the speeches Beneš was apparently most impressed by the following words by Churchill, pronounced reportedly with tears in his eyes: 'I don't know how things will develop, and I cannot say whether Great Britain will go to war on Czechoslovakia's behalf. I only know that the peace, which will only be made in the future, will not be made without Czechoslovakia.'[55] One of the organisers, A. H. Richards, provided a gloomier reflection of the event, in a letter to Churchill: 'Whilst recognising the delicacy and difficulty of his position, I did not think that 'Dr Benes' was particularly illuminating. I felt that it was a very sad occasion but well worth while for the measure of goodwill and good-cheer, it gave to one in whom – in spite of all – lamp of faith in Freedom burns bright within.'[56]

Czechoslovakia and the British war aims
The last ten days of August 1939 brought about the final wave of outward activity aimed at averting the approaching conflagration. However, the Foreign Office was already engaged in planning for the war. With respect to Czechoslovakia and its representatives the considerations of late August outlined most of the bones of contention for the years to come. When an information arrived that Beneš was surrounding himself with a circle of politicians and high-ranking officers and that he intended to proclaim the independence of Czechoslovakia on the outbreak of war, Roberts commented that although this was hardly consistent with the understanding that Beneš should refrain from political activities,

55) *Archiv Ústavu T. G. Masaryka*, Prague (hereafter *AÚTGM*), fond Edvard Beneš – Londýn (hereafter EB–L), box 111, record of Beneš's lunch with Churchill and other 40 personalities on July 27, 1939. See also Beneš, *Paměti*, p. 124; Zeman with Klimek, *The Life of Edvard Beneš 1884–1948*, p. 155.
56) *Churchill College Archive*, Cambridge, Churchill papers, CHAR 2/376, Richards to Churchill, 11 August 1939.

in the event of war the British 'should no doubt be glad to use him'. Although some information suggested that he did not have hold over his people, Roberts thought that Beneš could count upon the support of the great majority. The opinions within the Foreign Office, however, varied: Troutbeck, on the one hand, repeatedly called for some form of co-operation: 'The Czechs could probably, if encouraged, do as much or more to embarrass Germany as the Abyssinians could do to embarrass Italy.' He pointed out that the Czechs would be almost unanimously hostile to Germany and argued that the British should be in favour of giving them every support in their power. He was thinking of the best liaison to the Czechs and proposed the British Minister to Prague in the early 1920s, George R. Clerk. Meanwhile Reginald Leeper, the head of the recently founded Foreign Office Political Intelligence Department, secured the services of Bruce Lockhart to deal with South-East Europe including the Czechs and suggested that he 'keep in close touch with the Benesh organisation'. Trying to set the propaganda line with respect to a future of Czechoslovakia, Leeper argued realistically against speaking 'in terms short of complete independence'. As an initial step, however, he thought that the British should not go further than 'freedom for the Czechs from German domination'.[57]

Gladwyn Jebb, Cadogan's private secretary, on the other hand, was more sceptical. He warned against 'the re-emergence of that distasteful & indefensible mosaic' and preferred a reconstruction of 'the Austrian Empire – excluding Galicia, Transylvania, the Banat, Slovenia & Croatia, but including Bavaria, Württenberg & Baden'. In another paper, he accepted just 'autonomy' for the Czechs.[58] Cadogan toned down these far-reaching considerations, stating that there would be a long time to think about it during the war, but he set the very basic principles to be followed: for 'immediate purposes' he recommended to 'back Dr. Beneš if war breaks out. We can't refuse to inscribe the independence of Bohemia and Moravia on our banner.' Whether to incorporate it in a wider union or not was not to be settled off-hand.[59]

57) *PRO*, FO 371/22898, C 12826/7/12, Roberts' minute, 28 August, Troutbeck's minute, 29 August 1939, C 12865/7/12, Troutbeck's minute, 24 August 1939, Leeper's minute, 25 August 1939.
58) *Ibid.*, C 12826/7/12, Jebb's minute, 23 August 1939, C 12865/7/12, Jebb's minute, 28 August 1939.
59) *Ibid.*, C 12826/7/12, Cadogan's minute, 24 August 1939.

Meanwhile Beneš strove to establish solid foundations of the new resistance movement. Vital was the unequivocal support from Colonel Moravec and his intelligence officers who closely co-operated with the SIS and MI5. They provided Beneš with the vital links with home. Numerous Czechoslovak politicians and officials joined Beneš during summer: for instance the pre-Munich Deputy-Prime Minister, social democrat Rudolf Bechyně, or the chairman of the Czechoslovak (catholic) People's Party, Beneš's old friend Jan Šrámek, who at the age of sixty nine had escaped from the Protectorate, following Vansittart's advice.[60] Beneš set up a bureau, the civil part of which was headed by Jaromír Smutný, and the military one by General Sergej Ingr. The General had brought with him an important message from the central military resistance organisation in the Protectorate, calling upon Beneš to take the lead of the whole resistance movement.[61] This support was crucial for Beneš's aspirations to lead the struggle for re-establishment of Czechoslovakia, in competition with his major rivals – General Lev Prchala in Poland and Štefan Osuský in Paris. The Polish government supported Prchala and made him commander of the emerging Czechoslovak military unit in Poland, but by the end of August Beneš succeeded in getting even Prchala's pledge of obedience. Osuský, on the other hand, questioned Beneš's theory of the legal continuity of pre-Munich Czechoslovakia and came up with a 'ministerial theory': those plenipotentiaries, who had not given up their legations after 15 March, were the only legitimate representatives of Czecho-Slovakia (the post-Munich one with autonomous Slovakia). Beneš met twice with Osuský, as well as with Milan Hodža, the Slovak pre-Munich Prime Minister of Czechoslovakia and Beneš's lifelong rival. It seemed that agreement in the key questions was possible. On 24 August Beneš agreed with Osuský upon establishment of central political organ abroad and upon parallel efforts in London and Paris to achieve its recognition.[62] As Milan Hauner points out, Beneš had in his pocket one more trump, apart from the loyalty of the military both at home and abroad – the unlimited support from both children of the President Liberator Tomáš Garrigue Masaryk, Jan and Alice; this effec-

60) Firt, Julius, Cestou k únoru: Počátky byly v Londýně [On the way to February. The origins were in London], Svědectví, Vol. 12, 1973, No. 46, p. 216.
61) Šolc, Jiří, Ve službách prezidenta [In the president's services], Praha, Vyšehrad 1994, pp. 56–57.
62) Kuklík – Němeček, Hodža versus Beneš, pp. 40–44.

tively functioned like the generic legitimacy in a monarchical system.[63] In Detlef Brandes' words, neither the Czechoslovak exiles, nor the Allies could, at the end of the day, avoid Beneš as the leader of Czechoslovak resistance.[64] But it took a long time before the Allies fully realised this; meanwhile Beneš's suspicions grew and strengthened his determination to find an alternative to his previous foreign and security policies.

On the day of the German attack on Poland Troutbeck wrote a memorandum, approved by Strang, that set the pattern of British dealing with Czechoslovak problems in the ensuing months: It was expected that Beneš would soon proclaim Czechoslovakia's independence and perhaps himself as the head of her government and would also offer to recruit a Czechoslovak legion to fight alongside the allied armies. Together with his 'English friends' he would then start pressing the British government to proclaim the restoration of Czechoslovakia's independence as one of Britain's war aims. However, this was most objectionable. A restoration of pre-Munich Czechoslovakia, apparently desired by Beneš, was out of the question as such an aim would offend the Sudeten Germans, the Poles, the Hungarians and possibly even the Slovaks. Not even the term 'independence' was to be used, as it was 'to say the least a moot point whether the sovereign independence of any part of the former Czechoslovakia will ever again be practicable or desirable'. At the same time there were the strongest reasons for not omitting the 'liberation of the Czechs from German domination' in British war aims. Rather surprisingly, Troutbeck pointed out Britain's moral obligation to the Czechs and a certain degree of responsibility for their current plight, but above all he stressed the 'almost unanimous desire of all Czechs', whether resident abroad or in the Protectorate, to assist the Allies. The Slovaks, on the other hand, were regarded as 'primitive and irresponsible people' who materially mattered a great deal less than the Czechs. As it was not clear whether they were resentful of German domination, their liberation was not to be mentioned amongst war aims.

Although Beneš was considered 'far and away the most outstanding Czech figure in the world', there was as yet no proof of his prevalent influence amongst the Czechs in the Protectorate, who mattered most. Since

63) *Formování československého zahraničního odboje...*, p. 35.
64) Brandes, Detlef, Benešova politika v letech 1939–1945 [Beneš's policy in the years 1939–1945], *Dějiny a současnost* [History and present], Prague, Vol. 25, 2003, No. 1, pp. 36–38, here p. 36.

he was further 'personally abhorrent' in several countries, particularly in Poland and Hungary, Troutbeck recommended to 'walk warily' about any official recognition of him, although he would presumably have to be accepted as the *de facto* spokesman of the Czechs. An acceptance of an offer to create a Czech Legion should not commit the British further in their war aims.[65] Two days after British declaration of war on Germany, Cadogan set 'the liberation of the Czech people' as one of Britain's war aims, although 'without prejudice, for one moment, to their ultimate political structure and status'. Halifax agreed: 'It is no doubt one of the things we hope to see achieved – but I should not commit myself now as to the form such hoped for achievement might take.'[66] Kirkpatrick viewed the former frontiers of Czechoslovakia as 'impossible'. 'One would have thought that the Munich lesson ... had been learned by now,' Vansittart retorted and argued for a defensible frontier in the case of 'putting back a Czechoslovakia'. Nonetheless, even he recommended to avoid 'getting committed to anything fixed in a fluid world, when no one can say which way the tide will set'.[67]

The easiest task was to decide on British policy towards the 'independent' Slovakia. Immediately after the outbreak of war the British Consul in Bratislava, Peter Pares, appeared cut off from communication with London. The consulate was closed and on 3 September Sargent decided that he should be transferred to join Owen O'Malley's Legation in Budapest.[68] A couple of days later, the Foreign Office was considering whether the Slovak Consul Harminc ought not to be expelled. Sargent thought that every Slovak was 'capable of being bought for £5' and therefore he found it reasonable to assume that the representative of the 'so called Slovak Government' was, or might become at any time, a German agent. Strang reminded that Harminc's presence in Britain was the symbol of Britain's *de facto* 'recognition of that régime'. However, in view of the fact that the Slovak government disowned Harminc for having proclaimed himself on the Allied side, while Jan Masaryk gave his personal guaran-

65) *PRO*, FO 371/22899, C 13304/7/12 Troutbeck's memorandum, 1 September, Strang's minute, 4 September 1939.
66) *PRO*, FO 371/22898, C 13131/7/12, Cadogan's minute, Halifax's minute, 5 September 1939.
67) *PRO*, FO 371/22946, C 14840/13669/62, Kirkpatrick's minute, 20 September, Vansittart's minute, 23 September 1939.
68) *PRO*, FO 371/22904, C 13000/3145/12, various minutes, Sargent's minute, 3 September 1939.

tee of Harminc's loyalty to the 'cause', the Foreign and Home Offices permitted him to stay. Moreover, he continued to be recognised as the Slovak Consul in London.[69] In fact he joined the emerging movement of the Czechoslovak resistance.

Although Slovak troops participated in the German attack on Poland, the extension of the German occupation of Slovakia had made it possible to deal with that country in the same way as with Bohemia and Moravia. On 8 September 1939, Slovakia was proclaimed territory in German occupation and it was treated so for purposes of trading with the enemy, contraband, censorship etc. London asked the U.S. government to take charge of British interests in Slovakia.[70] British representatives abroad were not to maintain any official relations with their Slovak colleagues, but they should not discourage any unofficial overtures provided the initiative came from the other side.[71] The state of war did not, however, exist between Britain and Slovakia, and the Slovaks were not regarded as enemy nationals. It was to remain so until the end of the war, despite Slovakia's declaration of war on the United Kingdom in 1941.[72] The Slovak rulers were considered 'creatures of Germany ... not in a position to pursue an independent policy'.[73] Although during the first year of war the Foreign Office was intermittently getting reports suggesting that Slovakia was indeed independent and substantial part of its population quite contented with its current situation, and some officials even admitted that it might be so,[74] this did not have major impact on the course of

69) *PRO*, FO 371/22904, C 13221/2875/12, Sargent's minutes, 5 and 7 September, Kirkpatrick's minute, 6 September, Strang's minute, 7 September 1939.
70) *PRO*, FO 371/22904, C 13221/2875/12, Malkin's minute, 8 September 1939, C 17479//2875/12, Malkin's minute, 2 November 1939; FO 371/22901, C 13480/631/12, Halifax to O'Malley, No. 89, 14 September 1939; *H. C. Deb.*, 5th Series, Vol. 352, 9 October 1939, Cols. 1–2.
71) *PRO*, FO 371/24290, C 58/58/12, Halifax to Le Rougetel (Moscow), No. 2, 3 January 1940.
72) See Ivaničková, Edita, Britská politika a Slovensko v rokoch 1939–1945 [British policy and Slovakia in the years 1939–1945], In: *Slovensko na konci druhej svetovej vojny* [Slovakia at the end of the Second World War], ed. Valerián Bystrický, Bratislava 1994, p. 125–130; Idem, Zahraničnopolitická orientácia Slovenska v dokumentoch britskej Foreign Office (1939–1941), *op. cit.*, pp. 207–220.
73) *PRO*, FO 371/24290, C 309/58/12, Kirkpatrick's minute, 7 January 1940, C 1362/58//12, Kirkpatrick to Loraine, 30 January 1940.
74) See e.g. *PRO*, FO 371/24290, C 612/58/12, O'Malley to Kirkpatrick + enclosed memorandum by Pares, 6 January 1940, Makins' minute, 17 January 1940.

Britain's policy towards Slovakia. With the passage of time the quality and quantity of information coming from Slovakia was decreasing.[75]

Beneš launched his struggle for recognition skilfully – with a telegram to Chamberlain of 3 September, expressing 'the decision of the Czechs and Slovaks' to join the British in their struggle for a free Europe. Although he thus implied that he was the spokesman of the Czechs and Slovaks, as Troutbeck pointed out, he did not ask for any recognition. An answer was clearly necessary, as the message was published a day later. Sargent and Strang competed in their stressing that it should be non-committal: neither war aims, nor the Slovaks should be mentioned, Beneš 'must be regarded as a private individual'. Thus Troutbeck's draft became one great muddle and Halifax decided to write the Prime Minister's answer himself: the sufferings of the Czech people were not forgotten and the British looked forward to 'the release of the Czech people from foreign domination'.[76] The Prime Minister repeated this goal in the House of Commons on 13 September.[77] From non-recognition of the Protectorate, Britain now moved towards implying the liberation of the Czechs as one of its war aims. Nothing more and nothing less. Otherwise the war aims were defined in general terms of defeating Germany and re-establishment of international law and order.

The war aims, including the uneasy question of Czechoslovakia's future, was further examined in a response to Hitler's peace offer of 6 October. Halifax proposed to point out the 'difficulties' in any projected reply and to mention Poland, Czechoslovakia and disarmament in particular.[78] Similarly Churchill sent his Cabinet colleagues a note in which he argued that, with Czechoslovakia and Poland both 'subjected to a foreign yoke', no negotiations should begin until 'reparation' had been offered 'to the states and peoples who have been so wrongfully conquered', and until their 'effective life and sovereignty is unmistakably

---

75) See e.g. Roberts' minute of 4 August 1940: '...we know very little of what is really going on in Slovakia.' *PRO*, FO 371/24290, C 8121/58/12.

76) *PRO*, FO 371/22899, C 13303/7/12, Beneš to Chamberlain, 3 September, Troutbeck's and Strang's minutes, 4 September, Sargent's minute, 7 September, Halifax's draft and Chamberlain's minute, 8 September 1939. J. W. Bruegel is wrong when he says that Halifax watered down Chamberlain's original draft. Bruegel, The Recognition of the Czechoslovak Government in London, *op. cit.*, p. 2.

77) *H. C. Deb.*, 5th Series, Vol. 351, 13 September 1939, Col. 648.

78) Hill, *Cabinet Decisions on Foreign Policy*, p. 116.

to be restored'.[79] The Prime Minister would not rule out a sympathetic reference in his coming statement in the House to Czechoslovakia, but Poland was in his view the main concern.[80] The four Dominions, which had played such an important role in September 1938 in tipping the balance in the question whether or not to fight for Czechoslovakia, now urged the Allies to state their war aims clearly. A conference of neutral powers should be proposed that would decide on the boundaries of the reconstituted states of Poland and Czechoslovakia.[81] Eventually, on 12 October, Chamberlain mentioned in the House Hitler's overwhelming of Poland as well as previous overthrowing of Czecho-Slovakia as the two reasons why the British government could not accept his peace offer: 'Peace conditions cannot be acceptable which begin by condoning aggression. The proposals in the German Chancellor's speech are vague and uncertain and contain no suggestion for righting the wrongs done to Czecho-Slovakia and to Poland.'[82] Thus although in September it was Poland that was the reason for Britain's declaration of war on Germany, only a month later also the destiny of Czecho-Slovakia proved to be the reason for continued British involvement in the war.

Also in the key December communication to the French on the question of war aims, restoration of their liberties by the Slovak people appeared together with the Polish and Czech ones. But the government was careful 'not to define in precise terms' what they implied by 'the restoration of independence to Poland and Czecho-Slovakia'. The establishment of a number of small nation states, which had been 'viable' neither in the military nor economic sense, was viewed as one of major weaknesses of the inter-war settlement. Therefore the government was contemplating 'some form of closer association, at the least a system of financial and economic co-operation in Central and South-Eastern Europe'. For this purpose it intended to encourage closer co-operation between the Balkan States and also 'between the various refugee groups of Poles, Czechs, Slovaks and Austrians'.[83]

---

79) Gilbert, Martin, *Finest Hour. Winston S. Churchill 1939–1941*, London, Heinemann 1983, p. 56.
80) Hill, *Cabinet Decisions on Foreign Policy*, p. 120.
81) *Ibid.*, 125.
82) *H. C. Deb.*, 5th Series, Vol. 361, 12 October 1939, Col. 567.
83) *PRO*, FO 371/22947, C 20438/13669/62, W. P. (G) (39) 150, 15 December 1939.

Beneš was far from content with the vague British commitment as to the future of Czechoslovakia. He called on Halifax on 19 September, stressed the recent encouragement he had got from Roosevelt, and asked three questions: whether Britain was prepared to a) make restoration of Czechoslovakia one of its war aims, b) recognise some central organ acting on behalf of Czechoslovakia, c) help organise and equip Czech units. Halifax refused to commit to any war aims beyond the defeat of Hitler's Germany and promised to consult the War Office about the units. He, however, 'appreciated the force' of Beneš's arguments for the necessity of some central organ. The Foreign Secretary was highly accommodating; he himself even admitted a great responsibility of Britain for Czechoslovakia's misfortunes since last September.[84] Beneš left 'very much satisfied' with the results of the visit.[85] At a Cabinet meeting Halifax expressed his feeling that the request 'to accord a juridical basis to the Czech Government of which Dr. Benes was the head' should be granted. Also Churchill, in his capacity of the First Lord of the Admiralty, supported giving the 'oppressed peoples like the Poles and Czechs … the opportunity to take sides openly with us in the war', though without committing on territorial questions.[86] But the Foreign Office drew a significant distinction between the representatives of the two nations: It wished to safeguard a continuous existence of the Polish government and therefore even pressed President Mościcki, who was detained in Bucharest, to appoint his successor. In the case of the Czechs and Slovaks, however, a new organisation was to be built up, which was to be a slow process and there was 'everything to be said for not rushing it unduly'. Such an organisation had first to prove its case and ability to co-operate with the government in Prague, 'just as patriotic as the Czechs abroad' (ironically, this comparison was derived from Masaryk's assessment) and in a much better position to help the British.[87] Thus on 29 September, Halifax and Sargent dampened Beneš's hopes of a quick recognition: the government had first to be assured that the Central

84) *PRO*, FO 371/22899, C 14528/7/12, Halifax's minute, 20 September 1939.
85) *DČSZP 1939–1940*, No. 103, p. 229, footnote 1.
86) *Bod. Lib.*, microfilm, CAB 65/1, W. M. (39)21st Conclusions, 20 September 1939, W. M. (39)22nd Conclusions, 25 September 1939.
87) *PRO*, FO 371/22949, C 15019/15019/62, Roberts' minute, 27 September, Sargent's minute, 28 September, Cadogan's minute, 28 September 1939.

Organisation clearly represented the Czech nation. Beneš assured them that he was in direct contact with the government in Prague who were firm supporters of his activities, and that he 'definitely represented the whole Czech nation'.[88] However, the Foreign Office wanted to have this confirmed from other sources.

During the following days Beneš supplied the Foreign Office with an avalanche of documents and memoranda. But this activity could not reverse the previous FO's decision to wait and see before any recognition was to be considered. A memorandum informing the British about an 'internally constituted Czechoslovak Government', composed of Beneš as Prime Minister, Osuský (Foreign Minister), Ingr (Minister of National Defence) and Eduard Outrata (Minister of Finance), remained unanswered. These four were to be joined in the future by Masaryk, general Viest and also by one catholic Slovak and one minister of German nationality. The Cabinet was to be controlled by a National Council composed of former deputies, economic and financial experts and diplomats.[89] Indeed, a great deal of wishful thinking was entailed in this communication and this fact did not escape the attention of FO practitioners.

The Foreign Office also watched with misgiving the attempts to achieve the reconstitution of the Czechoslovak army both in Britain and in France. At an interdepartmental meeting on 28 September the general question of foreign units in Britain was discussed. The War Office did not contemplate the formation of Czech units, although it did not exclude their establishment in the future.[90] Makins, representing the FO, was concerned lest such prospective steps would involve any sort of political commitment, and he warned against an 'implied approval of the political ideas of Dr. Benes'. He was convinced that the formation of a Czech legion in England would 'involve the maximum of inconvenience with the minimum of military result'. It was considered that the Czechs should go directly to France for enrolment there. This

88) *PRO*, FO 371/22899, C 15436/7/12, Halifax's minute, 29 September 1939.
89) *Ibid.*, C 15437/7/12, Beneš to Sargent, 30 September 1939. The recent edition of Czech documents suggests that this document was a mere proposal of Beneš's note to Halifax. *DČSZP 1939–1940*, No. 107, pp. 236–237. However, it was actually sent to the Foreign Office.
90) Nevertheless, a small training camp for Czechoslovak volunteers was established in Birchington-on-Sea shortly after the outbreak of the war. *PRO*, HS 4/30, memorandum by Colonel J. Holland, 10 September 1939.

attitude, hardly deplorable from the practical point of view, enabled the government to make use of the Czechoslovak military potential for the Allied cause without entering into any political commitments. The more striking, however, was the Air Ministry's policy: while it was forming a Polish unit, it had turned down a proposal for Czech pilots 'owing to the language difficulty'.[91] Less than a year later, at the time of immediate threat to the British Isles, this alleged collective incapability was suddenly forgotten.

In a way, the FO's fears were well-founded, as in Beneš's plans the Czechoslovak armed forces were to play similar role as the Czechoslovak Legions during World War I. British worries grew when a treaty of the reconstitution of the Czechoslovak army in France was signed on 2 October by Daladier and Osuský – on behalf of a 'Provisional Czechoslovak Government'.[92] In a letter to Phipps the Foreign Office inquired by whom it had been signed and 'on behalf of what particular Czech body'. The Ambassador was asked to pass on the French the British suspicion about the real object of Beneš's proposals to set up military units in the United Kingdom – 'the securing of recognition for his central organisation, rather than the enrolment of an effective Czech-Slovak forces'. It further referred to Beneš's personal unpopularity in neighbouring states, particularly Hungary and Poland, as well as in Slovakia and allegedly also in the Czech parties which had been in power from the Munich Agreement to the German seizure of Prague. Therefore it seemed 'important not to recognise Dr. Benes immediately as the organiser and leader of the Czech and Slovak nations'. The recognition was not excluded for the future, but only after representative character of such an organisation had been confirmed. The French were warned against the danger of other bodies of dissident Czechs or Slovaks setting themselves up in opposition to Dr. Benes. Meanwhile the 'Czech [sic!] diplomatic missions' in London, Paris and other cities should serve as a nucleus around which a central organisation should be built.[93] This proposal coincided with Osuský's 'ministerial theory' and it also suited the French who were, as stated by the head of the European

91) *PRO*, FO 371/22899, C 16125/7/12, Conclusions of an interdepartmental meeting, Makins' minute, 29 September 1939, C 15436/7/12, Makins' minute, 3 October 1939. See also C 15436/7/12, Makins to Major Procter, WO and C 16125/7/12, Lord Hankey to Cadogan, 27 September 1939.
92) *DČSZP 1939–1940*, No. 110, pp. 241–245.
93) *PRO*, FO 371/22899, C 15436/7/12, Kirkpatrick to Phipps, 4 October 1939.

Department in the Quai d'Orsay, Henri Hoppenot, a day later 'rather embarrassed by Dr. Benes activities' and thought that he should remain in the shadow.[94] Indeed, the Quai d'Orsay was trying, in co-operation with Osuský, to outmanoeuvre Beneš of the emerging body. That was clearly unacceptable for most of the Czech exiles.[95] Hoppenot explained that Osuský had signed the agreement of 2 October on behalf of the provisional Czechoslovak government, so that it was clear that it was the 'Czechoslovak Army' and not the 'Osuski Army'. He further assured Phipps that 'no commitment would be entered into with Dr. Benes during his forthcoming visit' and any decision would be fully consulted with the British.[96] Thus the communication from London clearly contributed to the complete failure of Beneš's October visit to Paris.[97] He was cold -shouldered by many French politicians and Daladier refused to receive him even for a private talk.[98] This strengthened Beneš's conviction to orientate his further policy towards the U.S. and the U.S.S.R., and to achieve his immediate goals, quite paradoxically, towards Britain. Although he definitely did not think that what had been shown to him in England was 'wonderful cordiality', as he uttered to his friend Édouard Herriot when making comparison with the lack of enthusiasm in his welcome in France,[99] he hardly imagined that the French coldness had one of its origins in a British warning.[100]

94) *PRO*, FO 371/22899, C 15880/7/12, Phipps to Halifax, No. 751, 6 October 1939.
95) Kuklík – Němeček, *Hodža versus Beneš*, p. 52. Lockhart later informed the Foreign Office that Osusky had nearly succeeded in forming a Czechoslovak Provisional Government from which, apparently on the insistence of the Quai d'Orsay, Beneš was to be excluded. *PRO*, FO 371/24287, C 2655/2/12, Lockhart's memorandum, No. 23, 19 February 1940.
96) J. W. Bruegel claims that Hoppenot promised that 'no contact' would be entered with Dr. Beneš. However, it does not seem to be true. Bruegel, The Recognition of the Czechoslovak Government..., *op. cit.*, p. 4.
97) Roberts noted: 'It is just as well that Dr. Benes should have met with some difficulties in France and the French Government have clearly taken our warnings to heart.' *PRO*, FO 371/22899, C 17021/7/12, Roberts' minute, 23 October 1939.
98) *PRO*, FO 371/22899, C 17236/7/12, Lockhart's memorandum, 24 October 1939.
99) *Ibid.*, C 17021/7/12, Phipps to Halifax, No. 798, 20 October 1939.
100) In his memoirs Beneš says that on 10 February 1940, he was told that the Foreign Office had informed the Quai d'Orsay during his visit to Paris that it would not be possible to create a Czechoslovak government without Beneš's participation. It is indeed a peculiar interpretation of the FO communications to Paris that time. Beneš, *Paměti*, p. 142. In fact Sargent and Roberts managed to prevent Beneš from seeing Cadogan before his departure for Paris, although the latter was willing to see him any time. *PRO*, FO 371/22899, C 13228/7/12, Cadogan's minute, 2 October, Roberts' minute, 3 October 1939.

The first two months of war brought at least one positive change that contributed to strengthening of ties between the British and the Czechoslovaks. In a series of communications with senior FO officials during September and October Sir Robert Bruce Lockhart was asked to serve as an 'unofficial source of information about the Czechs'. He had spent several years in Czechoslovakia as a commercial secretary after World War I and he now became a liaison between the FO and the Czechoslovak organisation. It was considered that the Czechs would tell him more than to anyone else.[101] It was the most fortunate choice for the Czechoslovak exiles too: none of the British was to do more for the eventual recognition of Czechoslovak representation abroad than Bruce Lockhart. He did not hesitate to remind his colleagues that for 'all its failings, the former Czechoslovak Republic was the most successful, the most progressive, and the best-governed state in Central Europe'.[102] Sometimes his favouring of the Czechs went somewhat too far, such as his belief 'that of all the smaller nations of Europe they are the most capable of waging a determined and successful underground war against foreign oppression'.[103] He had a clear mind in the question of leadership of the Czechoslovak action abroad. He viewed Beneš as 'far the most able political organiser among the Czechs' and predicted that he would soon establish his position as the national leader of the liberation movement.[104] He repeatedly drew attention to the risks and dangers which might 'easily arise from an active or even passive discouragement of Dr. Beneš's leadership' whom he saw as a 'resolute fighter in war'.[105] He also argued against exaggerating the importance of Osuský, 'a pleasant, but vain and ambitious schemer' with no standing with the Czechs and Slovaks, but, apparently, some influence with certain French politicians, whose 'power for mischief' was 'greater than his power for creative good'.[106] Lockhart was soon delivering crucial reports of Beneš's regular contacts

101) *PRO*, FO 371/22899, C 15006/7/12, Leeper's minute, 9 September, Cadogan's and Halifax's minutes, 14 September 1939, C 15901/7/12, Roberts' minute, 11 October 1939; FO 371/22949, C 15019/15019/62, Strang to Leeper, 24 October 1939.
102) *Ibid.*, C 18016/7/12, Lockhart's memorandum, No. 8, 7 November 1939.
103) *Ibid.*, C 15006/7/12, Lockhart's memorandum, 12 September 1939.
104) *Ibid.*, C 15433/7/12, Lockhart's memorandum 'Situation in Czechoslovakia', 27 September 1939, C 15901/7/12, Lockhart's memorandum, 5 October 1939.
105) *PRO*, FO 371/22899, C 18016/7/12, Lockhart's memorandum, No. 8, 7 November 1939, C 17089/7/12, Lockhart's memorandum No. 6, 21 October 1939.
106) *Ibid.*, C 17089/7/12, Lockhart's memorandum, No. 6, 21 October 1939.

with resistance organisations inside the Protectorate as well as with the Protectorate government and President Hácha, which went as far as giving the later instructions on policy.[107] Although even Lockhart recommended caution in recognising any Czecho-Slovak organisation which did not present a satisfactory national front, he was constantly stressing to all Czech and Slovak politicians the need for unity and frequently trying even to mediate it. On the other hand, he pointed out to the FO officials that the petty intrigues were 'inevitable in the circumstances' and 'should not be taken very seriously'.[108] Both in the case of Beneš's quarrel with Osuský and later with Hodža, Lockhart supported the former and stressed his rationality and effectiveness.

Owen O'Malley, the British Minister in Budapest, delivered antipodal ideas about Czechoslovakia and about Beneš in particular. In mid-September he warned against 'anything like a pronouncement in favour of the reconstitution of Czecho-Slovakia' after the war, which 'would do much to drive Hungary into the arms of Germany'. The Foreign Office assured its Minister in Budapest about its intention to avoid 'any unnecessary irritation to Hungarian sentiment' and to keep the press etc., on the right lines. But there was something more than political realism in O'Malley's views: A month later he confessed to sharing Hungary's uneasiness at a prospect of Beneš's 'come-back': 'I cannot but feel that there are few public characters in Central European politics more likely to prove a source of embarrassment to British policy in years to come than this adroit little man. ...I should never expect him to take large-hearted or longsighted views of questions in which European as well as Czech interests are engaged.' O'Malley did not hesitate to look at things 'from the Hungarian angle' and therefore argued for every attempt to be made to dissociate the former President from the martyrdom of his people and their readiness to enter the war on the Allied side.[109] In general he was afraid that another 'golden age of émigrés' was about to dawn and he thought it was 'a pity as their political views are rarely sound'.[110]

107) *Ibid.*, C 18135/7/12, Strang's minute, 11 November 1939; FO 371/22900, C 18365/7//12, Lockhart's memorandum, 10 November 1939; FO 371/22900, C 18918/7/12, Lockhart's memorandum, 20 November 1939. On the essence of these communications see Pasák, *JUDr. Emil Hácha*.
108) *PRO*, FO 371/22899, C 17089/7/12, Lockhart's memorandum, 21 October 1939.
109) *Ibid.*, C 16878/7/12, O'Malley to Halifax, No. 132, 19 October 1939.
110) *PRO*, FO 371/22900, C 18635/7/12, O'Malley to Kirkpatrick, 7 December 1939.

At the end of October it seemed that O'Malley's views were gaining the upper hand. 'We fully share Mr. O'Malley's qualms about Dr. Benes,' Roberts minuted.[111] When the former President wished to address his fellow citizens on the BBC Czech broadcast on 28 October, the Czechoslovak state holiday, some officials, especially Strang, were most apprehensive that he might try to impress the world with the strength of his position especially in England: the BBC was instructed to 'politely intimate' to Beneš that there was no time.[112] There was no question, as Roberts recorded, of British or French government recognising 'any Czecho-Slovak Government at present or in the near future'.[113] 'Benes at 5, till 6.15,' Cadogan wrote in his diary on 25 October, obviously struck by the length of what seems to have been one of Beneš's never-ending monologues. 'He [is] obviously trying to get out recognition of his 'Provisional Government' – which he has failed to get in Paris.'[114] Cadogan gave him no encouragement and was careful not to commit the British government in any way. In fact Beneš merely asked for recognition of the Czechoslovak National Committee,[115] which had been set up in Paris on 17 October as a compromise solution of the temporary deadlock. And it was acceptable to the French, if only to encourage enlistment in the Czechoslovak army, which was going rather slowly.[116] The Foreign Office stressed to the French that the attitude of the two governments should be closely co-ordinated. Strang was anxious about a Czech game pretending 'in Paris that they enjoyed support in London and in London that they enjoyed support in Paris'.[117] Nevertheless, the French recognised the Committee by an exchange of letters between Osuský (i.e. not Beneš) and Daladier of 13 and 14 November, two days after the former had reluctantly joined the Committee, thus fulfilling a French *conditio sine qua non*. The Committee was 'qualified to represent the Czechoslovak people abroad and

111) *PRO*, FO 371/22899, C 16878/7/12, Roberts' minute, 24 October 1939.
112) *PRO*, FO 371/22899, C 17089, C 17340/7/12, Strang's minutes, 26 October 1939.
113) *PRO*, FO 371/22899, C 16878/7/12, Roberts' minute, 24 October 1939; FO 371/23089, C 16952/5606/18, Roberts' minute, 23 October 1939.
114) *Cadogan Diary*, diary entry for 25 October 1939, p. 226.
115) *PRO*, FO 371/22899, C 17305/7/12, Cadogan's minute, 25 October 1939.
116) Only about 2000 Czech and Slovak recruits enlisted during first seven weeks of war. *PRO*, FO 371/22899, C 17021/7/12, Phipps to Halifax, No. 798, 21 October 1939.
117) *PRO*, FO 371/22899, C 17483/7/12, Cadogan's minute, 26 October 1939, C 17465//7/12, FO to Campbell (Paris), 5 November 1939.

especially to implement the agreement of 2 October 1939 concerning the reconstitution of the Czechoslovak army'.[118]

The FO officials were now clear that Britain would have to sign a similar agreement with Dr. Beneš.[119] It seems that Lockhart's warnings against growing Soviet propaganda, which might find a fertile soil in both Slovakia and the Czech lands, were considered as sound. 'If we can do nothing for the democratic elements amongst the Czechs, the Czechs may be tempted to look to Moscow for their salvation,' Roberts noted.[120] However, there were also different considerations: the Germans might dismiss the Protectorate government at any time; and the recognition of the National Committee would put the British in a stronger position should they thereupon be faced with a request for recognition of 'Dr. Benes and his friends' as a Czech Government.[121]

Beneš tried to improve the wording of the letters, as distinct from those exchanged with the French government, so that it would be the object of the Committee to carry on the struggle for the liberation of the Czechoslovak Republic. But Cadogan dissuaded him from doing this.[122] Apparently, the British did not consider the whole question of recognition as very urgent.[123] It took the British governmental machinery five weeks before all the relevant departments expressed their agreement, the matter was approved by the War Cabinet[124] and Beneš invited to the final check. Meanwhile the Foreign Office smuggled into the text a formula stating that the Czechoslovak National Committee was qualified to represent *the Czechoslovak peoples*, instead of people. It was an attempt to express British doubts whether in fact the Czechs and Slovaks could be united in a single state after the war. The officials including Halifax

118) *DČSZP 1939-1940*, Nos. 145–146, pp. 309–311.
119) *PRO*, FO 371/22900, C 18519/7/12, Roberts' minute, 18 November, Strang's minute, 20 November 1939.
120) *PRO*, FO 371/22899, C 16390/7/12, Lockhart's memorandum, 10 October 1939, C 18135/7/12, Strang's minute 9 November 1939; FO 371/22900, C 18265/7/12, Lockhart's memorandum, 10 November 1939, C 18918/7/12, Lockhart's memorandum, 20 November 1939, C 19227/7/12, Roberts' minute, 30 November 1939.
121) *PRO*, FO 371/22900, C 19501/7/12, Roberts' minute, 4 December 1939.
122) *PRO*, FO 371/22900, C 18441/7/12, Cadogan's minute, 13 November 1939.
123) See Roberts' minute from 31 October 1939, when it seemed that the French recognition might be forthcoming. The author pointed out that a British recognition, however likely, was not so urgent, because the Czech army was being organised on the French soil. *PRO*, FO 371/22899, C 17465/7/12
124) *Bod. Lib.*, microfilm, CAB 65/2, W. M. (39) 111th Conclusions, 10 December 1939.

expected that Beneš would not be pleased with this difference of wording and they were ready to back down. But Beneš, rather surprisingly, did not raise the matter.[125] The letters were exchanged on 20 December and published two days later; the Committee, composed of eight members, was qualified to represent the Czechoslovak peoples and in particular 'to make such arrangements as may be necessary' in the territories under the jurisdiction of the British government 'in connexion with the reconstitution of the Czechoslovak army in France'.[126] The letters were 'very carefully drafted to avoid any far-reaching commitments to Dr. Benes...'[127] British diplomats abroad were instructed not to grant official recognition to representatives of the National Committee, but they were to give them unofficial co-operation, such as bag facilities, if required.[128] The continued recognition of the Czecho-Slovak legation headed by Lisický was now in the Foreign Office's view demonstrating British double *non*-recognition – of German occupation of the Protectorate and of Beneš's Committee as a government.[129]

Although during the end of 1939 the FO repeatedly emphasised that the Czechs and Slovaks must first settle their differences before any recognition might be forthcoming, it seems that the reasons for British wariness were deeper. When Lockhart criticised the Franco-British passivity towards the Czechs and warned against 'dangerous reactions in the Protectorate', which might be thus provoked, and against assisting those tendencies which, presumably, the British wished to check, the senior officials in the Foreign Office agreed that the exchange of letters was the furthest they could go at the moment. Cadogan mentioned the fact that

125) *PRO*, FO 371/22900, C 18519/7/12, Roberts' minute, 18 November, Strang's minute, 20 November, Cadogan's minute, 22 November, Halifax's minute, 24 November 1939, C 20582/7/12, Strang's minute, 18 November 1939. Jan Kuklík suggests that the English wording was even worse for Beneš than the French, as it spoke 'of the Czecho-Slovak Committee and Czech and Slovak peoples'. However, this is not correct, although these possibilities were also considered. Kuklík, The Recognition of the Czechoslovak Government in Exile and its International Status 1939–1941, *op. cit.*, p. 177.
126) *PRO*, FO 371/22900, C 20702/7/12, FO Memorandum, 20 December 1939. In early 1940 the British repeated to Beneš that the formation of units of a Czecho-Slovak army in the United Kingdom was not contemplated. *Hoover Institution Archive*, Stanford University, Palo Alto, Cal. (hereafter *HIA Stanford*), Eduard Táborský collection, Beneš to Sargent, 4 January, Sargent to Beneš, 19 February 1940.
127) *PRO*, FO 371/24287, C 1323/2/12, Roberts' minute, 18 January 1940.
128) *PRO*, FO 371/24288, C 5262/2/12, FO to Hayter (Shanghai), 12 April 1940.
129) *PRO*, FO 371/22290, C 20582/7/12, Roberts' minute, 30 December, Strang's minute, 9 January 1940, Cadogan's minute, 16 January 1940.

'the French are particularly chary of Dr. Benes'.[130] Quite naturally, close co-operation with France was by far the most important component of British strategy in the first ten months of war. It is true that, unlike the French, the British at least had not spread false information attempting, probably from the reasons of conscience, to point at Beneš as the culprit of the Munich fiasco.[131] Nor did they ignore him ostentatiously, and they were well aware that any Czechoslovak body without him would have little or no credibility and following. On the other hand, by the communication of 5 October 1939, London at least significantly strengthened the French chariness. Ironically, this set into the overall British pattern of influencing the French policy towards Central Europe, and especially towards Czechoslovakia, until March 1939, which was marked by constant effort to dissuade France from fulfilling her commitments or entering into new ones. Furthermore, despite the French intrigues with Osuský at Beneš's expense, it was France who eventually took the lead in the outward support of the Czechoslovak cause – first by the military agreement of 2 October, and then by recognising the National Committee. Indeed, it was the French army, supported only by a few British divisions, who was to face the whole power of the German Wehrmacht, and therefore the French wished to make as much use as possible of the potential Czechoslovak units, in spite of the awkward political commitments implied. The extremely butter-fingered British governmental machinery only added to the negative outward effect when it had taken more than five weeks before Britain recognised the Committee on similar lines as the French had done.

It was during this time of Beneš's complete disillusionment with the Western powers, that he had two crucial talks with Soviet Ambassador Ivan Maisky, one on 22 September and the other on 21 November. Maisky's and Beneš's records of the first talk do not match, while the content of the second talk we know only from Maisky's (semi-official) diary; a Czech record probably does not exist. It is clear that in September they talked about the future status of Ruthenia (the Sub-Carpathian Russia), but the question is whether Beneš saw it as a necessity or just an option for this inter-war Czechoslovak province to become a part of the USSR after

130) *PRO*, FO 371/22900, C 18918/7/12, Lockhart's memorandum, 11 November, Roberts' minute, 22 November, Strang's minute, 23 November, Cadogan's minute, 24 November 1939.
131) See Klimek, Edvard Beneš od abdikace..., *op. cit.*, pp. 192–193.

the war. After the Munich experience he also definitely wished a common border to be established between Czechoslovakia and the USSR, but it is questionable whether he said that he had 'no objections against the Soviet system being established in Czechoslovakia' when stressing above all the need to liberate the country from the German yoke, and whether he really 'accepted a federative tie between his country and the Soviet Union'.[132] However, these astonishing remarks fit into the context of Beneš's perception of the Nazi-Soviet Pact which differed substantially from the British, French or Polish ones. He viewed the Pact as a Soviet incentive for Hitler to unleash the war. And perhaps with the exception of Hitler himself, hardly anybody had desired the outbreak of war more than the Czechoslovak exiles in the spring and summer of 1939, as it meant the only hope for a future reestablishment of Czechoslovakia. Thus, through his contacts with Soviet diplomats, Beneš had cared to discount sincerity and earnestness of British efforts to make an alliance with the U.S.S.R. in the spring and summer of 1939[133] and was grateful for the Nazi-Soviet Pact as an inducement to war. He strove to remain in close contact with the only European 'non-Munich' Power throughout the whole of war, despite the Soviet recognition of Slovakia *de jure* and cancellation of the Czechoslovak Legation in Moscow in late 1939.[134] In March 1945, Molotov was to make full use of Maisky's records of his talks with Beneš, when pressing for the immediate cession of Ruthenia to the Soviet Union. At the same time the Soviet Commissar remarked that the question of Sovietisation was not on the agenda. Beneš only weakly responded that he did not remember what exactly he had then said to Maisky.[135]

Whatever the exact words that Beneš had said to the Soviet Ambassador, it is clear that by such far-reaching offers to the Soviet Union,

132) *DVP*, tom XXII (1939) – kniga 2, Nos. 625, 802, Iz dnevnika Majskogo, 22. 9., 21. 11. 1939, pp. 121–122, 326–237; *Dokumenty ČSR–SSSR*, Vol. I, No. 26, pp. 86–87, Beneš's record of his talk with Maisky, 22 September 1939.

133) *AVP*, fund Molotov's Secretariat, 1/217/20, Potemkin's diary, record of his talk with Fierlinger, 25. 6. 1939.

134) *Ibid.*, Vol. I, No. 20, pp. 74–75, Beneš's record of his talk with Maisky, 23 August 1939; *DHČSP*, No. 198, pp. 240–243, Smutný's record of Beneš's talk, 12 July 1941; Kural, Václav, *Vlastenci proti okupaci. Ústřední vedení odboje domácího 1940–1943* [Patriots against the occupation. The Central Committee of the Home Resistance 1940–1943], Praha, Karolinum 1997, pp. 77–87, 137; Brod, *Osudný omyl Edvarda Beneše*, pp. 28–29.

135) *Dokumenty ČSR–SSSR*, Vol. II, No. 253, pp. 520–523, Fierlinger's record of negotiations between Beneš, Masaryk, Fierlinger, Molotov and Zorin, 23 March [sic!, 24 March] 1939; Marjina, Nejen o Podkarpatské Rusi, *op. cit.*, pp. 48–51.

balanced by absolutely no reward, he seriously undermined not only the outcome of his war-time diplomacy, but the entire post-war international position of Czechoslovakia. And no bitterness about the British and French 'Munich' policy can take off this responsibility from him.

Towards the Provisional Government

In Karl Marx's view, 'emigré life is a school of scandal and meanness'.[136] Alexander I. Gercen called the exile 'a serious mental disease'.[137] The Czechoslovak case at least at the beginning of the war fully testified to the validity of these statements. Although practically none of the Czechoslovak politicians in exile was satisfied with the international status of the National Committee, for months the internal dissension provided the British and French with sufficient pretexts for refusing any further recognition. The major clash proceeded between Beneš and Hodža. It was bearing much of their mutual aversion from the years of *cohabitation* in 1935–38, but it also embodied the deeper Czecho-Slovak tension.[138] The long set of their meetings, interruptions, hopes for a *modus vivendi* and subsequent deterioration of the relationship was closely followed by Lockhart who supplied the Foreign Office with numerous memoranda including his own assessments.

Hodža fought for a promise of Slovak autonomy, which Beneš refused to give (arguing that such questions were to be settled by the nation itself after the war), and apparently also for his own position in the leadership of the Czechoslovak National Committee. There was, however, a paramount opposition to such a step amongst Czech émigrés.[139] Hodža declared himself 'the only representative of the Slovak nation in exile' and on 22 November 1939 he founded the Slovak National Council. Two months later it was supplemented by Czech opposition elements and the Czecho-Slovak National Council (CSNS) was set up. This body called for an enlargement of the Czechoslovak National Committee by including all members of the CSNS. It also called for subsequent declarations on the Slovak question and on Czecho-Slovakia's future active role in the Central European Federation.

136) Cited in *PRO*, FO 371/24288, C 7535/2/12, Lockhart's memorandum, 30 June 1940.
137) Cited in Feierabend, *Politické vzpomínky*, Vol. I, p. 327.
138) For further details see: Kuklík – Němeček, *Hodža versus Beneš*.
139) *DHČSP*, No. 26, p. 56, Ripka to Beneš, 28 October 1939.

The Foreign Office called for unity amongst Czecho-Slovak exiles while for many officials Hodža symbolised Slovakia (although he was not a Catholic).[140] He was considered a charming, amiable and amusing gentleman; there was a wide agreement in the Foreign Office that Beneš should find a place for him in the Committee and that the rift was making a very bad impression in Britain and France.[141] Some officials were impressed by Hodža's projects of various Central-European federations.[142] 'To my own mind,' Gladwyn Jebb argued, 'the federal ideas of Dr. Hodza, & his proposed economic union with Austria & Poland, are at least as worthy of investigation as the plans of Dr. Benes to restore the Czechoslovak sausage in all its original untenability.'[143] Nevertheless, it was Hodža who was gradually viewed as the element disrupting the Czecho-Slovak unity. While in Lochkhart's view Beneš was a war leader, Hodža was notable by his slowness and reluctance to take decision.[144] Lockhart perceived the creation of the Czecho-Slovak National Council as a breach of Hodža's former pledge never to undertake any action which might damage the Czechoslovak cause. Lockhart told him bluntly that the effect of this open disunity would be deplorable both in the Protectorate and in the West. He called Hodža's council 'a more than mediocre body', composed of 'nonentities', and 'surrealist in its oddity'. Hodža further undermined his own position by admitting that the people surrounding him were not the first 'Garnitur', perhaps not even the fifth one.[145] Some of them were completely unreliable and were to be detained in the summer of 1940, such as V. Borin-Ležák, who, as Lockhart reported, was a former Communist, but in 1939 organised a Czech Fascist group and left Prague with the apparent consent of the Gestapo. Hodža

140) Historians often tend to say that there was an 'overwhelming Czech representation' on the Czechoslovak National Committee. See e.g. Dockrill, The Foreign Office, Dr Eduard Benes and the Czechoslovak Government-in-Exile, 1939–41, op. cit., p. 703. In fact three of its eight members (Osuský, Slávik, Viest) were Slovaks, while Masaryk spoke of himself as of half-Slovak (although in fact he was just a 'quarter-Slovak').
141) PRO, FO 371/24287, C 2331/2/12, Lockhart's memorandum, 10 February, Leeper's minute, 11 February, Roberts' minute, 15 February, Strang's minute, 16 February 1940.
142) Hodža's ideas were later summarised in a book published in London. Hodža, Milan, Federation in Central Europe, London, Jerrolds 1942 (Slovak edition: Federácia v strednej Európe, ed. Pavol Lukáč, Bratislava, Kaligram 1997).
143) PRO, FO 371/24287, C 2455/2/12, Jebb's minute, 8 March 1940.
144) Ibid., C 2331/2/12, Lockhart's memorandum, 10 February 1940.
145) C 2655/2/12, Lockhart's memorandum, No. 23, 19 February 1940, C 2331/2/12, Lockhart's memorandum, No. 19, 10 February 1940.

himself did not even attempt to vindicate him.[146] Lockhart thought that Beneš must be left to deal with his opponents in his own manner.[147] Based on Masaryk's information, the Foreign Office even informed Paris that it considered the members of Hodža's committee too insignificant to account for anything.[148] The French government at this moment publicly backed the Czechoslovak National Committee and intervened against this 'subversive propaganda' – worried by possible disruptive effect of the Council's propaganda upon the Czechoslovak military units in France.[149] It seems that unlike previous October, this time the British communication strengthened Beneš's position in Paris.[150]

Apparently, the bulk of the Foreign Office was gradually and increasingly inclined to bet on Beneš, who – for all his defects and unpopularity – at least seemed to have his own people behind him. Roberts, pointing to the Beneš's friendly relations with the Polish government in exile,[151] argued that close Central European co-operation was also the former President's aim. Not the same importance was to be attributed to Beneš and Hodža: Beneš clearly represented the vast majority of the Czech people, and although he did not represent the bulk of the Slovak people, nor did Hodža, who 'represented very little except himself. ... The essential thing for the moment is to win the war and not to propound ideal paper solutions for the post-war reconstruction of Europe. Czech action, particularly in the Protectorate, may help us to win the war and to that extent we must encourage the Czech leader, Dr. Benes. There is no evidence whatsoever that the Slovaks can help us or want to help us.'[152] Also other officials agreed that very little support was to be expected from Slovakia during the war.[153]

146) *PRO*, FO 371/24288, C 4960/2/12, Lockhart's memorandum, No. 33, 31 March 1940, C 7535/2/12, Lockhart's memorandum, 30 June 1940.
147) *PRO*, FO 371/24287, C 2655/2/12, Lockhart's memorandum, No. 23, 19 February 1940.
148) *PRO*, FO 371/24290, C 878/48/12, Strang's minute, 15 January 1940, Kirkpatrick to Mack (Paris), 27 January 1940.
149) Kuklík, The Recognition of the Czechoslovak Government..., *op. cit.*, pp. 178–179; Kuklík, Jan – Němeček, Jan, *Proti Benešovi! Česká a slovenská protibenešovská opozice v Londýně 1939–1945* [Against Beneš! The Czech and Slovak anti-Beneš opposition in London 1939–1945] Praha, Karolinum 2004, pp. 44–45.
150) *PRO*, FO 371/24287, C 3308/2/12, Mack (Paris) to Kirkpatrick, 29 February 1939.
151) See Chapter 6.
152) *Ibid.*, C 2455/2/12, Roberts' minute, 11 March 1940.
153) *Ibid.*, C 2331/2/12, Lockhart's memorandum, No. 19, 10 February 1940, C 2950/2/12, Makins' minute, 3 March 1940.

Similarly the Foreign Office was gradually getting fed up with Hungary's exaggerated criticism of the British support to Beneš and his committee or warnings against backing of Czechoslovakia's territorial claims or using the word 'Czechoslovakia' at all – most of them strongly supported by O'Malley. After one of such outbursts against 'that jerry--built state' which 'should never reappear', made by Foreign Minister Count Csáky in the Hungarian Parliament, Sargent commented: 'I am glad that Count Csaky should have warned HMG against a danger of making premature promises – we must remember that the next time that Ct. Csaky and Mr. O'Malley press us to make promises to the Hungarian Govt. as to our future attitude towards Hungary's territorial claims against Roumania.'[154] In a talk with Lockhart he suggested sarcastically that Hungary be let have most of Slovakia: 'The Czechs w[oul]d then have a grievance. Nations – especially small nations – thrive on grievances. Whole strength of Hungary during last 20 years has lain in her grievances.'[155] Apparently the Foreign Office had no illusions about the real Hungarian aims, but from irritation or even contempt it was still a long way to a decision to write off Hungary completely. It was in Britain's strategic interest to keep it on the neutral path as long as possible.

Beneš's position was further strengthened by the testimonies of prominent refugees from the Protectorate. One Protectorate Minister and one high official, Ladislav K. Feierabend and Jaromír Nečas, both of them symbolising the connection and the continuity of the Prague government and the resistance abroad, as well as two younger Social Democratic members of the resistance, Bohumil Laušman and František Němec, escaped from the Protectorate and arrived in Britain during February and March. All of them stressed the unity of the home Czechs who were now solidly behind Beneš and condemned the disruptive activities of Hodža. Nečas, whom Lockhart rather naïvely assessed as 'a kind of Czech Mr. Greenwood and Mr. Maynard Keynes combined', stated that the whole Czech government in Prague, with only one exception, supported Beneš, whereas Hodža's separate action was not approved even by many of his own supporters in Slovakia. The Czecho-Slovak National Council was a problem not for politicians but for the French

154) *PRO*, FO 371/24427, C 3937/529/21, O'Malley to Halifax, No. 37, 9 March 1940, Sargent's minute, 23 March 1940.
155) *House of Lords Record Office*, London (hereafter *HLRO*), Bruce Lockhart papers, diary No. 32, 20 March 1940.

deuxième bureau and British intelligence service. Feierabend, 'an honest man' not only in Lockhart's view, brought a message from Rudolf Beran, the Agrarian leader, that Hodža 'must submit to the leadership of Dr. Beneš or risk complete ostracism'.[156] Feierabend stated that people in the Protectorate wished to see the creation of a Provisional government abroad headed by Beneš. Laušman and Němec emphasised the resistance potential of the Protectorate and the desire of the Czechs to be recognised as allies. This led Lockhart to stress the possible effectiveness of the military effort of the home Czechs whom the Allied governments might control and use should a 'proper encouragement' be provided.[157]

Being in London, Beneš tended to act as a person above the National Committee, dissociated from the intrigues in Paris. It was clearly his intention to create a government and the whole 'state machinery', but he intended to wait for the right 'psychological moment', being confident that when the time came, some Cabinet ministers (Churchill, Eden, Halifax and Stanley) would help 'the Czechoslovak cause'.[158] In late March he brushed up the proposal for the National Council, a quasi-parliament that would be comprised of all former ministers, deputies and senators, prominent personalities, certain officers and workers of the Czech and Slovak secret organisations. Hodža was to be offered a 'place of honour' in this body. Roberts warned against the ultimate goal of a provisional government entailed in that scheme and argued against any British encouragement to it until the government in Prague was liquidated or Hungary threw in her lot with Germany.[159] On 26 April, incidentally the day when the government decided to clear central Norway, Beneš talked to Cadogan, 'for hour and a quarter!', on the necessity for setting up and recognising the Czechoslovak government.[160] Detlef Brandes explains Beneš's decision to come up with this project, rather than with that of the quasi-parliament, by the effect of

156) Both Hodža and Feierabend were members of the Agrarian party.
157) *PRO*, FO 371/24287, C 2829, C 4073, C 4830/2/12, Lockhart's memoranda No. 24, 29, 31, 20 February, 16 March, 30 March 1940; Kuklík, The Recognition of the Czechoslovak Government..., *op. cit.*, p. 179.
158) *Edvard Beneš: Vzkazy do vlasti* [Edvard Beneš: Messages home], ed. J. Šolc, Praha, Naše vojsko 1996, No. 14, pp. 46–50, 8 February 1940.
159) *PRO*, FO 371/24287, C 4152/2/12, Lockhart's memorandum, No. 30, 13 March 1940; FO 371/24288, C 5750/2/12, Lockhart's memorandum, No. 37, 16 April, Roberts' minute, 18 April 1940.
160) *Cadogan Diary*, diary entry for 26 April 1940, p. 273.

recent admission of Poland and Norway to the Supreme War Council, Daladier's replacement by Reynaud and also Lockhart's reports of Halifax's positive attitude towards the Czechoslovak cause.[161] According to Beneš, the government in Prague no longer exercised any real power and Hácha was 'a complete cypher'. The continued recognition of this puppet government was most damaging. Beneš claimed to have his people behind him, but needed the authority to compel the refugees, often living on the refugee fund, to serve in the army, or to speak to the Polish and other governments on equal terms. He was clever enough to stress that the recognition would not involve any obligation as to the frontiers and even that in speaking of Czechoslovakia he did not mean to assume the pre-Munich frontiers.

The request was not rebuffed, but carefully examined on various levels and consulted with the French. Roberts recommended to await the events in the Danube basin, e.g. which way Hungary was going to jump, Makins thought that Benes was 'opening his mouth far too wide' (apparently his favourite phrase when speaking about Beneš) and thought that the request was premature. Sargent wished to know Lockhart's view. The liaison officer, now clearly supporting Beneš's plea, skilfully reversed the already well-worn argument of the need of unity: the recognition would put a stop to most of the Czech and Slovak dissensions and it would also stimulate the subversive movement both in the Protectorate and in Slovakia. Not much was to be expected from the Hungarians, while the Czechs and Slovaks were 'the most solid bulwark of Western Europe in the Danube basin'. Beneš possessed in Lockhart's view 'great virtues of courage and determination', commanded large measure of support of Czechs and also many Slovaks, was committed irrevocably to the Allied cause and therefore deserved their support. Lockhart, however, daringly predicted that Beneš could afford to wait little longer as he would benefit from the ministerial changes in Britain and possibly also from the development of events with respect to France. True, the French quickly agreed with the British suggestion that the recognition was premature; but it was already 18 May 1940 and the relevance of the French view

---

161) Brandes, *Großbritannien und seine osteuropäischen Alliierten 1939–1943. Die Regierungen Polens, der Tschechoslowakei und Jugoslawiens im Londoner Exil vom Kriegsausbruch bis zur Konferenz von Teheran*, p. 46. See also *DHČSP*, Nos. 66, 91, pp. 86–7, 91, Smutný's records of 14 March and 24 April 1940.

was soon to vanish.[162] A fortnight later, Hubert Ripka, a member of the National Committee, tried to make use of France's critical situation by direct approach to the new Prime Minister, 'anti-appeaser' Paul Reynaud, but it does not seem that he got any reply at all.[163] Nevertheless, after a month of investigation, the Foreign Office politely turned down Beneš's request: its further consideration should be preceded by 'a clear and public demonstration of the unity of the Czecho-Slovak action abroad', the suggested project of a larger representative body was recommended to be realised first.[164]

One of Lockhart's arguments for recognition was especially moving: 'In a war which we have not even begun to win excessive caution about the future of Europe is out of place. We should know who are our friends and back them. There is no small country in Europe where hate of Germany is so strong and where it can be better turned to our advantage.' On 2 June, after another talk with now embittered Beneš who spoke of a possible return to the United States and at the time that the evacuation of B.E.F. from the Continent was drawing to an end, Lockhart developed his argument further: 'Although it may be said truthfully enough that we are fighting the battle of liberty and that the small nations count for little, we have reached a stage in the war when even a minor contribution can help.' If the Czech assistance was not to be lost irretrievably, British policy had to be reconsidered. Encouragement of the Czechs and Slovaks would not preclude 'vague post-war dreams of a better and fairer Central Europe' while it was futile to think that the recognition would influence the attitude of Italy and Hungary. Having recently experienced another clear example of Hodža's unscrupulous trickery, Lockhart lost all confidence in him, declared that he had never kept his promises, and even proposed to warn Hodža that his activities were harmful to the Allied cause and the current hospitality of Britain and France could be reconsidered.[165] By then Lockhart himself was get-

162) *PRO*, FO 371/24288, C 6283/2/12, Cadogan's minute, 29 April, Roberts' minutes, 3 and 8 May, Makins' minute, 4 May, Sargent's minute, 7 May, Speaight to Campbell, 15 May, Campbell to Halifax, No. 388, 18 May 1940, C 6035/2/12, Lockhart's memorandum, No. 42, 12 May 1940. See also *DČSZP 1939–1940*, No. 230, pp. 470–479, Record of the points raised by Dr. Beneš in his conversation with Sir Alexander Cadogan on 26 April 1940.
163) Brandes, Detlef, *Großbritannien und seine osteuropäischen Allierten 1939–1943*, p. 47.
164) *PRO*, FO 371/24288, C 6283/2/12, Cadogan to Beneš, 25 May 1940.
165) *Ibid.*, C 6035/2/12, Lockhart's memorandum, No. 42, 12 May 1940, Lockhart's

ting desperate: he felt that the FO was taking no interest in 'his' Czechs and that he was only boring the Central Department whenever he raised a point about Beneš. Its superintending Under-Secretary, William Strang, whom Lockhart considered 'a poor creature – gutless and second-rate', had very seldom time to see him.[166] But Lockhart pressed hard. During what seems to have been a heated talk with Strang, he repeated many of his previous arguments, especially the potential for effective sabotage in the Protectorate, and he further reminded his always hesitant colleague that recently Jan Masaryk had hurriedly left for America, with the blessing of British ministers, to use his considerable influence and abilities in undertaking pro-Allied propaganda.[167] On the other hand, Lockhart added a gloomy warning that the Czech bourgeoisie in the Protectorate, felt abandoned by the Allies, could try to find a bargain with the Germans, while the working-class would turn in despair to Russia. Strang might have been 'fed up with Benes',[168] but he had to see him again. Beneš submitted a memorandum proposing establishment of the whole state machinery in exile. The government was to be composed of thirteen members – five of them Slovaks (i.e. far above the proportion of population) including one Catholic, with Masaryk as a Foreign Minister. The National Council (later renamed as 'State Council', but nicknamed by Makins as Beneš's 'personal parliament'[169]) would have its presidium composed of three members, 'perhaps' Bechyně, Hodža and one German Deputy. Beneš, however, protested to Strang against the argument of the alleged lack of unity and asked whether the Poles, Belgians, Norwegians or the Dutch were united; it was unfair to judge the Czechs and Slovaks more severely than the others. He stressed that he could secure the collaboration of most important politicians in exile, provided he could be sure of British recognition. But since Hodža was capable of blocking the recognition, he was enjoying his position and

memorandum, 2 June 1940. Lockhart was given an alleged letter to Beneš, but later recognised that it was a fake, as Hodža had in fact sent a different version that was much less 'reasonable'; *The Diaries of Sir Robert Bruce Lockhart 1939–1965*, 1 June 1940, p. 61.
166) *The Diaries of Sir Robert Bruce Lockhart 1939–1965*, 25 May 1940, p. 58.
167) Masaryk was considered by British and U.S. broadcasting experts as one of the best broadcasters in the world. *PRO*, FO 371/24288, C 4850/2/12, Lockhart's memorandum, No. 31, 30 March 1940.
168) *The Diaries of Sir Robert Bruce Lockhart 1939–1965*, 13 June 1940, p. 62; *PRO*, FO 371/24289, C 7295/2/12, Lockhart to Strang, 14 June 1940.
169) *PRO*, FO 371/24290, C 13739/2/12, Makins' minute, 1 January 1941.

would never agree with it. He further underpinned his proposals with another warning of the growing Soviet influence and reminded Strang of the thousands of Czechoslovak soldiers, hundreds of airmen and a number of political refugees now reaching the country: it would increase his authority if he could obtain recognition. Strang remained in his non--committal aloofness.[170]

Meanwhile numerous politicians started calling for the recognition of the Czechs – Sinclair, now the Secretary for Air, or a group of MPs (Mander, Noel-Baker, Lipson).[171] However, the crucial change of the attitude inside the Foreign Office came only with the fall of France. Even the hitherto major opponents now altered their views, following the change of circumstances: Thus Makins, although considering Beneš 'a somewhat tarnished figure' and warning that the British would 'regret one day' their prospective recognition of 'Dr Benes as a provisional government', enumerated on 24 June: 'Hungary may be written off. Italy is in the war and adversity has brought Czechs and Poles closer together. The Czechs have shown up well compared with some of our other Allies and the Czecho-Slovak National Committee and Army are moving to the United Kingdom. Our own position has changed for the worse and, having less to lose, we can perhaps afford to take on the Czechs.' Strang, Cadogan and Halifax soon agreed.[172] Apart from the arguments above, the FO Memorandum submitted to the Cabinet declared the need for some 'further gesture of encouragement' that would strengthen the will of the Czechs and Slovaks to resist after recent German successes. It also pointed out the danger of Czechs and Slovaks looking solely to the USSR. As the Czecho-Slovak cause was also popular in the United

---

170) *PRO*, FO 371/24289, C 7646/2/12, Strang's minute, 21 June 1940. The government got reports that there were 10–12,000 Czechoslovak soldiers in southern France waiting for transport to Britain. It was decided that the Admiralty should bring them over, together with the Poles. *Bod. Lib.*, microfilm, CAB 65/7, W. M. (40) 171st, 172nd, 177th Conclusions, 18, 19 and 23 June 1940. However, only over 3,000 Czechoslovak troops got to Britain, the others either dispersed or reached the ports too late.

171) *PRO*, FO 371/24288, C 6035/2/12, Butler's minute, 6 June, Mander to Butler, 19 and 21 June 1940, Halifax to Sinclair, 12 June 1940. Halifax used a peculiar argument that the 'recognition of the Czecho-Slovak cause would come better at some more favourable stage of war'. But any waiting for it at that time would have been equal to waiting for Godot.

172) *Ibid.*, C 7504/2/12, Makins' minute, 21 June 1940; FO 371/24289, C 7646/2/12, Makins' minute, 24 June, Strang's minute, 25 June, Cadogan's minute, 27 June, Halifax's minute, 27 June 1940.

States, the positives were considered as outweighing 'the disadvantages of proceeding to a new political act in respect of Central Europe'. The Czechoslovak army and refugees would require British financial assistance, should further recognition be given or not. The £ 7 million in gold deposited in London served as an additional argument for recognition as it could be used 'as security to any loan made to Dr. Benes'. Nevertheless, if he were able to secure the collaboration of the persons indicated by him, the government would be prepared to consider giving recognition. At a War Cabinet meeting on 3 July the issue went through, in Duff Cooper's words, 'without a murmur'.[173]

The recognition was preceded by an exchange of letters between Beneš and Halifax of 9 and 18 July. Several serious limitations were set up: the British refused to commit themselves to any particular frontiers in Central Europe, including Czechoslovakia. Indeed, the 'Provisional Czecho-Slovak Government' was to represent 'the Czech and Slovak peoples', not any state. (These terms in fact represented a step back from 'Czechoslovak' Committee and peoples.) It further did not attribute any legislative authority over Czecho-Slovak nationals or property to the new government, which was a concession to the Sudeten Germans and those Czechs and Slovaks in opposition to Beneš. And the Foreign Office strictly rejected Beneš's suggestion that by the non-recognition of the occupation after 15 March the British government had 'solemnly underlined the political and juridical continuation of the existence of the Czecho-Slovak Republic'. Of course, Beneš in his situation accepted all this and wished to settle the outstanding questions, such as the jurisdiction over Czecho-Slovak armed forces and civilians in Britain and the question of the gold, only *after* the recognition.[174] It was confirmed in Halifax's letter of 21 July and made public two days later. The same day Geoffrey Mander asked the Prime Minister in the House of Commons whether the Czechoslovak government would be in exactly the same position as the Polish one. Churchill who on 10 May had replaced Chamberlain as the British Prime Minister was advised to answer that there were 'certain technical distinctions', but he obviously disliked the formula and answered that there might 'be certain differences of form, but, in

173) *The Diaries of Sir Robert Bruce Lockhart 1939–1965*, 5 July 1940, p. 65; *Bod. Lib.*, microfilm, CAB 65/8, W. M. (40) 192nd Conclusions, 3 July 1940.
174) *PRO*, FO 371/24289, C 7646/2/12, Beneš to Halifax, 9 July 1940, Halifax to Beneš, 18 July 1940.

principle, there is no difference.'[175] The Czechoslovak anthem was for the first time played amongst other Allied anthems on the BBC on Sunday, 28 July 1940, after the British Council and several MPs urged the issue.[176]

The differences of form concerned mostly the titles: Strang recommended avoiding calling Beneš 'President of Czecho-Slovakia' and suggested the title 'President Benes, Head of the Czecho-Slovak Provisional Government' (which was a nonsense as it was Šrámek who became the Prime Minister) or 'the Czecho-Slovak President' (such as 'the French King') or simply 'President of the Republic'. It seems that Beneš later successfully outwitted Strang by emphasising that he was willing to avoid altogether the use of the word 'Czechoslovakia' and would call himself 'President of the Republic' or 'President of the Czechoslovak Republic' (!) or 'Czechoslovak President'.[177] In August *The Times* reported that 'The Czechoslovak President and Madame Beneš visited the King and Queen and remained to luncheon'.[178] Lockhart became 'the British representative to the Czechoslovak government' (not a Minister); his affection for 'his' Czechs is clear from the fact that despite his chronic indebtedness he was willing to risk an unfavourable Treasury reply to the question of representation allowance.[179] He soon reported that both Bechyně and Hodža accepted their nominations to the quasi-parliament and the negotiations with Jaksch, the leader of the Sudeten-German Social Democrats, were proceeding hopefully.[180] He spoke with considerable respect about some members of the new government, but pointed out the weak quality of the Slovak element. He was right in his assessment that the appointment of Masaryk and Ripka to the Foreign Ministry meant that the department would be 'under the direct control of Dr. Beneš'. 'The Government is probably as good as can be formed out of the existing material,' Lockhart concluded.[181]

---

175) *H. C. Deb.*, 5th Series, Vol. 362, 23 July 1940, Cols. 614–615; *PRO*, FO 371/24289, C 7646/2/12, Roberts' minute, 22 July 1940. Harry Hanak suggests that 'such diplomatic nuances were too much for Churchill'. Hanak, Prezident Beneš, Britové a budoucnost Československa, *op. cit.*, p. 23.

176) *H. C. Deb.*, 5th Series, Vol. 361, 23 July 1940, Cols. 1137–1138; *PRO*, FO 371/24289, C 7750/2/12.

177) *PRO*, FO 371/24289, C 7646/7/12, Strang's minutes, 19 and 25 July 1940.

178) *The Times*, 14 August 1940.

179) *PRO*, FO 371/24289, C 8267/2/12, Roberts' minute, 13 August 1940.

180) *Ibid.*, C 8159/2/12, Lockhart's memorandum, No. 57, 4 August 1940.

181) *Ibid.*, C 7973/2/12, Lockhart's memorandum, No. 54, 23 July 1940.

Conclusion

Unlike at the time of Munich and the March ides, the immediate impact of Czechoslovak matters on British foreign policy after the outbreak of war seems to be limited. On the other hand, the recognition of Beneš and his government meant in its effect a significant blow to any plans to redraw the map of Central Europe towards bigger units after the war. Some influential FO officials (Gladwyn Jebb in particular) had been seriously considering even a reestablishment of Austria-Hungary at the end of the war – a program to which Beneš represented clear anathema.[182] Indeed, he was aware of these considerations: In his ability to tell the others what they seemed to favour, he pointed out his new advocating of a federal solution for Central Europe: As he stressed to Cadogan in October 1939, he did not differ greatly from 'those in France [!] who were thinking along these lines'.[183] Similarly he earned a good deal of respect by his initial talks with the Poles during 1939–40.[184] But Beneš's primary aim was the restoration of Czechoslovakia in its pre-Munich boundaries. Regardless of any non-committal clauses about future frontiers the recognition of Beneš thus meant a great leap towards the shape of Central Europe after the war more in accordance with its inter-war structure rather than the pre-1918 one.[185]

The recognition was granted only after ten months of futile attempts and tough negotiations. It seems that Halifax, supported by Churchill, was prepared to recognise a Czech government headed by Beneš as early as on 20 September 1939. However, it was the Foreign Office who dominated Britain's foreign policies towards particular 'far-away countries' and it dissuaded its nominal chief from his intention. In various minutes and memoranda the following terms repeatedly occur: 'non--commitment', 'no encouragement', 'listen and say nothing'. The FO was seeking balance amongst various interests in and opinions about Central Europe, rather than embarking on the course which seemed most obvious from the perspective of prosecuting war – to support the natural allies. Some officials were consistent in their hostility to Beneš

---

182) *PRO*, FO 371/22899, C 17169/7/12, Jebb's minute, 24 October 1939.
183) *Ibid.*, C 17305/7/12, Cadogan's minute, 25 October 1939.
184) See e.g. *PRO*, FO 371/22899, C 17299/7/12, Roberts' minute, 26 October 1939. In the House of Commons, Butler called the initial conversations between Beneš and Sikorski 'a happy augury in the relations of these two peoples'. *H. C. Deb.*, 5th Series, Vol. 355, 30 November 1939, Col. 307.
185) I am developing this argument further in Chapter 6.

(Makins) or non-committal indifference (Strang), the attitude of others was fluctuating: Roberts who 'fully shared' O'Malley's qualms about Beneš, wrote at the same time that he was 'clearly the best of the bunch of Czech politicians' and two weeks later: 'With all his faults Dr. Benes appears to be the only experienced and really able leader among the Czech exiles.'[186]

Owen O'Malley is an example of crucial influence upon the foreign policy course of a Great Power, exerted by a plenipotentiary who, more than anything else, stresses the interests of the country where he is accredited. His influence, however, was more than balanced by Bruce Lockhart who supplied the Foreign Office with analyses based largely on information collected by the P.I.D., mostly from refugees. Indeed, it was sometimes far from objective. In its effect it supported the Czechoslovak cause.[187] For Lockhart too, the recognition of the Provisional government meant a milestone: for ten months he had worked to that end and had 'shown more restraint and perseverance than ever before' in his career. He asked himself if he might not have achieved the result more quickly if he had been more violent.[188] The answer is probably negative. Only when Britain's situation suddenly became more than critical, the Foreign Office decided to take on the Czechs. Nonetheless, Lockhart's activity, his dozens of cleverly argued memoranda, meant essentially that the recognition was looked into immediately, once the grand strategy made it possible. Those ten months of patient delivering of arguments made many officials think seriously about what they considered a bold step, unprecedented from the legal point of view. Indeed, J. W. Bruegel calls the recognition 'nothing short of a miracle'.[189]

It may seem that the Czechoslovak action in exile was extremely paralysed by internal dissension. But it was quite common also in other exile communities. An Austrian bureau in Paris for example was not recognised owing to internal troubles among the Austrian émigrés.[190] The Czechoslovak squabbles were certainly limited in comparison with

186) *PRO*, FO 371/22899, C 17236/7/12, Roberts' minute, 26 October 1939, C 17805/7//12, Roberts' minute, 8 November 1939.
187) The weekly summaries were edited in *Great Britain Foreign Office Weekly Political Intelligence Summaries*, Vol. I, Oct. 1939 – June 1940, London, Kraus International Publishers 1983 (hereafter *FO WPIS*).
188) *The Diaries of Sir Robert Bruce Lockhart 1939–1965*, 2 July 1940, p. 64.
189) Bruegel, The Recognition of the Czechoslovak Government..., *op. cit.*, p. 1.
190) *PRO*, FO 371/24291, C 1823/534/12, Roberts' minute, 21 February 1940.

the Polish governmental crisis of summer 1940, which culminated in a threat of physical violence from a number of officers from Prime Minister Sikorski's entourage to August Zaleski, unless he declined the request of President Rackiewicz to form a new government.[191] The British Minister to the Yugoslav government, George Rendel, considered intrigues among the Yugoslavs as being 'always with us' ever since that government arrived in London in June 1941, and governmental crises became more than common.[192] And a Dutch governmental crisis in late 1941 even led to considerations of penetrating the Allied governments by MI5 agents in order to learn of any 'intrigues or machinations' on the part of Allied Governments (inside and between them) 'in time to forestall their consequences'. (However, the plan was abandoned as the risks to good relations with the Allies were found as too great to be taken; the necessary information was to be obtained through ordinary diplomatic and other contacts.)[193] Beneš, after all, at some stages managed to get all his significant rivals (Prchala, Osuský, Hodža) on the track, though such temporary alliances were unstable. However 'tarnished a figure' Beneš might have been for some officials, the Foreign Office – unlike the Quai d'Orsay – was realistic enough to be aware that any attempts to outmanoeuvre him from the leadership of the Czechoslovak resistance were doomed to failure. If any recognition was to be given, it had to be to his organisation. However, it demanded a political decision, as from the legal point of view his legitimacy was more than questionable. Unlike in the case of other exile governments that sought a sanctuary in London, Beneš's claim was not based on continuity, but on a legal construction and, above all, on his real political influence underpinned by the Czechoslovak military contribution. Therefore the recognition came only at the moment, when the balance of advantage switched in favour of meeting Beneš's request.

To Beneš the ten months of the Allied hesitancy and procrastination only added salt to his Munich wounds, rather tragically for Czechoslovakia's future. And Beneš, whose position amongst Czechoslovak exiles had by then become, to say the least, dominant, was quite incapable of

191) Prażmowska, *Britain and Poland 1939–1943. The Betrayed Ally*, p. 64.
192) *PRO*, FO 371/26489, C 14162/13589/62, Rendel to Sargent, 20 December 1941; Brandes, *Großbritannien und seine osteuropäischen Allierten 1939–1943*, pp. 309–328.
193) *PRO*, FO 371/26489, C 13589/13589/62, Petrie to Cadogan, 3 December, Sargent to Petrie, 13 December 1941, C 14162/13589/62, Rendel to Sargent, 26 December 1941.

forgiving or even forgetting. For numerous Czechoslovak exiles, Britain remained the country of appeasement and 'Munich' throughout the war, and the Foreign Office a suspicious institution full of 'appeasers', allegedly conspiring even against Churchill and Eden. Even the most pro-western exiles perceived the adjective 'Provisional' as a sign that the Munich policy was still alive in Britain.[194] The 'President of the Republic' himself never really got over his 'Munich syndrome', which was only strengthened by the French hostility and British reserved attitude in the ensuing two years.[195] Now he was determined to use all his tactical skills in a 'fight' (rather than co-operation) for full recognition of his government, for revocation of Munich and its 'undoing'.

194) Feierabend, *Politické vzpomínky*, II, p. 27.
195) See e.g. *Válečné deníky Jana Opočenského*, 14 January 1943, p. 266; Feierabend, *Politické vzpomínky* II, pp. 235–237.

The legacy of Munich and the battles for history
While immediately after 15 March 1939 Beneš's tactics encompassed
not attacking Britain and France because of Munich, after Churchill's
rise to power his policy in this highly sensitive matter changed: Beneš
replaced his reserved attitude in reminding of Munich by a struggle
for its revocation.[1] Beneš was well aware that Churchill, Eden and the
leaders of the Labour Party, who occupied the positions in the new
coalition government, had opposed the 'Munich policy'. Indeed, they
themselves were aware that they owed much of their current reputation to that fact. Churchill and Eden, despite their undeniable effort
to build a national unity, were inclined to think of the divisions inside
the Conservative Party as of 'us' and 'them' along the 'Munich lines'.[2]
At critical junctions, such as the discussion whether 'to continue alone'
in mid-1940, Churchill did not hesitate to remind his colleagues of
his own 'lesson from Munich', however painful it must have been for
Chamberlain and Halifax.[3] Correspondingly, for one critical year he

1) In view of the evidence that I am submitting in this sub-chapter, one really wonders
about the following conclusion that Martin Brown reached in his book: 'Although the
spectre of the Munich Agreement had haunted Anglo-Czechoslovak relations ever since
its enactment, Beneš and his government had so far avoided any reference to this episode
and continued to do so until 1942 when they pressed for its revocation.' And the reason:
'...because this was such an emotive subject.' Brown, *Dealing with Democrats*, p. 137.
This statement is in my view utterly unfounded and unsustainable.
2) *Birmingham University Library*, Avon papers, AP 20/1/21, diary entry for 5 September
1941.
3) On 28 May, at the Cabinet meeting Churchill opposed Reynaud's apparent attempt to
get Britain to the conference table and end the war: 'If we once got to the table we should
then find that the terms offered us touched our independence and integrity. When, at
this point, we got up to leave the conference-table, we should find that all the forces of
resolution which were now at our disposal would have vanished.' Christopher Hill comments: 'The echo of Munich must have been painfully evident to Chamberlain, sitting at
the same table.' Hill, *Cabinet Decisions on Foreign Policy*, pp. 163, 315.

let Duff Cooper head the Ministry of Information, though he knew that 'Duff' was not 'the man for the job' and his activity caused much confusion. The reason was that 'nation owed much to Duff for his resignation at Munich'.[4]

Similarly the atmosphere in British public favoured Beneš's efforts. The pamphlet *Guilty Men*, written by three London journalists in the spring and distributed in July 1940, looked for the culprits of recent British war débâcle on the Continent and was above all imbued with contempt for Neville Chamberlain's appeasement policy. It was reprinted 22 times before October 1940 and the overall edition exceeded 217 thousand copies.[5] Eden thought that the future of the Tory Party would depend on getting young men into seats before the election. The reason was simple: 'No one could vote for men of Munich.'[6]

In September 1940 Beneš succeeded in obtaining the first important declaration on the topic of Munich from the British government. It was made by Winston Churchill in a BBC broadcast on the occasion of the second anniversary of the Munich conference. Beneš himself submitted a draft of a statement that might be made by Lord Halifax or the Prime Minister. Beneš's tedious historical account culminated in the key formulation that the 'so called Munich agreement no longer exists' and nobody could be bound by it. The Central Department saw in a statement 'the best way out of an awkward dilemma', although its officials agreed that the draft would not do and asked Bruce Lockhart to write a new one. Beneš again tried to implement a sentence to the effect that the broken pledge 'fully releases all parties to the Pact'. Roberts refused this in a telephone talk with Lockhart: 'Although we might no longer recognise this [German] acquisition [of Sudetenland], it was quite another thing to state that we did not recognise it, thus in fact implying that our object was the re-incorporation of the Sudetenland in a future Czechoslovak State,' Roberts reflected British non-committal attitude to the future shape of Central Europe. It seems from Roberts' words that the FO officials did not realise the sensitivity of the whole issue for all the Czechs, when he

4) *Birmingham University Library*, Avon papers, AP 20/1/21, diary entry for 27 May 1941.
5) Aster, Sidney, 'Guilty Men': The Case of Neville Chamberlain, In: *Paths to War. New Essays on the Origins of the Second World War*, eds. R. Boyce and E. M. Robertson, London, Macmillan 1989, pp. 233–268, here p. 234.
6) *Birmingham University Library*, Avon papers, AP 20/1/21, diary entry for 5 September 1941.

expressed his doubts 'that the Czechs at home were vitally interested in this problem at the moment, since their main object must [be] to free themselves from German domination'. He recommended restricting the broadcast to 'vaguer generalities'. Eventually Makins fiercely repelled this attempt ('It is not for Dr Benes to dictate the words of the S[ecretary] of S[tate].')[7]. Although at one moment Beneš told Lockhart that without a sentence to that effect it would be better not to broadcast at all,[8] he consoled himself with the fact that it was the Prime Minister who eventually sponsored the Czech broadcast and that he publicly presented 'the restoration of Czechoslovak liberties' as one of Britain's 'principal war aims'. At Masaryk's insistence the crucial sentence that the solemn pledges (of Munich) had been within six months ruthlessly broken was eventually supplemented by an important amendment: '...and the agreement destroyed'. At the same time the Czechoslovak government was reminded that by including these words the British had gone as far as they could.[9]

But this was not enough for many Czechoslovak politicians. When Feierabend proposed to thank the Prime Minister, his colleagues in the ministerial council refused.[10] At the same time, however, many exiles tried to attribute to Churchill's statement much broader meaning. The Central Department pointed out in a despatch to Washington this tendency of 'the Czechs here ... to read into it rather more than was actually said'.[11] Typical was a commentary 'Two Years after Munich' that accompanied full transcription of the statement in *The Central European Observer*, a fortnightly review published by the Czechoslovak government. It stated that from the destruction of 'Munich' it followed that neither Great Britain nor Czechoslovakia were any longer bound by it and that Churchill showed clearly that he regarded it as 'null and void'.[12] Ironically, although such statements and commentaries, often

7) *PRO*, FO 371/24292, C 10410/10410/12, Beneš's draft, Roberts' minutes, 20 and 24 September, Strang's minute, 22 September, Cadogan's minute, 23 September, Makins' minute, 24 September 1940.
8) *HLRO*, Bruce Lockhart papers, diary No. 34, 25 September 1940.
9) *PRO*, FO 371/24292, C 10410/10410/12, Churchill to Halifax, 26 September, Lockhart's draft, Strang to Masaryk, 28 September 1940.
10) *Válečné deníky Jana Opočenského*, 7 October 1940, p. 44; Feierabend, *Politické vzpomínky* II, p. 98.
11) *PRO*, FO 371/24292, C 10410/10410/12, Central Department to British Embassy, Washington, 5 October 1940.
12) *The Central European Observer*, 1 October 1940.

made by Czechoslovak representatives, followed the logic of what the Prime Minister had said, they brought the whole Czechoslovak action abroad into a precarious situation two years later when the British government finally said exactly this – that Munich was null and void.[13] Beneš himself was clearly trying to extract more from the British when he addressed a letter on that topic to Lockhart: Referring to a view from 'one political quarter' (Štefan Osuský)[14] he condemned its point that 'Mr. Churchill has intentionally avoided speeking [sic] about the restauration of the Czechoslovak Republic. ... To distinguish between the restauration of the Czechoslovak Republic and the restauration of Czechoslovak liberties seems to me to be quite meaningless.'[15] At the same time Lockhart was reporting to the Foreign Office that Beneš was 'obsessed with the belief' that the refusal of the British government to commit itself to the restoration of Czechoslovakia's former frontiers in fact implied 'Britain's adherence to the Munich line of 1938'.[16] Thus Lockhart's response, based on the previous instructions from the Foreign Office,[17] apparently aimed both to calm down the Czechoslovak exiles and at the same time to put an end to their attempts to commit Britain to a concrete form of post-war settlement: Churchill simply stated that the Munich Agreement had been destroyed, 'and any further elucidation or interpretation of this remark would be profitless'. Referring to Halifax's statement of 21 July 1940 about Britain's non-commitment to any particular frontiers in Central Europe, the letter explained that it

13) See chapter 6.
14) *HIA Stanford*, Eduard Táborský collection, box 8, envelope Documents concerning Štefan Osuský, Osuský's letter to Beneš, 3 October 1940, a handwritten comment on Lockhart's letter of 11 November 1940. See also Kuklík – Němeček, *Proti Benešovi!*, p. 113. However, the authors incorrectly date Osuský's letter as of 7 November 1940.
15) *AÚTGM*, EB-L, box 110, Beneš's letter to Lockhart, 10 October 1940. Anthony Polonsky says that the statement from 'one political quarter' only reflected previous Churchill's assurance in the House of Commons of 5 September – echoing the First World War experience and directed both to the British public and the U.S. government – that Britain had not made any commitment to post-war borders. Polonsky, Anthony, *The Great Powers and the Polish Question, 1941–1945. A Documentary Study in Cold War Origins*, London, LSE 1976, p. 77. However, Osuský unambiguously referred to Churchill's broadcast of 30 September 1940. *HIA Stanford*, Eduard Táborský collection, box 8, envelope Documents concerning Štefan Osuský, Osuský's letter to Beneš, 3 October 1940, Beneš's memorandum on Osuský's letter, undated.
16) *PRO*, FO 371/24287, C 10776/2/12, Lockhart to Halifax, 7 October 1940.
17) *PRO*, FO 371/24290, C 11069/2/12, Makins to Lockhart, 31 October 1940. Lockhart, however, 'slightly toned down' FO's instruction. FO 371/26389, C 11137/235/12, Roberts' minute, 10 November 1941.

'was intended to refer to all and any frontiers, including, of course, the so-called Munich line'.[18]

It is clear from British documents that Churchill's statement itself was not Prime Minister's initiative undertaken regardless of Foreign Office's hesitancy, or even against its will, as some historians claim in their futile effort to depict a fundamental dichotomy between Churchill and Eden on the one hand and the 'appeasers' in the Foreign Office on the other.[19] British policy was consistent enough in its reluctance, at least in the initial stage of the war, to commit itself to support any concrete shape of Continental frontiers before the end of the war. Even the Labour ministers repeatedly stressed in their talks with Czechoslovak exiles that it was too early to launch any discussions on the concrete war aims.[20]

The battle for history between Beneš and the appeasers took place also on the level of political propaganda and guilt for the inglorious end of Czechoslovakia. Throughout 1941 Beneš was writing a book called *The Fall and Rise of a Nation*, a story of Czechoslovakia's road from total destruction back to respectable position amongst the allies (1938–1941). In his foreword he intended to give credit to Bruce Lockhart, but also to some FO experts, namely Strang (!), Sargent and Roberts. No matter how much sincere Beneš was in these acknowledgements Lockhart knew that the text would have to be changed, as the Foreign Office disliked mentions of its officials in texts written by politicians.[21] What Lockhart, however, could not know, was the very fact that by the end of 1941 it would rest upon him to persuade Beneš not to publish his book at all. In the autumn of 1941 Beneš sent his text to the Foreign Office. Although Lockhart highlighted this fact as a sign of President's good will, this was also the only positive aspect of the whole matter found by experts in the centre of British diplomacy. Roberts and Makins put together dozens of concrete reservations. Sir Llewellyn Woodward, FO's historian and archivist, added others, stressing at the same time that the book was unbalanced, both in its content and style, and sometimes extremely

18) *AÚTGM*, EB-L, box 110, Lockhart's letter to Beneš, 11 November 1940; Beneš, *Paměti*, p. 297.
19) See e.g. Dockrill, The Foreign Office, Dr Eduard Benes..., *op. cit.*, p. 710.
20) *Archiv Ministerstva zahraničních věcí ČR* [Archive of the Foreign Ministry of the Czech Republic], Praha (hereafter *AMZV*), fund Londýnský archiv – důvěrný [London Archive – Confidential] (hereafter LA-D), box 61, 180,243/dův/40, G. Winter's records of his talks with H. Dalton and C. Attlee, 4 and 12 October 1940.
21) *HLRO*, Bruce Lockhart papers, diary No. 38, 3 May 1941.

exalted. As such it could hardly add to Beneš's reputation; it was written above all *ad majorem gloriam auctoris*, it did not provide the reader with any space for his or her own judgment, and sometimes it even distorted facts. 'I wish M. Benes could spare a couple of days to read Thukydides,' historian Woodward dreamt.[22] But Beneš was a politician, and a very pragmatic one: While towards Britain the text was quite tolerant, it was very critical of France, highly apologetic about the United States and most cordial towards Russia – including all the references to the period of the Soviet-German co-operation in 1939–41. 'The book is lacking in dignity,' William Strang minuted. 'There is a moving and inspiring story to be told about the recent history of Czechoslovakia, but this book does not tell it. Instead, there are repeated boasts by President Benes that he foresaw and foretold everything long before anyone else; there is fawning condonation of Soviet policy between August 1931 and June 1941; he plays up to the United States and occasionally misinterprets and tampers with our documents.'

The Central Department proposed to ask Beneš to check the text, page by page, with Woodward. Fearing that this would mean implicit sharing of responsibility for the resulting publication, however, the key officials eventually decided against this idea.[23] Instead, Beneš was to be discouraged from publishing the book, at least for the time being. This unenviable task fell on Lockhart who was considered one of a few persons with a real influence on Beneš. Even in this difficult matter he succeeded: After a two-hour conversation in Beneš's country residence in Aston Abbotts the President promised to postpone publication and, indeed, not to publish at all until he had agreed a date with the British.[24] Nevertheless, he was stricken and suspicious.[25] In discussing old

22) *PRO*, FO 371/26388, C 13503/216/12, Minutes by Roberts, Makins and Woodward, 1–9 October 1941, Lockhart's minute, 3 November 1941.
23) *Ibid.*, minutes by Strang, Cadogan, Eden and Law, 14–29 October 1941.
24) *HLRO*, Bruce Lockhart papers, diary No. 38, 11 November 1941. According to Beneš's own record, however, he undertook only to postpone the publication. Before that he would negotiate with Eden the frontier question and a general formula that would set up 'the principle of historical and natural border and revision with Hungary'. Then the term of formulation would come on the agenda. *AÚTGM*, EB-L, box 110, Beneš's record of his talks with Lockhart, 15 and 21 November 1941.
25) Substantial parts of the book later appeared in Beneš's wartime memoirs. 'The Fall and Rise' was eventually published 63 years later thanks to the care of Milan Hauner. See Beneš, Edvard, *The Fall and Rise of a Nation: Czechoslovakia 1938–1941*, ed. Milan Hauner, New York, Columbia University Press 2004. However, the editor's comment in

controversies, he made one 'good point', as Lockhart, often in a similar frame of mind as Beneš, noted: 'If Hitler had not attacked Poland and pushed us into the war, there would have been no Czechoslovakia. It would have disappeared, and we should have acquiesced.'[26] However contentious this 'virtual history' may be, it meaningfully reflects Beneš's view of Britain, upon which he based the formulation of his foreign policy.[27]

The shadows of the past also projected into fears of the future British political course, especially the fears of a compromise peace with Germany. Beneš was scared by certain conciliatory articles by some journalists (W. H. Dawson, G. Glasgow). Lockhart, who shared Beneš's worries and often even his broader political opinions, commented: 'Obviously there are many hidden appeasers in this country. They will not show their hand to-day, but later who knows?' He expected three peace moves by Hitler: One very soon and very extravagant in claims for Germany. That would be rejected out of hand. Another one made with very considerable concessions at the moment of near collapse. That would also be rejected because the British would know they were winning. Finally, one peace offer would come in a between stage when Hitler would offer to evacuate Western Europe if only he could keep his gains in Central Europe. 'This will be dangerous, for it will appeal to many Conservatives and if Hitler keeps all Central Europe he is master of all Europe and Germany wins the war and the peace.'[28] It is necessary to say that also the experts of the exile foreign ministry provided Beneš and Ripka with frequent reports on upcoming peace negotiations between Britain and Germany, the beginning of which was allegedly supported by a wide spectrum of British officials – ranging from financial experts in the City to Secretary of State for War David

his own review (!) of the book written for the leading Czech historical journal *Soudobé dějiny* is slightly surprising: 'The book was not published at the end, since it met with a fundamental criticism of the British Foreign Office that considered a temporary cession of Sudetenland, Slovakia (not to speak about Sub-Carpathian Russia) from the Czech lands as more acceptable a solution for quiet and peace in Central Europe where Britain did not want to be engaged even in the future.' See *Soudobé dějiny* [Contemporary history], Vol. XI, 2004, No. 1–2, p. 307. I do not think such an interpretation of the Foreign Office's attitude is acceptable in view of the relevant documentation.

26) *HLRO*, Bruce Lockhart papers, diary No. 38, 11 November 1941.
27) For further details see Smetana, Ozvěny Mnichova v zahraničněpolitických jednáních za 2. světové války, *op. cit.*, pp. 145–163.
28) *HLRO*, Bruce Lockhart papers, diary No. 38, 5 April 1941.

Margesson. Thus, 'new waves' of appeasement and pacifism in Britain were repeatedly detected.[29]

Beneš was in this connection very much frightened of the sudden flight by Rudolf Hess to Britain, followed by the 'hysteria', especially by an attempt to play him up as a great idealist, and also 'by the signs of appeasement in the Times' leader'. According to Lockhart, Beneš 'always fears – and fears rightly – the possibility of a compromise peace between England and Germany which would sacrifice Poles and Czechs.'[30] Of course, such fears were – at least under Churchill's premiership – unfounded and hardly justified. Nonetheless, Beneš had the experience of Munich and of numerous not entirely pleasant negotiations with British officials in the ensuing period. It is only paradoxical that he had correct reports on the origins of Hess's mission – that he was lured to Britain by the British Intelligence Service that had corresponded with him in the name of the Duke of Hamilton.[31] However, Beneš was rather inclined to attribute to the mysterious flight by the Führer's deputy the most conspiratorial explanations concerning the overall course of British foreign policy. He was not alone. On the opposite side of Europe, behind the Kremlin walls, the Soviet leaders saw in it an attempt on the part of the Nazi leadership to make a compromise peace with England and replace – allegedly in spite of Hitler's will – the policy of lasting friendship with Moscow by a military conflict. British warnings against concentration of German units in eastern Poland were then viewed in this context – either as a symptom of British participation in such a conspiracy, or at least as an effort to get the Soviet Union into war with Germany and then withdraw from the conflict altogether.[32] Also Beneš was afraid of Hitler's 'second' plan: containing more conquests in the East, no provocation of the U.S.A.,

29) *NA Praha*, fund Archiv Huberta Ripky (hereafter AHR), box 147, 1-3-2-1, 1608/dův/41, 2140/dův/41, Ducháček's reports of 5 June and 18 July 1941; *HIA Stanford*, Ivo Ducháček collection, box 1, diary entry for 2-7 June 1941; *Válečné deníky Jana Opočenského*, 21 May 1940, p. 117.
30) *HLRO*, Bruce Lockhart papers, diary No. 38, 14 May 1941.
31) *HIA Stanford*, Eduard Táborský collection, box 6, envelope Czechoslovak-British relations 1939–45, A strictly confidential report from a British military source, undated. The following two books provide similar explanations of the Hess riddle: Harris, John – Trow, M.J., *Hess: The British Conspiracy*, London, André Deutsch 1999; Allen, Martin, *The Hitler/Hess Deception*, London, HarperCollins 2003.
32) Gorodetsky, Gabriel, *Grand Delusion*, esp. pp. 267–274.

followed by a peace-offer giving back Western Europe but retaining all of Central Europe and the Balkans.[33]

It is evident that through this perception of Great Britain Beneš and his collaborators remained prisoners of 'Munich'. Any British military effort could hardly change this fact. Nor did the British representative with the Provisional Government do much to allay President's doubts about Britain's determination. On the contrary, his diaries show that Lockhart sometimes more than silently assented to Beneš's suspicions.

Establishing the governing structures in exile

In the second half of 1940 the Czechoslovak provisional government aimed to establish its own institutional framework. The President issued his first two decrees whereby a) the Czechoslovak State Council was set up as a consultative body of about 40 members, and b) the President was allowed to exercise legislative powers with the approval of the government.[34] For numerous reasons (the position of the Sudeten Germans etc.) the Foreign Office was afraid of Beneš and his government indulging in legislative authority in Britain. However, Beneš placated these worries by explanation that in fact he wanted to prevent the State Council embarking on legislation itself and that he only proposed to issue the essential minimum of decrees dealing with current business connected with the army etc., since he was 'fully aware of the dangers of legislative activity by a provisional emigré government'.[35] The State Council for the first time met on 11 December and the meeting was preceded by an exchange of letters between Beneš and Hodža, in which the latter called Beneš 'Mr. President' and assured him that there was nothing that stood in the way of his active participation in the State Council. Bruce Lockhart was happy about this proof of unity finally achieved amongst the Czechoslovak exiles and hurried to send English translations of the letters to the Foreign Office.[36] However, Hodža never really turned up at a State Council meeting.[37]

---

33) *HLRO*, Bruce Lockhart papers, diary No. 38, 31 May 1941.

34) *Dekrety prezidenta republiky 1940–1945. Dokumenty I* [Decrees of the President of the Republic 1940–1945. Documents I], eds. K. Jech and K. Kaplan, Brno, Doplněk 1995, No. 1–2, pp. 81–94. For further details see Kuklík, *Londýnský exil a obnova československého státu za druhé světové války*, pp. 41–69.

35) *PRO*, FO 371/24290, C 12210/2/12, Roberts' minutes, 11 November 1940.

36) *Ibid.*, C 13413/2/12, Lockhart to Halifax, No. 38, 12 December 1940, C 12111/2/12, Beneš to Hodža, 31 October, Hodža to Beneš, 2 November 1940.

37) Kuklík – Němeček, *Hodža versus Beneš*, pp. 129–130, 135–137.

The Provisional government achieved several remarkable successes on the international scene and in particular relation to the British hosts. Four months of negotiations with British authorities resulted in a British-Czechoslovak agreement concerning Czechoslovak Armed Forces. The land forces were to be completed by the mobilisation of Czechoslovak citizens living in the United Kingdom[38] and by drafting of volunteers, while the Czechoslovak air units were to be composed of personnel selected for service by a joint board composed of British and Czechoslovak representatives. Both the land forces and the air units were to be organised and employed under the British command, in its character as the Allied High Command. However, while the land forces were to be involved as one army and commanded by Czechoslovak officers, the Czechoslovak squadrons were incorporated in the RAF separately and, for practical reasons, the posts of squadron leaders were doubled in the first instance by British commanders.[39] These clauses only codified the already existing situation; two Czechoslovak fighter squadrons distinguished themselves in the battle of Britain and so did dozens of other airmen serving in British or Polish squadrons.[40] Indeed, British politicians regarded them as the best Czechoslovak propaganda.[41]

British opinion about the Czechoslovak land forces was more ambivalent and diversified. At the time of their transfer from France Anthony Eden uttered that he 'would much prefer to embark Polish troops'.[42] General John Dill, the Chief of the Imperial General Staff, similarly stressed the good quality of the Polish troops while on the account of their Czechoslovak counterparts he said that these 'were not of such high quality and would have to be carefully sorted out before rearming'.

38) However, the British were careful not to give Beneš and his collaborators a promise that they would assist to enforce compulsory military service in Britain. FO 371/24378, C 12081/12081/62, Ward's memorandum Conscription of Czechoslovaks in the United Kingdom, 7 November 1940.
39) *AMZV*, LA-D, box 180; *PRO*, FO 371/24368, C11579/1419/62, Text of British-Czechoslovak Agreement Concerning Czechoslovak Armed Forces, 25 October 1940.
40) In 1942–43, Beneš decided to press the British to grant independence to the air force. But this attempt did not succeed, as it was clear absurdity to grant such a small force any form of independent status. Indeed, it only irritated the Air Ministry and gave rise to notorious sentiments: 'Perhaps we have been too kind to the Czechs, but then we would have had Munich thrown in our face'. Cited from: Brown, The Czechoslovak Armed Forces in Britain, 1940–1945, *op. cit.*, pp. 176–178.
41) See e.g. *AMZV*, LA-D, box 61, G. Winter's record of his talk with H. Dalton, 4 October 1940.
42) *Bod. Lib.*, microfilm, CAB 65/7, W. M. (40) 172nd Conclusions, 19 June 1940.

He added prophetically: 'The ultimate disposal of unsuitable elements might prove difficult.'[43] Indeed, over 500 hundred soldiers, more than one seventh of the whole Czechoslovak unit, proved to be unsuitable as early as at the end of July due to their disobedience and waging of communist agitation against the war; they had to be interned by the British authorities.[44] Of course, newspapers did not ignore this crisis that shed peculiar light on Czechoslovakia's determination to take part in the deadly conflagration.[45] Bruce Lockhart visited the brigade in January 194 nd although he also noticed 'some splendid types of Slav manhood' amongst the soldiers, at the same time he reported of 'a considerable percentage of bespectacled intellectuals on whose frame the modern British battle-dress ... hung clumsily'.[46] On the other hand, the Special Operations Executive (SOE), an organisation set up in 1940 within the Ministry of Economic Warfare to instigate and support resistance in occupied Europe,[47] regarded the soldiers chosen from the brigade for conducting special operations on the Continent as belonging 'among the best of all SOE trainees' and appreciated their 'keenness, discipline, intelligence and courage'.[48] Despite occasional criticism of situation in the Czechoslovak brigade voiced by British officers,[49] it seems that the British were increasingly grateful for every contribution to their own war effort, however limited it was. Apart from the airmen, this applied primarily to the Czechoslovak battalion that helped the other Allies defend the besieged Tobruk in late 1941.[50] Correspondingly, the British led secret negotiations with the Soviet authorities in early 1941 on the

43) *Ibid.*, W. M. (40) 181st Conclusions, 26 June 1940.
44) Eduard Čejka writes about 539 soldiers while General Ingr referred in the Ministerial Council to 516 soldiers and 4 officers who refused obedience to the Czechoslovak authorities. See Čejka, *Československý odboj na Západě (1939-1945)*, pp. 234-235; Feierabend, *Politické vzpomínky* II, pp. 53-61, esp. 57, see also three testimonies written by eye-witnesses of those events on pp. 294-311.
45) See *HIA Stanford*, Eduard Táborský collection, box 6, envelope Czechoslovak-British relations 1939-45, A note of British feelings regarding Czechoslovakia, undated.
46) *PRO*, FO 371/26376, C 1132/6/12, Lockhart to Eden, 31 January 1941.
47) See Mackenzie, William J. M., *The Secret History of SOE: The Special Operations Executive*, London, St Ermin's 2000; Stafford, David, *Britain and European Resistance 1940-1945*, London, St. Antony's College (Oxford) – Macmillan 1983; Foot, M. R. D., *SOE. The Special Operations Executive 1940-1946*, 2nd edition, London, Pimlico 1999.
48) *PRO*, HS 7/108, 'SOE Country History, Czechoslovakia 1940-45', p. 7.
49) *DHČSP*, No. 192, pp. 232-234, Smutný's record of his talk with major Fillingham of the British military mission, 22 June 1941.
50) Čejka, *Československý odboj na Západě (1939-1945)*, pp. 327-338.

movements of Czechoslovak soldiers detained in the Soviet Union ever since Poland's fall to the Middle East. With the personal authorisation by the Prime Minister, payments for their transfers to Odessa were made directly to Gosbank in Moscow.[51] This very unusual and highly secret case of Anglo-Soviet co-operation enabled almost 500 Czechoslovak soldiers to be escorted in 8 transports to Palestine by early June 1941.[52]

The military agreement of November 1940 had also significant political repercussions as it influenced the position of the Sudeten-German democrats. Wenzel Jaksch, who was recognised by the Foreign Office merely as a 'President of the Sudeten German Social Democratic Party',[53] complained to Makins that the Sudeten Germans were no longer accepted into the British army unless the Czech authorities waived all claim to them. Makins assured Jaksch that the British government had done nothing to prejudice the position of the Sudeten Germans and that Jaksch's followers would no doubt be accepted, if suitable, in the R.A.F. 'Herr Jaksch clearly hoped that the option which his followers had enjoyed of joining the British army would be restored, but I held out no hope that this could be done.'[54] This change led to a numerical rise of the German-speaking members of the Czechoslovak army, reaching a tenth in 1942. Further, it worsened Jaksch's position in his long-drawn negotiations with Beneš about the Sudeten-German representation in the Czechoslovak state institutions.[55]

51) *PRO*, FO 371/26377-26379. Martin Brown first pointed out these negotiations. See also the brief reference to the troop movements in R. W. Seton-Watson published papers. Brown, *Dealing with Democrats*, pp. 156–157; *R. W. Seton-Watson and His Relations with the Czechs and Slovaks, Documents 1906–1951*, eds. J. Rychlík – T. Marzik – M. Bielik, 2 Vols., Praha – Martin, Ústav T. G. Masaryka and Matica Slovenská 1995, pp. 592–593.

52) Gebhart, Jan – Kuklík, Jan, *Velké dějiny zemí Koruny české XVa, 1938–1941* [The history of the lands of the Czech Crown – the big series], Praha, Paseka 2006, pp. 440–441.

53) In his reasoning why Jaksch's claim to be the accredited representative of 'the democratic forces in the Sudetenland' should be refused Roberts pointed out that his party polled four times less than Henlein's Sudeten German Party and only twice as much as the German Christian Socialists in the last pre-war elections. Jaksch did not pursue his claim further. *PRO*, FO 371/24291, C 1823/534/12, Jaksch to Makins, 1 February 1940, Roberts' minute, 21 February 1940, Makins to Jaksch, 29 February 1940.

54) *Ibid.*, C 11680/534/12, Makins' minute, 29 October 1940.

55) Brandes, *Cesta k vyhnání 1938–1945. Plány a rozhodnutí o „transferu" Němců z Československa a z Polska*, p. 69. For further details on the issue of the service of the Sudeten Germans in the Czechoslovak army see also: Raška, *The Czechoslovak Exile Government in London and the Sudeten German Issue*, Prague, pp. 89–94, 156–159; Idem, Edvard Beneš a otázka služby sudetoněmeckých antifašistů v československé armádě za druhé

On 10 December 1940, a British-Czechoslovak financial agreement was signed whereby the first credit of 7.5 million pounds was provided for the Czechoslovak provisional government to meet its military and other expenses.[56] At the same time those 26,793 kg of gold that had been blocked in the Bank of England with the direct account of the National Bank of Czechoslovakia ever since 15 March 1939, and its value was now reaching around 7.5 million pounds, were given to the government of the United Kingdom for the support of Allied war effort. The Treasury had by then refused vigorously the argument voiced by the Czechoslovak Minister of Finance Eduard Outrata that the gold should be preserved for post-war reconstruction of Czechoslovakia: unless all the Allies were willing to offer all their resources including gold as well as lives of soldiers and airmen for the common cause, there would not be anything to reconstruct after the war.[57]

These achievements in practical matters were followed by notable successes in the field of public relations. Czechoslovakia, its exiles and soldiers became fairly frequented topics in British newspapers; a few articles or at least references daily became standard, but a dozen or more were not exceptional.[58] 28 October, the Independence Day, was marked not only by Beneš's broadcast to the people of Czechoslovakia[59] and a mass at St. James's, Spanish Place where Lockhart with two representatives of the War Office, Norwegian chargé d'affaires and four Polish

světové války [Edvard Beneš and the question of the service of the Sudeten-German antifascists in the Czechoslovak army during the Second World War], In: *Na pozvání Masarykova ústavu* [At the invitation of The Masaryk Institute], Prague, Masarykův ústav AV ČR 2004, pp. 65–72.

56) It was to be followed by another two credits in 1942 and 1944.

57) *BEA*, OV 4/101, Waterfield to Cobbold, 14 September 1940; *PRO*, FO 371/24292, C 10783/8893/12, Kingsley Wood to Halifax, 9 October 1940, C13060/8893/12, Text of British-Czechoslovak Financial and Military agreement, 12 December 1940. See also Feierabend, *Politické vzpomínky*, II, enclosure 2/2, pp. 292–294. For further details see Smetana, *Nevyřízené účty*, *op. cit.*, p. 546.

58) The Czechoslovak Foreign Ministry closely watched these press reports. In February 1941, for example, the British press, both national and local, published 15,686 lines about Czechoslovakia. *NA Praha*, AHR, box 145, 1-13-4-1, Přehled československého ohlasu v britském tisku [Survey of Czechoslovak echoes in British press].

59) Interestingly enough, Beneš in his broadcast in the evening of 27 October presented amongst other things a rather 'revisionist' – in terms of post-war historiography – explanation of the events leading to the Munich Agreement: 'France, Britain, and of course all the others were unprepared. The events of the war have given sufficient proof of this. That is why we remained alone in 1938; that is why Munich took place.' *The Central European Observer*, 1 November 1940.

ministers were present, but also by appropriate share of the BBC air for 48 hours and adequately generous space of London newspapers. Canada honoured the day by extending formal recognition to the Provisional Government,[60] as the last of the Dominions, soon to be followed by Belgium and the Netherlands.[61] In January 1941 Anthony Eden, the newly appointed Secretary of State for Foreign Affairs, opened the Czechoslovak Institute in London, in a building offered by the British Council.[62] It was hoped to become a cynosure for the Czechoslovak community, numbering fifteen thousand, as well as a place where the British people would have opportunities to learn of the people of Czechoslovakia and vice versa. Eden, the anti-appeaser, did not fail to mention in his opening speech the recent Czechoslovak tragic sacrifice, which was in vain, and therefore humanity was in debt of the people of Czechoslovakia: 'Dr. Benes, in the long struggle for freedom no people has a finer record than yours.' The speech did not bear any trace of traditional British nostalgia for the Habsburg Empire: The Foreign Secretary drew a parallel between the 300 years of foreign rule before 1918 and the current foreign tyranny, but assured his Czechoslovak listeners that this time they would not have to wait for the liberation so long.[63]

The British treated the Czechoslovak provisional government the same way as they did the other Allied governments – apart from full diplomatic representation. The heads of states, the members of governments and the senior members of official staffs, including Czechoslovaks, as well as their wives and children enjoyed the same immunities and privileges as the heads of diplomatic missions to the United Kingdom. These included additional rations 'for entertainment purposes' (three times the size of an ordinary ration) or extra allowance of petrol for private motor vehicles. All Allied governmental officials were exempted from the paying income tax on their salaries as well as on income from British government securities (several specific war loans and bonds). British courts were to refuse to consider any suit against an Allied government without that govern-

60) *PRO*, FO 371/24290, C 11819/2/12, Lockhart to Halifax, No. 25, 31 October 1940.
61) *AMZV*, LA-D, box 129; *PRO*, FO 371/24289, C 11094/2/12, Dominions Office to Cadogan, 16 October 1944, Roberts' minute, 22 October 1940; Kuklík, The Recognition of the Czechoslovak Government..., *op. cit.*, p. 186.
62) The seat of the Institute was at 18 Grosvenor Place.
63) *AÚTGM*, EB-L, box 111, Anthony Eden's speech, 21 January 1941. Eden himself had an opportunity to feel at once how difficult this learning of the others might be; twice he had to ask the audience not to fire while he was speaking...

ment's consent and governmental buildings and premises used for official purposes were proclaimed as inviolable.[64] However, occasional Foreign Office circulars pointing out to other departments that Allied governments should be treated as Allies and not merely as foreigners ('simply as "damned foreigners"' in Makins' words) suggest that not everything worked smoothly when it came down to everyday business.[65]

The thorny way to full recognition – stage 1

Despite all the apparent progress the Czechoslovak provisional government was not legally recognised as the successor of former Czechoslovak governments in Prague before March 1939,[66] not to speak of being considered as the direct successor of pre-Munich governments. Beneš and his colleagues were determined to change this unsatisfactory situation, as Lockhart repeatedly warned the Foreign Office.[67] An impulse to Czechoslovak complaints about this 'highly illogical position' came in February when the U.S. government appointed Anthony Drexel Biddle Minister Plenipotentiary to the Dutch, Belgian and Norwegian governments, but not the Czechoslovak one. Beneš complained to Lockhart that if British attitude did not alter, nobody would be willing to go beyond the current position. This was confirmed by Polish procrastination in nominating a Minister to the Czechoslovak provisional government.[68]

An ideal opportunity arose at lunch with Anthony Eden. The more so, that the participants apparently got into a good mood after an excellent menu with oysters, sherry and claret. Eden listened with interest to Beneš's detailed exposition of the situation in the Balkans, made numerous notes and from time to time commented: 'I would not agree with you more.' He obliged to meet Beneš regularly and set up for him a lunch with the Prime Minister. At this opportune moment Masaryk went on an offensive: American attitude resulted from British recognition of

64) *PRO*, FO 371/26431, C 7238/84/62, Halifax's note to Allied diplomatic representatives, 19 December 1940.
65) *PRO*, FO 371/26463, C 1536/1536/62, Makins' minute, 11 February, circular letter signed by Cadogan, 19 February 1941.
66) *PRO*, FO 371/24292, C 10851/8893/12, Warr's minute, 21 October 1940, Roberts' minute, 23 October 1940.
67) *PRO*, FO 371/24289, C 9653/2/12 Lockhart to Halifax, 5 September 1940; FO 371/24290, C 11819/2/12 Lockhart's minute, 31 October 1940.
68) *HLRO*, Bruce Lockhart papers, diary No. 38, 8 February 1941. For further details see Chapter 6.

mere *provisional* Czechoslovak government and the fact that Britain had no Minister with the Czechs, only 'agent'. Other countries naturally followed British example, namely the Poles. Eden expressed surprise and promised to look into the matter at once. When Beneš referred to 'legal experts' who made difficulties, Eden retorted: 'Oh, I can deal with Malkin – a very good fellow. He can find a legal justification for almost anything I put up.'[69]

However, when Eden passed the matter on to his departmental experts, they, namely Roberts and Makins, expressed themselves against any change of status of the Czechoslovak government. (And Lockhart, apparently for tactical reasons, once again pretended that he agreed with his FO colleagues.) In their view the Czechs were treated 'very handsomely' and suffered only 'technical disabilities' such as the absence of full representation.[70] Until the 'entirely patriotic' Hácha's government in Prague, which was 'able to carry out an effective passive resistance to the Germans', had been disposed of,[71] Dr. Beneš's one in London was to remain purely a provisional administration. Makins doubted that the Americans would follow British lead anyway. Once again a statement that Beneš had made in a different situation, this time of 9 July 1940, was quoted against his current interests: 'In view of the fact that the free Czecho-Slovak nation will decide itself freely on all the steps necessary for the reconstitution of the final State organisation when the

---

69) *HLRO*, Bruce Lockhart papers, diary No. 38, 10 February 1941. Beneš's own record mentions briefly legal aspects of the provisional status and his promise to submit a memorandum. *AÚTGM*, EB-L, box 111, Beneš's record of his talk with Eden, 10 February 1941.

70) For example, when the Treasury organised the Chancellor's lunch with the Allied Ministers of Finance, Edvard Outrata was certainly invited, along with his Polish, Norwegian, Belgian and Dutch colleagues. Similarly, the Czechoslovaks were to be invited for the Inter-Allied Meeting that was planned to be called already in October 1940, but due to Greece's hesitation to take part and later war in the Balkans it did not take place before 12 June 1941. *PRO*, FO 371/26451, C 780/544/62, Waley to Makins, 23 January, Roberts to Waley, 25 January 1941; FO 371/24378, C 11724/11444/62, Cadogan's minute, 29 October 1940; FO 371/26451, 6593/544/62, Roberts' minute, 13 June 1941, speeches by the participants of the meeting.

71) Beneš himself, however, kept the British constantly informed of his contacts with the Protectorate government and President Hácha, and of Hácha's readiness to resign upon his (Beneš's) notice. *PRO*, FO 371/26388, C 336/216/12, Lockhart's memoranda, 8, 15, 24 and 26 January 1941. Thus three days before reading of Beneš's new demand, Roberts wrote: 'It is certainly important to maintain the Hacha-Elias Government in Prague, now that they clearly have a good understanding with Dr. Beneš.' *PRO*, FO 371/26381, C 1147/ /57/12, Lockhart to Strang, 4 February 1941, Roberts' minute, 12 February 1941. See also FO 371/26402, C 3893/3160/12, Lockhart to Strang, 14 April 1941.

war has been finished, we have decided to create a provisional system of State machinery...'[72] But once again Beneš found a way to push his will through the FO's obstinacy.

Lockhart worried that Eden's mission to Greece and the Middle East that eventually drew out from two weeks to almost two months,[73] would mean an end to all his promises, including that of Churchill's lunch with Beneš. Yet, before his departure Eden had asked the Prime Minister to invite Beneš to luncheon, attracting him by Beneš's 'impressive story' of underground organisations in the Protectorate, and by the following assurance: 'Moreover, the little man has had a harsh time and a further compliment from you would mean much to him.'[74] Churchill was quite ready to invite Beneš and the lunch took place on 26 February 1941. The Prime Minister assured his Czechoslovak partner that Eden had discussed with him the disadvantages implied by the provisional status. He also promised to visit the Czechoslovak troops soon. According to Lockhart's close associate from the Political Intelligence Department, general Dallas Brooks, Churchill also wrote the following instruction: 'All problems have to be considered now solely from point of view of winning and shortening the war.'[75] (It is not clear, however, who was the recipient.) Meanwhile other officials dealing with Czechoslovak matters pressed for full recognition: general Colin Gubbins, number 2 in the SOE, Rex Leeper, chief of the FO Political Intelligence Department, and Dallas Brooks; Roberts was the target of their pleading in the Ritz hotel on 9 April.[76]

Beneš was writing a long memorandum on the question of full recognition and intended to send it to the Prime Minister. Lockhart dissuaded him from that, although in Eden's absence Churchill was acting as Foreign Secretary and apparently found in foreign affairs a new thrill.[77] And it was he who eventually took the lead in the whole affair: On 19 April 1941, he visited together with his wife Clementine, three U.S. envoys (Harriman, Winant and Biddle) and a few officers the Czechoslovak brigade in Leamington. The Prime Minister received

72) *PRO*, FO 371/26394, C 1320/1320/12, Roberts' minute, 15 February, Makins' minute, 17 February 1941.
73) Avon, Earl of, *The Eden Memoirs. The Reckoning*, London, Cassell 1965, pp. 198–220.
74) *PRO*, FO 371/26395, C 1627/1627/12, Eden to Churchill, 11 February 1941.
75) *HLRO*, Bruce Lockhart papers, diary No. 38, 21 and 26 February 1941.
76) *Ibid.*, 9 April 1941.
77) *Ibid.*, 26 February, 19 March, 5 April 1941.

numerous presents of the soldiers' own making – drawings, coloured woodwork, embroidery, etc.[78] Upon the party's departure the troops broke into *Rule, Britannia*. The Prime Minister sang with them. Masaryk, always full of emotions, even saw tears in Churchill's eyes. Beneš had long talks with Churchill during the day by which almost any aspect of war, including general plan for the future, was discussed. He was enthusiastic about Churchill's historic imagination, his qualities of leadership, his prescience, and his quest of fundamentals. 'At last,' said Beneš to Lockhart the day after, 'I have met an Englishman who understands the fundamentals of this war and what it means to Europe.'[79] Even in his own record Beneš wrote: 'Generally he sees right.'[80] Indeed, an unusually positive evaluation of an Englishman written by Edvard Beneš... He also raised the question of full recognition and gave Churchill a short memorandum that the Prime Minister read on spot and said that it had to be 'put right'. He promised to take care of the matter himself.[81]

Churchill fulfilled his promise, but presumably not exactly the way Beneš had wished, as he sent the memorandum to the Foreign Office. It was accompanied by his comment: 'I see no reason why we should not give the Czechs the same recognition as we have given the Poles, and encourage the Americans to follow our example. In neither case should we be committed to territorial frontiers.' Eden identified with Churchill's views and asked the Central Department for observations.[82] However, the memorandum placed all blame for Czechoslovak difficulties upon the Foreign Office: Although the Czechoslovak government was recognised by the British government on 21 July 1940, the Foreign Office considered it always as 'provisional', without the rights of a fully recognised government (no British Minister was appointed to the Czechoslovak government, juridically it was not on the same level as the

78) Gilbert, Martin, *Finest Hour. Winston S. Churchill 1939–1941*, London, Heinemann 1983, p. 1066.
79) *HLRO*, Bruce Lockhart papers, diary No. 38, 20, 22 and 23 April 1941. See also Táborský, *Prezident Beneš mezi Západem a Východem*, p. 65.
80) V celku vidí správně." *AÚTGM*, EB-L, box 111, Beneš's record of Churchill's visit, 18 [sic!] April 1941; see also *AMZV*, LA-D, box 61, 1132/dův/41, report of Churchill's visit at the Czechoslovak brigade in Leamington, 19 April 1941.
81) *HLRO*, Bruce Lockhart papers, diary No. 38, 20 April 1941.
82) *PRO*, PREM 114/3A, M.456/1, Churchill to Eden, 20 April 1941; FO 371/26394, C 4078/1320/12, Eden's minute, 21 April 1941.

Polish government, in the official documents the Foreign Office avoided to speak of the „Czechoslovak Republic", etc.). This attitude caused that also the other Allied governments considered the Czechoslovaks as 'Allies of the second category'. Although official reasons for continuation of this policy invoked by the Foreign Office were 'legal' difficulties, the memorandum stated that in fact, 'it is the remnant of the Munich policy. Our people here and at home feel it as unjust and as a continuation of the Munich humiliation.'[83]

Lockhart was right in his expectation that the FO would not like these lines.[84] Maybe Eden submitted them to his officials with some satisfaction, as on the whole he did not regard their skills very highly. From his diary we know that he 'felt office to be dead, there was never a constructive suggestion from below, only a bureaucratic machine, gently ticking over'.[85] In each case the memorandum was perceived as offence inside the Foreign Office. Roberts rang Lockhart immediately to say the Office had received 'a rude communication', 'not at all a good document' from Beneš. Lockhart himself considered it 'a badly-worded document' and regretted that he could not have been in Leamington. He stressed to Roberts in the Foreign Office that – in Roberts' words – 'had he not been away during the last week he would have represented very strongly to Dr. Benes the complete lack of foundation for his suggestion that decisions favourable to the Czechs had been taken by H.M.G. as a whole, whereas the execution of these decisions had been allegedly hampered by the Foreign Office'. Roberts stressed that in the last few months the FO had successfully insisted that in practice the Czechs should be provided with exactly similar facilities as other British Allies. Lockhart on his part proposed to take 'strong exception' in private conversation with Beneš to the 'unfortunate phraseology'.[86] When he did so, the Czechoslovak President was 'penitent and rather upset' and wished to know how he could put the matter right at once. Lockhart suggested waiting until recognition had gone through and then paying a graceful tribute to the FO.[87] All this fuss, quite naturally, only added to already less than limited

83) *PRO*, FO 371/26394, C 4078/1320/12, Beneš to Churchill, 18 April 1941.
84) *HLRO*, Bruce Lockhart papers, diary No. 38, 20 April 1941.
85) *Birmingham University Library*, Avon papers, AP 20/1/21, diary entry for 2 June 1941.
86) *PRO*, FO 371/26394, C 4078/1320/12, Roberts' minute, 22 April 1941.
87) *HLRO*, Bruce Lockhart papers, diary No. 38, 23 April 1941. However, in his own record, one of his typical essays in self-delusion, Beneš presents an entirely different

popularity of the Czechoslovak President in the key governmental office. It was not restricted just to the Central Department. Malkin, the legal adviser, was 'very sore', while Strang boiled with rage: 'B[eneš]. is back at his old tricks again. He has been good for too long.' Lockhart soothed him in a half-an-hour conversation on 25 April pointing out President's English that was not good enough for him to realise how incorrect his language was. At the end, 'Strang was very nice, said all the Office were friends of the Czechs', and that the FO had recommended full recognition that should go through 'in three weeks'.[88]

Together with the 'short' memorandum, the Foreign Office also received from Beneš via Lockhart the 'long' and more official memorandum on the disabilities suffered by the Czechoslovak government owing to its provisional status. The text had been under preparation for months and presented both juridical and political case for full recognition.[89] Right at the beginning it announced the key thesis: 'The Czechoslovak Government in London and the whole of the Czechoslovak people at home adopt the standpoint that the Czechoslovak Republic continues to exist just as it existed before the 19th September, 1938.' This opinion was based on a consideration that starting with the Anglo-French plan, which had been forced upon Czechoslovakia, all significant territorial and juridical changes concerning Czechoslovakia happened forcibly or under threat of force and could not be recognised, as far as international law was concerned. This applied to the Munich Agreement, Beneš's resignation, the Slovak separation and the German occupation of Czechoslovakia. Therefore, juridically, the Czechoslovak Republic continued to exist just as it had existed before the September crisis.

picture of his talk with Lockhart: 'In the F.O. a big alarm and fear what will come out of it. Some of the concerned officials were frightened that it was an accusation from my side, they felt a little bit offended, but above all they were scared that W[inston]. Ch[urchill]. will go for them. And so the whole atmosphere changed immediately. – The effect was terrific – L[ockhart]. told me. The remark in the memorandum that the policy made by the F.O. so far is the remnant of the Munich policy cut to the quick.' *AÚTGM*, EB-L, box 110, Beneš's record of his talks with Lockhart, 23 April, 26 April 1941.
88) *HLRO*, Bruce Lockhart papers, diary No. 38, 25 April 1941.
89) In many respects the memorandum linked to a memorandum called *Mírové cíle československé* [Peace Aims of Czechoslovakia] that was in February 1941 prepared upon Lockhart's call and then discussed amongst Czechoslovak politicians. *Češi a sudetoněmecká otázka 1939–1945. Dokumenty,* No. 42, pp. 84–92; Brandes, *Großbritannien und seine osteuropäischen Allierten 1939–1943,* p. 115; Kuklík, *Londýnský exil...,* pp. 94–95.

These disputable legal arguments were effectively supported by political ones: Both the international situation and conditions in the Protectorate and Slovakia called for full recognition; Beneš further reminded his British partners of the share of the Czechoslovak military units in the fight against Germany, and stressed the potential of the underground organisation in the Protectorate with which the exile organisation was in constant clandestine contacts, as well as with Hácha's government itself. At the end, Beneš demanded recognition of juridical continuity of the pre-Munich Czechoslovak Republic, its President and Government, the same juridical position as the other Allied governments, and adoption of terms *the Czechoslovak Republic, the President of the Czechoslovak Republic, the Government of the Czechoslovak Republic*. The provisional character of the Czechoslovak government was to be understood in the future as only an internal concern of Czechoslovak democracy; 'this means that the present Government will, after the war, at once submit to the regulations of a democratic Czechoslovak Constitution'.[90]

Bruce Lockhart (and to some extent even Beneš himself) was aware how controversial and academic the legal argument was. Therefore he based his advocacy for the case of full recognition on stressing its political merits in the British struggle for winning the war. In his covering despatch addressed to Eden, he went so far as suggesting that of 'all the oppressed peoples, the Czechs are the best organised', and he stressed the military potential of the home Czechs who would be prepared to rise, one day, at their President's order. He highlighted the value of military and political intelligence supplied from former Czechoslovakia since the beginning of the war, and the close contacts existing between the Provisional Government in London and the home Czechs, again in a measure unprecedented amongst the Allies. 'Nor will it be contested,' Lockhart went on, 'that President Beneš enjoys a greater measure of authority and support in his own country than the leaders of other Allied foreign Governments enjoy in their countries. In one sense all these foreign Governments in our midst are provisional.' Although the Hungarians would probably be annoyed by full recognition, it would hardly alter 'by one hair's breadth' the line Hungary had already taken in the war. On the other hand, in Lockhart's rather naïve view, it 'would

90) *AMZV*, LA-D, box 129, memorandum Political and Juridical Relationship of the Czechoslovak Republic to Great Britain; see also *PRO*, FO 371/26394, C 4078/1320/12, Memorandum by Dr. Beneš, 18 April 1941.

be welcomed by all the other small States of Central and South-Eastern Europe, who all loathe and detest Germany and whose diplomatic hesitations since the war began are, at any rate to some extent, the result, partly, of Munich and, partly, of a deep-rooted fear lest, when we have won the war, we shall turn our back on Europe and abandon them'. So again, Munich came up on the agenda: Although during the seven years before the war British prestige declined in Europe, and nowhere more sharply than in Czechoslovakia, now Britain has recovered much of the lost ground. Nonetheless, the Czechs, with their sensitive memories of Munich, perceived the word 'provisional' as a slur to their national pride and also 'the last remnant of the Munich policy. I am in favour of avoiding references to Munich,' Lockhart wrote in another letter to Strang. 'It is unfortunate that the home Czechs, and indeed, all Czechoslovakia should remember it. But it would be tragic for our understanding of the whole situation in Central and South-Eastern Europe if we were to forget it altogether.' But above all, full recognition was in Lockhart's view the most practical form of immediate support to the home Czechs.[91]

Strang did not intentionally mislead Lockhart in his optimistic forecast of full recognition to be accorded in three weeks. The prospects actually looked promising at the end of April: The FO officials took Churchill's and Eden's comments as directives. Although Makins uttered that the 'two communications from Dr. Benes show him in his worst light and they are in fact replete with over-optimism and untruths', neither he doubted that Dr. Beneš's administration should now be recognised as the legal Government of the Czechoslovak Republic. The more so, that one of the reasons for holding back from full recognition, namely the effect on Hungary, had disappeared with the creation of the new László Bárdossy's government and Hungarian participation in the occupation of Yugoslavia. Two steps, however, were to be taken first: a) asking for Beneš's assurance that the position of Hácha's government in the Protectorate would not be prejudiced, and b) consulting the Dominions on the step proposed to be taken. Strang found Lockhart's arguments strong enough even to put the first condition aside.[92] Regarding the Dominions, however, Lockhart professed rightly that 'Smuts might be sticky'.[93]

91) *PRO*, FO 371/26394, C 4078/1320/12, Lockhart to Eden, 20 April 1941.
92) *Ibid.*, Roberts', Makins', Malkin's and Strang's minutes, 22–25 April 1941.
93) *HLRO*, Bruce Lockhart papers, diary No. 38, 25 April 1941.

Recognition of juridical continuity was in each case considered out of the question. From the legal point of view the right degree of recognition accorded to Beneš and his government was that of a provisional government. The Czechoslovak position was not like that of the Norwegian, Dutch or Yugoslav governments, who had moved themselves, without dissolution of continuity. It was not even the same as that of the Polish government where the transfer of authority to the new president and the new government took place – as Strang put it – 'in a regular manner'.[94] As Jan Kuklík has pointed out, here, rather paradoxically, the Czechoslovak exile paid for the British respect to the not very democratic Polish Constitution of 1935.[95] Nevertheless, the British had just Beneš's word for it that he and his administration were now in law the Head and Government of Czechoslovakia. 'To recognise him in that capacity is a matter not so much of law or fact as of faith,' concluded Strang, admitting that of course, there was a great deal to be said for such an act. Eden, on the contrary, drew an analogy with the Polish government that was only constituted after Poland had been over-run. He, however, was not prepared to commit himself 'to the pre-Munich boundaries of Czecho-Slovakia [sic!]', whatever he thought of the Munich settlement itself. And he found the minutes written by his officials so important that he wanted to have a discussion of the question in all its aspects, before taking any further step.[96]

Meanwhile Beneš, rather untimely, insisted on juridical continuity and intended to deliver another paper on that topic to the Foreign Office. Lockhart was not enthusiastic and Masaryk also disagreed – at least when talking to Lockhart. Nonetheless, Lockhart sounded Roberts on that question. Quite naturally, the reply was not favourable: The intention was to leave the whole question open. If Beneš kept hammering at it, he might force the British to take a definite attitude, which on legal merits might be unfavourable to the Czechs. After another round of Lockhart's persuasion and emphasis that it would certainly delay recognition, Beneš finally dropped the plan, although he wanted to discuss the question of formula with Eden anyway.[97]

94) *PRO*, FO 371/26394, C 4078/1320/12, Strang's minute, 25 April 1941.
95) Kuklík, *Londýnský exil...*, p. 96.
96) *PRO*, FO 371/26394, C 4078/1320/12, Strang's and Eden's minutes, 25 April 1941.
97) *HLRO*, Bruce Lockhart papers, diary No. 38, 30 April, 1 May, 3 May, 7 May 1941.

The process of recognition slowed down again, for various reasons. Roberts complained to Lockhart that it was hard to get hold of Eden, since he was very busy and full of Egypt and Near East questions. On Friday, 9 May, the meeting on Czechoslovak recognition was to be held under Eden's chairmanship. He put it off as 'not urgent'. Roberts said the department had all papers ready and that Eden 'had probably now realised he could not go far as he thought. Frank [Roberts] implied that he [Eden] made promises too rashly, i.e., without consulting his experts!'[98] It later turned out, however, that the reasons for the postponement were more prosaic: partly strong criticism to which sensitive Eden was exposed in the House of Commons a few days ago for Britain's military failures, partly just a busy day at the end of which he had some obligations to his wife's friend.[99] Although the Czechoslovak agenda did not (and naturally could not) top the list of the British Foreign Secretary's priorities, he was far from neglecting it. He promised Lockhart to hold the meeting soon and go long way to satisfy Beneš. He was also working together with the new U.S. Ambassador, John G. Winant, and wanted a parallel action. Lockhart worried lest it caused further delays. Eden promised that things would go through quite quickly and added some strong criticism of the Foreign Office.[100]

Lockhart's worries were not unfounded. Although he had been an eyewitness to the warm-hearted reception given to Beneš by Roosevelt during his stay in the United States in May 1939, he had certain doubts whether the President's enthusiasm for the Czechs would go the length of recognition, as Beneš himself expected.[101] Indeed, the U.S. policy towards the Czechoslovak government in London was non-committal, to say the least. Beneš entered into friendly contacts with Winant – who had visited Prague soon after Munich and unlike his predecessor Joseph P. Kennedy was very critical about appeasement – and he quickly won his support for U.S. recognition of his government, but the Ambassador's

98) *Ibid.*, 1 and 9 May 1941.
99) These were pieces of information that Lockhart obtained from Orme Sargent and Dallas Brooks. The latter said that Eden had a very busy day and was determined to drive Auriol Palmer down for his week-end party. *Ibid.*, 9 May 1941.
100) *Ibid.*, 10 May 1941.
101) In a congratulatory telegram on Roosevelt's victory in the presidential election Beneš went so far as hailing him as the saviour and defender of the oppressed peoples of Europe. 'What about H[is] M[ajesty's] G[overnment]?' justly asked Roberts. *PRO*, FO 371/24292, C 12087/12087/12, Lockhart to Halifax, 7 November 1940, Roberts' minute, undated.

despatches to that sense had only limited impact upon the U.S. position.[102] The U.S. government refused to negotiate recognition of the Czechoslovak provisional government, as in its view Czechoslovakia existed and was regularly represented in Washington by its Minister Vladimír Hurban. Although it was he who called for recognition of the London government, the State Department refused, pointing out the country's neutrality, which precluded recognising a revolutionary government. Lockhart learned via Beneš that Sikorski had been told in the State Department, when asking about the recognition of the Czechoslovak government, that the United States could not be expected to forestall the British attitude. But the U.S. government was two steps behind the British one, as Roberts promptly pointed out, since by then it recognised neither the National Committee nor the Provisional Government.[103] It therefore seems that the cold attitude originated elsewhere and had probably much to do with the highly critical assessments of Edvard Beneš supplied by the key U.S. diplomats in Europe. Throughout 1939, George F. Kennan from Prague and William C. Bullitt from Paris had been drawing a devastating picture of him.[104] Correspondingly, Sumner Welles refused to meet Beneš when he visited London in March 1940 during his peace mission, although he spoke with the Polish leaders. The situation repeated itself eleven months later in the case of Roosevelt's closest adviser Harry Hopkins. This only underlined the absence of Biddle's accreditation to the Czechoslovak provisional government.[105] In February 1941, Kennan, now the 1st secretary at the Berlin Embassy, wrote against recognition of Beneš's government, arguing that in the case of a revolt the Czech people would unite behind Hácha's government in Prague, rather than behind a committee in London. He based this rather unrealistic

102) *AÚTGM*, EB-V, box 155, Beneš's record of his talk with Winant, 28 March 1941; Bruegel, The Recognition of the Czechoslovak Government..., *op. cit.*, p. 10; Táborský, *Prezident Beneš mezi Západem a Východem*, p. 78.
103) *PRO*, FO 371/26405, C 6595/3261/12, Lockhart to Eden, No. 58, 16 June, Roberts' minute, 18 June 1941.
104) Kennan, George F., *Memoirs 1925–1950*, Boston-Toronto, Little, Brown and Company 1967; Idem, *From Prague After Munich. Diplomatic Papers 1938–1940*, Princeton (NJ), Princeton University Press 1968, pp. 7–8; Kalvoda, Josef, *Role Československa v sovětské strategii* [Czechoslovakia's role in Soviet strategy], Kladno, Dílo 1999, p. 117.
105) Hauner, Milan, Edvard Beneš a USA 1939–1942. Nad rukopisem nevydané publikace Jana Opočenského [Edvard Beneš and the U.S.A 1939–1942. Reading the unpublished book by Jan Opočenský], *Soudobé dějiny* [Contemporary history], Vol. III, 1996, No. 1, p. 15.

view, which ironically Hácha himself hardly shared,[106] on information from the now unofficial Protectorate representative in Berlin, František Chvalkovský. Kennan further recommended pro-Habsburg orientation and post-war creation of a federation in Central Europe, rather than reconstruction of Czechoslovakia under Beneš's leadership.[107] Kennan's judgments found their way to a memorandum composed in the Division of European Affairs of the State Department in the summer of 1941 that similarly did not recommend recognition.[108]

But let us return to London. The postponed meeting in the Foreign Office eventually took place on 21 May 1941. Makins wrote a record of it and it seems from the conclusions that his own arguments triumphed: Not only that the Dominions were to be consulted,[109] but a letter was to be sent to Dr. Beneš expressing doubts about the impact of full recognition upon the situation in the Protectorate: Hácha's government would have to take up an attitude. Either they would recognise Beneš, in which case they would be suppressed by the Germans, or they would refuse to recognise him, in which case the moral and propaganda effect would be unfortunate.[110] Lockhart was 'displeased' because the Central Department uselessly wasted a month for returning to this 'old bogey', and – perhaps even more importantly – because he was not asked to attend the meeting and therefore 'Strang & Co. could put anything they liked to the Secretary of State without anyone being able to check its correctness'. Makins assured him that all that was required was a written assurance

106) See Pasák, *JUDr. Emil Hácha,* passim.
107) *National Archives*, Washington, D.C. (hereafter *NARA*), Record Group (hereafter RG) 59, Department of State File 860F.01/461, Kennan's memorandum, February 5, 1941. The Division of European Affairs also paid attention to the views expressed by 'a source in the Protectorate' – by marking the following paragraph: '... The Czechoslovak emigré government was felt by the Czechs not to understand the problems of the Protectorate as they had developed, and thus to have lost its contact and much of its support. The people did not wish the reconstruction of Czechoslovakia – "an elongated sausage" which could not be maintained in a military or an economic sense – but felt that their future lay in their inclusion as an autonomous region within a larger political body which would constitute a political and economic unit...' *Ibid.*, 760F.64/304, Budapest telegram No. 64, 30 June 1941: Memorandum of Conversation with Source in the Protectorate.
108) *NARA*, RG 59, Department of State File 860F.01/461 1/2, memorandum 'The Question of Recognition of the "Czechoslovak Provisional Government" in London', undated, signed R. D. Coe.
109) *PRO*, FO 371/26394, C 5791/1320/12, Dominions Office telegram to the Governments of Canada, Commonwealth of Australia, New Zealand and to the Acting U.K. High Commissioner in the Union of South Africa, No. 95, 23 May 1941.
110) *PRO*, FO 371/26394, C 5553/1320/12, Makins' minute, 21 May 1941.

from Beneš that consequences of recognition would not cause violent reaction of wrong kind in the U.S.A.[111] Lockhart met Beneš and Masaryk immediately after they had received the written reply on recognition signed by Eden.[112] Thus he could observe their immediate reactions:

'The President was disappointed but dignified. He made no comment. Jan was annoyed or, at any rate, more outspoken. Rather bitter about Eden whose former sympathies (frequently expressed) had not taken him any further than Mr. Strang & Co. wished him to go. Then, referring to the letter, he sneered: "My dear provisional President" – "Yours provisionally, Anthony."'[113]

Although Beneš wrote up his 'assurance' of the generally positive impact of full recognition, including Hácha's government, almost immediately,[114] he could not understand the procrastination. He reproached that at the beginning of war he had to decide whether to denounce Hácha & Co. as traitors or to win them over. He said that for the sake of unity he chose the second course, but first would have been popular with the bulk of people. Lockhart assured him that there would be no great delay and that what 'our F.O. heroes of action' really wanted was a written assurance from him to cover them in case there were troubles in Prague and questions in Parliament. Beneš pointed out the importance of getting Czechs into Anglo-American camp. If Russia came into the war, he saw great danger that they would go pro-Russian – a warning that he was to repeat many times and that he had used a year earlier during negotiations on recognition of the Provisional Government.[115] He contrasted Eden's brave speeches from the time of Munich with his current attitude and spoke 'sadly about the ignorance and laziness of our diplomats and politicians'. Beneš was further depressed by Lockhart's news that he would be given another job,[116] though Lockhart accompanied it with an

111) *HLRO*, Bruce Lockhart papers, diary No. 38, 22 May, 23 May 1941. The FO files show that the question of Hácha's government was taken seriously in the Foreign Office. When a report came of a dismissal of some officials of Národní souručenství, the only permitted political party in the Protectorate, Makins commented: 'This does not seem to amount to much; but important change in the Czechoslovak [sic!] government might alter the position in regard to full recognition of Dr. Beneš.' *PRO*, FO 371/26381, C 5213/57/12 Makins' minute, 24 May 1941.

112) *PRO*, FO 371/26394, C 5553/1320/12, Eden to Beneš, 26 May 1941.

113) *HLRO*, Bruce Lockhart papers, diary No. 38, 28 May 1941.

114) *PRO*, FO 371/26394, C 5980/1320/12, Beneš to Eden, 28 May 1941.

115) See *PRO*, FO 371/24289, C 7646/2/12, Strang's minute, 21 June 1940.

116) He was to become Director-General of the newly set-up department called the

assurance that he would not take the new job unless recognition went through and that he would stay in close touch with the Czechs anyway. Beneš complained about his worst experience with British envoys in the inter-war period and said that he had hoped Lockhart would stay with the Czechoslovaks until the end of war and afterwards when he, Beneš, would need 'to have someone not only who understood his mind but was an expert on Central Europe'.[117]

The Central Department took Beneš's written assurance that further recognition would be beneficial not only to the Czechoslovak exiles but also to Czechoslovaks at home and to the Allied cause in general as satisfactory. 'Dr. Benes is, of course, a prejudiced party,' noted Roberts, 'but I see no reason to doubt that he is genuinely convinced of the arguments he sets out in his letter.' The letter therefore 'prepared the way for granting his request'.[118] However, the reactions of the first two Dominion governments, Australia and the Union of South Africa, were definitely opposed to any further recognition. While the Commonwealth government did not find any positive argument sufficiently strong to justify further recognition, general Smuts went even further and saw definite disadvantages in it. Nevertheless, the Foreign Office agreed to try to persuade the Dominions with the use of Beneš's letter about the argument that further recognition would be definitely helpful to the Allied cause and by stressing the reservations concerning the frontiers and juridical continuity. Although it was expected that this would be enough to overcome the Australian hesitations, the same did not apply to Smuts, who had been very much opposed even to recognition of the Provisional Government.[119] In the meantime, Eden wished that as little as possible be said to Dr. Beneš, 'for fear that we get into deep difficulties'.[120] However, the Dominions Office refused to send the appropriate telegrams, despite two emphatic requests that they should get

Political Warfare Executive and to have the rank of Deputy Under-Secretary of State for Foreign Affairs.

117) *HLRO*, Bruce Lockhart papers, diary No. 38, 29 and 31 May 1941.

118) *PRO*, FO 371/26394, C 5980/1320/12, Roberts' minute, 4 June 1941.

119) 'The memory of the commitments of the last war should counsel caution,' Smuts wrote and on the account of Beneš he added: 'I frankly dislike Benes's persistence. He has already occasioned too much trouble.' *PRO*, FO 371/24289, C 7646/2/12, Smuts to Halifax, 8 July 1940; FO 371/26394, C 4078/1320/12, Roberts' minute, 22 April 1941.

120) *Ibid.*, minutes by Roberts and Makins, 4 June 1941, minutes by Strang, Cadogan and Eden, all 5 June 1941.

them off quickly! They were held up by the Dominions Secretary, Lord Cranborne, who had discussed the matter with High Commissioners, all of whom had shown the strongest opposition to giving Dr. Beneš any further measure of recognition.[121]

It was impossible to conceal these growing difficulties from the Czechs for too long. At Masaryk's own request Eden met him on 12 June and told him about the fundamental reservations on the part of the Dominions, which meant at least postponement of full recognition. It does not seem that the Czechoslovak Foreign Minister was 'quite satisfied', as Cadogan minuted. On the contrary, according to Lockhart's diary, 'Jan was depressed'. Meanwhile Roberts and Makins agreed that it had been unwise of Churchill and Eden to raise Czech hopes and then darken them to ground again.[122] Indeed, Eden apparently wondered about Geoffrey Mander's letter of 14 June requesting him that he let him know in advance about the final decision for the 'full recognition'. The agitated Liberal MP was eager to put a question in the House, but the Foreign Secretary just marked the two crucial words with a question mark...[123] Five days later Lockhart, after another talk with the Foreign Secretary, informed Beneš and Masaryk that there would be further delay in the granting of 'fuller recognition'. They were both dejected. Lockhart tried to explain the reservations on the part of the Dominions by their worries of another European war and therefore favouring of larger groupings of states, but Masaryk pointed out the Poles and the others who had been recognised and then added rather bitter comment about the Czech aviators who had been killed fighting for Britain. Were they to be regarded as 'provisionally dead'?[124] Lockhart, who started asking himself whether he was not a deserter leaving a sinking ship, wrote a personal letter to Eden begging him to give Masaryk in their forthcoming talk as much encouragement as possible and to appoint a really acceptable successor to him for the Czechs. Lockhart suggested George Rendel, a Minister to Sofia.[125] This name did not arise much enthusiasm in Masaryk, but otherwise he apparently took as sincere Eden's apologetic tone, his assurances that the delays with recognition were highly embarrassing to him and his begging

121) *Ibid.*, C 5980/1320/12, Makins' minute, 14 June 1941, Sloan's minute, 24 June 1941.
122) *HLRO*, Bruce Lockhart papers, diary No. 38, 11–12 June 1941.
123) *PRO*, FO 371/26451, C 6163/544/62, Makins to Eden, 14 June 1941, Eden's minute, undated.
124) *HLRO*, Bruce Lockhart papers, diary No. 38, 19 June 1941.
125) *Ibid.*, 20 June 1941.

for patience and trust: 'It was clear that he was ashamed and that he felt, that undeserved wrong is being done to us.'[126]

Meanwhile a compromise solution, hoped to be acceptable both for the Dominions and the Czechs, was found in the Foreign Office: 1) the term 'provisional' was to be omitted in the future to describe the Czechoslovak government, though this would not mean that full recognition was accorded; 2) an official of ministerial rank was to be appointed. He would be called 'British diplomatic representative to the Czechoslovak Government' and a Czechoslovak 'diplomatic representative' was to be received in exchange. Lockhart at least agreed that the Czechs could be pacified by such a solution, if it was not himself who came up with that proposal, as Strang's record seems to suggest. Malkin added that all this would mean Dr. Beneš would not be regarded as the Head of a State and he would appear on the list of members of the Czechoslovak government (a Gordian knot of jurisprudence that he had already tried to cut several months ago[127]). Although it would be difficult to say whether the government was 'the Government of any foreign Power' or just 'Provisional Government' under the Diplomatic Privileges Act, even Malkin suggested that it might be possible 'to leave this question in decent obscurity'. The Dominions were to be consulted, and Eden stressed that 'this time we shall make it plain to Dominions that this is best we can do'.[128] Such was the situation and suggested solution of the uneasy 'Czechoslovak question' on the eve of *Barbarossa*.

The thorny way to full recognition – stage 2

The German attack on the Soviet Union turned not only the military situation, but also the whole of Second World War diplomacy upside down. Further, it opened wide range of new opportunities and options for Edvard Beneš and his policy. He took them up with his typical shrewdness and quickly made full use of them in the protracted negotiations on recognition. As early as on 25 June he entrusted to Lockhart

126) *AÚTGM*, EB-L, box 111, Masaryk's record of his talk with Eden, 20 June 1941.
127) *PRO*, FO 371/26394, C 2061/1320/12, Malkin's minute, 11 February 1941.
128) *Ibid.*, C 7206/1320/12, Strang's minute, 20 June, Malkin's minute, 21 June 1941, Eden's minute, 24 June 1941. The pertinent telegrams to Dominions were sent on 2 July 1941: *PRO*, FO 371/26394, C 5791/1320/12, Dominions Office telegram to the Governments of Canada, Commonwealth of Australia, New Zealand and to the Acting U.K. High Commissioner in the Union of South Africa, No. 131.

that Colonel Heliodor Píka, who had been sent to Moscow in April 1941 as a 'Czechoslovak military representative for the Soviet Union and Turkey' and who had hitherto been merely tolerated, was now receiving favours from the Soviet authorities.[129] Beneš further informed the British representative that the Russians started broadcasting in Czech to the Protectorate and in Slovak to Slovakia, while Molotov on the day of the German attack mentioned in his speech to the Soviet people also the wrongs committed on Czechoslovakia in 1938. Beneš warned against the dangerous political implications if a Soviet recognition preceded recognitions by the British and Americans, while Masaryk informed about ferment caused by the Soviet entry into the war in the Socialist camp, from where both criticism was voiced for not achieving British recognition and calls for obtaining recognition primarily from Moscow.[130] Lockhart sent an important report to the Foreign Office predicting that the Russians might grant the recognition in order to cause the maximum embarrassment to Germany in one of her main war arsenals. Although Beneš was in favour of any weapon necessary for the defeat of Germany, he did not, in Lockhart's view, wish to see Russia dominant in Central and Eastern Europe. However, 'Russia's entry into the war has stirred the imagination of many Czechs, who find it much easier to forget the Russo-German Pact of 1939 than the Munich dismemberment pact of 1938'. Cadogan considered all this a further argument for recognition of the Czechoslovak government, but he did not know how to get over the Dominion difficulties.[131] It was clear that the loyal but uninventive FO bureaucracy was unable to solve this quiz. Apparently an intervention from the highest political circles was necessary.

The definitive impulse for such an intervention came from Moscow: Relying on the information from Masaryk, Lockhart informed Eden that the Soviet Union recognised juridical continuity of the Czechoslovak Republic, considered the physical restoration of the Czechoslovak Republic one of its war aims, refrained from any interference in its

129) This was the beginning of the most successful intelligence mission. Píka's reports from the Soviet Union were regarded as first class and highly trustworthy within British governmental circles from Anthony Eden downwards. See e.g. various reports and commentaries in *PRO*, FO 800/874.
130) *HLRO*, Bruce Lockhart papers, diary No. 38, 25 and 26 June 1941; *PRO*, FO 371/ /26410, C 7140/7140/12, Lockhart to Eden, 26 June 1941.
131) *PRO*, FO 371/26410, C 7140/7140/12, Lockhart to Eden, No. 61, 26 June 1941, Cadogan's minute, 3 July 1941.

internal affairs, and was ready to resume mutual diplomatic relations as well as to form a Czechoslovak force in the U.S.S.R. to fight shoulder to shoulder with the Soviet troops. Lockhart stressed that 'this matter came entirely from the Russian side' and that Beneš and Masaryk were perturbed by the damage that the Soviet action might bring about for the Czechoslovak cause in the British governmental circles. On 10 July Masaryk repeated the same story to Eden himself.[132] Much of it was not quite true: the Soviet Ambassador Maisky did not tackle the question of juridical continuity and a diplomatic prelude on Beneš's part, clearly aimed at obtaining the Soviet recognition, had indeed preceded the Ambassador's communication.[133] Nevertheless, the message was clear: full Soviet recognition of the Czechoslovak government was impending. Therefore matters also started rolling on the British Imperial side. And they rolled very quickly, at least when measured by British diplomatic standards. It seems that the major reason for that change was Eden's decision to grant full recognition that he made at some moment between 10 and 14 July 1941. Yet, it is not quite clear what finally induced him: On 10 July (probably in the morning) he read another letter from Lockhart who reported on his conversation with Beneš. He found the President unbelievably depressed over British policy in connection with Russia's entry into the war and its possible consequences. Having read that, Eden instructed the Central Department to inform the Dominions and ask them for haste. He, however, attached a rather venomous comment: 'All the same I suspect that Dr. Beneš knows how to play his hand.'[134] And even more importantly, the urging telegram concerned the 'compromise solution' – with just obliterating the word 'provisional'

132) *Ibid.*, C 7680/7140/12, Lockhart to Eden, No. 63, 9 July 1941; *HLRO*, Bruce Lockhart papers, diary No. 38, 8 July, 10 July 1941.
133) On 30 June 1941, in a broadcast to the nation Beneš stated that the U.S.S.R. was again in the same relationship with Czechoslovakia as it had existed before Munich. Then he asked Píka to find out what the Soviet Government thought of that statement. On 8 July, Maisky informed Beneš that the Soviet Government considered the reconstitution of independent Czechoslovakia with the Czechoslovak national government as part of its political programme, that it further did not want to interfere in the internal affairs of Czechoslovakia, was ready to receive in Moscow a Czechoslovak Minister and also to set up a military unit on the Soviet territory. Beneš then said to Maisky that he considered this as a return to the mutual relationship that had existed before September 1938. *Dokumenty ČSR-SSSR*, Vol. I, No. 86, pp. 198–199, Beneš's telegraphic instruction to Col. Píka, 6 June 1941, No. 88, pp. 201–205, Beneš's record of his talk with Maisky, 8 July 1941.
134) *PRO*, FO 371/26388, C 7511/216/12, Lockhart to Eden, No. 62, 7 July 1941, Eden's minute, 10 July 1941.

and appointing merely a 'British representative'.[135] At 10:30, however, the Foreign Secretary met Jan Masaryk and promised to appoint a fully accredited Minister to the Czechoslovak government soon.[136] Lockhart was surprised, but Eden confirmed in his talk with him on 14 July that he had really said that to Masaryk. Lockhart recorded into his diary the ensuing impressive chapter in firm decision-making with Anthony Eden casting as the principal character:

'I then said this was not, as far as I know, the Central Department's plan which was to accredit a Minister but only to call him "British representative". Eden became petulant, raised telephone: "Mr. Strang, please!" – – "Not in room! Get him in two minutes then. Secretary of State speaking." ... "That You, William. What is all this Lockhart tells me about only appointing someone of ministerial rank and calling British representative? Is that right?" W.S. replies: "This is the idea." Eden. "I don't understand these terms – British representative – they're untidy. We've had enough of half-measures. We must go the whole hog now."'[137]

The Foreign Secretary certainly knew about the intended 'half--measure' from the time it had been conceived, but it seems that Jan Masaryk with his art of emotional persuading once again induced the British Foreign Secretary to stiffen Britain's policy – similarly as Masaryk had at least contributed from his position of Plenipotentiary to Halifax's 'sleepless night' on 24 September 1938 and the subsequent C-change in his foreign policy views.[138] However, for four crucial days Eden did not

135) *PRO*, FO 371/26394, C 7797/1320/12, Dominions Office telegram to the Governments of Canada, Commonwealth of Australia, New Zealand and to the Acting U.K. High Commissioner in the Union of South Africa, No. 146, 11 July 1941. The Dominions agreed between 11 and 13 July, but the Commonwealth Government expressed its expectation that the reservations 'will be made quite clear to Dr. Benes'. *Ibid.*, No. 429, 13 July 1941.
136) *HLRO*, Bruce Lockhart papers, diary No. 38, 10 and 11 July 1941. There is absolutely no evidence for Martin Brown's account that 'Eden sent for Bruce Lockhart the next day [8 July 1941 – V.S.]. The Foreign Secretary immediately overturned the Central Department's previous policy and demanded that Beneš and his government now be granted full recognition.' Brown, *Dealing with Democrats*, p. 147. The published diary, to which Brown refers, does not say a word about this episode (the less so on the page 119). Indeed, it does not mention the question of recognition in July 1941 at all...
137) *HLRO*, Bruce Lockhart papers, diary No. 38, 14 July 1941.
138) Masaryk expressed his 'wonder and disdain' that 'the British Prime Minister serves as a postman for a murderer and gangster... For my own personality I stated to Halifax that I considered the terrible Hitler's document [the Godesberg memorandum – V. S.] unacceptable and that we all would rather die, than live through such a humiliation.' *DČSZP 1938*, II, No. 706, p. 387. Jiří Ellinger points out the influence of this talk upon Halifax and the fact that this episode is otherwise entirely neglected by British historiography. Ellinger,

bother to inform anybody in his office about the change of his mind. Thus the Dominions were unnecessarily urged to reply to the 'compromise solution' at the time when the Foreign Secretary had already made a decision for an entirely different course! Due to such inconsistencies on Eden's part, one cannot really wonder that he was not terribly popular in the Foreign Office. Frank Roberts, undoubtedly a highly rational and efficient official, for example entrusted to Lockhart that he personally was not a great admirer of the Secretary of State.[139]

Nonetheless, Anthony Eden at least now did 'go the whole hog' when he raised the matter at the Cabinet meeting the same afternoon: Recalling the Russian recognition he recommended to do the same, notwithstanding the fact that 'the Benes Government' had not the same continuity as the other exiled governments. He stressed that this step would not commit Britain to any particular boundaries. Considering that Hugh Dalton had already a week earlier offered Lockhart to enlist the Labour Party to obtain recognition for the Czechs,[140] it seems that there was really no opposition. The Cabinet agreed and the Dominions were to be informed with a view to obtaining their assent.[141] Frank Roberts understood that 'the Dominion Governments should be given an opportunity of expressing their views, although they should not receive any encouragement to dissent from our decision or to think that they can deter us from this course of action'.[142] The telegram was drafted accordingly and sent on 16 July, late in the evening.[143] The same afternoon

Jiří, *Od usmiřování k válce. Neville Chamberlain a britská zahraniční politika, 1937–1940* [From appeasement to war. Neville Chamberlain and British foreign policy, 1937–1940], Unpublished PhD. Thesis, Prague, Charles University 2005, p. 216, footnote 122.

139) *HLRO*, Bruce Lockhart papers, diary No. 38, 9 May 1941. Lockhart's testimony throws certain doubts on Roberts' post-war claims that he regarded Eden 'as a man with a very keen and accurate sense of timing and a skilful negotiator'. Barker, Elisabeth, *Churchill and Eden at War*, London, Macmillan 1978, p. 25 + p. 312 – endnote 43.

140) *HLRO*, Bruce Lockhart papers, diary No. 38, 6 July 1941.

141) *Bod. Lib.*, microfilm, CAB 65/19, WM(41)69, 14 July 1941. I doubt, however, that the decision can be interpreted in the following words: 'The War Cabinet agreed but said the assent of the Dominions should first be obtained.' Barker, *Churchill and Eden at War*, p. 262.

142) *PRO*, FO 371/26394, C 7992/1320/12, Roberts' minute, 15 July 1941.

143) The key sentence reads as follows: 'We trust that you will not dissent from the course of action now proposed, which we feel we shall have to take in the course of the next few days.' *PRO*, FO 371/26394, C 8119/1320/12, Dominions Office telegram to the Governments of Canada, Commonwealth of Australia, New Zealand and to the Acting U.K. High Commissioner in the Union of South Africa, No. 159, 16 July 1941.

the King and the Queen cared to be kind to Beneš and Masaryk at a party for Inter-Allied Governments in the Buckingham Palace while both Churchill and Eden told the two Czechs that everything was or would very soon be 'all right' about recognition.[144] Next day the War Cabinet agreed that it was 'very desirable that full recognition ... of the Provisional Czechoslovakian Government [sic!] should be announced on 18 July in order to avoid undue emphasis being placed on the full recognition by Russia'.[145] The Dominions now got mere 17 hours to express their possible dissent. Of course, it was neither welcomed, nor expected.[146] When Masaryk, accompanied by Lockhart, came to the Foreign Office to obtain the official letter of recognition, Eden rang in his presence to the Dominions Office to learn about the Dominion response. Lockhart closely watched his reaction: '"Ah, Australia has agreed. No reply from the others." He turns to Jan. "Good! The Empire's united." Then with a smile: "I didn't give them much time to answer."'[147] Indeed, he did not. But it was a great pity for future Anglo-Czechoslovak co-operation that his determination to treat the whole issue of the Czechoslovak recognition so vigorously and decisively came only at the eleventh hour or, rather, literally five minutes past twelve. For at the end it was the Soviet Union that at least for four hours as the only Great Power recognised the Czechoslovak government without further adjectives.[148]

The key sentence of Eden's memorandum, which was soon repeated by its author in the House of Commons, announced the King's decision

144) *AÚTGM*, EB-L, box 110, Beneš's record of his talks with Lockhart, mid-June – 16 July 1941; *HLRO*, Bruce Lockhart papers, diary No. 38, 16 July 1941.
145) *Bod. Lib.*, microfilm, CAB 65/19, WM(41)71, 17 July 1941.
146) *PRO*, FO 371/26394, C 7992/1320/12, Dominions Office telegram to the Governments of Canada, Commonwealth of Australia, New Zealand and to the Acting U.K. High Commissioner in the Union of South Africa, No. 160, 17 July 1941.
147) *HLRO*, Bruce Lockhart papers, diary No. 38, 18 July 1941. In fact New Zealand also gave its consent. *PRO*, FO 371/26394, C 7992/1320/12, The Government of New Zealand to Dominions Office, No. 267, 17 July 1941; C 8119/1320/12, The Government of Australia to Dominions Office, No. 447, 18 July 1941.
148) *Dokumenty a materiály k dějinám československo-sovětských vztahů* [Documents and materials on the history of Czechoslovak-Soviet relations], 4/1, Praha 1982, No. 82, p. 149, Agreement between the U.S.S.R and the Republic of Czechoslovakia; Beneš, Edvard, *Šest let exilu a druhé světové války. Řeči, projevy a dokumenty z r. 1938–45* [The six years of exile and of the Second World War. Talks, speeches and documents from the years 1938–45], Praha, Družstevní práce 1946, p. 450. See also *Dokumenty ČSR–SSSR*, Vol. I, No. 93, pp. 212–214, Smutný's record of his talk with Beneš.

'to accredit an Envoy extraordinary and Minister Plenipotentiary to Dr. Beneš as President of the Czechoslovak Republic'.[149] His juridical position and that of his government were to be considered as identical with that of other Allied Heads of states and governments established in Britain. However, the question of juridical continuity was 'set aside … for further consideration at the appropriate moment' and the British government again refused any commitment with respect to any frontiers in Central Europe. Pending an outcome of the discussions with Sudeten German leaders, it also reserved its position as regarded 'the exercise of jurisdiction or authority in British territory over certain categories of former Czechoslovak nationals'.[150] While Masaryk was enthusiastic to the degree of his grateful kissing of Lockhart, Beneš was more restrained. He wanted to have the last paragraph concerning the Sudeten Germans removed and put into a separate and more private letter. As he said to Lockhart, meanwhile he was afraid to show the letter of recognition to his ministers and members of the State Council.[151] Lockhart presented the President's wish to Strang who was not obdurate: 'I expected you'd raise that point. Truth is we had to do the draft in such a hurry that we had no time to consult Czechs or you.'[152] It is not clear how much Lockhart felt persuaded by this reference to the time-pressure of three months. Nevertheless, the Central Department felt that this question had not been officially solved ever since the provisional recognition in July 1940, although it had cropped up in many practical connections, such as the Czechoslovak armed forces.[153] It was perceived as 'quite an advance' that the Czechs had agreed to accept the last paragraph of the letter at all and decided to meet the request.[154] During the 'recognition lunch' on 30 July, Eden told Beneš that the treaty had been altered and the contentious paragraph transferred into a separate letter, both of them dated 18 July 1941.[155]

149) *H. C. Deb.*, 5th Series, Vol. 373, 23 July 1941, Col. 861. Sir Philip Nichols was to take up the position. However, due to his illness it did not happen before October. By then, Bruce Lockhart was deputising for him.
150) *PRO*, FO 371/26394, C 7992/1320/12, Eden to Masaryk, (1), 18 July 1941.
151) *HLRO*, Bruce Lockhart papers, diary No. 38, 18 and 19 July 1941.
152) *Ibid.*, 23 July 1941.
153) See Chapter 6.
154) *PRO*, FO 371/26394, C 7992/1320/12, Roberts' minute, 26 July, Strang's minute, 27 July, Cadogan's minute, 28 July 1941.
155) *HLRO*, Bruce Lockhart papers, diary No. 38, 30 July 1941; *DHČSP*, No. 211, pp. 255–256, 30 July 1941; *PRO*, FO 371/26394, C 7992/1320/12, Eden to Masaryk, (2), 18 July 1941. Paradoxically, at the end it was Jan Masaryk who 'deserved' that at least the

A more difficult situation occurred when it turned out that in his re-corded broadcast on recognition Beneš had put in a long passage about frontiers and said that the British recognition meant that Sudetenland, Sub-Carpathian Russia and Slovakia would be returned to the Czecho-slovak Republic after the war. Ivone Kirkpatrick, now foreign policy adviser at BBC, noticed this statement. Strang and Roberts joined him in protesting that this should be attributed to the British government if it had just officially said that it took no commitments regarding fron-tiers. In a telephone conversation lasting twenty-five minutes Lockhart together with Masaryk talked Beneš out of his intention. The major argument was the critical stage in the Polish-Russian negotiations, in which the British were bringing pressure on the Poles not to insist on their inter-war eastern frontier; if they heard that the old frontiers had been given to Beneš, the whole thing would collapse. Here again, similarly as after Churchill's broadcast last September, Beneš tried to commit the British through his own interpretation of the statement. Of course, it by far exceeded, or even ran counter to what had actually been stated. Again he backed down, and this time perhaps even understood the British reasons. He pointed out some mistranslations and agreed to the two offending paragraphs being removed from the disc. Even if he had not agreed, however, the Foreign Office would have taken them out anyway.[156] That would certainly not have been an ideal contribution to future Anglo-Czechoslovak co-operation.

It remains to say a few words about Anglo-American co-operation in the issue of recognition. Eden sought a parallel action and kept the Americans informed of every intended step. A memorandum was handed to the U.S. Embassy in London, with the suggestion that 'nothing would contribute more to the encouragement of the Czechoslovaks' than some measure of recognition of Beneš's Administration on the part of the U.S. government. Halifax was asked to take any action in Washington to support the suggestion that Biddle be appointed as the U.S. representa-

paragraph with the reservations about the frontiers remained in the letter of recognition. He noticed that in its revised version it was omitted, due to a mistake of the FO typist. Another letter had to be prepared and Eden eventually had to sign the same letter three times. *HLRO*, Bruce Lockhart papers, diary No. 38, 6 August 1941; *PRO*, FO 371/26394, C 7992/1320/12, Roberts' minute, 8 August 1941.
156) *HLRO*, Bruce Lockhart papers, diary No. 38, 26 July 1941; *PRO*, FO 371/26394, C 8436/1320/12, Roberts' minute, 26 July 1941; *DHČSP*, No. 210, p. 255, 27 July 1941.

tive with the Czechoslovak provisional government in London.[157] But only after the Soviet and British governments had recognised, the State Department found it inappropriate that the U.S. government should hang entirely back. At the same time, however, Halifax reported that State Department officials had 'no great confidence in Dr. Benes personally, nor in his being a representative of Czechoslovakia universally acceptable to Czechoslovak nationals in and outside that country'.[158] Correspondingly, when Roosevelt on 30 July answered Beneš's letter of June 4 (although delivered by Hurban only on 24 July) asking for recognition,[159] it contained noble phrases of democracy, liberties and T.G. Masaryk's greatness, but a rather thin material result: The President announced that the U.S. government had decided to accredit an Envoy Extraordinary and Minister Plenipotentiary near the *Provisional* Government of Czechoslovakia in London.[160] The pertaining press release of 30 July stressed that the U.S. government entered into *formal* relations with the Provisional Government.[161] The FO officials wondered about such an anomalous appointment – that is a fully accredited *Minister* to a *provisional* government. The State Department explained that the words 'provisional' and 'established in London' reflected the alleged feeling among the Czechoslovak people that the members of the Hácha government (of the Second Republic) – which the U.S. government had not ceased recognising – had remained in the country and shared the hardships of its people, whereas those of the government in London were not doing so. In the American view the word *provisional* bore similar reservations as those covered in the British letter of *full* recognition.[162] The Americans thus came up with their own 'compromise solution', but the logic of the compromise was different from the one suggested by the British in June: instead of getting rid of the outwardly humiliating word 'provisional' while keeping legal distance, it offered a formal relationship but stuck to the 'slur to the national pride'.

157) *PRO*, FO 371/26394, C 7263/1320/12, Eden to Halifax, No. 474, 3 July 1941; FO 371/26388, C 7511/216/12, Eden to Halifax, No. 4018, 14 July 1941.
158) *PRO*, FO 371/26405, C 8196/3261/12, Halifax to Eden, No. 3414, 21 July 1941.
159) *AMZV*, LA-D, box 152, Beneš to Roosevelt, 4 June 1941.
160) *Ibid.*, Roosevelt to Beneš, 30 July 1941.
161) *PRO*, FO 371/26405, C 9089/3261/12, Press Release No. 365 from Department of State, 30 July 1941.
162) *PRO*, FO 371/26405, C 10468/3261/12, Hoyer Millar to Makins, 9 September 1941.

Anthony Drexel Biddel was eventually also appointed as Minister to the Czechoslovak *provisional* government on 28 October and only a year later the recognition was changed into a full and definitive one while Roosevelt for the first time addressed Beneš 'the President of the Republic of Czechoslovakia' in a telegram to him. Thus the United States accorded *de jure* recognition only as the 22nd state of the anti-Hitler coalition and the last of the Great Powers.[163] In spite of these delays Beneš considered highly the pure fact that the United States in July 1941, at the time of their neutrality, recognised his exile government, though only as provisional. For the procrastination, as well as for the fact that even in 1942 Washington did not take any commitment regarding frontiers, Beneš blamed the British and perceived it as a result of British behaviour.[164] Like other Beneš's critical assessments of Britain and her policy, also this one was unjust. It was Roosevelt's resolve to adjourn international politics in wartime, which for instance became the basis of his bitter quarrel with Charles de Gaulle over formation of a provisional government in France and caused many other inter-allied troubles during the war.[165] The articles 2 and 3 of the Atlantic Charter were the explicit expression of this policy. It refused territorial changes without the freely expressed agreement of the peoples concerned and proclaimed the right of all peoples to choose their governments.[166] The U.S. policy towards Czechoslovakia thus set

163) Edvard Beneš v USA v roce 1943. Dokumenty [Edvard Beneš in the United States in 1943], eds. J. Němeček, H. Nováčková, I. Šťovíček, *Sborník archivních prací* [Reports of archival works], Prague, Vol. 49, 1999, No. 2, pp. 469–564; *Formování československého zahraničního odboje...*, p. 44; *PRO*, FO 371/30826, C 10921/3899/12, Halifax to Eden, No. 575, 3 November 1942.
164) Feierabend, *Politické vzpomínky*, II, p. 236.
165) Gaddis, *The United States and the Origins of the Cold War 1941–1947*, pp. 13–14.
166) Czechoslovak attitudes towards the Atlantic Charter were more than reserved. The government in London was receiving reports from the Protectorate that the outcome of the Churchill-Roosevelt summit was 'being criticised fairly unfavourably by the people' and perceived as another set of concessions to the Germans. *HIA Stanford*, Eduard Táborský collection, box 10, envelope Reports from Czechoslovakia, A report from Prague, 25 August 1941. In a letter to Eden signed by Masaryk, the Czechoslovak government expressed its hopes that the application of points 2, 3 and 8 would result in securing such frontiers and guarantees especially for the neighbours of Germany, 'as to enable them to defend peace for themselves and for the world against any future attempts of aggression either by Germany or anyone else'. *AÚTGM*, EB-L, box 111, Masaryk's letter to Eden, 29 August 1941. By the end of the year, however, Beneš managed to present in his speeches his own political programme as 'an application of the eight Points of the Atlantic Charter'. *HIA Stanford*, Eduard Táborský collection, box 5, envelope Benes, Eduard, Speeches and writings, 1939–1944, Beneš's speech at the University of Glasgow, 7 November 1941.

into the overall pattern of non-commitment, whatever the President's kind words to Beneš in May 1939 might have been.[167]

Conclusion

British recognition of the Czechoslovak government in 1941 can certainly be viewed from several different angles. Much depends on whether the final result or the previous process of negotiations is assessed. As for the *result*, here again Bruegel's 'nothing short of a miracle' is valid, perhaps even more than for recognition of the Provisional Government a year ago.[168] The Czechoslovak Republic was legally re-created on the British soil and with the British consent. Although in view of many Czechoslovak exiles the British needed two years for something that the Soviets managed to grant in two weeks, this comparison is hardly sound. The Soviet rulers could easily make a foreign policy U-turn twice in two years and then even present all this as a continuous line of Soviet foreign policy. Since the Soviet appeasement of Hitler from 1939–41 did not result in any territorial losses to Czechoslovakia, many Czechs and Slovaks soon did believe the Soviet version of the previous events... British foreign policy, on the other hand, at least respected certain rules of both international law and constitutional procedures of particular countries. Beneš in fact offered a *modus vivendi* – the juridical continuity of the pre-Munich republic and of his own presidential function. But as it was based on illegality of everything that had happened under the threat of force, its acceptance by the British would have automatically meant that also British involvement in the Munich Agreement and the ensuing negotiations was illegal from the very beginning. Juridical continuity of the Czechoslovak Republic here clashed with continuity of British foreign policy. Although by 1941 few politicians and officials dissented from the view prevailing in the Foreign Office ever since October 1938, that is that Munich was a débâcle,[169] it was something else to say that the Prime Minister's signature of the Agreement had been invalid from the very beginning. Not even Churchill and Eden were ready to say that, despite the fact that they derived much of their reputation from criticism of appeasement.

Thus the recognition of the Czechoslovak government was accorded as a revolutionary act, unprecedented and unparalleled from the legal

167) See Chapter 4.
168) Bruegel, The Recognition of the Czechoslovak Government..., *op. cit.*, p. 1.
169) Lammers, From Whitehall after Munich, *op. cit.*

point of view. What General de Gaulle did not achieve in four years in Britain, Beneš managed to get in less than two years, although their original positions were not dissimilar. (And Beneš shared with the general his 'often baseless suspicions of Britain'.[170]) True, before 1940 Beneš was far more notable a figure than de Gaulle. For twenty years his name had been intrinsically connected with that of Czechoslovakia and therefore also his claim to chair the state structures in exile was less questionable than that of Charles de Gaulle. On the other hand, by 1941 de Gaulle was able to mustard military forces that both by their number and importance far exceeded the Czechoslovak ones.[171] There were perhaps three reasons for this dual British treatment of the two men and their efforts. Firstly, unlike de Gaulle, Beneš could prove that he had both the resistance structures and even the home government behind him.[172] Secondly, a number of the French in London were highly critical of de Gaulle and made their feelings known vehemently to influential British contacts.[173] Beneš, on his part, either managed to come to terms with his opponents, at least temporarily, or to convince the influential British circles of their unimportance. After Hodža's departure to the United States in 1941, they consisted virtually of nonentities and the British authorities treated them accordingly, especially if their activities seemed to undermine the Allied war effort.[174] Thirdly, there was a clear feeling on the part of Churchill, Eden and many other British politicians and officials (and certainly in the substantial part of British population) that Britain owed something to Czechoslovakia. Although not many explicit statements to that sense survived in the relevant documentation,[175] it was probably one of the

170) Barker, *Churchill and Eden at War*, p. 32.
171) Probably the best book on the topic of de Gaulle's exile in Britain is: Kersaudy, François, *De Gaulle et Churchill. La mésentente cordiale,* Paris, Perrin 2001 (Czech translation by Pavel Starý: *De Gaulle a Churchill. Srdečná neshoda*, Praha, Themis 2003).
172) As late as January 1942, Eden refused de Gaulle's proposal that he should take over SOE's French section with the following words: 'It would not, we fear, be prudent to rely ... on the assumption that the National Committee enjoys the adherence, open or secret, of a very large majority of French citizens.' Cited from: Barker, *Churchill and Eden at War*, p. 48.
173) *Ibid.*, p. 44.
174) Kuklík – Němeček, *Proti Benešovi!*, pp. 369–411.
175) There are, however, exceptions. See e.g. *AMZV*, LA-D, box 61, 169/dův/41, G. Winter's report on his talk with Miss Davies, director of the Labour Party's publication department, 20 January 1941. Troutbeck wrote as early as on 1 September 1939 in his memorandum: 'On moral grounds we cannot hold ourselves wholly blameless for their [the Czechoslovaks'] current plight...' *PRO*, FO 371/22899, C 13304/7/12, Troutbeck's memorandum, 1 September 1939.

reasons why the miracle of successful creation and recognition of the whole state structure of Czechoslovak institutions on the British soil could come about.

If, on the other hand, the *process* of recognition negotiations is to be assessed, it is hard to disagree with Bruce Lockhart who wrote into his diary a week before the recognition was granted: 'Our policy towards the Czechs has been bloody, but the worst part of it has been the raising of hopes and then the damping down process.'[176] It was not, however, the Foreign Office bureaucrats, the alleged 'Munichoids', as they were rather unjustly perceived by many Czechoslovak exiles, who slowed down the process. Although most of them considered the provisional status of the Czechoslovak institutions in Britain as adequate in the circumstances, once they got the political signal from Churchill and Eden for the recognition in April, they started operating towards that end and there was no division of opinion that it should be attained. The delays were caused initially by Eden himself, who had not enough time to deal with this minor issue, and later by the Dominions, namely Australia and general Smuts who disliked Beneš personally and had been against recognition of his government already in 1940. Martin Brown suggests that the Foreign Office was not obliged to consult the Dominions.[177] Also some Czech historians have called the care for the Dominions' opinion a mere pretext for Foreign Office's 'constant pro-crastination'.[178] However, it was clearly the Cabinet's aim to have the Commonwealth foreign policy co-ordinated in the time of war, as even the records of its pertinent meetings of 14 and 17 July clearly show. Five months later Eden grasped the position when asked by Stalin to agree with territorial changes in Central and Eastern Europe: 'I am afraid we have a troublesome Constitution, and ... we have to consult the Dominions, who are helping us in the war and naturally expect to be consulted as to what we arrange as regards national frontiers after the war.'[179] The *de jure* recognition of Beneš's government was intrinsically connected with the question of Central European frontiers. Therefore

176) *HLRO*, Bruce Lockhart papers, diary No. 38, 11 July 1941.
177) Brown, *Dealing with Democrats*, p. 144. The author cites Harold Nicolson's book *Diplomacy* (London 1939, p. 177): 'There is nothing which need prevent a Dominion Government from taking a wholly independent line in foreign policy.'
178) *DHČSP*, No. 204, p. 249 – note 1,18 July 1941.
179) *PRO*, FO 371/32874, N 109/5/38, record of an interview between Eden and Stalin, 16 December 1941.

seeking an agreement with the Dominions can hardly be interpreted as a sign of Central Department's attempt to procrastinate over the issue. For it were them, Strang *et cons*, who first wanted to overcome the Dominions' resistance – only to be stopped by Lord Cranborne. And then they quickly came up with a compromise solution aiming at least at cancellation of the humiliating provisional status! If they had been looking for a pretext to block full recognition, they could have argued that the Dominions' response made any further steps towards that aim impossible, at least for the time being. But there is no trace of such an attitude in the Foreign Office files.

The relevant British documents from the turn of June and July 1941 show clearly that it was only the Soviet initiative that finally brought the issue to a clear and concise solution. Otherwise the British would have only offered the 'compromise solution'. Beneš would have had no choice but to agree, though it is very likely that after some time, which would probably have been measured by month rather than years, he would have launched another diplomatic offensive for the full *de jure* recognition anyway.

Although in new circumstances, after the Soviet entry into the war, Eden distanced himself from the 'compromise solution' in a very spectacular way, he had been fully aware of the plan and had supported it from the very beginning. No initiative to override the Dominion obstacle came from his side, however, until 14 July – when it became clear that full Soviet recognition of the Czechoslovak government was a matter of days. This fact shows that again British policy towards Czechoslovakia suffered from lack of political leadership. That occurred only occasionally – first time in April and then only some three months later in the situation of acute danger of solely Soviet recognition with all the negative political consequences entailed. Neither Churchill with Eden, nor the Foreign Office wanted the Czechs to fall under the dominant Soviet influence. Here starts a continuous line of British policy that runs counter to the widespread ideas of an alleged British effort to attribute Czechoslovakia to a 'Soviet sphere', which are so popular especially in the Czech historiography.

Bruce Lockhart again played a pivotal role in the whole process of recognition. It seems that this time he showed less restraint than in the spring and summer 1940 and that he supported the Czechoslovak case more straightforwardly. He had a real influence on Eden, repeatedly made him find time for the Czechs and was relaying him the moods in the Czechoslovak camp.

The impact that the *process* had on the Czechoslovak exiles was, however, detrimental as it only supported their already strong mistrust of Britain. The British procrastination coincided with reports of Vansittart's retirement from the Foreign Office, which coupled with totally unfounded rumours of Horace Wilson's growing influence in the Foreign Office.[180] When the negotiations on full recognition of the Czechoslovak government protracted, the depressed President said in Lockhart's presence on 12 July 1941, that he did not understand British policy and 'could only assume that it was continuation of Munich'.[181] It seems almost impossible that at that stage of the war he could still be serious. However, as we shall see, that was not his last statement to that sense. Nonetheless, he continued with a bitter comment about possible impact of his failure to obtain recognition from the British upon the situation in the Protectorate: 'Home Czechs could say: Russians have recognised us. English haven't. Beneš and Masaryk who have always been "Westerners" have failed.'[182] According to his own record, he understood from Lockhart's 'diffident account' that 'perhaps' one of the reasons for postponements were 'conditions in the Conservative Party where was still a lot of people guilty of Munich'. From this alleged hint Beneš deduced that 'it is the real reason for postponements; the Munichoids are not only in the F.O., but above all in Parliament and the Conservative Party'. He was blunter in his talks with Lockhart when revealing the 'Munich tendencies' in British policy: Obviously some Cabinet members were still pursuing 'Munich policy' ['Mnichováctví'], though against Churchill's and Eden's will. He emphasised that 'the British government does not make its duty, that they are responsible for Munich, that I am not begging for anything, that I am just observing whether they are making their duty and undoing what they helped to cause'.[183] Beneš here started presenting and using Munich as a debt that the British had towards Czechoslovakia and were expected to pay back. It was only partly accomplished by granting full recognition to his government.

180) *Válečné deníky Jana Opočenského*, 22 May 1941, p. 117.
181) *Ibid.*, 12 July 1941.
182) *HLRO*, Bruce Lockhart papers, diary No. 38, 12 July 1941.
183) *AÚTGM*, EB-L, box 110, Beneš's record of his talks with Lockhart, mid-June – 16 July 1941.

The Polish-Czechoslovak Confederation
in British, Polish and Czechoslovak plans

On 22 November 1939, one day after his talk to Maisky, possibly about 'no objections against the Soviet system being established in Czechoslovakia' and his acceptance of a 'federative tie between his country and the Soviet Union', Beneš presented to the P.I.D. experts, Leeper and Lockhart, an entirely different vision of future Central Europe: Russia would not in his view seek to encroach on Western Europe if she felt secure against German aggression; the best bulwark against such German aggression would be a joint buffer state composed of Poland and Czechoslovakia that would at the same time mark 'the boundaries of Bolshevism'; the Polish part in this confederation would have to be a small ethnographical Poland that would not menace or excite Soviet Russia; the prerequisite for the formation of a Polish-Czech federation must be the abandonment of any dreams by the Poles of regaining their former territories now occupied by Russia. Beneš, however, feared that they would not do so until they were convinced that this was impossible. Therefore he thought that events must be allowed to develop further before he could conduct any detailed conversations with the Poles.[1] This communication encompassed several problems that arose during the subsequent four years of negotiations on remodelling of Central Europe, and it also adequately singled out the major stumbling block. The Polish politicians did not give up their eastern provinces until it was too late (and even then only some of them really did so). Beneš was not willing to wait so long. However abortive the whole series of negotiations on federalisation of Central Europe turned out to be at the end, it certainly represents a remarkable political initiative aiming at an alternative future of the whole region from the one that eventually befell it.

1) *PRO*, FO 371/23132, C 19148/72/55, Leeper to Strang, 22 November 1939, Jones' minute, 29 November 1939; see also pp. 183–185.

Edvard Beneš earned much of his growing prestige amongst British officials from his friendly contacts with the Polish exiles, especially Sikorski.[2] It seemed that in the situation of deadly menace to both nations, at least their exiled leaders were able to overcome eternal controversies and mutually hostile national stereotyping. Beneš had sufficient reports on what was expected of him. Even Hugh Dalton, the Labour Party foreign policy expert, criticised Czechoslovak failure to create alliance with Poland and pointed out that any Czechoslovak political action in Britain could succeed only if it had a broader Central European footing. The atmosphere in Britain was growingly pro-federative: even the Labour Party proclaimed on 8 November 1939 that 'Europe must federate or perish'.[3] At the same time Dalton strongly recommended building of a Polish-Czechoslovak bloc as a barrier against both Germany and Russia.[4] In one of his messages to the home resistance organisations from December 1939, Beneš emphasised that his public statements signalling willingness to limit the state sovereignty, including the federative projects, were '*above all a tactical matter*. For some time we will have to speak that way. It has much to do with the fact that England and France have not overcome their conceptions of a better arrangement of Central Europe both in minority and economic issues. ... Therefore we cannot say today that we are against federations...'[5] When in January 1940 the Polish government wished to connect its recognition of the Czechoslovak National Committee with an agreement on future Polish-Czechoslovak co-operation and mutual support of the Czechoslovak-German and Polish-Soviet frontiers, Beneš refused.[6] Later he turned the question of conversations on federation with Poland into his advantage: in crucial negotiations with the British on recognition, he effectively used the argument that

2) *PRO*, FO 371/22900, C 18918/7/12, Lockhart's memorandum, 20 November 1939.
3) Jaksch, Wenzel, *Cesta Evropy do Postupimi* [Europe's road to Potsdam], Praha, ISE 2000, p. 229.
4) *NA Praha*, AHR, box 146, 1-13-16-18, Hubert Ripka's talk with Hugh Dalton, 3 August 1939.
5) *Edvard Beneš: Vzkazy do vlasti*, No. 13, Beneš's report home, 9 December 1939; marked in the original.
6) Táborský, *Prezident Beneš mezi Západem a Východem*, p. 105; Brandes, *Großbritannien und seine osteuropäischen Allierten 1939–1943*, p. 77; Idem, Konfederace nebo Východní pakt? Polsko-československé vztahy za druhé světové války [The Confederation or the eastern pact? Polish-Czechoslovak relations during the Second World War], *Slovanský přehled* [Slavic survey], Prague, Vol. 28, 1992, No. 4, pp. 436–448, here p. 437.

inequality with the Polish government rendered any serious negotiations with his partners impossible.[7]

During the spring of 1940, the plan for a Polish-Czechoslovak federation was discussed in Polish political circles, including the Polish National Council.[8] The Foreign Office noted and welcomed Masaryk's utterance during his dinner with Robert Boothby that the Czechoslovak state 'could never be reconstituted in its old form' and that they were 'examining the possibilities and problems of federation'.[9] Some of the prominent Polish exiles, however, sought a co-operation with Hodža and other anti-Beneš – especially Slovak – exiles. Roberts called the idea of using the Slovaks against the Czechs foolish and Frank Savery, the 1st secretary at the British Embassy to the Polish government, advised the Poles to act in close touch with Beneš as with by far the most important personality.[10] Sikorski soon assured Beneš that he had warned members of his government that this nonsense must cease.[11] He really condemned Tytus Filipowicz, the former Polish Ambassador to the United States, for founding together with Hodža a Polish-Czech-Slovak club of cultural co-operation and all Polish ministers turned down the invitation to participate in it.[12] At the same time, however, Sikorski himself thought that Beneš had been wrong to exclude Hodža from the government and at a meeting of the Polish Cabinet he presented further contacts with the ex-Premier and a hidden support of him as a useful tool for further dealing with Beneš.[13] Reports about these contacts only fostered the

7) *PRO*, FO 371/24288, C 6283/2/12, Cadogan's minute, April 29; *DČSZP 1939–1940*, No. 230, pp. 470–479, Record of the points raised by Dr. Beneš in his conversation with Sir Alexander Cadogan on 26 April 1940. See also Beneš's report of his talks at Chatham House: *DHČSP*, No. 61, pp. 83–84, 9 March 1940.

8) *Czechoslovak-Polish Negotiations of the Establishment of Confederation and Alliance 1939–1944*, Prague, Publishing House Karolinum and the Institute of History, Academy of Sciences of the Czech Republic 1995, No. 14, p. 44, footnote 1.

9) *PRO*, FO 371/24287, C 1447/2/12, Waley to Makins, 27 January, Roberts' and Makins' minutes, 30–31 January 1940.

10) *PRO*, FO 371/24289, C 7815/2/12, Roberts' minute, 7 July, Savery to Roberts, 16 July 1940. Savery thought that the Polish government in France had been misled by the French government owing to the latter's hostility to Beneš.

11) *Czechoslovak-Polish Negotiations...*, No. 23, p. 53, Beneš's minutes of his conversation with Sikorski, 5 September 1940; *PRO*, FO 371/24292, C 9969/8531/12, Lockhart to Halifax, 12 September 1940.

12) *PRO*, FO 371/24292, C 9361/8531/12, Kennard to Halifax, 28 August 1940.

13) *Ibid.*, C 8920/8531/12, Bridge to Savery, 20 August 1940; Němeček, Jan, *Od spojenectví k roztržce* [From alliance to quarrel], Praha, Academia 2003, pp. 73, 77.

anti-Polish mistrust in the Czechoslovak circles and later gave rise to fears that the Poles in fact wished to create a tripartite federation dominated by Poland.[14] The Foreign Office went even further in its effort to promote a Polish-Czechoslovak rapprochement when it successfully suggested that generals Ingr and Sikorski might mutually visit the Polish and Czechoslovak troops in Scotland. The British Ambassador Howard Kennard told Sikorski on that occasion that the British government 'attached importance to the Polish Government entering into closer relations with the Czechs'.[15]

Soon the Foreign Office was stricken by the intensity of the Czechoslovak-Polish co-operation. In September 1940 the two leaders exchanged visits and agreed that the common and parallel interests represented in each case 75–80% of the sum total of their interests. General Sikorski above all welcomed Beneš's assurance that an arrangement with Poland must be a preliminary condition to any Russo-Czechoslovak understanding.[16] Lockhart commented on these developments with careful optimism: 'I hope, more strongly perhaps than I believe, that this useful and promising beginning may produce fruitful results.' The real bar, however, he saw in the feeling of most Poles that the Czechs and Slovaks were their social and cultural inferiors. He recommended promoting a Polish-Czechoslovak rapprochement 'by a tactful insistence on its desirability'. Roberts rightly remarked that the British had consistently acted on that line.[17] Sikorski's proclamation, that in the event of future scheme of federation for Eastern and Central Europe, Poland and Czechoslovakia would take the lead in any such movement, was viewed as 'a notable advance'.[18] Even more far-reaching were Beneš's views that he presented to Lockhart: He was prepared to accept a new federal formation for Central Europe that would replace 'the previous water-tight grouping of small nationalist states'. He did not see any objection to a federal combination of monarchies and republics. He saw the Czechoslovak-Polish federation as an essential factor in the establishment of a

---

14) *PRO*, FO 371/26376, C 6/6/12, Griffin's memorandum, 8 January 1941.
15) *PRO*, FO 371/24292, C 8531/8531/12, Roberts' minute, 14 August, C 8920/8531/12, Savery to Roberts, 22 August, Makins' minute, 27 August, C 9361/8531/12, Kennard to Halifax, 28 August 1940.
16) *Ibid.*, C 9969/8531/12, Lockhart to Halifax, 12 September 1940.
17) *PRO*, FO 371/24292, C 9969/8531/12, Lockhart to Halifax, 12 September, Roberts' minute, 20 September 1940.
18) *Ibid.*, Kennard to Halifax, 10 October, Roberts' minute, 14 October 1940.

real equilibrium in Central and Eastern Europe. In order to achieve this aim, Beneš was prepared to go so far as to accept a customs union, a single currency and common General Staff. The Czechoslovaks might be able to build a bridge between Poland and Russia while the Poles could play a similar role between the Czechs and Magyars. Lockhart appreciated the solid foundation of a Polish-Czechoslovak federation that a) avoided the risk of imposing an antiquated super-structure like the restoration of the Habsburg monarchy, b) filled out the dangerous vacuum in Central Europe, and c) would set an admirable example to the Balkan States. Roberts added a highly prophetic warning: The position of Russia after the war will be of vital importance to any policy of Polish-Czech federation: 'If Germany is completely defeated, then the Russians might regard such a federation as a new cordon sanitaire...' But if Germany was beaten but not broken, Russians might be glad to have a Slav bloc between them and the Germans. The British could not in his view go beyond encouraging on general lines the idea of Polish-Czech collaboration. Now even usually sceptical Makins consented: 'Czechs and Poles are thinking along the same lines, & something solid may emerge from their collaboration in adversity.'[19]

Indeed, the end of 1940 was marked by 'a very laudable rivalry to see which of the two parties can be the most cooperative'.[20] The Czech one came up with a proposal for the establishment of a permanent Polish-Czechoslovak Committee of co-operation composed of an Executive Committee and four sub-committees, the Polish party reciprocated with a draft of a joint resolution which Beneš accepted almost 'as it stood'. Apart from condemning the German terror in Poland and the Protectorate, it proclaimed determination 'to enter as independent and sovereign states into a close political and economic association which would become the basis of a new order in Central Europe'. 'It is a very good document.' 'Excellent,' Strang and Cadogan applauded.[21] It was decided to give it the maximum publicity, Charles Peake, head of the News De-

19) *PRO*, FO 371/24287, C 10776/2/12, Lockhart to Halifax, No. 13, 7 October, Roberts' minute, Makins' minute, 14 October 1940.
20) *PRO*, FO 371/24292, C 13276/8531/12, Roberts' minute, 16 December 1940.
21) *PRO*, FO 371/24292, C 11203/8531/12, Lockhart to Halifax, 16 October, C 11782/ /8531/12, Kennard to Halifax, 31 October, C 11838/8531/12, Lockhart to Halifax, 1 November, Strang's and Cadogan's minutes, 11 November 1940; *Czechoslovak-Polish Negotiations...*, No. 29, pp. 64–65, Declaration of the Provisional Czechoslovak Government and the Polish Government, 11 November 1940.

partment, called a conference of diplomatic correspondents with a clear intention: 'The leader writers of the principal morning papers will be bullied, bribed or cajoled into taking some notice of it.' His proposal to invite Strang or Makins was, however, turned down because the Foreign Office did not wish to appear too prominently in this spontaneous Polish-Czechoslovak action: 'We approve it wholeheartedly & desire the maximum publicity, but it should not appear that we sponsored the declaration.'[22] The Prime Minister 'warmly welcomed' the declaration in Parliament. The positive expectation was unanimous; Geoffrey Mander, the Liberal MP, described the projected Polish-Czechoslovak political and economic association after the war as 'the basis of a new order in central Europe and guarantee of its stability'.[23] The Polish-Czechoslovak tie-up was similarly welcomed also in the Labour Party leadership – by Attlee[24] or later by Hugh Dalton, the Minister of Economic Warfare, who called it 'the essential first step towards a satisfactory re-organisation of Middle Europe'.[25]

On 1 November 1940, Beneš sent Sikorski his memorandum *Échange des vues sur la collaboration polono-tchécoslovaque après la présente guerre* which presented a plan for *une conféderation sui generis* with two separated governments, parliaments and heads of two states, but with a federal Council composed of delegates of the two countries and a common parliamentary committee, the resolutions of which would be subordinated to the approval of the two parliaments. The state sovereignty would be limited in financial and commercial matters (with the object of a trade and monetary union), foreign policy would be common but diplomatic representation separated, the two armies would have unified equipment and the two General Staffs would be roofed by a common one. For attaining these aims, however, there were at least two necessary conditions: equalising of social structures of Poland and Czechoslovakia and good relationship between Poland and the Soviet Union.[26] Thus the

22) *PRO*, FO 371/24292, C 11838/8531/12, Roberts' minutes, 6 November, 11 November, Peake's minute, 9 November, Strang's minute, 11 November 1940.
23) *H. C. Deb.*, 5th Series, Vol. 367, 26 November 1940, Col. 73.
24) *AMZV*, LA-D, box 61, 243/dův/40, G. Winter's record of his talk with C. Attlee, 12 October 1940, see also 274/dův/41, G. Winter's report on his talk with A. Greenwood's secretary Henderson, 1 February 1941.
25) *PRO*, HS 4/63, S.O.'s minute, 17 October 1941.
26) *Czechoslovak-Polish Negotiations...*, No. 28, pp. 59–63, Beneš's memorandum to Sikorski, 1 November 1940; Němeček, *Od spojenectví k roztržce*, pp. 90–91.

policy towards the Soviet Union functioned already the other way round from what Beneš had promised to Sikorski and to which the General attached much importance:[27] something that was to be subordinated to Czechoslovak-Polish relations changed into a *sine qua non* for Polish-Czechoslovak co-operation. Indeed, the major stumbling block for the whole project was already brewing. Although the Central Department observed that the Czechs proposed to abandon very little of their sovereignty, generally it was considered reasonable to start with the concrete problems, rather than to 'spin grand designs out of academic cerebrations'.[28] These words by Strang also applied to various combinations of countries that would join in the federation.

Sikorski's reply confirmed the expectation of a radical redraft in the part of relations with Russia: a good will should be reciprocated; by then the Soviet Union did not recognise any of the two governments and Molotov negotiated with Hitler in Berlin. Poland should also have the right for her pre-war territorial integrity.[29] Roberts thought that Sikorski was near the mark in his comments, but it was 'clearly politically desirable that the Czech end of the Polish-Czech federation should make every effort to improve relations with the U.S.S.R.'[30]

Lockhart was aware that other serious obstacles lurked in the background, especially the grim spectre of Teschen (Těšín); in his view something had to be done to obliterate the memory rankling 'in every Czech mind ... of Colonel Beck's stab in the back' in the time of Munich. In any case Beneš was praised in the Foreign Office for his wise decision to leave this contentious matter out of discussions for the present. Among some Czechoslovaks there were suspicions of what might be called 'Poland's Great Power mania' and disquietude regarding the disparity in numbers between the two races (reaching a proportion of more than 2:1). In spite of all this, Lockhart viewed the achieved progress as 'eminently satisfactory' and some form of Polish-Czechoslovak federation as 'an attainable ideal'. But he warned against introduction of wider issues: other nations might join a Polish-Czechoslovak commonwealth only at a much later date, which primarily applied to Hungary. 'Any attempt at this stage

27) *PRO*, FO 371/24292, C 9969/8531/12, Kennard to Halifax, 20 September 1940.
28) *Ibid.*, C 11983/8531/12, Warr's minute, 11 November, Strang's minute, 14 November 1940.
29) *Czechoslovak-Polish Negotiations...*, No. 33, Sikorski's memorandum for Beneš, 3 December 1940.
30) *PRO*, FO 371/24292, C 13276/8531/12, Roberts' minute, 16 December 1940.

of the war to foist a wider scheme of federation on the small nations of Central Europe is almost certain to end in failure, and in that failure any hope of a satisfactory Polish-Czechoslovak agreement will disappear.' On the other hand, he viewed this project as an immediate necessity, as a test for any future scheme of federation in Europe and at the same time as a solid bulwark in Central Europe that might serve British interest in the event of Germany's collapse. For all these reasons he recommended making Polish-Czechoslovak federation a definite British war aim and giving it resolute support of British diplomatic effort.[31] The British representatives at the Polish government, Kennard and Savery, were strictly against, pointing out the deeply rooted anti-Czechoslovak sentiments in Poland which had hardly been entirely eradicated by the events of the last two years. The position and prestige of the Sikorski government in Poland was not strong enough as to be able to commit itself to any course of action that might be unpopular there. This fact, together with the pro-Russian Czech feelings, combined with the 'practical certainty' that at the end of the war Poland would have to make very considerable territorial sacrifices to Russia on her eastern frontiers, led Kennard to the conclusion: 'I should be very loath to see the idea of federation openly proclaimed at this stage of the war as one of the British war aims.' The ground should rather be carefully and gradually prepared beforehand.[32]

On the other side, numerous talks with Czechoslovak exiles, including officers, testified to the Czech fears of Polish ambitions and eventual absorption in a Greater Poland. 'I asked President Beneš to tell me frankly how seriously he regarded these rumours,' Lockhart reported to the Foreign Office. 'He replied that he had no complaints to make. He deprecated doubts and misgivings and would do his best to suppress them among his own countrymen.' Even alarms among Czechoslovak officers need not be taken seriously. Beneš – according to Lockhart's report – even defended Foreign Minister Zaleski against critical voices from Sikorski's entourage on the ground that he was a very lukewarm supporter of Polish-Czechoslovak collaboration: Although he was 'to some extent' prisoner of certain elements in the Polish Foreign Office who had

31) *PRO*, FO 371/24292, C 11838/8531/12, Lockhart to Eden, 1 November, C 11983/8531//12, Roberts' minute, 12 November 1940; FO 371/26376, C 6/6/12, Lockhart to Eden, 28 December 1940.
32) *PRO*, FO 371/26376, C 6/6/12, Savery's minute, 12 January 1941, C 528/6/12, Kennard to Strang, 15 January 1941.

been hostile to the Czechs, Beneš said that he had always been correct, and the President had never regarded him as anti-Czech. Lockhart ended his assessment of Beneš's policy by a conclusion that the President really wanted to create the Polish-Czechoslovak *bloc* that represented the only possible sea-wall that would stem the tide of revolution which might surge over Central Europe from Russia after a possible collapse of Germany.[33] However, the pertaining entry in Lockhart's diary tells a rather different story: 'Beneš afraid of Polish ambitions, afraid Poles wish to swallow Czechoslovakia. Very anti-Polish [sic! – probably anti-Czech] Foreign Office which, he considers, has learnt nothing and is still full of Beckists. Artsishevski [sic! – Arciszewski] more Beckist than Beck and a great anti-Czech. Zaleski, by whom B[eneš]. is disappointed, "lazy, immobile, and a prisoner to his conscience and to his surroundings".'[34] This is just one example of Lockhart's constant and very efficient effort to improve the picture of Beneš and his collaborators in the eyes of the Foreign Office. On the account of the Polish-Czechoslovak *bloc*, Lockhart's diary provides an interesting testimony in an August entry: two months after the Soviet entry into war, Beneš expressed his growing worries: '…if both Russia and Germany are beaten and rendered helpless, Polish megalomaniac dreams will resurge, and Poland will grab again all that can both in the West and in the East – with the same fatal results as last time.'[35] Indeed, not even this statement found a way to any of Lockhart's memoranda… There is a wide space open for possible explanations of the reasons that brought Lockhart to frequent misinforming of the Foreign Office, ranking just from Lockhart's Czechophilism and personal liking for Beneš and Masaryk up to hints of a possible financial motivation of the chronically indebted Robert Bruce Lockhart.[36]

The discussion in the Foreign Office in January 1941 on the appropriate measure of British support to the Polish-Czechoslovak talks ended in a compromise: Along with Lockhart's recommendations, now

33) *Ibid.*, C 508/6/12, Lockhart to Eden, 12 January 1941.
34) *HLRO*, Bruce Lockhart papers, diary No. 38, 11 January 1941.
35) *Ibid.*, 30 August 1941.
36) He was receiving money from the Czechoslovak Foreign Ministry after World War II, at regular intervals, for his propaganda work for Czechoslovakia. Jiří Brotan was the man who upon Masaryk's orders handed envelopes with U.S. dollars to Bruce Lockhart twice in 1945–46 ($ 20,000 in the first case and $ 16,000 in the second case). Brotan was a Foreign Ministry employee who later entrusted this testimony to Slovak historian Slavomír Michálek to whom I am grateful for this information and for allowing me to publish it.

more moderate, the Secretary of State was to 'emphasise gently' in his conversations with the Polish and Czechoslovak governments 'the importance of collaboration, and even federation, to both peoples and the unreality of frontiers in relation to the supreme consideration of national preservation'. Makins formulated the future political line and Cadogan decided on its distribution to other departments including Ministry of Information: It was out of the question to make the Polish-Czechoslovak confederation one of the *British* war aims, as it should rather become an aim of the two nations involved. Similarly it was not the concern of the British government to say what form the co-operation should have, but the British need not be 'too timid' in their encouragement of the general idea of closer association. With respect to the attitude of the home populations, there was a wide field open for a clever propaganda and if the Allies won, the exile governments would be strong enough. The obstacles were serious: the psychological distrust between the two peoples, the 'incurable tendency of the Poles to play with dissident Slovaks', to make overtures to Hungarians and 'generally to excite the suspicions of the Czechs'. Moreover, many Englishmen gave rise to much misunderstanding and confusion by their meddling in the internal politics of Allied governments. 'For all these reasons our official attitude and all branches of our propaganda should be quiet encouragement of the two Governments, and steady and unexaggerated advocacy of the closest possible collaboration between them.'[37] This was to remain the British political line with respect to the Polish-Czechoslovak negotiations in the ensuing year and a half: any initiative was to be left to the Poles and Czechoslovaks, the British did not intervene in the negotiations; although Eden's 'good offices' were 'always available', the two governments were to be allowed to speak for themselves.[38]

In the first half of 1941, it seemed that they really did so as the common project grew both in size and intensity of co-operation. Apart from the Co-ordination Committee, eight mixed Polish-Czechoslovak committees (five for permanent and three for current co-operation) were set up and seemed to be working smoothly. Both Polish and Czechoslovak newspapers wrote extensively about the co-operation. The two parties

37) *PRO*, FO 371/26376, C 508/6/12, Lockhart to Eden, 12 January 1941, C 528/6/12, Makins' minute, Strang's minute, Cadogan's minute, 19 January 1941.
38) *Ibid.*, C 2531/6/12, Foreign Office to Washington, 22 March 1941; *H. C. Deb.*, 5th Series, Vol. 374, 10 September 1941, Cols. 160–161.

agreed on co-ordination of their propaganda in the United States.[39] The Poles several times assured the Foreign Office that the idea of a Polish-Czechoslovak Commonwealth had full support of the underground political and resistance circles in Poland as well as the population itself.[40] Similarly Lockhart was given a message from the political centre of the secret organisations in Prague welcoming the news of the proposed federation, which was regarded as 'the most important initial step towards the creation of a new Europe'.[41]

On the other hand, the Foreign Office obtained more than enough information of mutual distrust and suspicions. Although Beneš with Sikorski undoubtedly viewed each other with considerable respect,[42] the FO officials also became listeners of numerous complaints from both sides. Foreign Minister Zaleski said to Kennard in December 1940 that his government still regarded the attitude of the Czechoslovak government in certain questions with some suspicion. This he instanced by the exclusion of general Prchala, whose relations with Poland had been friendly, from the Czechoslovak government.[43] Even Sikorski complained to Kennard that Beneš had not fully profited from the lessons of the past two years, and was still inclined to put the blame for what had occurred on others and to regard himself as an innocent victim. In this respect the Polish Prime Minister was certainly right, but Roberts saw behind his more critical attitude Beneš's disinclination to support the Polish views on the restoration of their old frontiers.[44] Another day Masaryk complained to Roberts that Sikorski had talked to him about the necessity for getting rid of 'the old school of statesmen connected with Geneva, meaning by this Dr. Beneš'.[45] The Poles, no doubt, often came up with completely unacceptable proposals, such as the plan for

39) *PRO*, FO 371/26376, C 3298/6/12, Lockhart to Eden, No. 35, 1 April 1941, C 2531//6/12, Lockhart to Eden, No. 24, 12 March 1941; Feierabend, *Politické vzpomínky*, II, pp. 69–71.
40) *PRO*, FO 371/26376, C 528/6/12, Strang's minute, 19 January, Roberts' minute, 30 January 1941, C 1132/6/12, Lockhart to Eden, 31 January 1941.
41) *Ibid.*, C 3231/6/12, Lockhart to Eden, 19 March 1941.
42) *PRO*, FO 371/24292, C 11838/8531/12, Lockhart to Eden, 1 November 1940; FO 371//26376, C 1132/6/12, Lockhart to Eden, 31 January 1941, C 6578/6/12, Lockhart to Eden, 16 June, Makins' minute, 20 June 1941.
43) *PRO*, FO 371/24292, C 13309/8531/12, Kennard to Halifax, 11 December 1940.
44) *PRO*, FO 371/26376, C 961/6/12, Kennard to Eden, 7 February 1941, Roberts' minute, 11 February, C 1611/6/12, Makins' minute, 18 February 1941.
45) *Ibid.*, C 10345/6/12, Roberts' minute, 16 September 1941.

Polish leadership of the combined army.[46] Trygve Lie, the Norwegian Foreign Minister, reported that there existed a Polish map showing territories in belonging of other countries which Poland intended to incorporate after the war – with a large slice of Czechoslovakia.[47] Nonetheless, Lockhart's diary shows that some of Beneš's devices were also rather lunatic, e.g. when he said in a January talk with Dalton, Jebb, Gubbins and Lockhart that the Poles should adopt the Czech spelling reform introduced by Hus.[48]

But most serious was the question of frontiers. An exchange of letters between Sikorski and Beneš on that topic from February 1941[49] was considered a retrograde step in Polish-Czechoslovak relation. Especially Sikorski was fairly criticised in the Foreign Office for his insistence on Poland's right to her borders as of September 1939. It opened the controversial issue of Poland's eastern frontier, to which the British did not feel committed, but did not wish to rub it into the Poles and thus to produce 'depression and suspicion in their minds'. Even more seriously, at least with respect to the mutual relationship, the letter raised the sensitive question of Teschen. Even Makins called Sikorski's letter 'far more foolish than that of Dr. Beneš'. Roberts hoped that Beneš, on his part, was just reserving the position when he stood by the pre-September 1938 frontiers. Lockhart recommended that it could be made known to both parties that the British government deprecated discussion of future frontiers by this stage of war.[50] By then it had been well known both to the Poles and Czechoslovaks. When later, in June 1941, Beneš came up with a proposal to make Těšín the federal capital of the Polish-Czechoslovak Commonwealth, Roberts commented that it was 'typical of his fertile but theoretical mind'. It could work as an ideal solution in any rising Anglo-Saxon community 'without established traditions and a strong sense of compromise', but hardly in the case of ancient European nations composing a federation.[51]

46) *PRO*, FO 371/26376, C 6251/6/12, Roberts' minute, 5 June 1941.
47) *Ibid.*, C 490/216/12, Dormer to the Foreign Office, 13 January 1941.
48) *HLRO*, Bruce Lockhart papers, diary No. 38, 17 January 1941.
49) *Czechoslovak-Polish Negotiations...*, No. 45, pp. 92–93, Sikorski's letter to Beneš, 10 February 1941, No. 47, pp. 99–102, Beneš's letter to Sikorski, 25 February 1941.
50) *PRO*, FO 371/26388, C 2249/216/12, Lockhart to Eden, No. 21, 4 March, Roberts' minute, 13 March, Makins' minute, 15 March, Cadogan's minute, 18 March 1941.
51) *PRO*, FO 371/26376, C 6578/6/12, Lockhart to Eden, 16 June, Roberts' minute, 20 June 1941.

Not everything went so smoothly in practical matters either, not even in the essential matter of diplomatic representation. The Polish Minister of Foreign Affairs August Zaleski appointed only at the end of November 1940 Alexandr Zawisza as a mere chargé d'affaires ad interim with the Czechoslovak provisional government.[52] The British reminded the Poles that an early appointment of a Minister would be desirable.[53] In March 1941, Sikorski asked Beneš for his *agrément* of Karol Popiel. But then the agreed candidate refused, as it would mean abandoning his political career. Indeed, Sikorski had not previously consulted either him or Foreign Minister Zaleski... Only in May the Poles offered Kajetan Morawski, but then it took a month before his name was approved; Beneš and Masaryk wanted to await Sikorski's return from the United States in order to make sure that Morawski's appointment had his approval. This already provoked Roberts to a sarcastic comment: 'There seems to be rather a "hoodoo" over this appointment.'[54]

Most importantly, a fundamental clash between two conceptions of the future Polish-Czechoslovak union arose soon. Although Zaleski was apparently exaggerating when complaining to Kennard that Beneš proposed a mere alliance much along the lines of the 'Little Entente', the Polish plans for close federation were apparently much more far-reaching than Beneš's 'confederation sui generis'. 'The Polish idea seems more sensible than that of the Czechs,' wrote Roberts, 'but the latter, as the smaller partner, are fearful of being absorbed by the Poles.'[55] This understanding for Czechoslovak hesitations remained a stable trace of the Foreign Office's attitude: the Czechs were the weaker party and already had had experience of the Poles trying to commit them much further than they thought desirable in regard to Polish-Russian relations. Accordingly British foreign-policy-makers refused numerous Polish calls for mediation or intervention that would have sought Czech agreement with a closer form of federation.[56] Discords and disagreements within

52) Němeček, *Od spojenectví k roztržce*, pp. 101–102.
53) *PRO*, FO 371/24292, C 13309/8531/12, Kennard to Halifax, 11 December 1940.
54) *PRO*, FO 371/26376, C 2196/6/12, Lockhart to Eden, 3 March 1941, C 4721/6/12, Kennard to Eden, 2 May, C 5549/6/12, Savery to Roberts, 21 May, Roberts' minute, 26 May 1941, C 6094/6/12, Lockhart to Eden, 4 June, C 6563/6/12, Dormer to Eden, 6 June 1941.
55) *PRO*, FO 371/26376, C 4721/6/12, Roberts' minute, 8 May 1941.
56) *Ibid.*, C 6251/6/12, Roberts' record of his talk with Dormer, 5 June 1941, C 6313/6/12, Dormer to Eden (record of his talk with Raczyński), 7 June 1941, C 6608/6/12, Dormer's

the Polish government – between Sikorski on the one hand and Zaleski's Foreign Ministry on the other – only strengthened the British in their decision to stay aloof.[57]

The Soviet entry into war meant a significant milestone also in the Polish-Czechoslovak negotiations. At the first stage it held up their development for a few months because of the Polish-Soviet negotiations, which resulted in the treaty of 30 July 1941 that meant a re-establishment of diplomatic relations and committed both parties to assist each other during the war. This caused a Polish governmental crisis with the resignation of three ministers charged with the Czechoslovak-Polish talks – Sosnkowski, Zaleski and Seyda. It also reminded the Czechoslovaks of the *pressing* problem of the Polish eastern border. But the prospects for progress in Polish-Czechoslovak talks did not seem bad. Indeed, rather surprisingly vis-à-vis later developments, Beneš expected that Russia's entry into war would help the Polish-Czechoslovak federation.[58] On 24 August Beneš received a message from Fierlinger that Molotov's deputy Vyshinsky had 'emphasised very eagerly his personal approval of such a confederation' which would in his view 'give rise to no objection or disputes'.[59] Beneš also asked Maisky formally to obtain a ruling on this subject from Moscow. The President hoped that if Russia continued to act as sensibly as she had done hitherto, it might be possible for the Polish and Czechoslovak governments to make, within the next few months, some agreed declaration of policy regarding confederation.[60]

In this respect President's optimism was justified: In November both parties came up with their written principles of the future tie. The major difference was clear from the titles (Constitutional Principles of the Federal Union of Poland and Czechoslovakia vers. Basic Principles of Czechoslovakia's and Poland's Confederative Association).[61] The Polish proposal, unlike the Czechoslovak one, was for a close union extending

record of his talk with Kot, 13 June 1941, C 10488/6/12, Dormer's record of his talk with Raczyński, 18 September 1941, C 13370/6/12, Eden to Dormer (record of his talk with Kulski), No. 137, 3 December 1941.

57) *Ibid.*, C 6578/6/12, Lockhart to Eden, 16 June, Makins' minute, 20 June 1941.

58) *HLRO*, Bruce Lockhart papers, diary No. 38, 30 August 1941.

59) *Dokumenty ČSR–SSSR*, Vol. I, No. 102, pp. 230–231, note 2; *PRO*, FO 371/26376, C 10191/6/12, Lockhart to Strang, 7 September 1941.

60) *HLRO*, Bruce Lockhart papers, diary No. 38, 30 August 1941; *PRO*, FO 371/26376, C 10191/6/12, Lockhart to Strang, 7 September 1941.

61) *Czechoslovak-Polish Negotiations...*, No. 75, pp. 154–156, No. 81, pp. 160–163.

to a common defence organisation and a common diplomatic service. On the other hand, it reflected that the Poles were frightened of the superior industrial and economic resources of Czechoslovakia. Therefore customs tariffs were to be maintained.[62] Paragraph 1 provided for the accession of other states, clearly to provide for cases such as Hungary. Lockhart saw the chief difference clearly: 'Poles want a Bundesstaat (otherwise want to swallow Czecho); Czechs insist on Staatenbund.'[63] Also the Foreign Office understood the Czech caution, even the reasons why they preferred the somewhat vaguer term 'confederation'. But the following Roberts' comment on the Polish proposal reflected the ambivalent feelings in the Central Department: 'The Czechs will naturally be suspicious of Polish attempts to make the confederation a very close union, since the Poles will outnumber the Czechs by nearly three to one. It is also much better that this union should grow up as an organic growth and should not be forced to grow too quickly. At the same time there is considerable force in the Polish thesis that unless the bonds of union are pretty close and definite the new arrangements will amount to little more than the old Little Entente which broke down immediately when pressure was brought upon it.'[64]

On 19 January 1942, the Declaration of the Czechoslovak and the Polish Governments on the agreement in the basic questions of confederation was adopted at the 5th meeting of the Czechoslovak-Polish Co-ordination Committee.[65] The signature and publication of the document was hastened by the conclusion of the Greco-Yugoslav Declaration of 15 January. The Co-ordination Committee issued a statement that congratulated the two Balkan governments on their initiation of the Balkan Union and expressed confidence that only its co-operation with the Confederation of states in Central Europe could 'assure security and develop prosperity of the vast region stretching between the Baltic

62) Anita Prażmowska apparently does not seem to be right when saying that the Polish proposal 'envisaged total economic integration, which the Czechoslovaks found unsatisfactory because they felt that this would restrict their economic development which was more advanced than Poland's'. Prażmowska, *Britain and Poland 1939–1943. The Betrayed Ally*, p. 142.
63) *HLRO*, Bruce Lockhart papers, diary No. 38, 21 December 1941. See also *Czechoslovak-Polish Negotiations...*, p. 39, note 2, Ripka's minutes of his talk with Beneš on 12 February 1940: 'It would be a certain kind of Staatenbund, not Bundesstaat.'
64) *PRO*, FO 371/26376, C 13252/6/12, Roberts' minute, 28 November 1941. See also Warr's minutes of 17 and 19 November in C 12580, C 12676/6/12.
65) *Czechoslovak-Polish Negotiations...*, No. 85, 86, pp. 168–173.

and the Ægean Seas'.[66] The Polish-Czechoslovak declaration itself was a compromise that proclaimed the aim to secure joint policy in the fields of foreign policy, national defence, economy and finance, social policy, communications, post service and telegraph. However, it did not tackle certain most sensitive issues, such as the diplomatic representation or the frontier questions. There were to be a joint General Staff charged with a preparation of defence, and in the time of war also a joint headquarters. In many respects the document did not go beyond declaring a common will to co-ordinate particular policies. Nonetheless, the Foreign Office appreciated the text as a 'very satisfactory document', as it went into much greater detail than previous statements. The more so that unlike the Balkan declaration, which had been concluded under British auspices and signed in the Foreign Office, the two Central European Allies produced their declaration on their own, with no British assistance. 'We certainly cannot object to point (1) stating that the two Governments desire their Confederation to embrace other states of the European area, although no doubt the Poles have in mind Lithuania as one of these states,' Roberts commented on the most controversial issue.[67] Eden welcomed both declarations in the House, joined by Mander, now Parliamentary Secretary to the Secretary of State for Air: 'That is exactly the sort of thing we want to have growing up.'[68]

The declaration meant the zenith of the Polish-Czechoslovak co--operation. It was, however, soon replaced by a sudden and ultimate deterioration of the relationship. Soviet foreign policy became a catalyst. The two parties responded differently to the Soviet geopolitical challenge – when it became clear that during his December visit to Moscow Anthony Eden had been presented with Stalin's territorial demands not dissimilar from his acquisitions resulting from the recent co-operation with Hitler. Polish Foreign Minister Edward Raczyński advised the Lithuanians to stand up for themselves in Europe and America and to seek Polish support in a federal union similar to that which the Poles

66) *PRO*, FO 371/ 30827, C 897/151/12, The Resolution, 19 January 1942.
67) *Ibid.*, Roberts' minutes, 23 and 26 January, Hancock's minute, 26 January, Makins' minute, 27 January, Cadogan's minute, 3 February 1942.
68) *H. C. Deb.*, 5th Series, Vol. 377, 27 January, 4 February 1942, Cols. 651, 1156–1157. See also a letter addressed to the Czechoslovak Minister, Maxmilián Lobkowicz, in which Eden on behalf of the British government warmly welcomed 'this further notable development in the relations between Czechoslovakia and Poland'. *PRO*, FO 371/ 30827, C 897/151/12, Eden to Lobkowicz, 4 February 1942.

were trying to bring about with the Czechs.[69] That was something utterly unacceptable to Beneš who had always been trying to stay on friendly terms with the Soviet Union and had achieved remarkable successes in that respect since 22 June 1941. On 27 December 1941, Lockhart informed Beneš about Stalin's territorial demands (Bessarabia, the Baltic States, territorial acquisitions in Finland). This brought the President to a real lecture in geopolitics that he gave Lockhart the following day: Russia 'will make her demands on us in three waves: (1) territorial rights (for security reasons) over Finland Gulf, Baltic States, Bessarabia. We should meet her here; after all, she is holding 80% of German forces; 50% of Japanese. Second line will be Poland, Ruthenia, Hungary, Balkans, Black Sea line. Here we can come to 50/50 arrangement. Third line will be Germany itself. If we play cards well, can resist here. If we have no policy, we lose all.'[70] In this highly realistic vision of post-war Europe, not dissimilar from the Stalin-Churchill 'percentage agreement' of October 1944,[71] the three Baltic States were written off.

Moreover, in the first months of 1942 it was becoming clear that Moscow's attitude towards confederations in Central and Eastern Europe was rather ambivalent, if not entirely negative. True, in December 1941 Stalin on his own said to Eden in Moscow that the Soviet Union would have no objection to the creation of 'these or those' state federations in Europe.[72] The Soviet leader had apparently read the British memorandum that had previously been submitted to Maisky, welcomed the Polish-Czechoslovak negotiations and expressed British hopes for establishment of a federal system in Central Europe and the Balkans. Eden now appreciated Stalin's attitude, adding that the arising Polish-Czechoslovak federation should be perceived as a positive fact while the Balkan countries would hopefully also find some form of federative

69) Raczynski, *In Allied London. The Wartime Diaries of the Polish Ambassador*, p. 106.

70) *HLRO*, Bruce Lockhart papers, diary No. 38, 28 December 1941.

71) For further details see Smetana, Vít, Sféry vlivu: mýtus, či realita? Jak se za války dělila Evropa [Spheres of influence: myth or reality? How Europe was being divided during the war], *Dějiny a současnost* [History and present], Prague, Vol. 27, 2005, No. 5, pp. 34–37.

72) Martin Brown claims that Eden in Moscow 'failed to secure Stalin's agreement for a proposed Czechoslovak-Polish post-war federation', and on another page writes that the British Foreign Secretary 'failed to secure the Soviet leader's approval for post-war federations'. Brown, *Dealing with Democrats*, pp. 187, 240. These unfounded statements do not withstand confrontation with either the British or the Soviet documentary evidence.

union. All these countries would 'thus have a better chance of preserving their political and economic independence...' Although the English and Russian records of the talk do not vary in substance, the latter does not contain an important additional note: '...against any attack which Germany was contemplating.'[73] Only a month later, however, the Soviet *Pravda* was about to publish a firm refusal of Raczyński's statements in a *Sunday Times* interview of 11 January 1942 on the necessity to construct a centre of power in 'the third Europe' – the area between Germany and Russia.[74] Upon Molotov's direct intervention the article was eventually not published and Moscow contented with a diplomatic note to the Polish government in which the Polish Foreign Minister was criticised for making statements concerning the future of the Baltic States.[75] However, an analysis written in February 1942 by Nikolaj V. Novikov, head of the IV.–European department of the Soviet People's Commissariat of Foreign Affairs, already stated that the two confederations, the Polish-Czechoslovak and Greco-Yugoslav, were directed not only against Germany, but also against the Soviet Union. According to Novikov both unions were considered as a barrier that would bar penetration of the Soviet influence into Europe and forestall Soviet march to the West in an event of Germany's collapse.[76]

In April 1942, the Soviet party dismissed a paragraph on the possibility of post-war federations, confederations or blocks from its draft of the Anglo-Soviet treaty.[77] When a month later in London Eden asked his Soviet counterpart about the reasons for that change, Molotov replied bluntly that it was caused by the attempts to 'direct some of these federations against the USSR'.[78] Eden retorted that the British government

73) Rzheshevskii, Oleg A., *Stalin i Churchill. Vstretshi. Besedy. Diskusii*, Moskva, Nauka 2004, No. 7, pp. 37–49, first talk with Eden on 16 December at 19 hours, esp. pp. 40, 42; *PRO*, FO 371/32874, N 109/5/38, record of an interview between Eden and Stalin, 16 December 1941. See also Avon, *The Eden Memoirs. The Reckoning*, p. 290.
74) Raczynski, *In Allied London*, pp. 356–360.
75) Gibianskii, Leonid J., Problemy vostotshnoi Evropy i natshalo formirovaniia Sovetskogo bloka, In: *Cholodnaia voina 1945–1963*, Moskva, Olma-press 2003, pp. 105–136, here p. 109. In fact, Raczyński mentioned only Lithuania.
76) *Ibid.*, p. 109.
77) Woodward, Sir Llewellyn, *British Foreign Policy in the Second World War*, Vol. II, London, H.M.S.O. 1971, p. 247.
78) *SSSR i germanskii vopros 1941–1949. Dokumenty iz archiva vneshnei politiki Rossiiskoi federatsii*, eds. G. P. Kynin and J. Laufer, tom I (1941–1945), Moskva, Mezhdunarodnye otnosheniia 1996, No. 24, pp. 159–161, Molotov to Stalin, 21 May 1942.

would never be a party to any such a scheme and promised to come up with a new formula. In the negotiations of 23 and 24 May, the two parties agreed again on the formula stressing the need of 'safeguarding and strengthening of the economic, military and political independence of all European countries. This should be done in suitable cases by means of regional understandings and confederations on the basis of friendly relations towards the Union of Soviet Socialist Republics and Great Britain.' But then the difficult negotiations about territorial questions were suspended, mostly as a result of the U.S. pressure, and an alternative British draft signed on 26 May.[79] It did not deal with territorial questions or frontiers and did not contain any mention of confederations either. The Foreign Office, however, assumed that the Soviet government would have been prepared to agree with the above formula.[80]

Already at the end of January 1942, the Czechoslovak government received first hints of Soviet discontent with the extent of Czechoslovak-Polish co-operation: In view of the 'Russian circles' the Declaration of 19 January went too far; the Czechoslovaks were not recommended binding their future with a regime, the foreign policy of which was unclear and economic policy showed conservative tendencies.[81] Statements made by the Soviet diplomats in London in early 1942 on the topic of the Czechoslovak-Polish Confederation were correspondingly reserved. Especially the Soviet Minister to the exile governments in London, Alexander J. Bogomolov, did not miss a single opportunity to criticise or even mock the Polish politicians in his talks with Beneš and Ripka, to strengthen the division between the two countries by stressing the good reputation of the Czechoslovak government in Moscow, and to voice the distrust on the part of the 'Soviet functionaries' of all those federative plans and combinations that might have anti-Soviet pricks.[82] In an attempt to dispel these apprehensions, Beneš lectured to Bogomolov in early February on the necessary conditions that would only enable the creation of the Confederation: '...a similar economic structure, removal

79) Woodward, *British Foreign Policy in the Second World War*, Vol. II, p. 252.
80) *PRO*, FO 371/30827, C 7636/151/12, FO Memorandum, 27 August 1942.
81) Táborský, Eduard, A Polish-Czechoslovak Confederation. A Story of the first Soviet veto, *Journal of Central European Affairs*, Vol. 9, 1950, pp. 379–395, here p. 388; Němeček, *Od spojenectví k roztržce*, p. 172.
82) *Dokumenty ČSR-SSSR*, I, No. 139, pp. 296–298, Beneš's record of his talk with Bogomolov, after 3 February 1942, Nos. 141, 154, 163, 168, pp. 301–303, 319, 331–333, 341–346, Ripka's records of his talks with Bogomolov, 9 February, 5 April, 15 May, 4 June 1942.

of the influence of aristocracy, Beckism, landlords, and a loyal agreement with the Soviet Union.'[83] Not even such a set of conditions, which were hardly acceptable for the Polish government in London, could influence the Soviet attitude. Edvard Beneš was gradually facing a dilemma whether to go further with the 'feudal' Poles or with the Soviets. Along with his world outlook and foreign policy priorities he decided for the latter. For unknown reason, however, he assured the Soviet part of his decision already during Molotov's visit to London in June 1942, and thus he voluntarily resigned the possibility at least to trade this fundamental concession in his future negotiations with the Soviets. As the Russian record reads, Beneš 'repeated that he would not accede to such a Polish-Czechoslovak Confederation which would be hostile to the interests of the USSR and that if he had to make a choice between Poland and the USSR, then he would undoubtedly choose the USSR'.[84] It seems that this proclamation originated in Beneš's gratefulness for the statement of the Soviet government about its adherence to the reconstitution of Czechoslovakia in her pre-Munich borders that he received from Bogomolov shortly before Molotov's arrival.[85]

A month later, the 'Soviet veto' on Czechoslovak participation in the Confederation arrived. Although it was not presented as an official statement of the Soviet government, but opinion of *'milieux soviétiques'* (a distinction that hardly mattered in the Soviet system), the message was clear enough: The Soviet government did not regard the Polish-Czechoslovak confederation as a step towards peace in Europe, but rather as a tool against the Soviet Union, and was therefore against any further negotiations aiming at its creation.[86] The term 'Soviet veto' itself, which

83) *Ibid.*, No. 139, pp. 296–298, Beneš's record of his talk with Bogomolov, after 3 February 1942.
84) Rzheshevskii, Oleg A., *Voina i diplomatiia. Dokumenty, kommentarii 1941–1942*, Moskva, Nauka 1997, No. 118, p. 260, Molotov's talk with Beneš, 9 June 1942. Beneš's own record, made with a delay of at least two days and therefore less reliable, does not contain this remark. *Dokumenty ČSR–SSSR*, I, No. 171, pp. 348–351.
85) *Dokumenty ČSR–SSSR*, I, No. 168, pp. 341–346, Ripka's record of his talk with Bogomolov, 4 June 1942.
86) *Ibid.*, No. 178, pp. 365–366, the Foreign Ministry's record of Masaryk's talk with Bogomolov, 15 July 1942. The record, written either by Masaryk himself or by somebody from his staff, is formulated as an official statement of the Soviet government. It does not seem to be correct, however, as Bogomolov himself in further negotiations denied that it was an official statement of the Soviet government. *Ibid.*, No. 182, pp. 371–376, Ripka's record of his talk with A. J. Bogomolov, 27 July 1942.

was used both by the Czech exiles at that time and by a substantial part of Czech historiography later on,[87] in fact meant that already in mid-1942 the Czechoslovak politicians accepted the main Soviet say in the issues of Czechoslovak foreign policy.

All this development had, of course, serious impact upon Czecho-slovak-Polish relationship and the cleavages widened. During the first half of 1942, since the adoption of the Declaration, the negotiations did not move one bit ahead, partly because Raczyński and Sikorski, the two major advocates of co-operation, spent long time in the United States. Indeed, the joint committees ceased meeting, one after another, by July 1942. Furthermore, the whole Czechoslovak representation was exasperated when the Polish National Council adopted the resolution of 17 March that referred to the co-operation of an independent Lithuania with the nations of Central Europe. Firstly, the Poles, in spite of the Polish-Czechoslovak Declaration, did not consult the Czecho-slovaks in any way before issuing that resolution, and secondly, such a policy was diametrically opposed to Russia's needs and intentions. The Czechoslovak government refused such a policy and Ripka stated in the State Council on 18 May that any military or political association with Poland 'is possible only if Polish policy is clearly and unmistak-ably pervaded by the spirit of friendship for her eastern neighbour, Soviet Russia'.[88] Beneš, Ripka and other Czechoslovak politicians were gradually giving the impression that they were paying less attention to the Polish-Czechoslovak relations than in the past.[89] Some of their ut-terances were really stunning and looked like a systematic preparation of the ground for future disentanglement from the Polish tie. Beneš for example doubted that Sikorski would be able to prevent bolshe-vism from becoming rampant in Poland at the end of the war, whereas Czechoslovakia with its disciplined people following his lead should then become 'an oasis of tranquillity'.[90] Next time he doubted that 'he would eventually have to treat with the same Poles as those with whom

87) Táborský, *Prezident Beneš mezi Západem a Východem*, pp. 98–141; Žáček, Rudolf, *Projekt československo-polské konfederace v letech 1939–1943* [The project of the Cze-choslovak-Polish confederation in the years 1939–1943], Opava, Slezský ústav Slezského zemského muzea v Opavě 2001, pp. 133–164.
88) *PRO*, FO 371/30827, C 6731/151/12, Nichols to Makins, 3 July 1942.
89) *PRO*, FO 371/30834, C 4047/326/12, Roberts' minute, 20 April, Makins to Nichols, 27 April 1942.
90) *Ibid.*, C 4047/326/12, Nichols to Makins, 14 April 1942.

he was now discussing matters in London'. Sikorski might well survive, 'but not the others'.[91] Ripka told Nichols in late May that he remained 'rather sceptical regarding future relations between the two countries'. Although he agreed with the British Minister to the Czechoslovak government that the frontier question was one of the main difficulties, 'the real difficulty at the moment was Russia'.[92]

The Poles were increasingly exasperated by the Czechoslovak emphasis on the necessity of the Soviet-Polish rapprochement, especially as the Polish-Soviet relations deteriorated. And they did not conceal their feelings from either the Czechoslovaks or the British. Raczyński, upon his return from the United States, complained to Ripka that the Polish-Czechoslovak relations entered a difficult if not a critical stage due to the difficulties the Poles were experiencing vis-à-vis the Russians and to the fact that the Czechs were giving the impression that they sided whole-heartedly with the Russians in these disputes and attached more importance to Russia than to Poland.[93] During a luncheon with Beneš on 20 May, Sikorski exploded that Czechoslovak friendship with Russia should not mean obeying 'orders from Moscow'. He could not tolerate Czechoslovaks classifying their friends into categories; they must decide for Poland or for the others.[94] Some three weeks later Sikorski complained to Eden that Beneš was behaving badly and – apparently under his impression that the British government was abandoning the Poles in its Treaty with the Russians – had shown 'signs of backing out of the proposed Polish-Czech confederation'. In Sikorski's view he was 'under Communist influence and seemed to be adjusting his policy away from Poland towards the Soviet Union'. Eden soothed the General that the British were still in favour of a Polish-Czechoslovak confederation and, indeed, of the extension of the confederation principle to other parts of Central and Eastern Europe. An article in that sense was not included in the Treaty only because of the Soviet worries lest some of the confederations be directed against them, although – according to Eden – the Soviet government was favourable in principle to the idea.[95]

91) *Ibid.*, C 5797/326/12, Nichols to Makins, 9 June 1942.
92) *PRO*, FO 371/30827, C 5534/151/12, Nichols to Strang, 28 May 1942.
93) *Ibid.*, C 4835/151/12, Nichols to Eden (report of his talk with Ripka), 8 May 1942.
94) *Czechoslovak-Polish Negotiations...*, No. 108, pp. 200–202, Ripka's minutes of Beneš's conversation with Sikorski and Raczyński, 20 May 1942.
95) *PRO*, FO 954/19, Eden to Dormer, 8 June 1942.

The officials in the Central Department, which dealt both with Czechoslovak as well as Polish affairs, regarded the relationship between the Czechs and the Poles as 'much the most important aspect of the Czechoslovak question'.[96] At the same time they noticed the growing Czechoslovak dependence on the Soviet wishes and apprehended the impact on the position of Poland, especially in view of the Soviet geopolitical ambitions revealed in the long negotiations before the signing of the Anglo-Soviet treaty of alliance of 26 May 1942.[97] The following debate of mid-May reveals some of the major dilemmas and geopolitical traps which British foreign policy was to face in the following three years. Strang forecasted that before too long Beneš would be called upon by the Russians to choose between Russia and Poland: '...in other words, to conclude a treaty with Russia which will make any Polish-Czechoslovak federal scheme empty of meaning, or even stand in the way of its conclusion. The Russians certainly intend to isolate and encircle Poland and to prevent the formation of a Baltic-Adriatic bloc, based on Poland in the north.' Makins even observed 'the general trend of the Soviet policy' amounting to extension of exclusive Russian influence over the whole of Eastern Europe, to be effected by the occupation of Finland, the Baltic States and Roumania, the closest possible association with Czechoslovakia and Yugoslavia, the crushing of Hungary and the encirclement of Poland. To Sargent all this evidently seemed rather fatalistic and therefore he asked Strang how to counter such a Soviet policy. 'I do not think we can counter the establishment of Russian predominance in Eastern Europe if Germany is crushed and disarmed and Russia participate in the final victory,' Strang replied. 'In that case the worst fears of the Poles, Yugoslavs, Greeks & Turks are justified,' Sargent retorted, 'and their only hope for the future lies in a Germany strong enough to counteract Soviet predominance. But I should be very sorry to have to reach such a distressing conclusion.'[98]

Although the Central Department appreciated occasional Czechoslovak assurances of the importance of collaboration with the Poles, by mid-June its officials felt that the devotion of Beneš and his govern-

96) *PRO*, FO 371/30834, C 5797/326/12, Makins' minute, 12 June 1942.
97) Woodward, *British Foreign Policy in the Second World War*, II, pp. 226–254; Kitchen, *British Policy Towards the Soviet Union During the Second World War*, pp. 100–123.
98) *PRO*, FO 371/30834, C 4668/326/12, Makins' minute, 7 May, Strang's minutes, 12 & 14 May, Sargent's minutes, 13 & 14 May 1942.

ment to that cause was not 'entirely wholehearted'. Indeed, Makins even felt 'very dissatisfied about the attitude of Dr. Benes in regard to his relationship to the Poles and the Russians'.[99] In his view already the full recognition combined with Russia's entry into the war had marked change in Beneš's by then collaborative attitude: 'The Russians made overtures to the Czechs, gave them assurances and flattered them, with the result that Dr. Benes has for some months past been casting sheep's eyes towards Moscow and has allowed Polish-Czech relations to deteriorate…' This attitude was 'the purest folly', since the principal hope of a satisfactory settlement in Eastern Europe lay, in Makins' view, 'in a really close relationship between Poland and Czechoslovakia and the final interment of the quarrel which played a significant part in the preliminaries to the present war'.[100] Apparently the Foreign Office's 'lesson from Munich' differed considerably from that of Edvard Beneš and most Czechoslovak exiles. On 13 June Lockhart delivered to the Foreign Office a report on Beneš's talk with Molotov of 9 June.[101] It confirmed Polish worst worries and the Central Department also concluded that Dr. Beneš had gone very far in arriving at a Soviet-Czechoslovak agreement at the expense of the Poles. The salient points were Molotov's recognition of the pre-Munich frontiers of Czechoslovakia, including the recognition of Teschen as part of Czechoslovakia, and Beneš's agreement with Molotov that Polish-Czechoslovak confederation would be dependent upon the Poles agreeing to satisfy Soviet demands generally and their territorial demands in particular. 'Dr. Benes has therefore in effect supported Soviet claims against those of his own partner, Poland,' the Central Department noted in its special memorandum. 'If we accept this position, we must abandon hope of effective Polish-Czechoslovak collaboration, and therefore of realising our scheme for an Eastern European Confederation.' The Secretary of State was again asked to remind the President in a clear

99) *PRO*, FO 371/30834, C 5797/326/12, Roberts' minute, 11 June, Makins' minute, 12 June 1942.

100) *PRO*, FO 371/30827, C 5534/151/12, Makins' minute, 7 June 1942.

101) *HIA Stanford*, Robert Bruce Lockhart collection, box 6, envelope 32, enclosure in Lockhart's minute of 13 June 1942; *The Diaries of Sir Robert Bruce Lockhart 1939–1965*, 13 June 1942, p. 178. Lockhart submitted the record as 'a private and personal communication'. Indeed, only due to the importance of the information he made an exception of his practice of never recording or repeating (after he ceased to be the British representative) his conversations with the President with whom he enjoyed 'a privileged and intimate friendship'. Thus, unusually, the report is not contained in the FO 371 series, but only in Bruce Lockhart papers. *PRO*, FO 800/873, Lockhart's report, 13 June 1942.

language of the importance of the Polish-Czechoslovak co-operation.[102] The memorandum even recommended application of the 'self-denying ordinance', the rule that was just recently proposed to the Soviets, was provoked by their attempts to sign a treaty with the Yugoslav government and generally forbade political treaties of the Great Powers with the 'lesser allies'.[103] But it was a clear nonsense because Molotov's communication could hardly be regarded as a treaty.

The key men in the Foreign Office, however, saw the matters quite differently. Eden himself thought that the faults might be 'pretty evenly divided' between Poles and Czechs, and that Makins was 'a little severe on Dr. Benes. Our Polish friends are not entirely without fault also. If Dr. Benes is slim, the Poles are impatient and impetuous.'[104] And Sargent, shortly afterwards, refused Roberts' suggestion to reconsider the forthcoming British statement on the revocation of Munich (see below) in view of Beneš's behaviour that was torpedoing Polish-Czechoslovak confederation and would hardly change with a further British concession. The Deputy Under-Secretary of State did not find enough evidence for such a statement: 'The unpalatable truth is that unless both Poles & Czechs can gain the good will of the Russians, there is very little chance of there being a confederation at all for it is the Russians who will be in a position to torpedo it.'[105] And, after all, Beneš soon informed Eden that a) the Soviet government 'had definitely been ready to accept the Czech-Polish Confederation' (!), the only condition being that it should not be directed against the Soviet Union, and b) no written documents had passed between the Russians and the Czechs, although the Czechs were expecting a written confirmation of Russia's recognition of their pre-Munich frontiers. Eden said that it would be against the spirit of the British-Soviet agreement or the 'self-denying ordinance', but Beneš objected that it would mean just a confirmation of what the Soviet government, which

102) *PRO*, FO 371/30827, C 5813/151/12, memorandum 'Polish-Czechoslovak Relations', 20 June 1942.
103) Eden submitted the proposal to Molotov on 9 June. On 4 July the Soviet Commissar instructed Maisky to say to Eden that the Soviet party agreed in principle and would like 'to have concrete proposals from the English side in this question'. But those never arrived. Thus, a year later, the two interpretations of this tacit agreement differed substantially. *SSSR i germanskii vopros 1941–1949*, No. 28, p. 165, Molotov's telegram to Maisky, 4 July 1942.
104) *PRO*, FO 371/30827, C 5813/151/12, Eden's minute, 7 June 1942; FO 371/30834, C 5797//326/12, Eden's minute, 14 June 1942.
105) *PRO*, FO 371/30827, C 6364/151/12, Sargent's minute, 21 June 1942.

was not bound by Munich, had already said. Upon this, according to Ripka's record, Beneš warned Eden that he might come up with the question of Munich in its all extent, including the unfulfilled guarantee of the new Czechoslovak frontier by Britain and France. Eden backed down. Otherwise, however, it seems that the conversation was cordial and confirmed a somewhat 'special relationship' between Eden and Beneš.[106]

In late July, however, Ripka informed Nichols of the growing 'difficulties' with the Russians over the confederation. The Central Department took it as a preparation of the ground for deterioration in Polish-Czech relations. 'The recent deterioration in Soviet-Polish relations has clearly presented the Czechs with an awkward problem,' Roberts admitted. 'But I think they would be better advised to keep their own counsel & not make it so easy for the Russians to play the Czechs off against the Poles.'[107] In view of the previous statements by Stalin and Molotov, combined with Beneš's misinforming Eden about his talk with Molotov, the officials were not sure to what degree Bogomolov's 'extreme suspicions' and his hostile arguing against the confederation represented real Soviet policy: 'The Soviet Government are certainly suspicious of the Confederation, but there seems no doubt that Bogomolov makes the very most of these suspicions, and indeed that both the Poles and the Czechs provide him with plenty of material for intrigue between them and against the Confederation.' Ripka said to Nichols that he did not wish the British to raise the question with the Russians anyway.[108] Thus from what the British knew, it all seemed as an issue that might be settled, if only handled sensibly and cautiously.

Beneš's realistic policy of seeking the Soviet approval in fact seemed to be in accordance with British policy throughout summer and autumn of 1942. On 29 September 1942, Eden said in his speech in Leamington that

106) The British Foreign Secretary went so far as asking the Czechoslovak President for his advice how to deal with the difficult Polish question: a settlement of the Polish frontiers depended on the compensation elsewhere, namely in Silesia and East Prussia. But Beneš agreed with Eden that caution was required and that it might be best not to press the Poles for the present as matters might change: '... what was impossible now might well be possible later, when the realities of the situation had made themselves felt.' In this he was to be entirely correct... *PRO*, FO 954/4, Cz/42/4, Eden to Nichols, 25 June 1942; *AÚTGM*, EB-V, box 79, Ripka's record of Beneš's talk with Eden and Nichols, 26 June 1942.

107) *PRO*, FO 371/30827, C 7401/151/12, Nichols to Strang, 24 July, David's minute, 28 July, Roberts' minute, 29 July 1942.

108) *Ibid.*, C 7636/151/12, Nichols to Strang, 29 July 1942, Strang to Nichols, 27 August 1942.

was later distributed to the Allied governments: 'We should continue to foster agreements of this kind (e.g. the Polish-Czech and Greek-Yugoslav Agreements) and to encourage the smaller States to weld themselves into larger *though not exclusive groupings*. Thus they would be better able, in collaboration with the Great Powers, to play their part in maintaining peace.'[109] The marked passage was designed to meet Russian susceptibilities and prevent Russian suspicions. A month earlier, the Foreign Research and Press Service (FRPS) – the British governmental 'think-tank' headed by Professor Arnold Toynbee under the auspices of the renowned Royal Institute of International Affairs (Chatham House), and seated in Balliol College in Oxford to draw in more academics and to escape the blitz – submitted to the Foreign Office its significant memorandum entitled 'Confederations in Eastern Europe'.[110] This blueprint was based on the unfinished projects of the Czechoslovak-Polish and Greek-Yugoslav confederations. In these plans, the first confederation was to incorporate Hungary and perhaps Austria, the southern confederation also Rumania and Bulgaria.[111] The paper was carefully examined in particular Foreign Office departments and two months later a meeting headed by Sargent decided that it should go forward, subject to final revision by the FRPS. Assuming that the object of the scheme was a) to provide durable safeguards against German penetration, b) to promote the security and prosperity of the area, and c) to accept the necessity of satisfying the strategic and political interests of the USSR, Foreign Office and Press Service was asked to consider particular questions. The last of them was: 'how best in any combination to meet what we may expect the Soviet Government to demand in order to guarantee their strategic security and their economic and political interests vis-à-vis any confederation or confederations?'[112]

The British were by then insisting that the two confederations should have good relations with Russia.[113] This condition primarily aimed to influence the Polish-Soviet relationship – to allay Soviet apprehensions and to make the Poles 'behave reasonably'. But the Foreign Office was careful to keep the balance between its particular policies. In late Sep-

109) *PRO*, FO 371/31535, U 1742/1742/70, Roberts' minute, 1 November 1942.
110) Robert W. Seton-Watson, now one of the key FRPS experts, provided the Czechoslovak government with this important paper. *NA Praha*, AHR, box 146, 1-13-15-5b.
111) *PRO*, FO 371/31500, U 420/61/72, Mabbott (FRPS) to Ronald, 3 August 1942.
112) *Ibid.*, Memorandum of 6 October 1942.
113) See e.g. *PRO*, FO 371/31535, U 1742/1742/70, Roberts' minute, 27 October, Warner's minute, 4 November 1942.

tember an idea brewed in the Northern Department that in view of the expected Russian dominant position in Eastern Europe after the war, combined with its current suspicious attitude towards the confederation plans, it should be made 'abundantly clear' to all the countries concerned that they would only get full British support to their confederation plans provided they could secure the goodwill of the Russians. Behind this proposal was a set of secret information suggesting that after the war the Soviet Union might concentrate on the restoration of France as a Russian puppet. 'If we adopt any other course, the Russian tendency will be to oppose our plans not only in Eastern Europe but in Western Europe as well.'[114] Representatives of the other interested Departments refused such a course. In Roberts' view the matter should not be re-garded purely from the Soviet angle: 'We are fighting this war to prevent German domination of Europe, and we have found Allies among the smaller nations of Europe because (1) they prize national independence, and (2) they expect our victory to produce a better Europe than the present German dominated Europe.' Since no European nation would in Roberts' view prefer a Europe dominated by Russia, there was a real danger of Germany rising again after the war as a sort of patron for the minor European States fearful of Russia. Therefore it was necessary to encourage the minor Allies to strengthen their own position, to some extent independently from Britain and Russia. 'Nor do I feel that the Soviet Government can possibly prefer such a France, even if it adopts a Communistic system of government, to Great Britain or the U.S.A. as an Ally.' (If 'France' is replaced by 'Eastern Europe' or 'East Germany', this sentence marks the major error of Western Sovietology in the war and even early post-war years. In a long run, the Kremlin rulers clearly did *not* regard their co-operation with the Anglo-Saxon powers as more important than proliferation of communism and expansion of the area under Moscow's control.) Generally, Roberts went on, Russian doubts could only be dissolved if and when they were 'satisfied regarding the relations between the U.S.S.R. and the Anglo-Saxon Powers', and were therefore 'confident that the proposed federations will not simply be a revival of the old Cordon Sanitaire of 1919'.[115] It was decided to keep

114) *PRO*, FO 371/32918, N 4912/50/38, FO Memorandum (G. M. Wilson), 23 September 1942.
115) *Ibid.*, Roberts' minute, 1 October, Dixon's minute, 2 October 1942; FO 371/30827, C 9156/151/12, Roberts' minute, 26 September 1942.

things as they were, but to handle the matter very carefully because the Russians would regard British and U.S. attitude as one of the tests of their real intentions towards them.[116]

The records of the Soviet-Czechoslovak talks, both Czech and Soviet, from the summer and autumn of 1942 show that also Beneš and Ripka were denying Soviet accusations that confederation plans, such as the Polish-Czechoslovak one, were intended as an instrument against the Soviet Union. Even the Foreign Office by then thought that Beneš was 'doing his best to persuade the Russians of the utility of the proposed Polish-Czech Confederation'. At the same time, however, the President repeated again and again that without Soviet approval there would, of course, be no confederation.[117] For that case he was trying to induce the Soviet government to an unambiguous official statement: 'Provoke me to a rift with the Poles in the confederation issue,' Bogomolov presented Beneš's words of September 1942 to his Moscow masters. 'Give me an official notification of it, so that I could tell that to the Poles and English.' But the Soviet diplomacy was unwilling to do the 'dirty job' of interrupting the Polish-Czechoslovak negotiations instead of Beneš.[118]

The FRPS submitted the ordered papers in early 1943.[119] By then the fate of the northern federation had in fact been sealed. When no official statement arrived from Moscow, but its negative attitude was more than obvious, Beneš attempted to get consent of the Great Powers for a simple Czechoslovak-Polish treaty of alliance and friendship oriented against Germany.[120] The British agreed, expecting that it would not be a substitute but a necessary step towards the practical realisation of the

---

116) Christopher Warner, head of the Northern Department, was thus alarmed at Sumner Welles' and Adolf Berle's advocacy of one big confederation from the Baltic to the Mediterranean to be imposed if necessary by the U.S. and Britain by force. And Sargent called for early consultations with the Americans. *PRO*, FO 371/32918, N 4912/50/38, Warner's minute, 2 October, Sargent's minute, 3 October 1942.

117) *Dokumenty ČSR-SSSR*, I, No. 182, Ripka's record of his talk with Bogomolov, 27 July 1942, Nos. 183, 187, 199, pp. 377–381, 389–390, 407–408, Beneš' records of his talks with Bogomolov, 31 July, 27 August, 30 October 1942; Prečan, Dokumenty sovětské éry v ruských archivech, *op. cit.*, p. 622; *PRO*, FO 371/30827, C 9156/151/12, Roberts' minute, 26 September 1942.

118) Cited from: Prečan, Dokumenty sovětské éry v ruských archivech, *op. cit.*, p. 622.

119) *PRO*, FO 371/35261; published also in: Bán, András D., *PAX BRITANNICA: Wartime Foreign Office Documents Regarding Plans for a Postbellum East Central Europe*, Highland Lakes, Atlantic Research 1997.

120) *PRO*, FO 954/4, Cz/42/8, Eden to Nichols, No. 250, 2 November 1942.

confederation.[121] But the Soviets, or again *'milieux soviétiques'*, did not – refusing to recognise any significant difference between confederation and alliance.[122] From December 1942 onwards, Beneš with his colleagues started to sound a possibility of concluding an alliance treaty with the Soviet Union.[123] Thus the British Foreign Secretary was entirely wrong in his expectation that 'Dr. Beneš would choose the Polish connexion if he was forced to make a choice, but that in present circumstances he did not wish to have to make that choice'.[124] Eden's sobering was all the more painful when, half a year later, he finally recognised where Beneš's foreign policy priorities actually lay.

The question of the Czechoslovak frontiers and the origins of 'permanent solution' of the Sudeten German issue[125]

A week after the full recognition of the Czechoslovak government was granted, Beneš lamented to his Chancellor Jaromír Smutný about British non-committal attitude to the future Czechoslovak frontiers: 'I had a similar experience in the last war; but when somebody gave me a recognition, then he had it all lost. Then I already hold him and, bit by bit, keep pushing him further. Now and here again, they [the British] already feel that they have it all lost, that I already have both Sudetenland and Subc[arpathian] Russia. Only some time is needed. Then they are only afraid of one thing: if they gave us the whole frontier now, they

121) *Czechoslovak-Polish Negotiations...*, No. 147, p. 279, Eden to Masaryk, 19 November 1942; No. 149, p. 280–281, Masaryk to Raczyński, 20 November 1942; *PRO*, FO 371/30828, C 10614/151/12, Roberts' minute, 7 November, Strang's minute, 8 November, Eden's minute, Malkin's minute, 12 November 1942.
122) *AVP*, fund Vyshinski's Secretariat, 295/31/43, Bogomolov's record of his talk with Fierlinger, 8. 1. 1943.
123) *Dokumenty ČSR-SSSR*, I, Nos. 207, 210, pp. 418–419, 423–424, Ripka's records of his talks with V. A. Valkov, 14 & 29 December 1942.
124) *PRO*, FO 954/19, Eden to Dormer, 16 October 1942.
125) To avoid the term 'final solution', which is intrinsically connected with the Jewish Holocaust, I chose the term 'permanent solution' used by President Beneš's secretary Eduard Táborský in April 1942 when he sought a publisher for his study on the problem of the transfer of minorities in Central Europe as a 'permanent solution of minority questions'. Prof. Ernest Barker of the Cambridge University Press refused the manuscript, pointing out apart other things that the technique of transfer of populations was at that time connected with Hitler's policy. *HIA Stanford*, Eduard Táborský collection, box 6, envelope Czechoslovak-British relations, Táborský to Prof. Barker, 15 April 1942, Barker to Táborský, 20 April 1942.

are afraid that we would feel too strong and we would not wish to go to some confederation...'[126]

By early 1941 'the restoration of the whole of the former territory of Czechoslovakia, both in relation to Germany, and to Hungary and Poland' (although with possible minor border rectifications) became Czechoslovakia's fundamental peace aim.[127] However, this had not always been so. Apart from the specific issue of Sub-Carpathian Russia,[128] the Sudeten German minority was the reason for not having pressed for territorial restoration earlier. It was generally agreed that Sudeten Germans must be prevented from causing another tragedy like the one in 1938. Plans for the massive expulsion had been brewing, especially in the Czech non-Communist resistance, since the early stages of the German occupation.[129] But Beneš himself had called such plans in his early talks with the representatives of the *Treuegemeinschaft sudetendeutscher Sozialdemokraten* in September 1939 as 'foolishness'.[130] His own plan for the reduction of the number of Germans in Czechoslovakia was comprised of population expulsion, but also of ceding territory with its inhabitants. As Francis Raška has put it: 'The protection of the basic foundation of Czechoslovak statehood justified, in Beneš's opinion, the sacrifice of some of the original state concepts, specifically the historic frontiers.'[131] Beneš further formulated a concept of national homogenisation by the method of internal population transfers. As he informed the experts in the Royal Institute of International Affairs in Oxford, the Germans were to be concentrated in two districts in western and northern Bohemia where they could get 'local government'.[132] When Beneš tried to push this cantonal plan through, however, he encountered a fierce opposition, especially on the part of the home resistance organisations, but also from his closest collaborators in London.[133] But he did not give up the concept which found its way to the memorandum 'Czechoslovakia's

126) *DHČSP*, No. 210, p. 255, 27 July 1941.
127) *Češi a sudetoněmecká otázka 1939–1945*, No. 47, pp. 84–92, Memorandum Mírové cíle československé; *R. W. Seton-Watson and His Relations with the Czechs and Slovaks*, No. 215, pp. 602–615, Czechoslovakia's peace aims, 1941.
128) See Chapter 4.
129) Raška, *The Czechoslovak Exile Government in London and the Sudeten German Issue*, pp. 38–39.
130) *Ibid.*, p. 40.
131) *Ibid.*, p. 37.
132) *DHČSP*, No. 61, pp. 83–84, 9 March 1940, pp. 101–103, 5 April 1940.
133) Brandes, *Cesta k vyhnání 1938–1945*, pp. 88–98.

peace aims'.[134] A minor debate has developed in the Czech-German historiography, whether in the period from summer 1940 to May 1941 Beneš abandoned his plan for the transfer of certain territories, as Václav Kural has written,[135] or whether it remained continuously one of principal methods whereby Beneš wanted to solve the difficult minority issue, as has been suggested by Detlef Brandes rejoined by Francis Raška.[136] For the purpose of this book, however, it is more important to follow how the British authorities were informed about the Czechoslovak plans, what their reaction was and how they themselves contributed to the debate on this complicated issue.[137]

Some historians have stated that in the beginning of the war the British and French governments still felt bound by the Munich Agreement.[138] There is, however, little evidence for such a conclusion ever since the agreement had been destroyed by Germany in March 1939. And it was certainly not the case from Churchill's accession to power onwards. The Foreign Office clearly wished an agreement to be reached between Beneš and Jaksch with a result of the Sudeten German representatives being admitted to the State Council. For such a development, had it actually occurred, would have clearly strengthened Czechoslovak claim for the border districts, it seems that as early as in the second half of 1940 the Foreign Office tacitly considered a likely return of these districts to the Czechoslovak state.

In a lengthy report to the Foreign Office, based on a series of long conversations with the President, Lockhart presented Beneš's vision of the future Czechoslovak state: Starting from the eastern strip, it was inopportune to raise the question of Ruthenia (Sub-Carpathian Russia), but

134) *Češi a sudetoněmecká otázka 1939–1945*, No. 47, pp. 84–92, Memorandum Mírové cíle československé.
135) Kural, Václav, *Místo společenství konflikt! Češi a Němci ve velkoněmecké říši a cesta k odsunu* [Conflict instead of community! The Czechs and Germans in the Sudeten German Reich and the road to transfer], Praha, Ústav mezinárodních vztahů 1994, p. 144.
136) Brandes, Detlef, Eine verspätete tschechische Alternative zum Münchener Diktat, Edvard Beneš und die sudetendeutsche Frage, *Vierteljahrshefte für Zeitgeschichte*, 1994, No. 2, pp. 221–241; Idem, Opožděná česká alternativa k mnichovskému diktátu [A belated Czech alternative to the Munich Dictate], *Dějiny a současnost* [History and present], Prague, Vol. 15, 1993, No. 2, pp. 29–36. Raška, *The Czechoslovak Exile Government in London and the Sudeten German Issue*, p. 49.
137) Admitting that Beneš might have been sincere, at least when talking to Lockhart, the following analysis would rather confirm Brandes' and Raška's views.
138) Raška, *The Czechoslovak Exile Government in London and the Sudeten German Issue*, pp. 31, 35; Brown, *Dealing with Democrats*, p. 255.

at the end of a victorious war he expected that Ruthenia would 'fall into his lap like a ripe plum'. 'I have commended his prudence,' Lockhart stressed properly. But due to growing anti-Hungarian sentiments following twenty years 'of an enlightened administration', he thought that it would be a mistake to assume that by the return of Ruthenia to Hungary the British would be rid of a troublesome problem. 'In the event of a British victory Ruthenia is likely to opt for re-inclusion in a reconstituted Czechoslovakia, or to be forcibly "protected" by Russia.' The Slovaks, according to Beneš, had to decide their own future: 'If they wish to stay out, they may remain out.' But any federation should be 'a real federation and not home rule for Slovakia plus Slovak political rule in Prague'. In the frontier issue, Beneš only wished some rectification of the *present* Slovak-Hungarian border (namely return of Košice), otherwise he had 'no irredentist ambitions and no desire to re-incorporate the Hungarian portions of Slovakia'. Future existence of Czechoslovakia, however, depended on a satisfactory solution of the German-Bohemian problem, where a return to status quo ante was impossible. 'Assuming, and in my opinion rightly, that the restoration of Czechoslovakia on the basis of the Munich line is a political and economic impossibility, and that a new Czechoslovakia must preserve, if not the old historic frontiers, at least the frontiers corresponding to the geographical, economic and military structure of the country, President Beňeš [sic] has found his own solution of the problem. He has borrowed it from Hitler. It is an exchange of populations.' Germans from the central and northern districts were to be transferred to western Bohemia and Beneš was prepared to concede to Germany a strip of the western frontier in exchange for a piece of Reich territory in the north. A proper Czech Lebensraum would thus be found in central Bohemia and Moravia and a German-Bohemian Lebensraum in the west. Lockhart saw this plan as the only practical solution, 'provided always that the German-Bohemians are not given a raw deal'. On the other hand, negotiations between Beneš and Jaksch were in his view doubtful, but would have a better 'chance for success when Germany has suffered some reverses and Herr Jaksch has rid himself of the illusion that he enjoys the special favour of the British Labour Party'.[139]

The departmental minutes attached to this Lockhart's report are, indeed, extremely interesting. Roberts seemingly noted that Beneš's

139) *PRO*, FO 371/24287, C 1447/2/12, Lockhart to Halifax, 7 October 1940.

cautiousness in demanding back the return of Ruthenia and of some portions of the Slovak territory was probably inspired by tactical regards. With respect to the Sudeten question, Roberts noticed that Beneš was prepared to abandon the old argument of the historic frontiers. On the other hand, the 'Munich line certainly cut across all the racial, natural, military and economic divisions'. Although the solution of the whole difficult problem would obviously depend on the extent of Germany's defeat, and details were missing about the proposed transfers, Roberts saw 'a good deal to be said for concentrating the Germans so far as possible in Western Bohemia'. It seemed to him clear that such predominantly German area would not come under any Czech federation but would remain in Germany 'or in whatever smaller German neighbouring state emerged from the war'. Negotiations between Beneš and Jaksch were in his view to continue to prolong indefinitely as Jaksch or any other Sudeten leader could hardly be expected to agree to the Czechoslovak plan. Roberts thought, however, that it was not a bad thing, since there was no real basis for agreement and both parties could thus have their hands free to deal with the situation after the war. Seemingly, the advantages of the British tenet of non-commitment were gradually being projected on the others... Makins, sceptical as always, called most of Beneš's plans 'castles in Spain', but concurred with Roberts that an agreed solution of the Sudeten problem was not to be expected. But the next minute, written by Strang, probably superseded in its radical attitude everything that had by then been written by any British official: 'M. Benes's ideas have a good deal to commend them... There will be no peace for the new Czech State unless the German minority are swept right out of it.'[140] This statement, recorded by one of the highest officials in the centre of British foreign policy, illustrates the gradual radicalisation of British views. It was undoubtedly influenced by the Blitz and went hand in hand with growing anti-German (instead of merely anti-Nazi) feelings of British public opinion and calls for revenge.[141] However, this was not an isolated opinion on the British side. Already in the beginning of the war the Royal Institute of International Affairs started investigating the possibilities of population

140) *Ibid.*, Roberts' and Makins' minutes, 14 October, Strang's minute, 17 October 1940.
141) See e.g. *AMZV*, LA-D, box 61, 480/dův/40, G. Winter's record of his talk with James Smith Middleton, Secretary General of the Labour Party, 20 November 1940.

'transfers', in consequence of direct request by Halifax. In May 1940, its expert prof. John David Mabbott supplied the first version of his memorandum that recommended organised 'transfers' of the German population as the best solution to the minority problem in Czechoslovakia (in addition to cessation of some border territories and expected exodus of Germans immediately after the war) and he also investigated possibilities of 'transfers' in other European countries. This was the first of such memoranda that were later produced by the FRPS and widely circulated within Whitehall.[142]

The British government did not feel committed towards Hungary in any way and the regards for her attitudes in the beginning of the war gradually waned after April 1940, when the Hungarians permitted the passage of German troops through its territory, and changed into serious considerations of declaring war on Hungary in the autumn of 1941.[143] The British did not feel bound by the terms of the Vienna Award which was considered 'a departure from the agreement reached at Munich'.[144] In January 1941, Cadogan strictly refused a suggestion made by George Barcza de Nagyalásóny, the Hungarian Minister and a strong Anglophile, that the agreement between the Hungarian and Czechoslovak governments had been reached 'in accordance with the modus procedendi contained in the Annex to the Munich Agreement' and that the fact that Britain had ceased to recognise the validity of the Munich Agreement as a result of the state of war between Britain and Germany should not affect the part of the Annex referring to the settlement of the Hungarian-Czechoslovak question: The British government had 'no responsibility whatever for a settlement reached by two of the Munich Powers in their absence, and without their consultation on its terms. Cadogan further questioned Barcza's claim, that the British government had recognised the territorial settlement under the Vienna Award as final, by direct references to the Hungarian acquisitions of March 1939: apparently the Hungarian government itself did not regard the Award as final. 'So much for the finality of the Vienna Award! I am puzzled to

142) Brandes, *Cesta k vyhnání 1938–1945*, pp. 32–33; Brown, *Dealing with Democrats*, pp. 277–280.
143) *PRO*, FO 371/26418, C 13319/10893/12, Roberts' minute, 13 November 1941; *AÚTGM*, EB-L, box 111, Ripka's record of Beneš's talk with Eden and Nichols, 13 November 1941.
144) *PRO*, FO 371/24290, C 13413/2/12, Cadogan to George de Barcza (Hungarian Minister), 28 December 1940.

know which frontier it is that you suggest that His Majesty's Government have acknowledged or made themselves responsible for.'[145]

Ruthenia, however, was considered as one of the typical controversial issues only to be solved at the peace conference after the war. The British attitude was non-committal on both sides: Until the end of 1941, the Czechs were being discouraged from talking about the Ruthenian question, and references to it were banned 'so far as possible' on the Czechoslovak BBC programmes. In reaction to a Czechoslovak complaint, the Ministry of Information was instructed in March 1941 to draw its attention also to analogical references on the Hungarian programmes.[146] When thinking about the future status of Hungarian acquisitions in Slovakia, the Foreign Office felt bound to 'consider our obligations towards our Czechoslovak Allies'.[147] But here, as well as in the Sudeten issue, it preferred a compromise solution.[148]

The FO experts, however, were correct in their estimation that the chances for a Beneš-Jaksch agreement were not bright, if only because of the proposed transfer of German population. In December 1940, the Foreign Office noticed another Beneš's statement proposing both expulsion and transfer of territories: he spoke 'in talkative company' in Oxford not only about the extreme west triangle (including Carlsbad), but also about another two territories in the north. One million of Germans 'would be "guilty" and would therefore remove themselves'. If, after all this, there remained more than 1 million Germans (the highest still acceptable number), 'he would simply deport them'. The remainder could stay, but with no minority rights.[149] On 25 January 1941, Jaksch informed Makins of the deadlock in the negotiations. The latter doubted any possibility of British intervention, demanded by Jaksch: '... the peoples concerned should work out their own arrangements and it was not our habit to seek to impose our own solution until we were obliged

145) *PRO*, FO 371/26389, C 235/235/12, George Barcza to Cadogan, 6 January 1941, Cadogan to George Barcza, 30 January 1941.
146) *PRO*, FO 371/26401, C 3031/3031/12, Ripka to Lockhart, 21 March, Lockhart to Eden, No. 31, 31 March, Strang to M. Peterson (Ministry of Information), 5 April 1941.
147) *PRO*, FO 371/24428, C 13673/529/21, Roberts' minute, 29 November 1940.
148) See e.g. *PRO*, FO 371/26388, C 2249/216/12, Roberts' minute, 13 March 1940.
149) *PRO*, FO 371/24290, C 13015/2/12, Latham's minute, 2 December 1940. See also Raška, *The Czechoslovak Exile Government in London and the Sudeten German Issue*, pp. 48–49. That all this was said in Oxford is clear from Makins' letter to Leeper of 28 April 1941, in: FO 371/26392, C 3939/639/12.

to do so.'[150] Jaksch undoubtedly found certain support amongst some British officials and also in the Labour Party (Noel-Baker, M.P.; William Gillies, leader of the party's International Section, and others).[151] But even there it was by no means universal: Hugh Dalton reported to Lockhart that, 'in Labour Party circles, Jaksch's name is mud!'[152] Dalton himself considered him 'a vain little man' and discounted his claims of great influence. 'He is like the frog who tried to inflate himself into an ox.'[153] And although in the Foreign Office Jaksch could come to see Makins 'any time he wished', and Roberts thought he was 'reasonable and well-intentioned', the officials repeatedly stressed that he represented less than 1/6 of the Sudetens, who were in their big majority 'the originators of the old Pan-German movement from which Nazism evolved'. His position was further weakened by the cessation of a dissident group (the Zinner group). Therefore the reluctance of the Czechs to commit themselves very far with Jaksch was viewed as 'not unnatural'. Two of three Jaksch's requirements of January 1941 were found unacceptable by the Foreign Office – to disapprove transfers of population and to state as one of British war aims that the Sudeten Germans, 'purged from the spirit of Nazism', would be invited to co-operate in 'a Czechoslovak or greater Central European federation, on a basis of self-government'. Transfers were by then generally regarded as 'at least a partial solution' while the latter statement should – as in the case of Czechoslovak-Polish talks – become 'their war-aim', rather than British one.[154] What the Central Department did support, however, was a special BBC service for the Sudeten German opposition, and by July 1941 pushed it through in spite of the serious reservations of P.I.D. and later also the Ministry of Information's disagreement.[155] 'We feel very strongly,' wrote Leeper, 'that these broadcasts to the German minority in Czechoslovakia (not to the Sudetens!) can only be undertaken with the approval and co-

150) *PRO*, FO 371/26392, C 918/639/12, Jaksch to Makins, 25 January 1941; Makins' minute, 3 February 1941.
151) Raška, *The Czechoslovak Exile Government in London and the Sudeten German Issue*, p. 100; *HIA Stanford*, Eduard Táborský collection, box 8, envelope Other materials concerning Wenzel Jaksch & the Sudeten German Social Democrats, Report on attitudes of Wenzel Jaksch, 1941.
152) *PRO*, FO 800/869, Jebb to Lockhart, 14 November 1940.
153) *PRO*, HS 4/63, Minister's minute N.S. 70, 16 December 1941.
154) *PRO*, FO 371/26392, C 918/639/12, Jaksch to Makins, 25 January, Roberts' minute, 31 January 1941.
155) *Ibid.*, C 6399/639/12, Miss Wrangham (M. of I.) to Roberts, 10 June 1941.

-operation of the Czechs.' Roberts disagreed that they *must* be regarded as a minority in a future Czechoslovak state: 'Personally I think the future Czech state should receive back the old historic and strategic frontier of the Bohemian Kingdom [!], but it seems to me ostrich-like to ignore the very real Sudeten problem, as this letter tends to.'[156] Makins' reply to Leeper pointed out 'a very real Sudeten problem' and – referring to previous Beneš's statements – it stressed that the President himself was 'not too anxious to regard them or even to retain them as "a German minority in Czechoslovakia".'[157]

How much the FO officials were therefore disappointed when they found out that in an interview to the Dutch paper *Free Netherlands* Beneš said exactly this ('We know that this territory will again belong to our Republic.')! 'Dr. Benes is rapidly falling back into his former narrow & intransigent mood,' reacted Makins.[158] But Beneš soon explained to Lockhart that his statements had been misunderstood, and he presented an updated solution of the Sudeten German problem, whereby 800–900 thousand Germans would be transferred to Germany with their territory in western and northern Bohemia, another 1,1 million would be sent to Germany as a compensation, in addition to 300 to 400 thousand who would flee. 300 thousand would be 'exchanged' for Austrian Czechs and only 400 thousand German democrats would thus remain in the new republic and receive Czechoslovak citizenship. Such a projected settlement made any agreement between Beneš and the Sudeten German representatives purely theoretical. This Lockhart's report, although mentioned in other FO papers, later disappeared from the Foreign Office archives together with departmental minutes and a small map of supreme importance, only to be found decades later by Detlef Brandes in Jaromír Smutný's papers at Columbia University in New York.[159] It is very likely that this mysterious disappearance of the report and above all the map, which with the passage of time became highly uncomfortable for Beneš as a testimony of his territorial generosity, was one of numerous services that Bruce Lockhart did for 'his Czechs'.

156) *Ibid.*, C 3939/639/12, Leeper to Makins, April 16, Roberts' minute, 23 April 1941.
157) *Ibid.*, Makins to Leeper, 28 April 1941.
158) *Ibid.*, C 4941/639/12, Roberts' minute, Makins' minute, 7 May 1941.
159) Brandes, Opožděná česká alternativa k mnichovskému diktátu, *op. cit.*, pp. 30–36. Lockhart's report is mentioned in: *PRO*, FO 371/26392, C 10002/639/12, Roberts' minute, 10 September 1941.

Negotiations between Beneš and Jaksch resumed in the late summer, but there was not much room for agreement: a massive transfer of Sudeten population into Germany, by then openly advocated by the members of the Czechoslovak government,[160] 'was one which no Sudeten leader could for one moment entertain';[161] at the same time the Central resistance organisation in the Protectorate (Ústřední vedení odboje domácího – ÚVOD) vehemently argued against admitting of Sudeten Germans to the State Council. Beneš was warned that such a step might shake even his own authority.[162] On 26 September Jaksch informed the Foreign Office that 'full agreement' had been reached with Beneš that open collaboration in London would *not* be to the mutual benefit of the two peoples, since it might lead to hostile agitation among both Czechs and Sudeten Germans at home.[163] The German terror, unleashed after Heydrich's arrival to Prague on 29 September, made agreement virtually impossible, which the Central Department officials clearly realised.[164]

At the same time the Foreign Office registered growing Czechoslovak tendency to claim the pre-Munich frontiers. When Philip Nichols finally presented his credentials to Beneš, he remarked that the British people had at that moment of trial (a month after Heydrich's accession to the position of Reichsprotektor) a greater admiration for the Czech nation than ever before. 'This started the President off on the events of Munich, the part he had played and the temper of the Czech people to-day.' After stressing that he could not have acted otherwise and that his action had been justified by later developments, he implied that the old frontier was the only possible one for Czechoslovakia; 'otherwise

160) See e.g. *PRO*, FO 371/26388, C 5999/216/12, Ripka's article 'A new Central Europe' in *The Central European Observer*, 30 May 1941.
161) *PRO*, FO 371/26392, C 10002/639/12, Makins' report of his talk with Jaksch, 4 September 1941.
162) 'Národ, v němž není rodiny nepostižené násilnictvím Němců, by to nesnesl. Jsme povinni včas varovat.' [A nation, in which no single family has been spared German brutality, would not stand it. We are obliged to warn in time.] *HIA Stanford*, Eduard Táborský collection, box 10, envelope Reports from Czechoslovakia 1941, a report from ÚVOD, August 30, 1941. See also Raška, *The Czechoslovak Exile Government in London and the Sudeten German Issue*, p. 52.
163) A gentleman's agreement was, however, reached on the painstaking issue of Sudeten-German military service: prompted by the growing anti-German feelings in the Czechoslovak forces, the Czechoslovak authorities undertook to make no attempt to bring pressure on the Sudetens to join the Czechoslovak forces. *PRO*, FO 371/26392, C 10814/639/12, Makins' record of his talk with Jaksch and Paul, 26 September 1941.
164) *Ibid.*, C 11057/639/12, Roberts' minute, 7 October 1941.

Prague was completely at the mercy of the Germans and an independent Czechoslovakia an impossibility.' Nichols limited himself to pointing out that the historic Czech-German frontier was one the oldest in Europe.[165] But the Foreign Office regarded the question of the future frontiers of Czechoslovakia 'quite as difficult a one as that of the eastern frontiers of Poland' and generally did not wish to depart from the line that the British consistently held, namely that they could not recognise or support the establishment in the future of any particular frontiers in Central Europe. If only on account of their 'commitment to the U.S. to accept no "commitments"',[166] which was further confirmed by the clause 2 of the Atlantic Charter that deprecated any territorial changes which did not accord with the freely expressed wishes of the people concerned. The Czechoslovak requirement to broadcast to the Czechs at home that the future state must include Sudetenland, the part of Slovakia occupied by Hungary, and Sub-Carpathian Russia, was refused accordingly, since anything said on the BBC would inevitably be regarded as having the approval of the British government.[167]

The British were annoyed by Beneš's speech in Aberdeen on 10 November 1941: Not only that he spoke about frontiers, that he stressed previous British shortsightedness, superficiality and selfishness compared to his own unfailing prescience, but he even suggested that post-war Germany might be called upon to make rectifications for her pre-1938 frontiers to the profit of her neighbours and be compensated in the colonial sphere! Strang asked Eden to hint to Beneš that as he was recognised as a head of state, this imposed upon him 'a special obligation of discretion in matters which might arouse controversy in the country in which he is received as a guest. He is talking far too much.'[168] But Eden was not that severe. He had recently been asked by Lockhart to meet Beneš at regular monthly intervals and was undoubtedly pleased by Lockhart's remark that Beneš was devoted to him and that he would find him 'far easier to handle than most of the other Allied representatives'.[169] Eden's 'hint' at a

165) *PRO*, FO 371/26412, C 11972/8214/12, Nichols to Eden, 27 October 1941.
166) *PRO*, FO 371/26389, C 11137/235/12, Roberts' minute, 10 October, Cadogan's minute, 13 October 1941.
167) *Ibid.*, C 11137/235/12, Beneš's memorandum communicated by Lockhart, 3 October 1941, minutes by Millard, Roberts, Makins, Sargent, Cadogan, 9–13 October 1941.
168) *PRO*, FO 371/26388, C 13398/216/12, Nichols' minute, Strang's minute, 12 November 1941.
169) *Ibid.*, C 13503/216/12, Lockhart's minute, 3 November 1941.

dinner in the Foreign Office was thus a very mild one: the report of what Beneš had said had caused his colleagues and himself 'some disquiet'. The President in turn explained to him that 'the problem represented by German populations and minorities should be more widely shared, the British Empire not excluded'. Following this exchange, Eden assured his subordinates: 'I am, however, hopeful that as a result of what I said Dr. Benes will be more guarded in the future in any reference he may make to the colonial problem.'[170] Quite typically for Czechoslovak way of recording uncomfortable information, Ripka's record of this conversation does not contain any reference to an exchange on this topic...[171] When Beneš was further reprimanded by Nichols, he produced an ingenious theory that although reference to colonies had appeared in the text as published, he had not in fact mentioned colonies when speaking in Aberdeen at all. He suggested that this might be said in reply to Captain Graham's question in the House of Commons. 'I am afraid,' worried Roberts, 'that this is rather too ingenious a solution as all the reports of Dr. Benes's speech which I have seen include this particular reference.' And Makins added: 'Dr Benes' suggestion is almost insulting, especially when considered with his behaviour over the article in Foreign Affairs.'[172] Indeed, to that prestigious journal Beneš had submitted a text suggesting exactly the same solution of the German problem, and he instructed the editor to leave those references out only after his talk with Eden.[173] 'Dr. Beneš is also billed to speak out shortly at Chatham House on "The Europe we are fighting for", or some such title,' warned Strang. 'He is having the time of his life, being President of Czechoslovakia, and having GB and America for a platform. He never stops talking.' Nichols suggested that regular talks with Eden might restrain him from speaking so often in public, but Strang remained sceptical.[174]

170) *Ibid.*, C 12636/216/12, Eden to Nichols, 13 November 1941.

171) *AÚTGM*, EB-L, box 111, Ripka's record of Beneš's talk with Eden and Nichols, 13 November 1941.

172) *PRO*, FO 371/26388, C 13437/216/12, Roberts' minute, 28 November 1941; The article called for 'a transfer of populations on a very much larger scale than after the last war'. Beneš, Edvard, Organisation of Postwar Europe, *Foreign Affairs*, Vol. 20, No. 2 (January 1942), p. 238.

173) *Ibid.*, Nichols' minute, 27 November 1941; FO 371/30825, C 2456/138/12, Hancock's minute, 11 March 1942.

174) *PRO*, FO 371/26388, C 13437/216/12, Strang's minute, 11 November 1941, C 13503/ /216/12, Lockhart's minute, 23 November, Strang's minute, 29 November 1941.

Yet, even this irritation by the President's Aberdeen speech had its limits: Firstly, Beneš also stressed in it the necessity of federal blocs in Europe (an East European federation and a Balkan bloc), which Sargent found very useful and hoped that he had not been reproved for this particular passage.[175] Secondly, although the Czech section of the BBC. broadcasted the speech, which made Kirkpatrick wash heads of the Czech editors responsible for this, no dementi or dissociation was issued (although the Czech editors suggested that, and Maxmilián Lobkowicz, the Minister to Britain who got a rather twisted version of this incident, protested against the alleged Foreign Office's instruction to that sense...).[176] Thirdly, when the Hungarian Parliament registered a solemn protest against another of Beneš's Aberdeen statements – that the Hungarians would be compelled to disgorge the territories which they had acquired through German support – the detestation of Hungary's policy and its protagonists prevailed in the Foreign Office. Strang recorded the generally perceived difference: 'Dr. Benes has been very mischievous: but I must confess that I do not very much care what the Hungarians think or do. ...I do not think we should go out of our way to disavow him, or to try in any way to placate the Hungarians.'[177] And fourthly, when it turned out that Captain Graham would not withdraw his parliamentary question, Richard Law, Butler's successor as the Parliamentary Under-Secretary of State, simply pointed out in response certain misinterpretations of Beneš's words and stated no responsibility of the British government for anything what might have been said on that occasion. It was Mander who then reminded of one of the most admirable traces of wartime Britain: 'Is it not the case that allied States are perfectly free to express their views in anyway they please in this country?' Law affirmed.[178]

Throughout the autumn of 1941, the Central Department officials thought that Beneš's previous 'sensible' policy of seeking compromise solution of the Sudeten German and Hungarian problems was abandoned and they found this allegedly sudden change to have resulted

175) *Ibid.*, C 13398/216/12, Sargent's minute, 27 November 1941.
176) *PRO*, FO 371/26418, C 12675/10893/12, Roberts' minute, 13 November 1941.
177) *Ibid.*, C 13319/10893/12, Murray to Roberts, 14 November, Roberts' minutes, 13–14 November, Strang's minute, 13 November, Cadogan's minute, 14 November, Lockhart's minute, 20 November 1941.
178) *H. C. Deb.*, 5th Series, Vol. 376, 3 December 1941.

from the full recognition last July.[179] In December Ripka came up with a proposal that broadcasts in German for the Sudeten population should be included in the Czech programmes. As his other statement, that agreement had been reached between Beneš and Jaksch on the Sudeten German representation in the State Council, was not found 'altogether in accordance with the facts', and it would only have a bad propaganda effect among the Sudetens and in Germany, the department wanted to remain firm: '… all that would be achieved would be a further success for the Czechs in driving us down the slippery slope of agreeing to the reconstitution of Czechoslovakia as she existed before Munich. This may or may not be a good thing in itself, but it is certainly undesirable to commit ourselves at this stage.' Such a step was conditioned by *previous* admission of the Sudeten Germans to the State Council. The FO officials were aware that it would mean implicit recognition of the Sudetenland as a part of the Czechoslovak Republic. But being on the defensive, they at least wanted to use this forthcoming *commitment* as the only incentive for Beneš to come to arrangement with Jaksch and his collaborators, whom the Central Department was not willing to sell 'down the river'.[180] Nobody cared, however, that the current situation – when Jaksch was allowed to broadcast fortnightly in the German programmes – gave the impression that the British government regarded the Sudeten lands as part of Germany, no matter that he was not 'an authorised spokesman addressing the Sudetenland'.[181]

On 16 December 1941, in response to the British declaration of war on Finland, Hungary and Rumania and the U.S. entry into the war, the Czechoslovak government distributed amongst the Allied governments a memorandum that rejected as illegal all the territorial changes that befell Czechoslovakia since September 1938, and maintained the principle of juridical continuity of the pre-Munich Czechoslovak Republic. It also

179) *PRO*, FO 371/26389, C 11137/235/12, Roberts' minute, 10 October 1941; FO 371/ /26388 C 13398/216/12, Roberts' minute, 12 November 1941.
180) *PRO*, FO 371/26392, C 13205/639/12, Nichols to Eden, 26 November 1941, C 13260/639/12, Roberts' minute, 3 December, Makins' minute, 10 December 1941.
181) *PRO*, FO 371/30834, C 1101/326/12, Roberts' minute, 20 January 1941. It was Lockhart who eventually pointed out this necessary impact – only in April 1942 when he finally found out that Jaksch had been broadcasting for 9 months! FO 371/30834, C 2408/326/12, Lockhart's minute, 10 April 1942. See also Garnett, David, *The Secret History of PWE. The Political Warfare Executive, 1939–1945*, London, St Ermin's 2002, esp. pp. 184–185, 206, 210–211.

contained Czechoslovak declaration of a state of war with all countries which were in a state of war with Great Britain, the U.S.S.R. and the United States of America. However, with Germany and Hungary Czechoslovakia had been in a state of war, according to the memorandum, since those two countries 'committed acts of violence against the security, independence and territorial integrity of the republic'. (Poland was not included in this category...) Makins called the memorandum a further and an important step in the diplomatic campaign of the Czechoslovak government 'to force us to recognise Czechoslovak claims which are constantly increasing in scope and importance'. Although it was in his view 'very natural' that the Czechoslovak government should act in this way, unless Britain's existing policy was to be 'completely stultified' the British could not allow the Czechoslovaks to get away with it. Makins also noted the introduction of 'a new concept of international relations, namely that of a retrospective declaration of war'. Nichols' suggestion that the various points in the note be passed over in silence was thus refused. The argument that the Soviet government was likely to accept all the Czech claims did not matter – in view of the quantity of commitments that the Russians had given to Czechoslovakia during the last six months. Thus the British, in response to the Czechoslovak note, reserved their position as set forth in the letter of recognition of 18 July 1941.[182]

Two days before Christmas, Beneš presented to Nichols a rather different plan for the future of Czechoslovakia. It was based on three principles: renunciation of Munich, restoration of Czechoslovakia's *natural frontiers* and retention of certain number of Germans. As it was not possible to get rid of 3.2 million people, he now proposed cession of territory with 600–700 thousand Germans and expulsion of 300–400 thousand war-guilty ones. Basing himself on the proposition that for every German that he got rid of with territory he ought to be entitled to get rid of two without, he wished to 'send away' a further 1.2 million. At the end there would remain a million of Germans, of whom half a million would probably opt to become Czechs and be assimilated. As a compensation for the cession of territory, he would ask for minor modifications in Czechoslovakia's favour on the North Bohemian frontier. In Slovakia he was willing to cede to Hungary one-third of the territory

182) *PRO*, FO 371/26405, C 13955/3261/12, Ripka to Nichols, 16 December, Proclamation of a State of War, 16 December, Nichols to Eden, 17 December, Makins' minute, 28 December, Eden to Nichols, 31 December 1941.

lost as a result of the Vienna Award. According to the above principle of two expelled Magyars without territory for every one with territory, he would get rid of the entire Hungarian minority. All this would happen under international supervision and financing, but with a considerable contribution on the Czechoslovak part. Rather surprisingly, there was general agreement at the Foreign Office that this was as good a solution as possible of the minority problem after the war. This plan was put in contraposition to Stalin's plan for the integral restoration of the pre-Munich frontiers of Czechoslovakia. Even Makins noted that Beneš's ideas were 'not altogether impossible and something could probably be made of them. The trouble is that his ideas get larger and larger as time passes.' Eden suggested that Beneš should be encouraged 'to some extent in this, if only to pin him down'.[183]

These overtures signalled Beneš's third big diplomatic offensive, this time aiming at securing the pre-Munich frontier and getting approval for the transfer of Sudeten German. The long-drawn negotiations were to last over seven months – to complete mortification of its major protagonists (and also to exhaustion of more than one reader of the pertinent documentation[184]).

As it had been the case in numerous other issues, also in this bid Beneš found an ally or, indeed, insinuator in Bruce Lockhart. His diary shows that he stressed to the President the importance of the pre-Munich frontiers, although at the same time Lockhart was assuring the Foreign Office that he was doing his best 'to keep Dr. Beneš off the frontier question'.[185] During his informal farewell as the diplomatic representative, in December 1941, Lockhart said to Beneš his 'five points: (1) frontiers to-day more important than peoples; (2) N. West frontier of Rudohoře [sic! – probably Krušné hory, Krušnohoří] and Krkonoše essential to Czechs – had preserved them for 1500 years; (3) solution of problem is transfer of populations; (4) no minority treaties – only right of self-de-

183) *PRO*, FO 371/26388, C 14276/216/12, Nichols to Makins, 22 December 1941, Roberts' minute, 4 January, Makins' minute, 5 January, Eden's minute, 5 January 1942.
184) Apart from my work, I would refer to Francis Raška's book. Although the author otherwise follows the negotiations related to the Sudeten German issue with admirable attention to details, here he limited himself to some general observations on the *way* and *methods* that these talks were pursued. Raška, *The Czechoslovak Exile Government in London and the Sudeten German Issue*, pp. 58–60.
185) *PRO*, FO 371/26389, C 11137/235/12, Lockhart to the Central Department, 23 November 1941.

termination is right to leave country, and (5) our policy has prevented an agreement between Jaksch and B. which otherwise would have taken place long ago and is now handicapping the Czechs in their negotiations with the Poles – and is therefore hampering Polish-Czech federation. B. agreed.'[186] How that might have been achieved – in view of the fact that from October 1940 onwards Beneš presented to Jaksch massive transfer of German population as one of the key methods how to solve the Sudeten German problem – is unclear.

However, from the turn of the year Lockhart participated in diplomatic negotiations only occasionally and more indirectly, although Beneš naturally kept his closest British 'agent' fully informed of his aims and the development of negotiations.[187] Philip Nichols, Lockhart's successor, soon proved to be a willing listener and sometimes even advocate of Beneš's reasoning, although he more than Lockhart understood the Foreign Office's responses. Thus he managed to play the role of an intermediary and eventually came up with a compromise solution that was later adopted. Beneš, assisted by Ripka (Masaryk was in the United States), was the driving force of the negotiations while the FO Central Department, sometimes assisted by Cadogan and Eden, represented the party which constantly resisted the exerted pressure, a breakwater that repelled most of the ingenious arguments delivered by Beneš.

In mid-January 1942, Roberts finally noted that it was not so that Beneš's policy oscillated between attempts to secure for Czechoslovakia the pre-Munich frontiers on the one hand and plans to cede territories inhabited exclusively by the Germans on the other hand: 'Dr. Benes is ... doing all he can to commit us to accept the general principle of the restoration of the old frontiers of Czechoslovakia, with minor alterations in certain Sudeten districts.'[188] On 16 January 1942, Beneš complained to Nichols about Jaksch's broadcasts and explained that due to growing anti-German feelings both in the Protectorate and amongst the exiles and in the Army, he could not admit Sudeten Germans into the State Council, although the agreement had been reached in principle. At this occasion the President went on an offensive: The Sudeten question

186) *HLRO*, Bruce Lockhart papers, diary No. 34, 27 December 1940.
187) Kuklík, *Londýnský exil...*, pp. 126, 171–175; *AÚTGM*, EB-L, box 110, Beneš's record of his talk with Lockhart, Leeper and Brooks, 30 May, Memorandum handed to Lockhart, 3 June, Beneš's records of his talks with Lockhart, 23 May, 4 June and 13 June 1942.
188) *PRO*, FO 371/30834, C 326/326/12, Roberts' minute, 16 January 1942.

needed early solution as with the approach of victory the public opinion would radicalise, and Beneš needed an instrument to exert his moderating influence. Further, he had always wished to keep the balance between the east and the west, but it would not help his policy if Czech public opinion regarded the U.S.S.R. as their only saviours. Thirdly, although he recognised the repeated British reservations over the question of frontiers due to the commitments to the U.S. government, he urged that Czechoslovakia had the right to be considered as a special case. No other country, e.g. Poland or Yugoslavia, had been called upon to make such sacrifices. As Czechoslovakia had acted in the interest of Europe as a whole, and her attitude after Munich was a dignified one, 'perhaps some recompense' was due to her. It would be useful if the British government could place on record that, juridically speaking, Munich and the Vienna Award had no existence in the eyes of the British government and therefore the *status quo ante* was restored.[189] This was in his view a 'flank attack' on a position he could not occupy by a frontal attack. Roberts was quick to refute all these arguments: 1) Beneš has the most assured position with his fellow-countrymen. 2) Although Czechoslovakia was treated very badly, her sufferings cannot be compared with those of Poland or Yugoslavia. 3) Russian policy is based on opportunism and can afford to give sweeping promises to the Czechs one day with complete disregard to earlier Soviet policy (e.g. breaking off diplomatic relations). Roberts argued reasonably that the British could not and should not compete with the Soviets on that plane. But the following sentence reflects the complete British disregard to the trauma that Munich had caused to the Czech nation and to Beneš in particular: 'It should not be too difficult for Dr. Benes to convince himself and his people that British, and we hope American, policy will be more consistent and more reliable if less immediately encouraging.'

Eden thus went to his lunch with Beneš on 21 January armed with sufficient arguments from the FO experts.[190] The President asked him for some understanding with the British government on the future constitution of Czechoslovakia for three reasons: a) to reach 'some agreement concerning the frontiers' and thus to make possible an agreement over the Sudeten Germans, b) to reach final conclusions with the Poles, c) to

189) *Ibid.*, C 1101/326/12, Nichols to Eden, 19 January 1942.
190) *Ibid.*, Roberts' minute, Cadogan's minute, 20 January, Eden's minute, 21 January 1942.

give encouragement to his followers in the Protectorate. While Poland or Yugoslavia would be, at the end of the war, considered from the point of view of their old frontiers, this did not apply to Czechoslovakia, which, as a result of Munich, had made a quite unparalleled sacrifice. Beneš asked the British government to repudiate Munich 'formally and juridically' and thus to restore status quo ante (with a reservation, at least according to Nichols' record, to discuss with the Great Powers and Czechoslovakia future frontiers and their implications). Ripka recorded that Beneš showed Eden the 'Munich maps', which he always carried with him (!), upon which the Foreign Secretary glossed to Nichols: 'Look at that criminal absurdity.' There was no other solution, said Beneš, apart from keeping the historical frontiers and reducing the number of the Germans down to around one million. Ripka, however, challenged the method of cession of territories for obtaining smaller ones as compensation and said that there would be a strong opposition against this President's project amongst Czechoslovak politicians. Whether this was orchestrated in advance or not, the episode did not appear in the English record and the Foreign Office continued to discount Beneš's argument of his moderating influence upon his compatriots. Eden said that Britain was not bound by the Vienna Award and as for Munich, the British already stated that the Germans had violated that agreement, 'and that it was therefore no longer valid; but a distinction must be drawn between the end of Munich and what flowed from the recognition of that fact'. Nevertheless, he reminded his Czechoslovak partners that he and Churchill had been against Munich (a remark that is missing in the English record...) and understood the Czechoslovak point, but that they were limited by their undertakings to President Roosevelt about non-commitments with respect to frontiers. He asked Beneš for a memorandum stating his views and he expressed his feeling that it 'might not be impossible' for the President, Ripka and Nichols to find a formula acceptable for both sides.[191]

Beneš soon came up with a formula hardly acceptable for the British whereby they would say that the decisions concerning Czechoslovakia,

191) *PRO*, FO 954/4, Cz/42/1, Eden to Nichols (a memorandum in fact written by Nichols), No. 13, 21 January 1942; *AÚTGM*, EB-V, box 79, Ripka's record of Beneš's talk with Eden and Nichols, 21 January 1942. Also Táborský recorded the episode with the map in his diary: *HIA Stanford*, Eduard Táborský collection, box 2, Táborský's diary, 22 January 1942.

which had been brought about since 1938, could not be considered as valid and her pre-Munich legal status was re-established. Nichols was doubtful. The Foreign Office disagreed. It was easier for its officials because in the meantime Ripka made a tactical mistake when at a lunch with Makins he gave 'a categorical assurance' that if the British government assured the Czechoslovak government that the admission of Dr. Jaksch and other Sudeten German representatives in the National Council would mean the withdrawal of Eden's letter of 18 July 1941, they would admit the Sudeten representatives immediately.[192] Jurisdiction over the Sudeten Germans in exchange for their admittance to the State Council was considered acceptable as it, indeed, followed the logic of this letter. Strang, again very surprisingly, proposed to add that the British government did not regard as binding any territorial changes which had been effected in Czechoslovakia since August 1938 for the benefit of Germany and Hungary. But Cadogan saw no reason for that and Malkin later brought about legal arguments against it.[193] Soon it turned out that the suggested deal was not satisfactory to Beneš, nor was its modified version giving to the Czechoslovak government the exercise of jurisdiction in British territory over all nations of the former Czechoslovak Republic (i.e. including the population of Ruthenia).[194] Ripka tried to save face by stating that he had had in mind Eden's *first* letter. But since its withdrawal would have meant withdrawing the full recognition of the Czechoslovak government, this statement by him cannot really be taken fully seriously.

Any attempt to find a more comprehensive formula seemed doomed to failure. The Foreign Office was also influenced by its 'long experience of Benes's methods of negotiation ... designed to achieve his objects one by one, and by an almost painless and imperceptible process to commit His Majesty's Government explicitly or implicitly to the principle of the restoration of the Czechoslovak State with the frontiers it possessed before Munich.' The officials were not willing to follow Beneš into 'his juridical labyrinth' and could not help suspecting 'that all his ingenious formulae and his frequent references to the theory of juridical continuity

192) *PRO*, FO 371/30834, C 845/326/12, Makins' minute, 30 January 1942.
193) *Ibid.*, Strang's minute, Cadogan's minute, 4 February 1942, C 1644/326/12, Strang's minute, Malkin's minute, 17 February 1942.
194) *Ibid.*, C 1401/326/12, Nichols to Makins, 5 February 1942, C 1461/326/12, Nichols to Makins, 6 February 1942.

are designed to achieve his ends by a less direct approach'. Accepting the formula invalidating every decision concerning Czechoslovakia since Munich would call into question the validity of the Czechoslovak Financial Claims Act, the Refugee Trust Fund etc. None of the other countries had her frontiers guaranteed by Britain, which Beneš himself knew or at least had himself twice stated in the State Council (11 December 1940, 25 November 1941), and it would be up to each of them to present its own case at a peace conference.[195]

Again and again, over and over, Beneš was stressing: 1) the 'Munich debt' that on moral basis Britain had towards Czechoslovakia, greater than to any other country, and to himself personally, 2) the need for his country to get – for the case of peace conference – equality when compared with Poland or Yugoslavia (he sometimes even 'strengthened' this argument by alleged Czechoslovak inferiority to Germany and Hungary), 3) his need to have an instrument to calm down radical and chauvinist tendencies, especially in view of the possible shortness of time with the Allied victory approaching.[196] Beneš produced dozens of other arguments, but naturally none of them capable or convincing enough to change the general doctrine of Britain's policy based on her tacit agreement with the U.S. government.

By mid-February negotiations were reaching a deadlock and Beneš was correspondingly loosing his patience: He complained that everything had to be dragged out of the British and he did not see the need for that since Czechoslovakia had suffered more than any other country. By sustaining and supporting Jaksch (through his broadcasts etc.) the British government might be 'nursing a second Henlein in their bosom'. The Central Department thought that Beneš probably had 'lost his sense of proportion'. It was reminded that while Jaksch had made unconditional surrender to Beneš, the latter had declined to fulfil his part of the bargain (i.e. to admit Sudeten Germans to the State Council) – hence the Sudeten German pamphlet criticising the Czechoslovak plans and policy, about which Beneš also complained. The officials were equally surprised by Beneš's peculiar argument that Czechoslovakia would go

195) *Ibid.*, C 845/326/12, Makins to Nichols, 4 February 1942.
196) *Ibid.*, C 845/326/12, Nichols to Foreign Office, 5 February 1942, C 1644/326/12, Nichols to Makins, 9 February 1942, C 1645/326/12, Nichols to Makins, 9 February 1942, C 4047/326/12, Nichols to Makins, 14 April 1942, C 5797/326/12, Nichols to Makins, 9 June 1942.

to the peace conference in a position of moral inferiority vis-à-vis Germany and Hungary.[197] The Foreign Office would have been even more astonished if they had known what Beneš was at the same time saying to the SOE. To general Gubbins he complained about British reluctance to solve the outstanding question of Sudetenland, which only emphasised Russia's recognition of all Czechoslovakia's just and legitimate claims. It is worth quoting the explanation that the President offered and Gubbins recorded: All this was 'due to the fact that the Foreign Office liked to keep him, as it were, on a string so that he must always be in the position of a suppliant, which to him indicated a lack of sincerity on the part of someone or some clique in the Foreign Office who did not want to have to deal with him on a completely frank and equal basis, which would be the case if there was no major point outstanding between them. As a further reason for this attitude he suggested that there were too many "Men of Munich" still in power or making their influence felt through the Foreign Office.' They were not prepared 'to admit their mistakes or to believe the real depth of German perfidy'. He was, on the other hand, grateful to SOE that unlike FO they were in no way supporting Jaksch.[198] Since SOE could scarcely influence the course of British foreign policy and such remarks probably sooner or later – via Gladwyn Jebb and others – reached the FO officials, it is hard to see how all this could be intended to assist Beneš's policy. By employing such methods, the President only added to the aversion that the key FO officials – who had crucial influence on what sort of policy towards Czechoslovakia was being made – felt in relation to Beneš. Bypassing the Foreign Office was scarcely possible in the British political system.

On 23 March Beneš had another lunch with Eden. The President displayed worries lest Russia, by appearing more generous than Britain, should make it more difficult for Czechoslovakia to follow the policy of balance between east and west. Ripka then asked the British Foreign Secretary to declare at least some general principles that would be acceptable even for the United States. Eden was doubtful.[199] By early April Minister Nichols and the Central Department agreed that it would be

197) *Ibid.*, C 1645/326/12, Nichols to Makins, 9 February, Makins to Nichols, 23 February 1942.
198) *PRO*, HS 4/16 and HS 4/9, M to C.D., 21 February 1942.
199) *PRO*, FO 954/4, Cz/42/3, Eden to Nichols, 23 March 1942; *AÚTGM*, EB-V, box 79, Ripka's record of Beneš's talk with Eden and Nichols, 23 March 1942.

better to leave the question alone and take no further action.[200] But the leaders of the Foreign Office realised that if the Anglo-Soviet treaty were signed as then proposed, i.e. with all the proposed territorial commitments, they would be faced with yet another Beneš's offensive which they could not probably withstand. William Strang at the same time questioned the U.S. argument: 'If we do stand out, I do not think the American argument is the best one to use. I have never been quite convinced that the State Dept. would mind very much if we told Dr. B. that we would support his pre-Munich frontiers' apart from Teschen. 'The State Dept., without consulting us, have told the Free French (and, I think, Vichy also) that they intend to restore the integrity of France and her possessions. ... If, therefore, we really wanted to help Dr. Benes, it would be open to us to put the case to the State Dept. and get their reaction. The best argument against Benes is that we don't want to commit ourselves about frontiers anywhere: but we may soon be driven of this ground.' [201]

Beneš was not willing to wait for too long and returned to the charge soon after Easter with a revised formula: it said that the *legal* status of Czechoslovakia which existed before her conflict with Germany in 1938 was re-established and that Czechoslovakia would join with the Great Powers to determine her *final* settlement relating to frontiers and other questions. Nichols read it and a 'long and at times vigorous conversation' ensued. He saw the bone of contention in the term 'legal status': 'Again and again he [Beneš] argued that this ought not to be difficult for us and again and again I argued that we could not deny the fact that Munich had existed, and that these facts could not be denied by a stroke of the pen'. While Poland and Yugoslavia now juridically retained their pre-war frontiers, Czechoslovakia had to rest content with her Munich frontiers. And to the home Czechs Beneš attributed the suspicion that at the end of the war Britain might once again make peace with Germany repeating all the features of Munich. Nichols used all sorts of argument to point out how ridiculous such suspicions were. But at the same time he warned the Foreign Office: 'Munich has obviously made an indelible impression, if indeed it has not had a pathological effect, upon the homeland.' Since Nichols himself thought that Beneš was earnest in his worries and that

200) *PRO*, FO 371/30834, C 3484/326/12, Nichols to Makins, 30 March, Cadogan's minute, 9 April, Eden's minute, 10 April 1942.
201) *Ibid.*, Strang's minute, 3 April, Cadogan's minute, 9 April 1942.

both the 'humiliation' argument and the 'dependence on Russia' argument had some force in them, he went, of his own initiative, to FO legal expert Malkin and together they drafted a revised formula. Although Nichols had certain doubts if it would satisfy the President, who was out for all he could get, he might agree if it were presented to him as the furthest the British could go. The first sentence later became the basis of the compromise: Since Germany had destroyed the arrangement concerning Czechoslovakia reached in 1938, the British government regarded itself as 'free from any engagements in this respect, and in the final settlement of the Czechoslovak frontiers to be reached at the end of the war will in no wise be influenced by the change effected in and since 1938'. This was regarded as unobjectionable but the Central Department, worried of similar demands from other countries of the region, refused the second sentence stating that at the peace settlement Britain would make every effort to secure for Czechoslovakia such frontiers as to ensure her strength and stability. 'Clearly Dr. Benes supposes that, having decided to meet the Russians over their frontiers, we cannot refuse to meet him over the Czechoslovak frontiers,' Roberts commented. 'I presume, however, that our intention is to regard the Russian case as one apart, and resolutely to refuse to deal with other European frontiers at this stage in the same way.'[202] Although a meeting of the key officials that Eden held at the Foreign Office on 21 April admitted a possibility to accord to Czechoslovakia more or less its pre-Munich frontiers, it did not recommend making any public and obligatory statement to this sense. In each case, it was decided to wait until the negotiations with the Soviet Union had been concluded.[203]

But the treaty in its final form, after the U.S. intervention, did not tackle territorial questions whatsoever.[204] On 4 June Beneš met with Eden upon the Foreign Secretary's request. The President appraised the Anglo-Soviet treaty and then again pressed for 'undoing' of Munich: He accepted the reservation concerning the frontiers which applied to

202) *Ibid.*, C 4047/326/12, Nichols to Makins, 14 April, Roberts' minute, 20 April 1942.
203) Kuklík, Jan – Němeček, Jan, Cesta k oduznání Mnichova za druhé světové války, In: *Mnichovská dohoda. Cesta k destrukci demokracie v Evropě* [Munich agreement. The way to destruction of democracy in Europe], ed. J. Němeček, Praha, Karolinum 2004, pp. 132–144, here p. 136; *PRO*, FO 371/30834, C 4047/326/12, Nichols to Makins, 14 April, Roberts' minute, 20 April, Strang's minute, 22 April, Makins to Nichols, 27 April 1942.
204) Woodward, *British Foreign Policy in the Second World War*, Vol. II, Appendix I, pp. 663–665.

all Central European countries, but demanded to have the previous reservations concerning juridical continuity of the pre-Munich republic and jurisdiction over Sudeten Germans 'solved'. A year had lapsed from the note of recognition containing those reservations and Beneš was not willing to wait any longer. The British attitude was 'unjust, unmerited and unjustified'. It was in his view unthinkable that the government of Churchill and Eden wished to continue the 'Munich policy'.[205] When he repeated this sentence to Nichols the following day in a heated discussion – which was provoked by the latter's doubts about acceptability for the British of Beneš's new formula on juridical continuity – Nichols retorted that 'it was fantastic to hold this for a moment and that he [Beneš] could hardly believe himself what he was saying'. Nevertheless, Beneš stuck to it that if the present government did not take steps effectually and juridically to put an end to Munich, it was in effect continuing the Munich policy. That moment Nichols offered the first sentence of the formula that he had drafted with Malkin almost two months earlier and that had by then remained in cold storage, upon Foreign Office's recommendation. The President replied that some such formula would be 'the very minimum' that would give him some satisfaction. With respect to the paragraph about jurisdiction, the President accepted linking it *confidentially* with admitting of the Sudeten representatives to the State Council, but only on the condition that it would happen 'in an appropriate moment'.[206]

The Foreign Office now agreed to offer Beneš the 'Nichols-Malkin formula' plus once again the old paragraph about jurisdiction. Roberts recorded an important advantage *pro futuro* of such an agreement: 'The offer ... might also help to dispose of any Czech request which we understand may be forthcoming for an Anglo-Czech treaty based upon the Anglo-Soviet precedent.'[207] On 25 June Eden wanted to show Beneš the pertaining formula during their lunch, but in the light of what he had just heard about Beneš's talks with Molotov he found it 'not perhaps entirely suitable' and promised to 'see whether it could not be slightly

205) *AÚTGM*, EB-L, box 111, Beneš's record of his talk with Eden in the Foreign Office, 4 June 1942.
206) *PRO*, FO 371/30834, C 5797/326/12, Nichols to Makins, 9 June 1942; *AÚTGM*, EB-L, box 110, Beneš's record of his talk with Nichols, 5 June 1942.
207) *PRO*, FO 371/30834, C 5797/326/12, Nichols to Makins, 9 June, Roberts' minute, 11 June, Makins' minute, 12 June, Malkin's minute, 13 June, Eden's minute, 14 June 1942, C 6363/326/12, FO Memorandum, 20 June 1942.

modified in a manner agreeable' to Beneš.[208] But in the ensuing days the Foreign Office effectively blocked all the attempts to improve it, whether they came from Nichols or from Beneš himself.

On 1 July Nichols, whom by then Sargent called 'a more than 100% Czechophile',[209] suggested that the Foreign Office produce an additional paragraph whereby both sides would reserve their position as regarded juridical continuity, but the British government would say that this question should not 'constitute an obstacle to harmonious and good relations between the two countries'. This in fact followed a previous proposal by Ripka and a conversation with Beneš who had pointed out a need for an instrument to punish persons guilty of acts committed between Munich and the outbreak of war. Nichols replied that no real advance on the question of juridical continuity was acceptable for the British and that any contentious cases might be solved ad hoc. On the account of jurisdiction, Beneš refused the conditional formula, by which Jaksch was in his view put on an equality with himself, and asked the British to trust him, to withdraw the reservation regarding jurisdiction at once, and to leave it to him to come to an agreement with the Sudeten leaders at an appropriate moment.[210]

'Dr. Benes is a very experienced negotiator, which no doubt explains why we are always asked at the last moment for further concession,' Roberts noted, thus launching a series of arguments why none of the two proposals were acceptable. However the position of 'Jaksch and his friends' was not 'of the very first importance in regard to the war effort', the Office was not prepared 'to throw them completely to the wolves' and give Beneš a 'blank cheque' in regard to the Sudeten Germans. He argued to them by British moral obligation and possible criticism in Parliament. However, now Beneš had to pay for his comparison between Jaksch and Henlein,[211] that he had made in a moment of irritation, as well as for his frequent references to the bitter anti-Sudeten feelings amongst his compatriots, which had prevented him from ad-

208) *PRO*, FO 954/4, Cz/42/4, Eden to Nichols, 25 June 1942; *AÚTGM*, EB-V, box 79, Ripka's record of Beneš's talk with Eden and Nichols, 25 July 1942.
209) *AÚTGM*, EB-L, box 111, Ripka's record of his talk with Sargent, 17 June 1942.
210) *PRO*, FO 371/30834, C 6590/326/12, Nichols to Makins, 1 July 1942.
211) In fact it was not a sudden outburst but rather Beneš's conviction. On 13 June 1942, he said to Lockhart that British policy concerning Jaksch was in fact 'a new Henleinism' ("nové henleinovství"). Of course, Lockhart agreed. *AÚTGM*, EB-L, box 110, Beneš's record of his talk with Lockhart, 13 June 1942.

mitting the Sudeten leaders to the State Council: 'Dr. Benes asks us to trust him unconditionally about the Sudetens, although his hands are likely to be tied by his own followers, and refuses to trust us in regard to the question of juridical continuity.' Roberts further quoted the pertinent sentence in the War Cabinet paper that Eden was about to present to his colleagues: '...I should hope that Dr. Beneš will leave aside the question of juridical continuity, which is a matter of historical fact, and is in any case a question for the Czechoslovak people themselves and not one on which H.M.G. should be asked unilaterally or in agreement with Dr. Benes to express an opinion.' Makins, after a few words of criticism about Nichols' readiness to come with alternative formulae, proposed to give Beneš the declaration, take it or leave it, as 'the longer we negotiate the more he will ask'. The last sentence of Makins' minute, in itself truthful enough, shows again the roots of mutual Anglo-Czechoslovak misperceptions and misunderstandings: 'No good can come of further argument about past history, which no formula can change.' Cadogan agreed and Malkin, from his juridical point of view, added that the question of guilt of the Czechoslovak nationals for action taken by them before August 1939 would anyway have to be decided by the Czechoslovak courts.[212]

The memorandum went to the War Cabinet as a whole, including the conditional formula on jurisdiction, although with a suggestion that that section would not be published. The text made it clear how limited the new commitment was: 'The passage regarding the effect of the Munich Agreement, although it may help Dr. Beneš, does not, in fact, mean any change in the existing situation or involve His Majesty's Government in any new commitments.' However, the memorandum further summed up Beneš's plans for the solution of the Sudeten German question and linked them with the estimation by FRPS from last February that the number of Germans who might require to be transferred to Germany would range from 3 to 6,8 million people.[213] Although transfer of population on such a scale would be a formidable undertaking, it was – the memorandum continued – at the same time

212) *PRO*, FO 371/30834, C 6180/326/12, Roberts' minute, 20 June 1942, C 6590/326/12, Roberts' and Makins' minutes, 2 July, Malkin's and Cadogan's minute, 4 July, signed by Eden on 5 July 1942, C 6867/326/12, Roberts to Nichols, 17 July 1942.
213) *PRO* FO 371/30930, C 2167/241/18, Memoranda on Frontiers of European Confederations and the Transfer of German Populations, 20 February 1942.

impossible to avoid some measures of that kind in post-war Europe. Unless, however, they were not carried out in an orderly and peaceful manner the paper prophesied that the Czech and Polish populations would expel the German minorities forcibly. The question was whether Beneš and the Sudeten German representatives were to be let known. The paper did not recommend discussing the application of the principle 'until a much later stage'. At the end, Eden asked his colleagues to negotiate with Dr. Beneš on the basis on the annexed formula and for the approval 'for the general principle of the transfer to Germany of German minorities in Central and South-Eastern Europe after the war in cases where this seems necessary and desirable, and authority to let this decision be known in appropriate cases'.

The Cabinet approved the paper on 6 July[214] and the next day Eden showed the formula to Beneš who 'smiled enigmatically', accepted the formula on Munich, but referring to the German reprisals consequent upon death of Heydrich he refused the paragraph concerning jurisdiction. As to juridical continuity, Eden assured the President that points, which might arise as a result of differing views on it, should be dealt with by ad hoc agreements. Eden took it that Beneš agreed that it should not be mentioned in the present document.[215] In slight contradiction with what had just been approved, he also informed Beneš about the planned transfers of populations.[216] But nothing about transfers was to be given in writing 'at this stage'.[217] Jaksch was informed that the British were considering transfers of populations as a method of future settlement in countries like Czechoslovakia or Poland a month later, during one of his periodical calls at the Foreign Office, since 'a special summons to Dr. Jaksch alone among minority leaders might give the impression that we regard him as more important and representative a figure than in fact we do'.[218] Jaksch regretted this communication but 'did not seem unduly surprised' and warned that if it were actually applied, the British 'must expect the strongest opposition from the Sudeten Germans whatever their political views'. According to Roberts, Jaksch departed 'in a more resigned frame of mind'. Indeed, he was gradually loosing his ground;

214) *Bod. Lib.*, microfilm, CAB 65/31, W. M. (42) 86th Conclusions, 6 July 1942
215) *PRO*, FO 954/4, Cz/42/5, Eden to Nichols, 7 July 1942.
216) *PRO*, FO 371/30835, C 6867/326/12, Nichols to Makins, 9 July 1942, C 7307/326/12, Nichols to Roberts, 22 July 1942.
217) *Ibid.*, Roberts to Nichols, 4 August 1942.
218) *PRO*, FO 371/30835, C 7307/326/12, Roberts' minute, 27 July 1942.

it was another blow after Eden had in late June decided to terminate his periodical broadcasts in the German BBC programs, following fierce criticism from Lord Vansittart, Lockhart and Beneš himself.[219]

By mid-July, after yet another unsuccessful attempt to secure immediate jurisdiction over the Sudeten Germans (this time the British were asked to withdraw the reservation of 18 July 1941 in exchange for the Czechoslovak promise to arrange for the Sudeten German represenation in the State Council 'at the appropriate moment before the end of the war'), Beneš agreed to drop the whole paragraph, shelve it 'for the present' and proceed only with the Munich formula. This only added to the reputation of Jan Masaryk who had only recently returned from the United States and the Foreign Office had no doubts that it was he who deserved credit for this sudden reasonableness on the Czechoslovak side.[220] The technical modalities were agreed on 17 July on a windy aerodrome outside Exeter where Beneš decorated Czechoslovak fighter pilots and Nichols, by then already mortified by the long dragged negotiations,[221] at least got some fresh air: Beneš chose to receive the Munich formula in a letter, rather than in a form of a question and answer in the House.[222] Of course, this provided another opportunity at least to express officially the Czechoslovak standpoint. Thus the Foreign Office did not get just 'a simple acknowledgement' as it wished.[223] The proposed answer contained a statement maintaining 'the Czechoslovak political and juridical position with regard to the Munich agreement and the events which followed it'. To this Eden was prepared to resign, but in co-operation with Nichols the Foreign Office managed to shelve other fuzzy remarks which were only likely to attract unwelcome parliamentary attention.[224]

219) Raška, *The Czechoslovak Exile Government in London and the Sudeten German Issue*, pp. 108–110.
220) *PRO*, FO 371/30835, C 6867/326/12, Nichols to Makins, 9 and 15 July 1942.
221) *Ibid.*, C 6867/326/12, Makins' minute, 11 July 1942.
222) *Ibid.*, C 7210/326/12, Nichols to Roberts, 20 July 1942.
223) *Ibid.*, Roberts to Nichols, 20 July 1942.
224) The letter, as proposed in its original version, referred to 'the other questions, which are certainly of far less political importance than those settled in your note and which may arise later as the consequences of the events connected with Munich', which were stated to be capable of resolution 'easily and without major difficulties in the spirit of friendship and collaboration existing between both our countries'. Roberts commented: 'This development is typical of the whole course of these negotiations, since the Czechs always want to get just a little bit more than we are prepared to offer.' *Ibid.*, C 7361/326/12, Nichols to Roberts, 24 July, minutes by Roberts, Malkin, Strang and Eden, 27–28 July 1942, C 7210/326/12, minutes by Allen and Roberts, 31 July, Strang's minute, 1 August 1942.

The letters were dated 5 August 1942. The British note, signed by Eden, after recalling the recognition of July 1941 and Churchill's broadcast of September 1940, stated: '...as Germany has deliberately destroyed the arrangements concerning Czechoslovakia reached in 1938, in which His Majesty's Government in the United Kingdom participated, His Majesty's Government regard themselves as free from any engagements in this respect. At the final settlement of the Czechoslovak frontiers to be reached at the end of the war they will not be influenced by any changes effected in and since 1938.' Masaryk, who signed the Czechoslovak reply, expressed his warmest thanks in the name of the whole Czechoslovak people, at the time suffering so terribly under the Nazi yoke, and after making the statement about the juridical position, stressing the significance of the new note 'as a highly significant act of justice towards Czechoslovakia' and assuring Eden of the 'real satisfaction' and 'profound gratitude' to his 'great country and nation' on the part of the Czechoslovak government, ended up with the important sentence: 'Between our two countries the Munich Agreement can now be considered as dead.'[225] In Parliament, later in the day, Eden, after presenting the gist of the letters, paid tribute on behalf of the British government to 'the tenacious and courageous stand' of the Czechoslovak people against their ruthless German oppressors: 'Acts such as the destruction of Lidice have stirred the conscience of the civilised world and will not be forgotten when the time comes to settle accounts with their perpetrators.' The Poles, who as well as the Americans had been informed in advance, secured an assurance that the repudiation of the Munich Agreement did not apply to the Polish acquisition of Teschen: Eden, in his reply to a planted parliamentary question, expressed his confidence that the frontier between the two Allied countries would be 'dealt with on the basis of the close and friendly relations' which now happily existed between them.[226] The Foreign Office noted the friendly broadcast by Masaryk which contrasted with the 'rather grudging' speech by Beneš. Although the latter was broadcasted on the occasion of the Anglo-Czechoslovak exchange, it was primarily devoted to the Russian attitude and to Beneš's conversations with General de

225) *Ibid.*, C 7210/326/12, Eden to Masaryk, 5 August, Masaryk to Eden, 5 August 1942; Beneš, *Šest let exilu a druhé světové války*, pp. 465–467.
226) *H. C. Deb.*, 5th Series, Vol. 382, 5 August 1942, Cols. 1004–1005; Raczynski, *In Allied London*, p. 119.

Gaulle.[227] 'However, we are quite used to this sort of thing by now,' Frank Roberts, the key British official dealing with Czechoslovak affairs throughout the war, sarcastically commented on the nature of this uneasy friendship.[228]

Conclusion

Jaromír Smutný, the President's Chancellor, wrote twenty years later (and once again in exile) that with the revocation of Munich, followed by the symbolic enhancement of the status of British and Soviet Legacies to Embassies, Dr. Beneš had considered the task that he had given to himself and the resistance movement abroad as fulfilled.[229] But in fact what he achieved in August 1942 was a rather slim result, considering the previous eight months of frenetic diplomatic activity. The formula only followed the logic of what Churchill had said almost two years ago: If the Munich settlement had been destroyed by the Germans, Britain clearly could not feel bound by it. And Beneš with his collaborators did consider Churchill's broadcast and Lockhart's letter of 7 November 1940 as a proof that the British government did not recognise the validity of the Munich Agreement any more – as it is clear from a legal analysis by the President's secretary and legal expert Eduard Táborský of late 1940.[230] Thus it would not be a terrible overstatement to say with respect to the British declaration of 1942 that rarely was so little achieved after such a long and intensive set of friendly negotiations... It seems from Beneš's

227) On the topic of the French renunciation of Munich from the very beginning see: Kuklík – Němeček, Cesta k oduznání Mnichova..., *op. cit.*, pp. 138–142; *Československo-francouzské vztahy v diplomatických jednáních 1940–1945*, Nos. 104–107, pp. 173–181. Cadogan attached to the agreement of 29 September 1942 his interesting comment that only underlined the difference of positions of the Czechoslovak government on the one hand and the French National Committee on the other by 1942: '...I really can't take this harlequinade seriously. It doesn't much matter what the French National Ctee. promises to anyone. And the idea that this c[oul]d. be used in any way as a means of pressure on us to do more is simply fantastic.' *PRO*, FO 371/30835, Cadogan's minute, 12 October 1942.
228) *PRO*, FO 371/30835, C 7933/326/12, Roberts' minute, 16 August 1942.
229) Smutný, Jaromír, Edvard Beneš a československý odboj za druhé světové války [Edvard Beneš and Czechoslovak resistance in World War II], *Svědectví* [Testimony], Paris, Vol. 21, 1963, pp. 50–60. Eduard Táborský, Beneš's other assistant, has been more sober in his reflection of President's evaluation of the achievement, saying that Beneš saw that the British note was the best he could get at that moment. Táborský, *Prezident Beneš mezi Západem a Východem*, p. 68.
230) *HIA Stanford*, Eduard Táborský collection, box 8, envelope Other materials concerning Wenzel Jaksch & the Sudeten German Social Democrats, Táborský's legal opinion concerning the status of the Sudeten Germans, 1940.

subsequent policy that in 1942 he realised that he was approaching the very limits of commitment that he could hope to obtain from the British during the war. Only in March 1945 the British agreed to grant the Czechoslovak government *full political authority* over the territory of Czechoslovakia in the frontiers from 31 December 1937.[231]

Beneš clearly saw a continuation of the Munich policy and influence of 'Munichoids' in all the procrastination as well as in the insufficient and rather unsatisfactory result of the long negotiations. But it was undeserved. The Foreign Office was not motivated in its policy by any effort to preserve the fruits of the Munich settlement. Its officials, in agreement with Churchill and Eden, primarily strove to avoid numerous entanglements and commitments that would dangerously narrow the manoeuvring space for British foreign policy in the fluid and unstable world that was yet to emerge from the war. They were afraid that a commitment conceded to one exile representation would set off an avalanche of mutually contradictory demands from all those exiles now seated in London. The commitment granted to Beneš in 1942 was therefore of a limited nature and rather helpful for his propaganda purposes than having any practical, not to say legal, meaning. What was perhaps more important was the promise of British support for the post-war transfer of the Sudeten Germans. With that achievement in hands, Beneš lost the last reason for seeking a deal with Jaksch. The Central Department also realised that there was little the British could do to foster an agreement between Beneš and Jaksch – the more so that the latter wrote protesting letters against the British renunciation of Munich to U.S. State Secretary Cordell Hull and Canadian Prime Minister Mackenzie King.[232] The deal actually never materialised. And the President and his collaborators in their further negotiations with British, Soviet and American politicians and officials were gradually limiting the area which was to be cessed to Germany after the war, and at the same time they were increasing the number of Germans to be transferred without territory.[233] At the same time the British officials

231) Prečan, Vilém, British Attitudes towards Czechoslovakia, 1944–45, *Bohemia*, Vol. 29, 1988, No. 1, pp. 73–87.
232) *PRO*, FO 371/30835, C 8119/326/12, Roberts' minute, 1 September 1942, C 7809//326/12, Roberts' minute, 7 August 1942; Jaksch, *Cesta Evropy do Postupimi*, pp. 258–259.
233) Brandes, Opožděná česká alternativa k mnichovskému diktátu, *op. cit.*, pp. 30–36.

also increasingly preferred 'considerable transfers of population' – as opposed to ejecting just the 'guilty' Germans – as a remedy to be used 'on a fairly large scale'.[234]

It is important to ask to what degree the British renunciation of Munich was influenced by the terror that the Germans had unleashed in the Protectorate after the assassination of Heydrich, especially in view of some allegations that Beneš had sent the two parachutists, Gabčík and Kubiš, to the Protectorate with a cold-blooded consideration that if they succeeded the subsequent reprisals would help him to achieve his political goals.[235] It seems that the role was by no means crucial. In his report of 9 June – the day of German annihilation of Lidice, but recording a talk with Beneš from four days ago – where Nichols urged that the acceptable formula be offered to Beneš, the Minister mentioned only his *feeling* that Beneš *felt* that the reprisals put further obligation on the British to do something to discharge the debt that they, in Beneš's view, owed to Czechoslovakia. In Beneš's own record the reprisals were mentioned only as an argument why Jaksch et al. could not be admitted to the State Council.[236] In the departmental minutes, in which the process of building of agreement based on Nichols' proposal is recorded, the Nazi terror is not mentioned at all. Only Makins commented on the topic of the 'Munich debt', in a minute that can at the same time serve as an example of both usually moderate and calm reactions to Beneš's frequent insinuations directed against the protagonists of British foreign policy and to a different perspective on the events of 1938–1942: 'Dr. Benes is never tired of saying, among other things, that H.M.G. owe the Czechs a debt which they have not paid. Considering that we are fighting this war in part at all events for the liberation of his country, and have recognised him as head of the State and his Government as the legal Government, and are supporting him and his followers in every possible way, this is an exaggerated point of view.'[237] On 25 June Eden promised to reconsider the formula in the light of Beneš's talk with Molotov. And in the ensuing days the Foreign Office refused all the new suggestions, although the officials were at the same time read-

234) *PRO*, FO 371/30835, C 9161/326/12, Cadogan's minute, 29 September 1942.
235) See e.g. Uhlíř, Jan Boris, *Ve stínu říšské orlice* [In the shadow of the Reich spread-eagle], Praha, Nakladatelství Aleš Skřivan ml. 2002, p. 143.
236) *PRO*, FO 371/30834, C 5797/326/12, Nichols to Makins, 9 June; *AÚTGM*, EB-L, box 110, Beneš's record of his talk with Nichols, 5 June 1942.
237) *PRO*, FO 371/30834, C 5797/326/12, Makins' minute, 12 June 1942.

ing the Czechoslovak resolutions protesting against the Nazi terror in the Protectorate, Canadian senators called for obliterating of German villages as a reprisal and even Cadogan went out of his way by putting on the record: 'I hope Heydrich suffered during the days when he was dying.'[238] The reprisals eventually did appear in the memorandum for the Cabinet – as a psychological reason to give Beneš 'such satisfaction as possible'. But that meant only an approval of a decision that had already been adopted in the office which dealt almost exclusively with all the foreign policy issues of not primary importance – the Foreign Office. Eden really did not need to pile up arguments for renunciation of Munich in a Cabinet led by Churchill and Attlee. Nevertheless, publicly the renunciation of Munich purported as a direct British response to the Nazi atrocities committed on the Czechs.

The terror, however, served the Czechoslovak politicians for obtaining support for retribution that they started planning and preaching. 'This German behaviour has been so outrageous even by German standards that we can hardly criticise the Czechoslovak Govt. for having gone further than we should wish in specifying the measures of retribution to be taken after the war,' Roberts wrote on 24 June 1942.[239] But this did not go so far as to offer Beneš a British instrument to try people guilty of crimes committed in the period from Munich to the outbreak of war. And, as I have pointed out, calls for radical solution of the minority issue in post-war Europe had been commonplace amongst British officials ever since the autumn of 1940.

The Soviet factor was again important. But unlike in 1940 or 1941, this time the FO officials were not impressed by the President's argument about the danger of the turn of most Czechs towards the Soviet Union. The Foreign Office felt that Britain could not compete with the Soviet rulers in opportunism anyway and thought that Beneš's position amongst his compatriots both at home and abroad was strong enough to stand out such move. After all, two years ago he had used his enormous popularity amongst the Czechs at home as a crucial argument for recognition... It seems that only Bruce Lockhart, a good psychologist who knew Beneš well, realised the broader dangers entailed in the

238) *HIA Stanford*, Eduard Táborský collection, box 3, envelope Various documents from 1942, extracts from *The Evening News* and *Evening Standard*, 12 June 1942; *PRO*, FO 371/30848, C 5663/5404/12, Cadogan's minute, 10 June 1942.
239) *PRO*, FO 371/30848, C 6232/5404/12, Roberts' minute, 24 June 1942.

growing disparity between the British and the Soviet commitment to Czechoslovakia, especially in view of Beneš's intended journey to Russia the coming summer. On 1 May 1942, after an hour-and-a-half long conversation with the President, he wrote into his diary: 'Beneš is going to Russia this summer. He will, of course, play Russia against us. But if he goes with empty hands – and nothing settled – from here, the Russians will push him farther than he wants to go.'[240] Yet, eventually the journey was postponed by one and a half year.

The Soviet dimension in 1942 is, however, even more illustrative for comparison of political capabilities of Great Powers on the one hand and other Allies on the other hand. Throughout the spring of 1942 the British were prepared to concede to the Soviet Union its territorial acquisitions of 1939–40. But that was considered an exceptional case, for obvious reasons. Although hardly any other exile leader was able to pursue his foreign policy goals so stubbornly and with such inventiveness in application of various negotiating techniques like Beneš, not even he was able to surpass the foreign policy priorities resulting from Britain's policy to the other two Great Powers. Only if Britain had approved the Soviet frontiers of 1941 in the alliance treaty with Moscow, Beneš would have got a chance to get British approval of Czechoslovakia's pre-Munich frontiers. It is clear from the Foreign Office files that the officials expected such an offensive and they felt that they would hardly be able to withstand it.

If for Beneš Munich meant probably the most serious trauma in his life, the repetition of which he was determined to avoid in the future at all costs, the protagonists of British foreign policy, if and when thinking about the future of Central Europe, primarily wished to prevent recurrence of the unstable inter-war mosaic of mutually grudging and spiteful little countries. The federations clearly played crucial role in such deliberations. Therefore it is astonishing if Anita Prażmowska addresses the question why mere 'utterances' in favour of the Polish-Czechoslovak declaration of 1940, the Greek-Yugoslav agreement and in favour of 'smaller states weld[ing] themselves into larger though not exclusive groupings' were not followed by a real policy on the matter. Regardless of the fact that she quotes a minute written by somebody else, from a different day and even on a slightly different topic as compared to the

240) *The Diaries of Sir Robert Bruce Lockhart 1939–1965*, 1 May 1942, p. 161.

information she sets forth,[241] even her explanation of 'the government's preoccupation with much weightier matters in the conduct of war' is hardly acceptable.[242] Yes, the British wished to have their plans consulted with the Americans – only to be replied that maybe after New Year[243] – and were thinking about the appropriate moment to address the Russians with a similar enquiry. It is also true that an inter-departmental committee on politico-strategic matters was only set up in October 1942. However, the author ignores the whole detailed elaboration of the FRPS plans, to which the Foreign Office attached much importance, as well as Eden's stressing of the importance of confederations for future peace in Europe during his negotiations with Stalin and Molotov in December 1941 and May 1942. While neglecting the relevant Foreign Office files, she also fails to see the motivation that was behind the mere cautious encouragements to the Polish-Czechoslovak confederation – the fear that more outward support might arise suspicions and thus spoil the whole hopefully developing project. When referring to Poland, Prażmowska may be right that mere occasional 'utterances' in support of the federations combined with discouragement of some Polish-led initiatives aiming to encourage anti-Soviet unity of the London based governments-in-exile inflamed the 'already visible and profound distrust of British motives towards the Soviet Union'.[244] However, this hardly applies to all the exiled governments.

On the Czechoslovak side, even the cautious British support to the federation project of Poland and Czechoslovakia raised suspicion about its real motives. Gustav Winter, the Social-Democratic correspondent

241) See Prażmowska, *Britain and Poland 1939–1943. The Betrayed Ally*, p. 144. In fact the minute was not Roberts', but Ronald's, not of 23 October 1942, but of 31 October 1942, and not written in response to an enquiry by the Foreign Minister of the Dutch exile government about 'British views on the future balance of power in Europe', but rather about British 'plans for the future of Eastern Europe and the Balkans'. *PRO*, FO 371/31535, U 1742/1742/70, Law's minute, 23 October 1942, Ronald's minute, 31 October 1942.

242) Prażmowska, *Britain and Poland 1939–1943. The Betrayed Ally*, p. 144.

243) In March 1943, Eden agreed with Sumner Welles that an ideal solution would be a creation of two federations, one composed of the Balkan states and the other of the remaining countries of Eastern Europe. Welles preferred inclusion of Hungary to the Balkan confederation and Austria to the other one. *FRUS*, 1943, Vol. III, p. 24. For the development of American plans for federations in Eastern Europe see: Lundestad, Geir, *The American Non-Policy towards Eastern Europe 1943–1947*, Oslo, Universitetsforlaget 1978, pp. 347–356.

244) Prażmowska, *Britain and Poland 1939–1943. The Betrayed Ally*, pp. 143–144.

in Paris in the inter-war period and foreign policy expert in the time of war, talked in March 1941 with William Gillies, the Labour Party foreign policy secretary. According to Winter's record, the latter argued for regional security pacts: 'If Czechoslovakia makes federation with Poland, how could she object against possible England's agreement with a few Atlantic states on some special interests?' Winter's conclusion was obvious: 'This statement only confirmed my previous opinion why all the British politicians welcomed with such an enthusiasm the Czechoslovak-Polish negotiations. In the case of need the English would have in it an alibi for their own security pacts.'[245]

It is very difficult, if not impossible, to establish the actual degree of Czechoslovak devotion to the confederation project. Clearly it was much lower than in the case of the Poles;[246] and the British officials were well aware of that fact. On the one hand, it was the 'ultimate aim of Czechoslovakia', proclaimed in a memorandum that was distributed to various British agencies to create after the war 'a federative Central European union, consisting of Poland and Czechoslovakia, which could be joined by other Central European states, should they not themselves bring into existence federal unions in another form'.[247] On the other hand, however, there were widespread doubts about the whole project and opposition to it, ranging from Prime Minister Šrámek to the majority of the State Council's members and to Fierlinger in Moscow. Those who argued for the confederation in these internal discussions usually stressed that internationally Czechoslovakia could not get along without its goodwill and serious effort to reach agreement.[248] No wonder that especially Polish historiography blames not only Soviet policy, but also President Beneš for the failure of the project – the argument being that Beneš made use of British favouring of the federation projects to strengthen the Czechoslovak position, and only to abandon the plan

245) *AMZV*, LA-D, box 61, 877/dův/41, G. Winter's records of his talk with W. Gillies, 26 March 1941.
246) See e.g. the excellent comparison of the efforts undertaken by respective sides in the military field by Jiří Friedl: Friedl, Jiří, *Na jedné frontě. Vztahy československé a polské armády za druhé světové války* [For the same cause: Czechoslovak-Polish military relations during the Second World War], Praha, Ústav pro soudobé dějiny 2005, esp. pp. 201–205.
247) *R. W. Seton-Watson and His Relations with the Czechs and Slovaks*, No. 215, pp. 602–615, Czechoslovakia's peace aims, 1941.
248) Němeček, *Od spojenectví k roztržce*, p. 110.

on the first possible occasion.[249] Czech historians dealing with Polish-Czechoslovak relations during the Second World War usually claim that the Czechoslovak effort in the negotiations was sincere.[250] It was – some of them say – the Soviet Union that stood up to the confederation while the British gave up the federative plans in view of the Soviet opposition; therefore no wonder that also the exiled representatives of the small Czechoslovakia dropped the project...[251] However, while Edvard Beneš did so in November 1942 at the latest, the British were to present their plans as late as at the conferences in Moscow and Tehran in the autumn of 1943, and Churchill personally even during his Moscow negotiations with Stalin in October 1944.[252]

If the preparatory works for the union with the Poles did not mean for Edvard Beneš a purpose-made tool, then at least a well-calculated advantage in his struggle to achieve his major goals vis-à-vis the British government – full recognition for his government, renunciation of Munich and its legal consequences, and approval for a radical solution of the minority question in post-war Czechoslovakia.[253]

249) See e.g. Wandycz, Piotr S., *Czechoslovak-Polish Confederation and the Great Powers, 1940–1943*, Bloomington, Indiana University 1956.
250) Němeček, *Od spojenectví k roztržce*; Žáček, *Projekt československo-polské konfederace v letech 1939–1943*.
251) Such was for example Doc. Vilém Prečan's argumentation in his polemic with me at the international conference *Munich agreement, the way to destruction of democracy in Europe* on 25 October 2003.
252) Most recently, Leonid Gibianskii pointed out these British efforts. Gibianskii, Problemy vostotshnoi Evropy i natshalo formirovaniia Sovetskogo bloka, *op. cit.*, p. 110.
253) Brandes, *Großbritannien und seine osteuropäischen Allierten 1939–1943*, p. 290. The author points out the notable coincidence between Beneš's agreement with the confederation and Eden's undertaking to agree with the post-war transfer of the Sudeten Germans from Czechoslovakia. However, Brandes rules out that Beneš used the negotiations on the establishment of confederation merely as a tool for obtaining British consent with the transfer. See Němeček, *Od spojenectví k roztržce*, p. 97.

This book, on a general level, is primarily a polemic with the following frequented statements that are of key importance for assessments of both British and Czechoslovak foreign policy:

1) that the policy of appeasement as carried out by Neville Chamberlain and his Cabinet gave Germany a free hand in Eastern Europe;

2) that the Chamberlain Cabinet continued in the policy of appeasement not only after Munich, but also in the spring and summer of 1939 and to a certain degree even after the outbreak of the war;

3) that the 'Munich policy' influenced British dealings with Czechoslovakia long after Chamberlain's departure from the premiership and that it was the real cause of delays in the full recognition of the government in exile and in the renunciation of Munich as well as the real cause of refusal to guarantee the return to Czechoslovakia's pre-Munich borders and to accept the construction of juridical continuity of pre-Munich Czechoslovakia;

4) that the fact that the British needed three years for granting full recognition and renouncing the tangible results of the Munich Agreement while the Soviets managed to give the same in three weeks testifies to the formers' willingness (if not their intention) to hand Czechoslovakia over to the Soviet sphere of influence.

While I do not wish to repeat again the contents of conclusions in particular chapters, I would like to draw several general observations from the overall analysis of British policy towards Czechoslovakia from Munich to its renunciation in 1942. This policy apparently suffered from the lack of political leadership throughout the whole period. As a result, the sociological phenomenon of bureaucratic changelessness played a central role in the Anglo-Czechoslovak relationship. Various British governmental departments often continued in their previous work, unless they got a clear political directive that they should do otherwise. Such a directive often did not come, simply for the ministers had other urgent matters to deal with. When researching the period prior to the outbreak of war, however, I did not come across any single case of attempting to bribe Germany at the Czechoslovak expense. On the contrary, many of the episodes that have been traditionally attributed by both Czech and also part of British historiography to the continuation or even new waves of appeasement in British policy were in fact caused by the desire of particular departments to carry on in their business or by untimely respect to various other commitments. These were either of legal character (e.g. the dealing with the Bank for International Settlements) or political commitments to other Great Powers (the question of frontiers). Munich was clearly much more present in the minds of the Czechoslovak exiles than in the actual British foreign policy conduct ever since March 1939 – either generally or in the specific policy towards Czechoslovakia. This disparity applies all the more to the situation after September 1939 or indeed after May-June 1940.

While between 15 March 1939 and the outbreak of war there was no real partner on the Czechoslovak side to influence British policy (to a lesser degree this applies also for the period from Munich to 15 March), from August 1939 it became increasingly clear that it would once again be Edvard Beneš. Although he was certainly not popular amongst many British politicians and officials, they were at the same time aware that they would not be able to avoid him as the leader of any Czechoslovak action in exile. The question was what form such action would have. The Foreign Office, and particularly its Central Department that played the key role in British dealings with Czechoslovakia, was soon flooded with memoranda asking for recognition and later for a higher degree of it. Thus Beneš almost immediately became the dynamic force in the Anglo-Czechoslovak relationship, whereas the British governmental bodies were mostly passive and responsive. The process of recognition was slowed down by the dissensions amongst Czechoslovak émigrés but primarily by British respect for the position of several neutral countries. Only when these nations oriented their policy more clearly towards Germany, and France collapsed, recognition of the Provisional government became possible. Robert Bruce Lockhart deserved more than anyone else that it happened almost immediately; for months he had been cautiously but permanently delivering arguments towards that end. The most important one was the fact that Beneš was in clandestine contacts with the home resistance and with the Protectorate government. Ironically enough, this fact later changed into an argument *against* full recognition for his government and himself as the President of the Czechoslovak Republic. Although the Prime Minister's initiative launched the process of full recognition in April 1941, it broke down due to the Dominions' reluctance to grant further recognition. Another political directive was needed. It came only as a result of the quick Soviet recognition following the German attack. Then Eden realised the danger of the dramatic rise of the Soviet influence amongst the Czech population and politicians as a result of British *non-recognition* and found a way to overcome the Dominions' reservations.

'President Benes' policy is to commit us, our policy is to avoid commitment,' Roger Makins, head of the Central Department, formulated in one of his minutes the merits of tensions between Beneš and the Foreign Office.[1] The President constantly criticised the British for 'lack of policy', for being unprepared for a possible German collapse. This was in his thinking connected with the uncertain status of the former Czechoslovak territories ceded to Germany, Hungary and Poland in 1938. But here all his initiatives failed as a result of Britain's commitment to the U.S. government's non-commitment in territorial matters. Although the British government was considering breaching this principle in response to Soviet demands to secure the territorial acquisitions from 1939–40, it did not want to do the same in the case of other countries, including Czechoslovakia.

Munich certainly *was* the central issue in the Anglo-Czechoslovak relationship at least until its renunciation. In the initial stage the British had to deal with numerous practical problems that this unstable settlement and its early collapse produced. Later, Munich developed into a major political argument frequently used by Edvard Beneš in his efforts for achieving his goals which generally aimed at 'undoing' of Munich. By overstressing it, however, he at the same time undermined his own policy. This applied to the relationship with Britain, when his methods added to the irritation on the part of key officials dealing with Czechoslovakia who hardly felt any 'guilt' because of Munich. It also gradually diverted Czechoslovak foreign policy from the course of even balance between West and East; constant reminding of Munich naturally strengthened its

---

1) *PRO*, FO 371/26 388, C 13503/216/12, Makins' minute, 28 November 1940.

eastern orientation. Munich also resonated in internal British political debates, independently of Beneš and his policy. After 15 March 1939 it significantly enhanced the reputation of the 'anti-appeasers', and after their gradual accession to power it influenced their planning for the future and even political decisions such as Prime Minister's staffing. Nevertheless, while on the British part Munich was only one of many historical arguments, on the Czechoslovak part it gradually developed into a real 'syndrome'.

The President's feeling that Britain had a moral debt to Czechoslovakia because of Munich was not universally shared amongst British politicians and officials. Therefore, they dealt with the Czechoslovak affairs in a standard way, using their customary methods. These often included slowness of bureaucratic machinery and always subordination to major political priorities and overall political directives. In the context of rather naïve expectations that Czechoslovakia should get a preferential treatment, as a way of repaying the 'Munich debt', all this seemed to most of the Czechoslovak exiles like an intentional procrastination and – a continuation of the 'Munich policy'. As such it provided at least a mental underpinning for looking for an alternative foreign policy course that would replace relying on the West. Until the beginning of 1942 it seemed, however, that this was found in a close co-operation with Poland. This coincided with British plans for federalisation of the area between Russia and Germany. Thus the British supported the plan for a post--war Czechoslovak-Polish confederation and agreed that it should have friendly relations with the Soviet Union. By the end of 1942, however, the Polish-Soviet relations turned out to be an insurmountable obstacle and Beneš decided to secure an alliance with the USSR.

One of the aims of this book, though not the central one, was to look at the resonance of British foreign policy amongst Czechoslovak politicians and its impact upon Czechoslovak foreign policy. This brings me to looking for alternatives: Could an entirely different policy have changed the foreign policy orientation of Czechoslovakia? I suggest that the answer is in the negative. There is plenty of evidence that Edvard Beneš had decided to re-orient the Czechoslovak foreign policy soon after Munich and that he himself repeatedly deflected it from the preached balance between East and West. Tragically enough, the British hesitation, procrastination and non-committal attitude strengthened him in his feeling that his new foreign policy course was in fact the only possible one.

Edvard Beneš presented his 'lesson from Munich' in a clear and concise form during his talk with Molotov in London in June 1942: For so many years Czechoslovakia was a trustworthy ally of France, only to be betrayed by her at the end. In its geographical situation, surrounded by Austria, Germany, Poland (!) and Hungary, the country is now forced to look for a mainstay. This cannot be Germany, taking into account its anti-Czechoslovak tendencies. 'For the period of 20 years Czechoslovakia was oriented towards the West, especially towards France. Now the situation sharply changes and if the USSR becomes Czechoslovakia's neighbour, then orientation towards the USSR will best agree with the interests and likings of the Czechoslovak people. It is necessary to build up such form of Europe, in which a repetition of Munich would not be possible.'[2] This was not an isolated statement by Beneš.[3]

Although there was hardly a lack of goodwill on the part of Churchill, Eden and some officials to be forthcoming in their responses to various Czechoslovak demands and initiatives, British foreign policy was at the same time constrained by numerous more important regards, ranging from commitments to the other two Great Powers to respect for the attitudes of Dominions, Colonial issues, etc. Beneš's complaints that whenever he asked the British for a concession he had to undergo a painful process of extracting it were not unfounded, especially when compared to the easiness with which he was by then obtaining the same or similar concessions from the Soviet Union – ever since 22 June 1941. The FO officials, however, deluded themselves by their expectation that in spite of the Soviet opportunism it should not be too difficult for Dr. Beneš to convince himself and his people that British and American policy would be more consistent and more reliable if less immediately encouraging. This misperception was to have serious impact on the future of Czechoslovakia.

2) Rzheshevskii, *Voina i diplomatiia. Dokumenty, kommentarii 1941-1942*, No. 118, s. 260, record of Molotov's conversation with Beneš, 9 June 1942.
3) See e.g. the records of his talk with Polish minister Zygmunt Kaczyński in August 1943, summed up in: Němeček, *Od spojenectví k roztržce*, pp. 240–241.

Archival material
Public Record Office (The National Archives), London (PRO)
FO 371 Foreign Office general correspondence
FO 800 Papers of Lord Halifax
FO 800 Papers of Robert Bruce Lockhart
FO 954 Papers of Earl of Avon
PREM 3 Prime Minister's Office: operations papers
PREM 4 Prime Minister's Office: confidential papers
CAB 23 Cabinet Minutes and Conclusions, 1938–1939
CAB 24 Memoranda for Cabinet Meetings, 1938–1939
CAB 27 Minutes and Papers of the Foreign Policy Committee of the Cabinet, 1938–1939
CAB 65 War Cabinet Minutes, Conclusions and Confidential Annexes
CAB 66 War Cabinet and Cabinet Memoranda
CAB 67 War Cabinet Memoranda (WP (G) series)
CAB 68 War Cabinet Memoranda (WP (R) series)
CAB 120/737 War Cabinet, Czechoslovakia
CAB 127/158 Repercussions of the Munich Agreement
CAB 121/359 Cabinet, Policy towards Czechoslovakia
CAB 122/485 Cabinet, Civil Affairs – Czechoslovakia
HO 294 Home Office, Czechoslovak Refugee Trust Fund: Records
T 160 Treasury, Czechoslovak Gold
T 210 Treasury, Czechoslovak Financial Claims
WO 106 War Office, Directorate of Military Operations and Intelligence
WO 190 Situation in Czechoslovakia
WO 193 War Office, Directorate of Military Operations
HS 4 Special Operations Executive, Czechoslovakia
HS 7/108 SOE Country History, Czechoslovakia 1940–45

House of Lords Record Office, London (HLRO)
Robert Bruce Lockhart Papers

School of Slavonic and East European Studies, University of London (SSEES)
Karel Lisický Collection

Bank of England Archive, London (BEA)
files relating to Czechoslovakia – 1939–1945

Bodleian Library, Oxford (Bod. Lib.)
Clement Attlee Papers

Arthur Greenwood Papers
Viscount Simon Papers
microfilms of Cabinet Papers – series CAB 23, CAB 24, CAB 65, CAB 66

Churchill College, Cambridge
Alexander Cadogan Papers
Winston S. Churchill Papers
Frank Roberts Papers
William Strang Papers
Robert Vansittart Papers

University of Birmingham Library, Birmingham
Earl of Avon Papers
Neville Chamberlain Papers

Archiv Ministerstva zahraničních věcí ČR
[Archive of the Foreign Ministry of the Czech Republic] Praha (AMZV)
Londýnský archiv – důvěrný [London Archive – Confidential] (LA-D)
Londýnský archiv [London Archive] (LA)

Archiv Ústavu T. G. Masaryka [Archive of The T. G. Masaryk Institute]
Praha (AÚTGM) – so called Beneš Archive (BA)
Edvard Beneš – druhá světová válka [Edvard Beneš – World War II]
fond 40 – Kancelář prezidenta republiky [fund 40 – Presidential Office]

Národní archiv [National Archive] Praha (NA Praha)
fund No. 1 – Hubert Ripka (AHR)
fund Pozůstalost Dr. Huberta Ripky [Dr. Hubert Ripka papers]
fund Předsednictvo ministerské rady [Presidium of the Council of Ministers]

Archiv vneshnei politiki, Moscow (AVP)
fund Sekretariat Litvinova
fund Sekretariat Molotova
fund Sekretariat Vyshinskogo
fund Referentura po Czechoslovakii

National Archives, Washington (NARA)
U.S. Department of State Archives, 1939–42, Record Group 59

Hoover Institution Archives, Stanford University, Palo Alto, Cal. (HIA Stanford)
Robert Bruce Lockhart collection
Ivo Ducháček collection
Eduard Táborský collection

Published collections of documents *

British Documents on Foreign Affairs – reports and papers from the Foreign Office confidential print, Part III, *From 1940 through 1945*, Series A, *The Soviet Union and Finland*, 5 Vols., Bethesda (MD), University Publications of America 1998.

British Documents on Foreign Affairs – reports and papers from the Foreign Office confidential print, Part III, *From 1940 through 1945*, Series F, *Europe*, 26 Vols., Bethesda (MD), University Publications of America 1997.

British 'White Papers' on Munich Crisis and Agreement, Misc. Nos. 7, 8 and 11 (1938), resp. Cmd. 5847, 5848 and 5908.

České a československé archivní dokumenty v Archivu Hooverova institutu [Czech and Czechoslovak archival documents in Hoover Institution Archive], eds. J. Kuklík – J. Němeček, *Soudobé dějiny* [Contemporary history], Vol. 5, 1998, No. 1, pp. 95–116.

Česko-slovenská národní rada v Paříži 1940. Dokumenty [Czecho-Slovak National Council in Paris, 1940. Documents], eds. J. Kuklík – J. Němeček, *Moderní dějiny* [Modern history], Prague, Vol. 6, 1998, pp. 175–237.

Československo-francouzské vztahy v diplomatických jednáních 1940–1945 [Czechoslovak-French relations in diplomatic negotiations 1940–1945], eds. J. Němeček – H. Nováčková – I. Šťovíček – J. Kuklík, Praha, HÚ AV ČR – SÚA – UK – Karolinum 2005.

Československo-sovětské vztahy v diplomatických jednáních 1939–1945, Dokumenty 1–2 [Czechoslovak-Soviet relations in diplomatic negotiations 1939–1945. Documents I–II], eds. J. Němeček – H. Nováčková – I. Šťovíček – M. Tejchman, Praha, SÚA 1998–1999. (*Dokumenty ČSR–SSSR*)

Češi a sudetoněmecká otázka 1939–1945. Dokumenty [The Czechs and the Sudeten German question. Documents], ed. J. Vondrová, Praha, Ústav mezinárodních vztahů 1994.

Cesta ke Květnu [The road to May], 2 Vols., eds. M. Klimeš – P. Lesjuk – I. Malá – V. Prečan, Praha, Nakl. Československé akademie věd 1965.

Czechoslovak-Polish Negotiations of the Establishment of Confederation and Alliance 1939–1944, Prague, Publishing House Karolinum and the Institute of History, Academy of Sciences of the Czech Republic 1995.

Dekrety prezidenta republiky 1940–1945. Dokumenty I–II [Decrees of the President of the Republic 1940–1945. Documents I–II], eds. K. Jech – K. Kaplan, Brno, Doplněk 1995.

Documentary Background of World War II, 1931 to 1941, ed. J. Gantenbein, New York, Columbia University Press 1948.

Documents Diplomatiques Français, 1932–1939, 2e Série (1936–1939), Tome XIII–XIX, Paris, Ministère des Affaires Etrangères 1979–1986. (*DDF*)

Documents on British Foreign Policy, 1919–1939, 3rd series, 1938–1939, 9 Vols., London, His Majesty's Stationery Office 1949–57. (*DBFP*)

Documents on German Foreign Policy, Series D (1937–1945), Washington, Government Printing Office 1948–1957. (*DGFP*)

Documents on International Affairs 1939–1946, 2 Vols., Oxford, Oxford University Press 1951–1954.

Documents on Polish-Soviet Relations 1939–1945, 2 Vols., London, General Sikorski Historical Institute 1961, 1967.

* Czech, Slovak and Polish sources are also translated into English. German, Russian and French ones are entered in the original language only. In case that a book has been published both in a 'world language' and Czech/Slovak, then this is mentioned. Such books are entered according to the language of the original publication.

Dokumenty a materiály k dějinám československo-sovětských vztahů [Documents and materials on the history of Czechoslovak-Soviet relations], 4/1-2, Praha 1982, 1984.

Dokumenty československé zahraniční politiky. Československá zahraniční politika v roce 1938. Svazek II (1. červenec - 5. říjen 1938) [Documents on Czechoslovak Foreign Policy. Czechoslovak Foreign Policy in 1938, Volume II (1 July - 5 October 1938)], Praha, ÚMV - UK - Karolinum - HÚ AV ČR 2001. (*DČSZP 1938, II*)

Dokumenty československé zahraniční politiky. Od rozpadu Česko-Slovenska do uznání československé prozatímní vlády 1939-1940 (16. březen 1939 - 16. červen 1940) [Documents on Czechoslovak Foreign Policy. From the break-up of Czecho-Slovakia until the recognition of the Czechoslovak provisional government (16 March 1939 - 16 June 1940)], Praha, ÚMV - UK - Karolinum - HÚ AV ČR 2002. (*DČSZP 1939-1940*)

Dokumenty československé zahraniční politiky. Od rozpadu Česko-Slovenska do uznání československé prozatímní vlády 1939-1940. Příloha: Zápisy ze zasedání Československého národního výboru 1939-1940 [Documents on Czechoslovak Foreign Policy. From the break-up of Czecho-Slovakia until the recognition of the Czechoslovak provisional government. Annex: Minutes of the meetings of the Czechoslovak National Committee 1939-1940], Praha, ÚMV - UK - Karolinum - HÚ AV ČR 1999. (*DČSZP - ČSNV*)

Dokumenty vneshnei politiki, tom XXII (1939) - kniga 1-2, tom XXIII (1940-22 iiunia 1941) - kniga 1-3, Moskva, Mezhdunarodnye otnosheniia 1992, 1998. (DVP)

Dokumenty z historie československé politiky 1939-1943 [Documents from the history of Czechoslovak politics 1939-1943], eds. L. Otáhalová - M. Červinková, Praha, Academia 1966. (*DHČSP*)

Edvard Beneš v USA v roce 1943. Dokumenty [Edvard Beneš in the United States in 1943], eds. J. Němeček - H. Nováčková - I. Šťovíček, *Sborník archivních prací*, Vol. 49, 1999, No. 2, pp. 469-564.

Edvard Beneš: Vzkazy do vlasti [Edvard Beneš: Messages home], ed. J. Šolc, Praha, Naše vojsko 1996.

The Foreign Office and the Kremlin. British Documents on Anglo-Soviet Relations, 1941-1945, ed. G. Ross, Cambridge, Cambridge University Press 1984.

The Foreign Office List and Diplomatic and Consular Year Book, Years 1938-1948, London, Harrison and Sons Ltd. 1938-1948.

Foreign Relations of the United States, 1938-1943, Washington, D.C., Government Printing Office 1955-1968. (*FRUS*)

Great Britain Foreign Office Weekly Political Intelligence Summaries, Vols. I-XXV, 1939-1946, London, Kraus International Publishers 1983. (*FO WPIS*)

Ján Papánek, Za vojny Benešovi. Dokumenty - výběr, 1939-1945 [Ján Papánek, To Beneš during the war. Documents - selection, 1939-1945], ed. S. Michálek, Bratislava, Veda 1997.

Kennan, George F., *From Prague After Munich. Diplomatic Papers 1938-1940*, Princeton (NJ), Princeton University Press 1968.

Komintern i vtoraia mirovaia voina, tom I (1939 - 22 iiunia 1941), tom II (posle 22 iiunia), eds. N. C. Lebedeva - M. M. Narinskij, Moskva, Pamiatniki istoricheskoi mysli 1994.

Nazi-Soviet Relations 1939-1941. Documents from the Archives of the German Foreign Office, eds. R. J. Sontag - J. S. Beddie, Washington, Department of State 1948.

Parliamentary Debates, House of Commons, London, H.M.S.O., 5th Series, 1938-1942. (*H. C. Deb.*)

Parliamentary Debates, House of Lords, London, H.M.S.O., 5th Series, 1938–1942. (*H. L. Deb.*)

Pax Britannica: Wartime Foreign Office Documents Regarding Plans for a Postbellum East Central Europe, ed. A. D. Ban, Boulder, Columbia University Press 1997.

Soviet Peace Efforts on the Eve of World War II, 2 Vols, ed. V. Filin et al., Moscow, Novosti Press Agency Publishing House 1973. (*SPE*)

SSSR i germanskii vopros 1941–1949. Dokumenty iz archiva vneshnei politiki Rossiiskoi federatsii, eds. G. P. Kynin – J. Laufer, tom I (1941–1945), Moskva, Mezhdunarodnye otnosheniia 1996.

Velká Británie a československo-sovětská smlouva z r. 1943 [Great Britain and Czechoslovak-Soviet treaty of 1943], ed. I. Šťovíček, *Historie a vojenství* [History and military], Prague, Vol. 43, 1994, No. 1, pp. 161–172.

Published diaries, correspondence, political pamphlets, collections of speeches and memoirs

Amery, Leo, *The Empire at Bay. The Leo Amery Diaries 1929–45*, eds. J. Barnes – D. Nicholson, London, Hutchinson 1988.

Amery, L. C. M. S., *My Political Life: The Unforgiving Years 1929–1940*, London, Hutchinson 1955.

Attlee, Clement R., *As It Happened*, London, Heinemann 1954.

Avon, Earl of, *The Eden Memoirs. The Reckoning*, London, Cassell 1965.

Beneš, Bohuš, *Amerika šla s námi* [America went with us], 2nd edition, Zürich, Konfrontace 1977 (first published as *Amerika jde s námi* [America goes with us], London, Čechoslovák 1941).

Beneš, Edvard, *An Appeal to the American People*, Chicago, The University of Chicago 1939.

Beneš, Edvard, *Czechoslovakia's Second Struggle for Freedom*, London, Czechoslovak Institute 1941.

Beneš, Edvard, *Democracy Today and Tomorrow*, London, Macmillan 1939.

Beneš, Edvard, *Mnichovské dny. Paměti* [The days of Munich. Memoirs], Praha, Svoboda 1968.

Beneš, Edvard, *Paměti. Od Mnichova k nové válce a k novému vítězství*, Praha, Orbis 1947 (English edition: *Memoirs of Dr. Eduard Beneš. From Munich to a New War and a New Victory*, Boston, 1954).

Beneš, Edvard, *Šest let exilu a druhé světové války. Řeči, projevy a dokumenty z r. 1938–45* [The six years of exile and of the Second World War. Talks, speeches and documents from the years 1938–45], Praha, Družstevní práce 1946.

Beneš, Edvard, *Towards a Lasting Peace. Three Speeches Delivered*, London, Czechoslovak Ministry of Foreign Affairs 1942.

Bitva o Československo v britském veřejném mínění [The battle of Czechoslovakia in the British public opinion], eds. B. Beneš – J. Šuhaj, London, Čechoslovák 1941.

Bohlen, Charles E., *Witness to History 1929–1969*, New York, Norton & Company 1973.

The Diaries of Sir Alexander Cadogan, 1938–1945, ed. D. Dilks, New York, G. P. Putnam's Sons 1972.

Chamberlain, Neville A., *The Struggle for Peace*, London, Hutchinson 1939.

Churchill and Roosevelt, the Complete Correspondence, 3 Vols., ed. W. F. Kimball, Princeton (NJ), Princeton University Press 1984.

Churchill Speaks: Winston S. Churchill in Peace and War: Collected Speeches, 1897–1963, ed. R. Rhodes James, Leicester, Winward 1981.

Churchill, Winston S., *The Second World War: I. The Gathering Storm; II. Their Finest Hour; III. The Grand Alliance; IV. The Hinge of Fate; V. Closing the Ring, VI. Triumph and Tragedy*, London, Cassell 1948–1954.

The Churchill War Papers, Vol. I., *At the Admiralty, September 1939 – May 1940*, ed. M. Gilbert, London, Heinemann 1993.

The Churchill War Papers, Vol. II., *Never Surrender, May 1940 – December 1940*, ed. M. Gilbert, London, Heinemann 1994.

The Churchill War Papers, Vol. III., *The Ever Widening War, 1941*, ed. M. Gilbert, London, Heinemann 2000.

Winston Churchill, Companion Vol. V., *The Coming of War, 1936–1939*, ed. M. Gilbert, London, Heinemann 1975.

Ciechanowski, Jan, *Defeat in Victory*, London, Gollancz 1947.

Clementis, Vladimír, *Odkazy z Londýna* [Messages from London], Bratislava, Obroda 1947.

Colville, John, *The Fringes of Power. Downing Street Diaries 1939–1955*, 2 Vols., London, Sceptre 1985, 1986.

Duff Cooper, Alfred, *Old Men Forget*, New York, Dutton 1954.

Dalton, Baron Hugh, *Hitler's War Before and After*, Middlesex, Harmondsworth 1940.

Dalton, Baron Hugh, *The Fateful Years: Memoirs 1941–1945*, London, F. Muller 1957.

The Political Diary of Hugh Dalton 1918–40, 1945–60, ed. B. Pimlott, London, Cape 1986.

The Second World War Diary of Hugh Dalton 1940–45, ed. B. Pimlott, B., London, Cape/LSE 1986.

Drtina, Prokop, *Československo můj osud: kniha života českého demokrata 20. století* [Czechoslovakia – my fate: A book of life of a Czechoslovak democrat of the 20th century], 2 Vols., 2nd edition, Praha, Melantrich 1991–1992 (first published in Toronto, Sixty Eight Publishers, Corp. 1982).

Einzig, Paul, *In the Centre of Things. The Autobiography of Paul Einzig*, London, Hutchinson 1960.

Feierabend, Ladislav Karel, *Politické vzpomínky* [Political memoirs], 3 Vols., Brno, Atlantis 1994, 1996 (first published in 4 Volumes in Washington, D.C. at the author's expense in 1965–67).

Fierlinger, Zdeněk, *Ve službách ČSR. Paměti z druhého zahraničního odboje* [In the services of the Czechoslovak Republic. Memoirs of the second resistance abroad], 2 Vols., Praha, Svoboda 1947 and 1951.

Formování československého zahraničního odboje v letech 1938–1939 ve světle svědectví Jana Opočenského [Forming of the Czechoslovak resistance abroad in the light of Jan Opočenský's testimony], ed. M. Hauner, Praha, Archiv akademie věd 2000.

Halifax, Earl of, *Fullness of Days*, London, Collins 1957.

Harriman, W. Averell, and Abel, Eli, *Special Envoy to Churchill and Stalin 1941–1946*, London, Hutchinson 1976.

The Diplomatic Diaries of Oliver Harvey 1937–1940, ed. J. Harvey, New York, St. Martin's Press 1970.

The War Diaries of Oliver Harvey 1941–1945, ed. J. Harvey, London, Collins 1978.

Henderson, Sir Nevile, *Failure of a Mission: Berlin 1937–39*, London, Hodder and Stoughton Ltd. 1940.

Hodža, Milan, *Federation in Central Europe*, London, Jerrolds 1942 (Slovak edition: *Federácia v strednej Európe*, ed. P. Lukáč, Bratislava, Kaligram 1997).

Jaksch, Wenzel, *Europas Weg nach Potsdam. Schuld und Schicksal im Donauraum*, Stuttgart, Deutsche Verlags-Anstalt 1958 (English edition: *Europe's Road to Potsdam*, London, Thames and Hudson 1963; Czech edition: *Cesta Evropy do Postupimi*, Praha, ISE 2000).

Wenzel Jaksch – Edvard Benes. Briefe und Dokumente aus dem Londoner Exil, 1939–1943, ed. F. Prinz, Köln, Verlag Wissenschaft und Politik 1973.

Kennan, George F., *Memoirs 1925–1950*, Boston-Toronto, Little, Brown and Company 1967.

Kirkpatrick, Ivone, *The Inner Circle. Memoirs*, London, Macmillan 1959.

Korbel, Josef, *The Communist Subversion of Czechoslovakia 1938–1948*, Princeton, Princeton University Press 1959.

Laštovička, Bohuslav, *V Londýně za války: zápasy o novou ČSR 1939–1945* [In London during the war: struggles for new CSR], 3rd edition, Praha, Svoboda 1978.

Lipski, Józef – Raczyński, Edward – Stroński, Stanislaw, *Trzy podróże gen. Sikorskiego do Ameryki* [Three journeys of gen. Sikorski to America], London 1949.

Lockhart, Sir Robert Bruce, *Comes the Reckoning*, London, Putnam Comp. 1947 [Czech edition: *Přichází zúčtování*, Praha, Fr. Borový 1948].

Lockhart, Sir Robert Bruce, *Jan Masaryk. A Personal Memoir*, London, Putnam 1956.

The Diaries of Sir Robert Bruce Lockhart 1915–1938, ed. K. Young, London, Macmillan 1973.

The Diaries of Sir Robert Bruce Lockhart 1939–1965, ed. K. Young, London, Macmillan 1980.

Macmillan, Harold, *Winds of Change 1914–1939*, London, Macmillan 1966.

Maisky, Ivan, *Memoirs of a Soviet Ambassador, The War 1939–1943*, London, Hutchinson 1967.

Jan Masaryk. Depeše z Londýna [Despatches from London], ed. V. Olivová, Praha 1996.

Masaryk, Jan, *Volá Londýn* [London calling], Praha, Panorama 1990.

Mikolajczyk, Stanislaw, *The Rape of Poland: Pattern of Soviet Aggression*, New York, Whittlesey House 1948.

Moravec, František, *Master of Spies. The Memoirs of General František Moravec*, London, Bodley Head (Czech edition: *Špión, jemuž nevěřili*, Toronto, Sixty-Eight Publishers 1977).

Nicolson, Sir Harold George, *Diaries and Letters, 1930–1962*, 3 Vols., ed. N. Nicolson, London, Collins 1966–1971.

Opočenský, Jan, *Edvard Beneš. Essays and Reflections Presented on the Occassion of his Sixtieth Birthday*, London, G. Allen and Unwin Ltd. 1945.

Válečné deníky Jana Opočenského [Jan Opočenský's war-time diaries], eds. J. Čechurová – J. Kuklík – J. Čechura – J. Němeček, Praha, Karolinum 2001.

Osuský, Štefan, *Pravda víťazí. Pohled do zrkadla druhého odboje* [The truth triumphs. Looking to the mirror of the second resistance], London 1942.

Osuský, Stephen, *Beneš and Slovakia*, London 1943.

Raczynski, Edward, *In Allied London. The Wartime Diaries of the Polish Ambassador*, London, Weidenfeld and Nicolson 1962.

Raczynski, Edward, *The British-Polish Alliance. Its Origins and Meaning*, London, Sikorski Historical Institute 1948.

Ripka, Hubert, *Československá zahraniční politika: výklad ministra Huberta Ripky ve Státní radě dne 7. ledna 1942* [Czechoslovak foreign policy: Minister Hubert Ripka's speech in the State Council on 7 January 1942], London, Čechoslovák 1942.

Ripka, Hubert, *Likvidace Mnichova* [Liquidation of Munich], London, Čechoslovák 1943.

Ripka, Hubert, *Munich: Before and After*, New York, Howard Fertig 1969.

Ripka, Hubert, *O středoevropské problematice* [On Central European problems], London, Čechoslovák 1943.

Ripka, Hubert, *Russia and the West*, Lecture delivered on 25th February at the Institut Francais – London, London, Czechoslovak Institute 1942.

Ripka, Hubert, *S Východem a Západem*, London, Čechoslovák 1944 (English edition: *East and West*, London, Lincolns-Prager 1944).

Roberts, Frank, *Dealing with Dictators. The Destruction and Revival of Europe 1930–1970*, London, Weidenfeld & Nicolson 1991.

R. W. Seton-Watson and His Relations with the Czechs and Slovaks, Documents 1906–1951, eds. J. Rychlík – T. Marzik – M. Bielik, 2 Vols., Praha – Martin, Ústav T. G. Masaryka and Matica Slovenská 1995.

Simon, Viscount, *Retrospect*, London, Hutchinson 1952.

Strang, William, *Home & Abroad*, London, A. Deutsch 1956.

Táborský, Eduard, *Pravda zvítězila. Deník druhého zahraničního odboje*, [The truth has triumphed. The diary of the second resistance movement abroad], Praha, Fr. Borový 1947.

Táborský, Eduard, *Prezidentův sekretář vypovídá. Deník druhého zahraničního odboje, díl II.* [President's secretary giving evidence. The diary of the second resistance movement abroad, Vol. II], Zürich, Konfrontace 1983.

Táborský, Eduard, *The Czechoslovak Cause: An Account of the Problems of International Law in Relation to Czechoslovakia*, London, H. F. & G. Witherby 1944 (Czech edition: *Naše věc. Československo ve světle mezinárodního práva za druhé světové války*, Praha, Čechoslovák 1946).

Taylor, A. J. P., *Czechoslovakia's Place in a Free Europe. The substance of the lecture given at the Czechoslovak Institute in London on April 29th*, 1943, London, Czechoslovak Institute 1943.

Templewood, Viscount, *Nine Troubled Years*, London, Collins 1954.

Vansittart, Lord, *The Mist Procession*, London, Hutchinson 1958.

Welles, Sumner, *Seven Major Decisions*, London, H. Hamilton 1951 (American edition: *Seven Decisions that Shaped History*, New York, Harper 1951).

Winter, Gustav, *Očima Západu: 3 přednášky* [Viewed by the West: 3 lectures], London, Čechoslovák 1944.

Newspapers, polls

The Central European Observer
Čechoslovák
Daily Express
Daily Telegraph
Manchester Guardian
News Chronicle
The Times

Gallup International Public Opinion Polls. Great Britain 1937–75, Vol. I, ed. G. H. Gallup, New York, Random House 1976.

Public Opinion 1935–46 (collected Gallup Poll data), Princeton, Princeton University Press 1951.

Biographies

Birkenhead, W. F. S. 2nd Earl of, *Halifax: the Life of Lord Halifax*, London, H. Hamilton 1965.

Bryant, Chris, *Stafford Cripps. The First Modern Chancellor*, London, Hodder & Stoughton 1997.

Carlton, David, *Anthony Eden: A Biography,* London, Allen Lane 1981.

Clarke, Peter, *The Cripps Version. The Life of Sir Stafford Cripps*, London, Allen Lane 2002.

Colvin, Ian, *Vansittart in Office*, London, Victor Gollancz Ltd 1965.

Davis, Kenneth Sydney, *FDR, into the Storm, 1937–1940*, New York, Random House 1993.

Feiling, Keith, *The Life of Neville Chamberlain*, London, Macmillan 1946.

Gilbert, Martin, *Prophet of Truth. Winston S. Churchill 1922-1939*, London, Heinemann 1976.

Gilbert, Martin, *Finest Hour. Winston S. Churchill 1939-1941*, London, Heinemann 1983.

Gilbert, Martin, *Road to Victory. Winston S. Churchill 1941-1945*, London, Heinemann 1986.

Kershaw, Ian, *Hitler 1936-1945. Nemesis*, London, The Penguin Press 2000.

Lias, Godfrey, *Beneš of Czechoslovakia*, London, George Allen & Unwin Ltd 1940.

Mackenzie, Sir Compton, *Dr. Beneš*, London – Toronto, G. G. Harrap 1946 (Czech edition: *Dr. Beneš*, Praha, Družstevní práce 1947).

Rhodes James, Robert, *Bob Boothby*, London, Hodder & Stoughton 1991.

Rhodes James, Robert, *Anthony Eden*, London, Weidenfeld & Nicolson 1986.

Rose, Norman, *Vansittart, Study of a Diplomat*, London, Heinemann 1978.

Roberts, Andrew: *'The Holy Fox': a Biography of Lord Halifax*, London, Weidenfeld & Nicolson 1991.

Šolc, Jiří, *Ve službách prezidenta* [In the president's services; František Moravec], Praha, Vyšehrad 1994.

Taylor, A.J.P., *A Biography of Beaverbrook*, New York, Simon and Schuster 1972.

Young, Kenneth, *Churchill and Beaverbrook: a Study in Friendship and Politics*, Eyre & Spottiswoode 1966.

Zeman, Zbyněk – Klimek, Antonín, *The Life of Edvard Beneš 1884-1948, Czechoslovakia in Peace and War*, Oxford, Clarendon Press 1997 (Czech edition: Zeman, Zbyněk (only), *Edvard Beneš 1884-1948*, Praha, Mladá fronta 1999).

Other books

Adams, R. J. Q., *British Politics and Foreign Policy in the Age of Appeasement, 1935-1939*, Stanford, Stanford University Press 1993.

Adamthwaite, Anthony, *France and the Coming of the Second World War, 1936-1939*, London, Totowa 1977.

Addison, Paul, *The Road to 1945: British Politics and the Second World War*, London, Jonathan Cape 1975.

Allen, Martin, *The Hitler/Hess Deception*, London, HarperCollins 2003.

Andrew, Christopher, *Secret Service: The Making of the British Intelligence Community*, London, Sceptre/Heinemann 1986.

Aster, Sidney, *1939. The Making of the Second World War*, London, Deutsch 1973.

Aster, Sidney, *British Foreign Policy, 1918-45. A Guide to Research and Research Materials*, Wilmington (Del), Scholarly Resources 1991.

Barker, Elisabeth, *British Policy in South-Eastern Europe in the Second World War*, London, Macmillan 1976.

Barker, Elisabeth, *Churchill and Eden at War*, London, Macmillan 1978.

Bartlett, Christopher John, *British Foreign Policy in the Twentieth Century*, London, Macmillan Education 1989.

Bátonyi, Gábor, *Britain and Central Europe, 1918–1933*, Oxford, Clarendon 1999.

Bell, P. M. H., *The Origins of the Second World War in Europe*, London, Longman 1986.

Bell, P. M. H., *John Bull and the Bear. British Public Opinion, Foreign Policy and the Soviet Union 1941–1945*, London, Edward Arnold 1990.

Beloff, Max, *The Foreign Policy of Soviet Russia*, Vol. II, *1936–1941*, London-New York-Toronto, Oxford University Press 1949.

Brandes, Detlef, *Großbritannien und seine osteuropäischen Alliierten 1939–1943. Die Regierungen Polens, der Tschechoslowakei und Jugoslawiens im Londoner Exil vom Kriegsausbruch bis zur Konferenz von Teheran*, München, R. Oldenbourg Verlag 1988 (Czech edition: *Exil v Londýně 1939–1943. Velká Británie a její spojenci Československo, Polsko a Jugoslávie mezi Mnichovem a Teheránem*, Praha, Karolinum 2003).

Brandes, Detlef, *Der Weg zur Vertreibung 1938–1945. Pläne und Entscheidungen zum 'Transfer' der Deutschen aus der Tschechoslowakei und aus Polen*, München, R. Oldenbourg 2000 (Czech edition: *Cesta k vyhnání 1938–1945. Plány a rozhodnutí o „transferu" Němců z Československa a z Polska*, Praha, Prostor 2002).

Brendon, Piers, *The Dark Valley. A Panorama of the 1930s*, London, Pimlico 2001.

Brod, Toman – Čejka, Eduard, *Na západní frontě. Historie československých vojenských jednotek na Západě v letech druhé světové války* [At the Western front. History of the Czechoslovak military units in the West in the years of the Second World War], Praha, Naše vojsko 1965.

Brod, Toman, *Osudný omyl Edvarda Beneše* [Edvard Beneš's fateful mistake], Praha, Academia 2002.

Brown, Martin David, *Dealing with Democrats. The British Foreign Office and the Czechoslovak Émigrés in Great Britain, 1939 to 1945*, Frankfurt am Main, Peter Lang 2006.

Butler, James Ramsay Montagu – Gibbs, Norman Henry – Gwyer J. M. A. – Howard, Michael – Ehrman, John, *Grand Strategy*, 6 Vols., London, H. M. S. O. 1956–1976.

Carley, Michael Jabara, *1939. The Alliance That Never Was and the Coming of World War II*, Chicago, Ivan R. Dee 1999.

Carlton, David, *Churchill and the Soviet Union*, Manchester, Manchester University Press 2000.

Čejka, Eduard, *Československý odboj na Západě (1939–1945)* [The Czechoslovak resistance in the West (1939–1945)], Praha, Mladá fronta 1997.

Charmley, John, *Chamberlain and the Lost Peace*, London, Papermac 1991.

Charmley, John, *Churchill: The End of Glory*, London, Hodder and Stoughton 1993.

Cienciala, Anna, *Poland and the Western Powers 1938–1939. A Study in the Interdependence of Eastern and Western Europe*, London, Routledge & K. Paul 1968.

Cockett, Richard, *Twilight of Truth: Chamberlain, Appeasement, and the Manipulation of the Press*, London, Weidenfeld & Nicolson 1989.

Colvin, Ian, *The Chamberlain Cabinet*, London, Gollancz 1971.

Cowling, Maurice, *The Impact of Hitler: British Politics and British Policy 1933–1939*, Cambridge, Cambridge University Press 1975.

Craig, Gordon – Gilbert, Felix (eds.), *The Diplomats 1919–1939*, Princeton (NJ), Princeton University Press 1953.

Crowson, N. J., *Facing Fascism. The Conservative Party and the European Dictators, 1935–1940*, London, Routledge 1997.

Dallek, Robert, *Franklin D. Roosevelt and American Foreign Policy, 1932–1945*, Oxford, Oxford University Press 1979.

Dejmek, Jindřich, *Nenaplněné naděje. Politické a diplomatické vztahy Československa a Velké Británie (1918–1938)* [Dashed hopes. Czechoslovak-British political and diplomatic relations (1918–1938)], Praha, Karolinum 2003.

Dugelby, Thomas B., *The BREN Gun Saga*, Toronto, Collector Grade Publications 1999.

Einzig, Paul, *Appeasement Before, During and After the War*, London, Macmillan 1942.

Folly, Martin H., *Churchill, Whitehall and the Soviet Union, 1940–1945*, London, Macmillan Press 2000.

Foot, M. R. D., *SOE. The Special Operations Executive 1940–1946*, 2nd edition, London, Pimlico 1999.

Friedl, Jiří, *Na jedné frontě. Vztahy československé a polské armády za druhé světové války* [For the same cause: Czechoslovak-Polish military relations during the Second World War], Praha, Ústav pro soudobé dějiny 2005.

Gaddis, John Lewis, *The United States and the Origins of the Cold War 1941–1947*, 2nd edition (first published in 1972), New York, Columbia University Press 2000.

Gannon, Franklin R., *The British Press and Nazi Germany 1936–1939*, Oxford, Clarendon Press 1971.

Garnett, David, *The Secret History of PWE. The Political Warfare Executive, 1939–1945*, London, St Ermin' Press 2002.

Gates, Eleanor M., *End of the Affair: The Collapse of the Anglo-French Alliance, 1939–1940*, Berkeley, University of California Press 1981.

Gebhart, Jan – Kuklík, Jan, *Druhá republika 1938–1939* [The Second republic 1938–1939], Praha – Litomyšl, Paseka 2004, pp. 236–238.

Gebhart, Jan – Kuklík, Jan, *Velké dějiny zemí Koruny české XVa, 1938–1941* [The history of the lands of the Czech Crown – the big series], Praha, Paseka 2006.

Gilbert, Martin – Gott, Richard, *The Appeasers*, London, Weidenfeld & Nicolson 1967.

Gilbert, Martin, *The Roots of Appeasement*, London, Weidenfeld & Nicolson 1966.

Glees, Anthony, *Exile Politics during the Second World War. The German Social Democrats in Britain*, Oxford, Clarendon Press 1982.

Gorodetsky, Gabriel, *Grand Delusion. Stalin and the German Invasion of Russia*, New Haven and London, Yale University Press 1999.

Gorodetsky, Gabriel, *Stafford Cripps' Mission to Moscow*, Cambridge, Cambridge University Press 1984.

Grant Duff, Shiela, *A German Protectorate. The Czechs under Nazi Rule*, London, Macmillan 1942.

Harris, John – Trow, M.J., *Hess: The British Conspiracy*, London, André Deutsch 1999.

Haslam, Jonathan, *The Soviet Union and the Struggle for Collective Security in Europe 1933–39*, London, Macmillan 1984.

Heumos, Petr, *Die Emigration aus der Tschechoslowakei nach Westeuropa und den Nahen Osten 1938–1945: politisch-soziale Struktur, Organisation und Asylbedingungen der tschechischen, jüdischen, deutschen und slowakischen, Flüchtlinge während des Nationalsozialismus,* München, Oldenbourg 1989.

Hill, Christopher, *Cabinet Decisions on Foreign Policy. The British Experience. October 1938–June 1941*, Cambridge, Cambridge University Press 1991.

Hinsley, Francis Harry, *British Intelligence in the Second World War*, 5 Vols., London, H. M. S. O. 1979–1990.

Howard, Michael, *The Continental Commitment. The Dilemma of British Defence Policy in the Era of Two World Wars*, London, Penguin Books Ltd. 1974.

Kacewicz, George V., *Great Britain, the Soviet Union and the Polish Government in Exile (1939–1945)*, The Hague, Martinus Nijhoff 1979.

Kalvoda, Josef, *Czechoslovakia's Role in Soviet Strategy*, Washington, D.C., University Press of America 1978 (Czech edition: *Role Československa v sovětské strategii*, Kladno, Dílo 1999).

Kamenec, Ivan, *Slovenský stát* [The Slovak State], Praha, Anomal 1992.

Kennedy, Paul, *The Realities behind Diplomacy*, London, Fontana 1981.

Kersaudy, François, *De Gaulle et Churchill. La mésentente cordiale*, Paris, Perrin 2001 (Czech translation by Pavel Starý: *De Gaulle a Churchill. Srdečná neshoda*, Praha, Themis 2003).

Kimball, Warren F., *Forged in War. Churchill, Roosevelt and the Second World War*, London, HarperCollins 1997.

Kissinger, Henry Alfred, *Diplomacy*, New York, Simon & Schuster 1995.

Kitchen, Martin, *British Policy Towards the Soviet Union During the Second World War*, London, Macmillan 1986.

Kokoška, Jaroslav – Kokoška, Stanislav, *Spor o agenta A-54* [The dispute about the agent A-54], Praha, Naše vojsko 1994.

Křen, Jan, *Do emigrace. Buržoazní zahraniční odboj 1938–1939* [Into the exile. The bourgeois resistance abroad 1938–1939], Praha, Naše vojsko 1963.

Křen, Jan, *V emigraci. Západní zahraniční odboj 1939–1940* [In the exile. The western resistance abroad 1939–1940], Praha, Naše vojsko 1969.

Kuklík, Jan, *Londýnský exil a obnova československého státu za druhé světové války* [The exile in London and the reconstruction of the Czechoslovak state during World War II], Praha, Karolinum 1998.

Kuklík, Jan, *Vznik Československého národního výboru a prozatímního státního zřízení ČSR v emigraci* [The creation of the Czechoslovak National Committee and the provisional state regime of the Czechoslovak Republic in Exile], Praha, Karolinum 1996.

Kuklík, Jan – Němeček, Jan, *Hodža versus Beneš*, Praha, Karolinum 1999.

Kuklík, Jan – Němeček, Jan, *Proti Benešovi! Česká a slovenská protibenešovská opozice v Londýně 1939–1945* [Against Beneš! The Czech and Slovak anti-Beneš opposition in London 1939–1945], Praha, Karolinum 2004.

Kural, Václav, *Místo společenství konflikt! Češi a Němci ve velkoněmecké říši a cesta k odsunu* [Conflict instead of community! The Czechs and Germans in the Sudeten German Reich and the road to transfer], Praha, Ústav mezinárodních vztahů 1994.

Kural, Václav, *Vlastenci proti okupaci. Ústřední vedení odboje domácího 1940–1943* [Patriots against the occupation. The Central Committee of the Home Resistance 1940–1943], Praha, Karolinum 1997.

Kvaček, Robert – Chalupa, Aleš – Hejduk, Miloš, *Československý rok 1938* [The Czechoslovak year 1938], Praha, Panorama 1988.

Lockhart, Sir Robert H. Bruce, *What Happened to the Czechs?*, London, Batchworth Press 1953.

London, Louise, *Whitehall and the Jews 1933–1948. British Immigration Policy, Jewish Refugees and the Holocaust*, Cambridge, Cambridge University Press 2000.

Lukas, Richard C., *The Strange Allies. The United States and Poland, 1941–1945*, Knoxville, University of Tennessee Press 1978.

Lukes, Igor, *Czechoslovakia between Stalin and Hitler. The Diplomacy of Edvard Beneš in the 1930s*, Oxford, Oxford University Press 1996.

Lundestad, Geir, *The American Non-Policy towards Eastern Europe: 1943–1947*, Tromsö, Universitetsforlaget 1978.

Luža, Radomír V., *The Transfer of the Sudeten Germans: a Study of Czech-German Relations, 1933–1962*, London, Routledge and Kegan Paul 1964.

Lvová, Míla, *Mnichov a Edvard Beneš* [Munich and Edvard Beneš], Praha, Svoboda 1968.

Mackenzie, William J. M., *The Secret History of SOE: The Special Operations Executive*, London, St Ermin's 2000.

Mastny, Vojtech, *Russia's Road to the Cold War: Diplomacy, Warfare, and the Politics of Communism, 1941–1945*, New York, Columbia University Press 1979.

Medlicott, W. N., *British Foreign Policy since Versailles, 1919–1963*, 2nd edition, London, Methuen 1968.

Medlicott, W. N., *Contemporary England, 1914–1964*, London 1967.

Michie, Lindsay W., *Portrait of an Appeaser. Robert Hadow, First Secretary in the British Foreign Office, 1931–39*, London, Praeger 1996.

Middlemas, Keith, *Diplomacy of Illusion: The British Government and Germany, 1937–39*, London, Weidenfeld & Nicolson 1972.

Miner, Steven Meritt, *Between Churchill and Stalin. The Soviet Union, Great Britain and the Origins of the Grand Alliance*, North Carolina, The North Carolina Press 1988.

Němeček, Jan, *Od spojenectví k roztržce* [From alliance to quarrel], Praha, Academia 2003.

Neville, Peter, *Appeasing Hitler. The Diplomacy of Sir Nevile Henderson, 1937–39*, London, Macmillan 2000.

Neville, Peter, *Hitler and Appeasement. The British Attempt to Prevent the Second World War*, London – New York, Hambledon Continuum 2006.

Newman, Simon, *March 1939. The Making of the British Guarantee to Poland*, Oxford, Clarendon Press 1976.

Ovendale, Richard, *Appeasement and the English-Speaking World*, Cardiff, University of Wales Press 1975.

Overy, Richard, *Why the Allies Won*, 2nd edition (first published in 1995), London, Pimlico 2006.

Parker, R.A.C., *Chamberlain and Appeasement. British Policy and the Coming of the Second World War*, London, Macmillan Press 1993.

Parker, R.A.C., *Churchill and Appeasement*, Basingstoke and Oxford, Macmillan Press 2000.

Pasák, Tomáš, *JUDr. Emil Hácha (1938–1945)*, Praha, Horizont 1997.

Polonsky, Anthony, *The Great Powers and the Polish Question, 1941–1945. A Documentary Study in Cold War Origins*, London, LSE 1976.

Pozdeeva, L. V., *London – Moskva. Britanskoe obshchestvennoe mnenie i SSSR 1939–1945*, Moskva, Institut vseobshchei istorii RAN 2000.

Prażmowska, Anita J., *Britain, Poland and the Eastern Front 1939*, Cambridge, Cambridge University Press 1987.

Prażmowska, Anita J., *Britain and Poland 1939–1943. The Betrayed Ally*, Cambridge, Cambridge University Press 1995.

Raška, Francis Dostál, *The Czechoslovak Exile Government in London and the Sudeten German Issue*, Prague, The Karolinum Press 2002.

Robbins, Keith, *Munich 1938*, London, Cassell 1968.

Roberts, Geoffrey, *The Soviet Union and the Origins of the Second World War: Russo-German Relations and the Road to War, 1933–1941*, New York, St. Martin's Press 1995.

Rothwell, Victor, *Britain and the Cold War, 1941–47*, London, Cape 1982.

Rupnik, Jacques, *Histoire du Parti communiste Tchécoslovaque (Des origines à la prise du pouvoir)*, Paris, Presses de la Fondation nationale des sciences politiques, Paris 1981 (Czech edition: *Dějiny komunistické strany Československa. Od počátků do převzetí moci*, Praha, Academia 2002).

Rzheshevskii, Oleg A., *Voina i diplomatiia. Dokumenty, kommentarii 1941–1942*, Moskva, Nauka 1997.

Rzheshevskii, Oleg A., *Stalin i Churchill. Vstretshi. Besedy. Diskusii*, Moskva 2004.

Shirer, William L.: *The Collapse of the Third Republic – An Inguiry into the Fall of France in 1940*, London, Heinemann 1970.

Stafford, David, *Britain and European Resistance 1940–1945*, London, St. Antony's College (Oxford) – Macmillan 1983.

Strang, Lord William, *The Foreign Office*, London, George Allen & Unwin Ltd. 1955.

Survey of International Affairs, 1938, Vol. III, Royal Institute of International Affairs, Oxford, Oxford University Press 1953.

Survey of International Affairs, 1939–1946: The World in March 1939; The Eve of the War 1939; Hitler's Europe; The Realignment of Europe, Royal Institute of International Affairs, Oxford, Oxford University Press 1952–58.

Táborský, Eduard, *President E. Beneš Between East and West 1938–1948*, Stanford, Hoover Institution Press 1981 (Czech edition: *Prezident Beneš mezi Západem a Východem*, Praha, Mladá fronta 1993).

Taylor, A. J. P., *The Origins of the Second World War*, London, Hamilton 1961.

Taylor, Telford, *Munich. The Price of Peace*, London–Sydney–Auckland–Toronto, Hodder and Stoughton 1979.

Terry, Sarah M., *Poland's Place in Europe. General Sikorski and the Origin of the Oder-Neisse Line, 1939–1943*, Princeton, Princeton University Press 1983.

The Oxford Companion to the Second World War, eds. I. C. B. Dear – M. R. D. Foot, Oxford – New York, Oxford University Press 1995.

Wandycz, Piotr S., *Czechoslovak-Polish Confederation and the Great Powers, 1940–1943*, Bloomington, Indiana University 1956.

Watt, Donald Cameron, *How War Came, the Immediate Origins of the Second World War, 1938–1939*, London, Heinemann 1989.

Watt, Donald Cameron, *Too Serious a Business: European Armed Forces and the Approach to the Second World War*, London, Temple Smith 1975.

Wheeler-Bennett, Sir John, *Munich: Prologue to Tragedy*, New York, Duell, Sloane & Pearce 1948.

Woodward, Sir Llewellyn, *British Foreign Policy in the Second World War*, 5 Vols., London, H. M. S. O. 1970–76.

Žáček, Rudolf, *Projekt československo-polské konfederace v letech 1939–1943* [The project of the Czechoslovak-Polish confederation in the years 1939–1943], Opava, Slezský ústav Slezského zemského muzea v Opavě 2001.

Articles

Aster, Sidney, 'Guilty Men': The Case of Neville Chamberlain, In: *Paths to War. New Essays on the Origins of the Second World War*, eds. R. Boyce – E. M. Robertson, London, Macmillan 1989, pp. 233–268.

Aster, Sidney, Viorel Virgil Tilea and the Origins of the Second World War: An Essay in Closure, *Diplomacy & Statecraft*, Vol. 13, 2002, No. 3, pp. 153–174.

Beneš, Edvard, Organisation of Postwar Europe, *Foreign Affairs*, Vol. 20, No. 2 (January 1942).

Blaazer, David, Finance and the End of Appeasement: The Bank of England, the National Government and the Czech Gold, *Journal of Contemporary History*, Vol. 40, 2005, No. 1, pp. 25–39.

Brandes, Detlef, Benešova politika v letech 1939–1945 [Beneš's policy in the years 1939–1945], *Dějiny a současnost* [History and present], Prague, Vol. 25, 2003, No. 1, pp. 36–38.

Brandes, Detlef, Die britische Regierung kommt zu einem Zwischenergebnis. Die Empfehlungen des britischen Interdepartmental Committee on the Transfer of German Populations vom Mai 1944. In: *Occursus, Setkání, Begegnung. Sborník k poctě 65. narozenin prof. dr. Jana Křena* [Essays in honour of 65th birthday of Prof. Dr. Jan Křen], eds. Z. Spousta – P. Seifter – J. Pešek, Praha, Karolinum 1996, pp. 45–68.

Brandes, Detlef, Eine verspätete tschechische Alternative zum Münchener Diktat, Edvard Beneš und die sudetendeutsche Frage, *Vierteljahrshefte für Zeitgeschichte*, 1994, No. 2, pp. 221–241.

Brandes, Detlef, Konfederace nebo Východní pakt? Polsko-československé vztahy za druhé světové války [The Confederation or the eastern pact? Polish-Czechoslovak relations during the Second World War], *Slovanský přehled* [Slavic survey], Prague, Vol. 28, 1992, No. 4, pp. 436–448.

Brandes, Detlef, Opožděná česká alternativa k mnichovskému diktátu [A belated Czech alternative to the Munich Dictate], *Dějiny a současnost* [History and present], Prague, Vol. 15, 1993, No. 2, pp. 29–36.

Brown, Alan, The Czechoslovak Armed Forces in Britain, 1940–1945, In: *Europe in Exile. European Exile Communities in Britain 1940–45*, eds. M. Conway – J. Gotowitch, New York – Oxford, Berghahn Books 2001, pp. 167–182.

Bruegel, Johann Wolfgang, The Recognition of the Czechoslovak Government in London, *Kosmas – Journal of Czechoslovak and Central European Studies*, Vol. 2, 1983, No. 1, pp. 1–13.

Bruegel, Johann Wolfgang, Na okraj Mastného knihy o vzniku studené války [A note on Mastny's book about the origins of the Cold War], *Svědectví* [Testimony], Paris, 1981, No. 64. pp. 835–840.

Bystrický, Valerián, Otázka garancie hraníc Československa po mníchovskoj konferencii [The question of the guarantee of the Czechoslovak frontiers after the Munich conference], *Slovanský přehled* [Slavic survey], Prague, Vol. 12, 1990, No. 2, pp. 115–125.

Clement, Piet, The Bank for International Settlements during the Second World War. In: *Nazi gold: The London Conference, 2–4 December 1997*, London, Stationery Office 1998, pp. 43–60.

Červinková, Milada, Views and Diplomatic Activity of Dr. Edvard Beneš in the Period of Preparation for the Czechoslovak-Soviet Treaty of 1943, *Historica*, Vol. 17, 1969, pp. 235–274.

Cornwall, Mark, Elizabeth Wiskemann and the Sudeten Question: A Woman at the 'Essential Hinge' of Europe, *Central Europe*, Vol. 1, 2003, No. 1, pp. 55–75.

Cornwall, Mark, The Rise and Fall of a 'Special Relationship'?: Britain and Czechoslovakia, 1930–1948, In: *What difference Did the War Make?*, eds. B. Brivati – H. Jones, Leicester, Leicester University Press 1993, pp. 130–150.

Dejmek, Jindřich, Britský appeasement: bilance půlstoletí trvající historiografické diskuse [British appeasement. Survey of the half century of historiography discussion], *Český časopis historický* [Czech historical journal], Prague, Vol. 98, 2000, No. 1, pp. 130–141.

Dejmek, Jindřich, Československá diplomacie v době druhé republiky (říjen 1938 – březen 1939) [Czechoslovak diplomacy in the time of the Second Republic (October 1938 – March 1939], In: *Pocta profesoru Janu Kuklíkovi* [Essays in honour of professor Jan Kuklík], Praha, Karolinum 2000, pp. 9–26.

Dockrill, Michael, The Foreign Office, Dr Eduard Benes and the Czechoslovak Government-in-Exile, 1939–41, *Diplomacy & Statecraft*, Vol. 6, 1995, No. 3, pp. 701–718.

Firt, Julius, Cestou k únoru: Počátky byly v Londýně [On the way to February: The origins were in London], *Svědectví* [Testimony], Paris, Vol. 12, 1973, No. 46, pp. 212–267.

Foster, Alan J., An Unequivocal Guarantee? Fleet Street and the British Guarantee to Poland, *Journal of Contemporary History*, Vol. 26, 1993, No. 1, pp. 33–47.

Fry, Michael Graham, Agents and Structures: The Dominions and the Czechoslovak Crisis, September 1938, *Diplomacy and Statecraft*, Vol. 10, 1999, No. 2&3 – Special Issue on The Munich Crisis, 1938. Prelude to World War II, pp. 291–341.

Gebhart, Jan – Kuklík, Jan, Exil a domov – Počátky spojení [The exile and home – the beginnings of the communication], *Historické listy* [Historical papers], Prague, 1995, No. 4, pp. 28–31.

Gibianskii, Leonid J., Problemy vostotshnoi Evropy i natshalo formirovaniia Sovetskogo bloka, In: *Cholodnaia voina 1945–1963*, Moskva, Olma-press 2003, pp. 105–136.

Goldstein, Erich, Neville Chamberlain, the British Official Mind and the Munich Crisis, *Diplomacy and Statecraft*, Vol. 10, 1999, No. 2&3 – Special Issue on The Munich Crisis, 1938. Prelude to World War II, pp. 276–292.

Hanak, Harry, Great Britain and Czechoslovakia, 1918–1948. An Outline of Their Relations, In: *Czechoslovakia Past and Present*, Vol. I., ed. M. Rechcígl, The Hague, Czechoslovak Society of Arts and Sciences in America – Mouton 1968, pp. 770–800.

Hanak, Harry, Prezident Beneš, Britové a budoucnost Československa [President Beneš, the British and the future of Czechoslovakia], *Historie a vojenství* [History and military], Prague, Vol. 44, 1995, No. 1, pp. 13–39.

Hanak, Harry, Sir Stafford Cripps as British Ambassador in Moscow, May 1940 to June 1941, *English Historical Review*, Vol. 94, 1979, pp. 48–70.

Hanak, Harry, Sir Stafford Cripps as British Ambassador in Moscow, June 1941 to January 1942, *English Historical Review*, Vol. 97, 1982, pp. 332–344.

Haslam, Jonathan, Soviet-German Relations and the Origins of the Second World War: The Jury Is Still Out, *Journal of Modern History*, Vol. 69, 1997, No. 4, pp. 785–797.

Hauner, Milan, Czechoslovakia as a Military Factor in British Considerations of 1938, *The Journal of Strategic Studies*, Vol. 1, 1978, No. 2, pp. 194–222.

Hauner, Milan, Edvard Beneš v Chicagu 1939 a počátky druhého odboje [Edvard Beneš in Chicago 1939 and the beginnings of the second resistance], *Historie a vojenství* [History and military], Prague, Vol. 45, 1996, No. 2, pp. 31–55.

Hauner, Milan, Čekání na velkou válku 1939 /I.-II./. Edvard Beneš mezi Mnichovem, 15. březnem a porážkou Polska [Waiting for a great war. Edvard Beneš between Munich, March 15 and the defeat of Poland], *Dějiny a současnost* [History and present], Prague, Vol. 21, 1999, No. 4, pp. 12-15, No. 5, pp. 36-39.

Hauner, Milan, Edvard Beneš a USA 1939-1942. Nad rukopisem nevydané publikace Jana Opočenského [Edvard Beneš and the U.S.A. 1939-1942. Reading the unpublished book by Jan Opočenský], *Soudobé dějiny* [Contemporary history], Prague, Vol. III, 1996, No. 1, pp. 7-22.

Ivaničková, Edita, Britská politika a Slovensko v rokoch 1939-1945 [British policy and Slovakia in the years 1939-1945], In: *Slovensko na konci druhej svetovej vojny* [Slovakia at the end of the Second World War], ed. V. Bystrický, Bratislava 1994, p. 125-130.

Ivaničková, Edita, Československo-maďarské vzťahy v stredoeurópskej politike Veľkej Británie (1938-1945) [Czechoslovak-Hungarian relations and the 1938-1945 policy of Great Britain towards Central Europe], *Historický časopis* [Historical journal], Bratislava, Vol. 46, 1998, No. 2, pp. 250-260.

Ivaničková, Edita, Zahraničnopolitická orientácia Slovenska v dokumentoch britskej Foreign Office (1939-1941) [Foreign policy orientation of Slovakia in documents of the British Foreign Office (1939-1941)], *Historický časopis* [Historical journal], Bratislava, Vol. 44, 1996, No. 2, pp. 207-220.

Janáček, František, Pakt, válka a KSČ. První týdny po 23. srpnu a 1. září 1939 [The Pact, the war and the Communist Party of Czechoslovakia. First weeks after 23rd August and 1st September 1939], *Historie a vojenství* [History and military], Prague, 1969, pp. 425-457.

Janáček, František – Němeček, Jan, Reality a iluze Benešovy 'ruské' politiky 1939-1945 [Realities and illusions of Beneš's 'Russian' policy, 1939-1945], In: *Edvard Beneš, československý a evropský politik* [Edvard Beneš, Czechoslovak and European politician], Praha 1994, pp. 71-95.

Jožák, Jiří, K historii čs. zahraniční akce v USA (15. 3. - 1. 9. 1939) [Towards the history of the Czechoslovak exile action in USA (15 March - 1 September 1939)], *Historie a vojenství* [History and military], Prague, Vol. 40, 1991, No. 5, pp. 43-77.

Kitchen, Martin, Winston Churchill and the Soviet Union during the Second World War, *Historical Journal*, Vol. 30, 1987, No. 2, pp. 415-436.

Klimek, Antonín, Edvard Beneš od abdikace z funkce presidenta ČSR (5. října 1938) do zkázy Československa (15. března 1939) [Edvard Beneš from his resignation the presidency of the Czechoslovak Republic (5th October 1938) to the destruction of Czechoslovakia (15th March 1939)], In: *Z druhé republiky. Sborník prací Historického ústavu armády České republiky* [Inside the Second Republic. Collection of studies, published by the Historical Institute of the Czech Army], Praha 1993, pp. 155-241.

Kokoška, Stanislav, Několik poznámek k československé částečné mobilizaci v květnu 1938 [Several notes on Czechoslovak Partial Mobilisation in May 1938], In: *Pocta profesoru Janu Kuklíkovi* [Essays in honour of professor Jan Kuklík], Praha, Karolinum 2000, pp. 99-114.

Kopeček, Michal – Kunštát, Miroslav, „Sudetoněmecká otázka" v české akademické debatě po roce 1989 ['The Sudeten German issue' in Czech academic discussion after 1989], *Soudobé dějiny* [Contemporary history], Prague, Vol. 10, 2003, No. 3, pp. 293-318.

Křen, Jan, Hodža a slovenská otázka v zahraničním odboji [Hodža and the Slovak question in the resistance abroad], *Československý časopis historický* [Czechoslovak historical journal], Prague, Vol. 16, 1968, pp. 193-214.

Kubů, Eduard, Czechoslovak Gold Reserves and Their Surrender to Nazi Germany, In: *Nazi Gold: The London Conference, 2-4 December 1997*, London, Stationery Office 1998, pp. 245-248.

Kuklík, Jan, The Recognition of the Czechoslovak Government in Exile and its International Status 1939-1942, *Prague Papers on History of International Relations*, Vol. 1, 1997, pp. 173-205.

Kuklík, Jan - Němeček, Jan, Cesta k oduznání Mnichova za druhé světové války, In: *Mnichovská dohoda. Cesta k destrukci demokracie v Evropě* [Munich agreement. The way to destruction of democracy in Europe], ed. J. Němeček, Praha, Karolinum 2004, pp. 132-144.

Kuklík, Jan - Němeček, Jan, K počátkům druhého exilu E. Beneše 1938-1939, [Towards the origins of E. Beneš's second exile, 1938-1939], *Český časopis historický* [Czech historical journal], Prague, Vol. 96, 1998, No. 4, pp. 803-823.

Lammers, Donald, Fascism, Communism and the Foreign Office, 1937-39, *Journal of Contemporary History*, Vol. 6, 1971, No. 3, 66-96.

Lammers, Donald, From Whitehall after Munich: The Foreign Office and the Future Course of British Policy, *The Historical Journal*, Vol. 16, 1973, No. 4, pp. 831-856.

Lockhart, Sir Robert Bruce, The Second Exile of Edward Beneš, *Slavonic and Eastern European Review*, Vol. 28, 1949.

Lukeš, Igor, Benesch, Stalin und Komintern. Von Münchener Abkommen zum Molotow--Ribbentrop-Pakt, *Vierteljahrshefte für Zeitgeschichte*, Vol. 41, 1993, No. 3, pp. 325-353.

Luža, Radomír V., The Russo-Czechoslovak Alliance, *East European Quarterly*, Vol. 19, 1985, No. 1, p. 113-118.

Manne, Robert, The British Decision for Alliance with Russia, May 1939, *Journal of Contemporary History*, Vol. 9, 1974, No. 1, pp. 3-26.

Manne, Robert, Some British Light on the Nazi-Soviet Pact, *European Studies Review*, Vol. 11, 1981, No. 1, pp. 83-102.

Manne, Robert, The Foreign Office and the Failure of Anglo-Soviet Rapprochement, *Journal of Contemporary History*, Vol. 16, 1981, No. 4, pp. 725-755.

Marjina, Valentina V., Brána na Balkán. Slovensko v geopolitických plánech SSSR a Německa v letech 1939-1941 [The gate to the Balkans. Slovakia in the geopolitical plans of the USSR and Germany], *Soudobé dějiny* [Contemporary history], Prague, Vol. 1, 1993/1994, No. 6, pp. 827-846.

Marjina, Valentina V., K historii sovětsko-československých vztahů v letech 1938-1941. Nad deníkem Ivana M. Majského [Towards the history of the Soviet-Czechoslovak relations, 1938-1941. Reading the diary of Ivan M. Maisky], *Soudobé dějiny*, [Contemporary history], Prague, Vol. 6, 1999, No. 4. pp. 514-533.

Marjina, Valentina V., Nejen o Podkarpatské Rusi. Jednání Beneš-Molotov v Moskvě v březnu 1945 [Not only about the Sub-Carpathian Russia. The negotiations Beneš-Molotov in Moscow in March 1945], *Dějiny a současnost* [History and present], Prague, Vol. 18, 1996, No. 4, pp. 48-51.

Marjina, Valentina V., Politika SSSR po czechoslovackomu voprosu nakanune Velikoi Otechestvennoi voiny (sentiabr' 1940 - iiun' 1941 g.), *Mezhdunarodnye otnosheniia i strany Centralnoi i Yugo-Vostochnoi Evropy*, Moskva, Institut slavianovedenia i balkanistiki 1989, pp. 117-129.

Marjina, Valentina V., Poslednii vizit v Moskvu (mart 1945 goda). Dokumentalnii otcherk, *Slavianovedenie*, 1996, No. 6, pp. 77-88.

Marjina, Valentina V., Sovetsko-germanskii pakt o nenapadenii i nachalo vtoroi mirovoi voiny v ocenke czeshskoi obshchestvennosti, In: *Politicheskii krizis 1939 g. i strany Centralnoi i Yugo-Vostochnoi Evropy*, Moskva, Institut slavianovedenia i balkanistiki 1989, pp. 117–129.

Marjina, Valentina V., SSSR i czechoslovackii vopros. 1939 god, In: *Mezhdunarodnye otnoshenia i strany Centralnoi i Yugo-Vostochnoi Evropy*, Moskva, Institut slavjanovedenia i balkanistiki 1990, pp. 95–128.

Marjina, Valentina V., E. Beneš: Vtoroi vizit v Moskvu (dekabr 1943 g.), In: *Vtoraia mirovaia voina. Aktualnye problemy*, ed. O. A. Rzheshevskii, Moskva, Nauka 1995, pp. 151–165.

Mastny, Vojtech, The Beneš-Stalin-Molotov Conversations in December 1943: New Documents, *Jahrbücher für Geschichte Osteuropas*, Vol. 20, 1972, No. 3, pp. 367–402.

Neilson, Keith, Stalin's Moustache: The Soviet Union and the Coming of War (review article), *Diplomacy & Statecraft*, Vol. 12, 2001, No. 2, p. 197–208.

Němeček, Jan, Československá diplomatická mise v Moskvě (březen – prosinec 1939) [The Czechoslovak diplomatic mission in Moscow (March – December 1939)], *Moderní dějiny* [Modern history], Prague, Vol. 4, 1996, pp. 221–275.

Němeček, Jan, Československý zahraniční odboj a sovětsko-finská válka 1939–1940 [The Czechoslovak resistance abroad and the Soviet-Finnish war], *Moderní dějiny* [Modern history], Prague, Vol. 3, 1995, pp. 139–157.

Němeček, Jan, Edvard Beneš a Sovětský svaz 1939–1940 [Edvard Beneš and the Soviet Union 1939–1940], *Slovanské historické studie* [Slavic historical studies], Prague, Vol. 23, 1997, pp. 179–193.

Němeček, Jan, Edvard Beneš a Sovětský svaz 1939–1945 [Edvard Beneš and the Soviet Union], *Slovanský přehled* [Slavic survey], Prague, Vol. 87, 2001, No. 3, pp. 313–343.

Němeček, Jan, Likvidace československé zahraniční služby po 15. březnu 1939 [Liquidation of the Czechoslovak foreign service after 15 March 1939], *Acta Universitatis Carolinae – Philosophica et Historica 1, Studia Historica* XLVIII, Prague 1998, pp. 143–158.

Němeček, Jan, Okupace českých zemí 1939 a Společnost národů [The occupation of the Czech Lands and the League of Nations], *Moderní dějiny* [Modern history], Prague, Vol. 5, 1997, pp. 149–163.

Němeček, Jan, Slovenská národní rada 1939 [Slovak National Council 1939], *Soudobé dějiny*, Vol. 3, 1996, No. 1, pp. 123–129.

Newman, Michael, The Origins of Munich: British Policy in Danubian Europe, *The Historical Journal*, Vol. 21, 1978, No. 2, pp. 371–386.

Nováčková, Helena – Šťovíček, Ivan, Edvard Beneš o jednání v Moskvě v prosinci 1943 [Edvard Beneš about the negotiations in Moscow in December 1943], *Soudobé dějiny* [Contemporary history], Prague, Vol. 3, 1996, No. 2–3, pp. 321–349.

Otáhalová, Libuše – Otáhal, Milan, O problematice plánů na uspořádání střední a východní Evropy za druhé světové války [On plans for the post-war arrangement of Central and Eastern Europe during the Second World War], *Sborník historických prací* [Reports of historical works], Prague, Vol. 15, 1967, pp. 163–199.

Pavlowitch, Stevan K., Out of Context – The Yugoslav Government in London 1941–1945, *Journal of Contemporary History*, Vol. 16, 1981, No. 1, pp. 89–118.

Polonsky, Anthony, Stalin and the Poles 1941–7, *European History Quarterly*, Vol. 17, 1987, No. 4, pp. 453–492.

Prečan, Vilém, British Attitudes towards Czechoslovakia, 1944–45, *Bohemia*, Vol. 29, 1988, No. 1, pp. 73–87. (Czech version: Vztah Britů k Československu v letech 1944–45, In: Vilém Prečan, *V kradeném čase*. *Výběr ze studií, článků a úvah z let 1973–1993*, Brno, Doplněk 1994, pp. 38–59).

Prečan, Vilém, Dokumenty sovětské éry v ruských archivech – nový pramen k československým dějinám 1941–1945 [Documents of the Soviet era in Russian archives – a new source to the Czechoslovak history 1941–1945], *Soudobé dějiny* [Contemporary history], Prague, Vol. 2, 1995, No. 4, pp. 609–628.

Pruessen, Ronald W., Od symbolu ke katalyzátoru a znovu k symbolu. Vývoj amerického chápání Československa a východní Evropy v letech 1943–1948 [Symbol to catalyst to symbol. The evolution of US perceptions of Czechoslovakia and Eastern Europe, 1943–1948], *Soudobé dějiny* [Contemporary history], Vol. 5, 1998, No. 2–3, 238–246.

Raška, Francis Dostál, Edvard Beneš a otázka služby sudetoněmeckých antifašistů v československé armádě za druhé světové války [Edvard Beneš and the question of the service of the Sudeten-German antifascists in the Czechoslovak army during the Second World War], In: *Na pozvání Masarykova ústavu* [At the invitation of The Masaryk Institute], Prague, Masarykův ústav AV ČR 2004, pp. 65–72.

Roberts, Geoffrey, The Soviet Decision for a Pact with Nazi Germany, *Soviet Studies*, Vol. 44, No. 1, 1992, pp. 57–78.

Robbins, Keith, Konrad Henlein, the Sudeten Question and British Foreign Policy, *The Historical Journal*, Vol. 12, 1969, No. 4, pp. 674–697.

Ross, Graham, Foreign Office Attitudes to the Soviet Union 1941–1945, *Journal of Contemporary History*, Vol. 16, 1981, pp. 512–540.

Seton-Watson, Christopher, R. W. Seton-Watson and the Czechoslovaks 1935–1939, In: *Great Britain, the United States and the Bohemian Lands*, eds. E. Schmidt-Hartmann – S. Winters, Munich, Oldenbourg 1991.

Sharp, Tony, The Origins of the 'Tehran Formula' on Polish Frontiers, *Journal of Contemporary History*, Vol. 12, 1977, No. 3, pp. 381–393.

Smetana, Vít, Beneš a Britové za druhé světové války [Beneš and the British during the Second World War], In: *Na pozvání Masarykova ústavu* [At the invitation of The Masaryk Institute], Prague, Masarykův ústav AV ČR 2004, pp. 73–86.

Smetana, Vít, Británie a československé zlato. 'Case study' britského appeasementu? [Great Britain and the Czechoslovak gold: A case study of British appeasement?], *Soudobé dějiny* [Contemporary history], Prague, Vol. 8, 2001, No. 4, pp. 621–658.

Smetana, Vít, Dejmkovo velké dílo pod drobnohledem [Dejmek's magnum opus under the microscope], *Soudobé dějiny* [Contemporary history], Prague, Vol. 11, No. 4, pp. 97–116.

Smetana, Vít, Levicový intelektuál v Churchillových službách. Moskevská mise sira Stafforda Crippse [Left wing intellectual in Churchill's services. Sir Stafford Cripps' Moscow mission], *Dějiny a současnost* [History and present], Prague, Vol. 18, 1996, No. 6, pp. 40–43.

Smetana, Vít, Mise Plukovníka Perkinse v kontextu britské politiky vůči Československu a pomoci jeho odbojovému hnutí na sklonku 2. světové války [Colonel Perkins' mission in the context of British policy towards Czechoslovakia and help for its resistance movement towards the end of the Second World War], *Historie a vojenství* [History and military], Prague, Vol. 50, 2001, No. 3, pp. 692–736.

Smetana, Vít, Nevyřízené účty. Problém československých aktiv v britských bankách a snahy britské administrativy o jeho řešení po 15. březnu 1939 [Accounts to be dealt with. The problem of Czechoslovak assets in British banks and British Government's attempts at its settlement after 15 March 1939], *Český časopis historický* [Czech historical journal], Prague, Vol. 102, 2004, No. 3, pp. 521–551.

Smetana, Vít, Old Wine in New Bottles? British Policy towards Czechoslovakia, 1938–39 and 1947–48, In: *Czechoslovakia in a Nationalist and Fascist Europe 1918–1948*, eds. M. Cornwall – R.J.W. Evans, Proceedings of the British Academy No. 140, Oxford – New York, Oxford University Press 2007, pp. 143–167.

Smetana, Vít: Ozvěny Mnichova v zahraničněpolitických jednáních za 2. světové války [The echoes of Munich in foreign policy negotiations during World War II], In: *Mnichovská dohoda. Cesta k destrukci demokracie v Evropě* [Munich agreement. The way to destruction of democracy in Europe], ed. J. Němeček, Praha, Karolinum 2004, pp. 145–163.

Smetana, Vít, Robert Bruce Lockhart and his patronage of Czechoslovak exiles and their political programme in Britain during the Second World War, In: *Exile and Patronage. Cross-cultural Negotiations beyond the Third Reich*, eds. A. Chandler – K. Stokłosa – J. Vinzent, Berlin, Lit Verlag 2006, s. 167–177.

Smetana, Vít, Sféry vlivu a Československo: oběť, nebo spoluarchitekt? [Spheres of influence and Czechoslovakia: victim or co-architect], In: *Československo na rozhraní dvou epoch nesvobody*, eds. Z. Kokošková – J. Kocian – S. Kokoška, Praha, Národní archiv – Ústav pro soudobé dějiny AV ČR 2005, pp. 58–65

Smetana, Vít, Sféry vlivu: mýtus, či realita? Jak se za války dělila Evropa [Spheres of influence: myth or reality? How Europe was being divided during the war], *Dějiny a současnost* [History and present], Prague, Vol. 27, 2005, No. 5, pp. 34–37.

Smetana, Vít, Sovětská hrozba očima Foreign Office na podzim 1939 [The Soviet menace viewed by the Foreign Office in autumn 1939], *Dějiny a současnost* [History and present], Prague, Vol. 18, 1996, No. 5, pp. 46–50.

Smetana, Vít, Vítězství geopolitiky nad ideologií. Sovětsko-německý pakt 1939 [The victory of geopolitics over ideology. The Soviet-German pact 1939], *Dějiny a současnost* [History and present], Prague, Vol. 21, 1999, No. 4, pp. 24–29.

Smetana, Vít, Zatracené závazky. Britové, Francouzi a problém garance pomnichovského Československa [Damned Commitments: The British, the French, and the problem of guaranteeing the security of Czechoslovakia after the Munich Agreement], *Soudobé dějiny* [Contemporary history], Prague, Vol. XI, 2004, No. 1–2, pp. 88–109.

Smutný, Jaromír, Edvard Beneš a československý odboj za druhé světové války [Edvard Beneš and Czechoslovak resistance in World War II], *Svědectví* [Testimony], Paris, Vol. 21, 1963, pp. 50–60.

Strang, Bruce, Once More unto the Breach. Britain's Guarantee to Poland, March 1939, *Journal of Contemporary History*, Vol. 31, 1996, pp. 721–752.

Strang, Bruce, Two Unequal Tempers: Sir Ogilvie-Forbes, Sir Nevile Henderson and British Foreign Policy, 1938–39, *Diplomacy and Statecraft*, Vol. 5, 1994, No. 1, pp. 107–137.

Šustek, Vojtěch, Státní rada v Londýně v letech 1940–1941 [The State Council in London, 1940–1941], *Sborník archivních prací* [Reports of archival works], Prague, Vol. 44, 1994, No. 2, pp. 239–333.

Táborský, Eduard, Beneš and the Soviets, *Foreign Affairs*, Vol. 27, Jan. 1949, pp. 302–314.

Táborský, Eduard, A Polish-Czechoslovak Confederation. A Story of the first Soviet veto, *Journal of Central European Affairs*, Vol. 9, 1950, pp. 379–395.

Táborský, Eduard, Benešovy moskevské cesty [Beneš's Moscow journeys], *Svědectví* [Testimony], Paris, Vol. 1, 1957, pp. 193–214.

Táborský, Eduard, The Triumph and Disaster of Eduard Beneš, *Foreign Affairs*, Vol. 36, 1958, pp. 669–684.

Táborský, Eduard, Politics in Exile, 1939–1945, In: Mamatey, Victor S., and Luža, Radomír, *A History of the Czechoslovak Republic*, Princeton (NJ), Princeton University Press 1973, pp. 322–342.

Táborský, Eduard, Beneš a náš osud [Beneš and our fate], *Svědectví* [Testimony], Paris, Vol. 57, 1978, pp. 17–50.

Velecká, Hana, Agónie appeasementu. Britská politika a rozbití Československa 15. 3.–31. 8. 1939 [The agony of appeasement. British policy and the break-up of Czechoslovakia 15. 3.–31. 8. 1939], *Český časopis historický* [Czech historical journal], Prague, Vol. 99, 2001, No. 4, pp. 788–822.

Velecká, Hana, Britská pomoc uprchlíkům z Československa od okupace do vypuknutí války v roce 1939 [British assistance to Czechoslovak refugees, from the German occupation till the outbreak of war in 1939], *Soudobé dějiny* [Contemporary history], Prague, Vol. 8, 2001, No. 4, pp. 659–691.

Watt, Donald Cameron, An Intelligence Surprise: The Failure of the Foreign Office to anticipate the Nazi-Soviet Pact, *Intelligence and National Security*, Vol. 4, 1989, No. 3, pp. 512–534.

Watt, Donald Cameron, British Intelligence and the Coming of the Second World War in Europe, In: *Knowing One's Enemies: Intelligence Assessment between the Two World Wars*, ed. E. R. May, Princeton, Princeton University Press 1984, pp. 237–270.

Watt, Donald Cameron, Chamberlain's Ambassadors, In: *Diplomacy and World Power. Studies in British Foreign Policy 1890–1950*, eds. M. Dockrill – B. McKercher, Cambridge, Cambridge University Press 1996, pp. 136–170.

Watt, Donald Cameron, Francis Herbert King. A Soviet Source in the Foreign Office, *Intelligence and National Security*, Vol. 3, 1988, No. 4, pp. 62–82.

Woodward, Sir E. Llewellyn, Some Reflections on British Policy, 1939–1945, *International Affairs*, Vol. 31, July 1955, pp. 273–290.

Wright, Quincy, The Munich Settlement and International Law, *American Journal of International Law*, 1939, No. 33.

Young, Robert J., French military intelligence and Nazi Germany, 1938–1939, In: *Knowing One's Enemies: Intelligence Assessment between the Two World Wars*, ed. E. R. May, Princeton, Princeton University Press 1984, p. 271–309.

Żurawski vel Grajewski, Radosław, Starania dyplomacji czechosłowackiej o cofnięcie uznania rządu brytyjskiego dla umowy monachijskiej (sierpień 1941 – sierpień 1942 r.) [Efforts of the Czechoslovak diplomacy to undo the British consent with the Munich Agreement (August 1941 – August 1942)], In: *Czechosłowacja w stosunkach międzynarodowych w pierwszej połowie XX wieku* [Czechoslovakia in international relations in the first half of the 20th century], ed. A. M. Brzeziński, Warszawa, Wydawnictwo Naukowe 2003, pp. 69–128.

Żurawski vel Grajewski, Radosław, Z historii stosunków brytyjsko-czechoslowackich w okrsie II wojny światowej (lipiec 1940 – lipiec 1941) [From the history of British-Czechoslovak relations in the course of World War II (July 1940 – July 1941), In: *Z polityki zagranicznej Wielkiej Brytanii w I połowie XX wieku* [From British foreign policy in the first half of the 20th century], ed. A. M. Brzeziński, Łódź, Wydawnictwo Uniwersytetu Łódzkiego 2002, pp. 102–127.

Theses

Child, Victoria, *British Policy towards the Soviet Union 1939–1942 with Special Reference to the Baltic States*, Unpublished D.Phil. Thesis, Oxford University 1994.

Ellinger, Jiří, *Od usmiřování k válce. Neville Chamberlain a britská zahraniční politika, 1937–1940* [From appeasement to war. Neville Chamberlain and British foreign policy, 1937–1940], Unpublished PhD. Thesis, Prague, Charles University 2005.

Smetana, Vít, *Enigma zahalená tajemstvím. Britská politika a Sovětský svaz v roce 1939* [Enigma wrapped in a mystery. British policy and the Soviet Union in the year 1939], Unpublished M.A. Thesis, Prague, Charles University 1997.

BIOGRAPHICAL NOTES*

Robert J. G. BOOTHBY, from 1958 baron Boothby, K.B.E. (1900–1986), British politician, educated at Eton and Magdalen College, Oxford. At the age of 24 he became Conservative M.P. for East Aberdeen and Kincardineshire, served as Parliamentary Private Secretary to the Chancellor of the Exchequer, 1927–9 and Parliamentary Secretary (Junior Minister) to the Minister of Food, 1940–1. He resigned following the investigation by the Parliamentary Committee of his concealed interest in further dealing with the Czechoslovak balances blocked in Britain. After the war he became one of the leading exponents of a united Europe and also worked at the BBC.

Brendan BRACKEN, from 1952 1st Viscount Bracken of Christchurch, P.C. (1901–1958), British politician, educated in Sydney, Australia and at Sedbergh School. A pro-British son of an Irish Nationalist and separatist was a newspaper proprietor, founded and edited *The Banker*, bought *The Economist* and became Chairman of *The Financial News*. He was Conservative M.P. for North Paddington, 1929–45 and for Bournemouth, 1945–51. He served as Churchill's Parliamentary Private Secretary, 1940–1, very successful Minister of Information, 1941–5 and briefly First Lord of the Admiralty, 1945.

Richard Austin BUTLER, later 1st Baron Butler of Saffron Walden, K.G., C.H. (1902–1982), British official and politician, educated at Marlborough and Pembroke College, Cambridge, *fellow* at Corpus Christi, 1925–9. From 1929 he was Conservative M.P. for Saffron Walden Division of Essex. He served as Parliamentary Under-Secretary of State at India Office, 1932–8 and at the Foreign Office, 1938–41; Minister of Education, 1941–5; Chancellor of the Exchequer, 1951–5; Lord Privy Seal, 1955–7; Home Secretary, 1957–62; Deputy Prime Minister, 1962; Foreign Secretary, 1963–4. A staunch supporter of Chamberlain's policy of appeasement, he later became a loyal colleague and admirer of Churchill. He was the leading influence in reviving the fortunes of the Conservative Party after its defeat in 1945, but twice, in 1957 and 1963, he failed to be chosen Prime Minister.

Sir Alexander George Montagu CADOGAN, G.C.M.G., K.C.B. (1884–1968), British diplomat and official, educated at Eton and Balliol College, Oxford, entered the Diplomatic Service in 1908, became head of the League of Nations section at the Foreign Office before appointment as Minister at Peking, 1934–5 and Ambassador, 1935–6; Deputy Under-Secretary of State, 1936–7 and Permanent Under-Secretary of State at the Foreign Office, January 1938 – February 1946; Permanent British Representative to the United

---

* Those politicians who during their career became prime ministers, presidents or dictators, and their biographical notes are thus easily accessible in numerous encyclopaedias, are not included. This applies to Clement Attlee, Edvard Beneš, Neville Chamberlain, Winston Churchill, Édouard Daladier, Anthony Eden, Zdeněk Fierlinger, Emil Hácha, Adolf Hitler, Milan Hodža, Vyacheslav Molotov, Benito Mussolini, Władysław Sikorski and Joseph Stalin.

Nations Organisation, 1946–50. His diaries, published in 1971, caused astonishment by their outspoken comments.

Alfred Duff COOPER, from 1952 1st Viscount Norwich, G.C.M.G., D.S.O. (1890–1954), British politician and diplomat, educated at Eton and New College, Oxford. He served with distinction as a lieutenant of the Grenadier Guards in the campaigns of 1918, then in the Foreign Office as Principal Private Secretary to two Ministers. He was a Conservative M.P. for Oldham, 1924–9 and for St. George's Division of Westminster from 1931; Financial Secretary to the War Office, 1928–9 and 1931–4 and to the Treasury, 1934–5; Secretary of State for War, 1935–7; First Lord of the Admiralty, 1937 – October 1938. He resigned owing to disagreement with governmental foreign policy. Churchill made him Minister of Information in 1940, but he was not considered a success and was replaced by Brendan Bracken a year later. He then became Resident Cabinet Minister for Far Eastern Affairs in Singapore and President of the Far Eastern War Council, 1941–2. In 1943 he became governmental liaison to the Free French and subsequently successful British Ambassador at Paris, 1944–8. He is the author of autobiography *Old Men Forget* (1953).

Edward Hugh John Neale DALTON, from 1960 Baron Dalton, known as Hugh Dalton, P.C. (1897–1962), son of the chaplain to Queen Victoria and tutor to the future King George V, educated at Eton and King's College, Cambridge. During World War I he served as a lieutenant on the French and Italian fronts. As a member of the Labour Party he failed in four attempts to get to Parliament in the early 1920s, before finally becoming M.P. for Peckham Division of Camberwell in 1924 and Bishop Auckland Division of Durham in 1929. He served as junior Foreign Office Minister in the second Labour government, 1929–31. Dalton opposed MacDonald's National Government and thus lost his seat in 1931. He taught at the London School of Economics before re-entering Parliament after the 1935 general election. He was a stark critic of appeasement and Munich. In 1940 Churchill appointed him Minister of Economic Warfare and he created the Special Operations Executive (SOE). In 1942 he became Minister of the Board of Trade. After the Labour victory in 1945 he became Chancellor of the Exchequer. He nationalised the Bank of England in 1946, but the following year was forced to resign after leaking secret budget details to a journalist and was replaced by his enemy Stafford Cripps. Dalton returned to the government in 1948 as Chancellor of the Duchy of Lancaster and served as Minister of Town and Planning in 1950–51. He wrote two books about his political career, *Call Back Yesterday* (1953) and *High Tide and After* (1962).

Paul EINZIG (1897–1973), British journalist specialising in economic and from World War II also political issues. He worked as a commentator of the *Financial News* in the 1930s and criticised governmental monetary policy, including the transfer of the Czechoslovak gold to Germany in 1939. He is the author of numerous books about monetary problems, position of central banks as well as economic systems in totalitarian regimes.

Edward Frederick Lindley Wood, from 1925 Baron Irwin, from 1934 Viscount HALIFAX, K.G., O.M., G.C.S.I. (1881–1959), British politician, educated at Eton and Christ Church, Oxford, later *fellow* at All Souls. Conservative M.P. for the York district Ribon, 1910–25. He served as Churchill's Under-Secretary of State for Colonies, 1921–2; Minister of Education, 1922–4; Minister of Agriculture, 1924–5; Viceroy of India, 1926–31; President of the Board of Education in the National Government, 1932–5; Secretary of State for War, 1935; Lord Privy Seal, 1935–7; Lord President of the Council, 1937–8; Secretary of State for Foreign

Affairs, 1938–40. At a crucial period in Anglo-American relations, in 1941–6, he was Ambassador to the United States. He was president or governor of 30 charity organisations and also Chancellor of the Oxford University, 1933–59.

Sir Nevile Meyrick HENDERSON, G.C.M.G. (1882–1940), British diplomat, entered the Diplomatic Service in 1905, served at Embassies in St. Petersburg, Tokyo, Rome, Paris, Constantinople and Cairo, then became Minister at Legations in Belgrade, 1929–35 and in Buenos Aires, 1935–7; from 29 April 1937 to 3 September 1939 he was Ambassador in Berlin, retired in March 1940. He is the author of memoirs *Failure of a Mission: Berlin, 1937–39* (1940).

Konrad HENLEIN (1898–1945), German politician in Czechoslovakia, educated at the Commerce Academy in Jablonec nad Nisou. He served voluntarily in the Austro-Hungarian Army during World War I and worked as a banking official in 1919–25. He became a gym-teacher in 1925 and chairman of the *Deutscher Turnerverband* in 1929, founded *Sudetendeutsche Heimatfront*, became its chairman in 1933 and transferred it into *Sudetendeutsche Partei* (SdP) in 1935. He was a deputy in the National Assembly, 1935–8, and as a chairman of the SdP presided over the movement favouring autonomy and later separation of the Sudeten German districts. He became *Reichskommissar* for the Sudeten German territories, deputy in the *Reichstag* and leader of the NSDAP in the Sudeten German province after Munich, head of the Civil Service in the Protectorate from mid-March to mid-April 1939 and then *Reichsgauleiter* of the Sudeten German province and also *Gruppenführer* and later *Obergruppenführer* SS. He committed suicide in May 1945.

Sir Samuel HOARE, from 1944 1st Viscount Templewood, P.C., G.C.S.I., G.B.E., C.M.G. (1880–1959), British politician, educated at Harrow and New College, Oxford. He was Conservative M.P. for Chelsea, 1910–45, served as Assistant Private Secretary to the Colonial Secretary in 1905; Secretary of State for Air, 1922–9; Secretary of State for India, 1931–5 and for Foreign Affairs, June-December 1935; First Lord of the Admiralty, 1936–7; Home Secretary, May 1937 – September 1939; Lord Privy Seal, 1939–40; Secretary for Air, 1940; Ambassador to Spain, 1940–4.

Robert Spear HUDSON, from 1952 Viscount Hudson of Pewsey, C.H. (1886–1957), British official and politician, educated at Eton and Magdalen College, Oxford. He served in the Diplomatic Service, 1911–1920; was Conservative M.P. for Whitehaven Division of Cumberland, 1924–9 and for Southport, 1931–7; Parliamentary Secretary to Minister of Labour in the National Government, 1931–5; Minister of Pensions, 1935–6; Parliamentary Secretary to Minister of Health, 1936–7; Secretary to the Department of Overseas Trade, 1937–40; Minister of Shipping, 1940 and of Agriculture and Fisheries, 1940–5. In 1953–7 he was Chairman of the Board of Governors at the Imperial Institute.

Sir Thomas Walker Hobart INSKIP, from 1939 1st Viscount Caldecote, C.B.E., P.C., K.C. (1876–1947), educated at Clifton and King's College, Cambridge. He became a Barrister in 1899, served in the Naval Intelligence Division from 1915 and at the Admiralty as head of the Naval Law Branch, 1918–9. He was Conservative M.P. for Central Bristol, 1918–29 and for Fareham, 1931–9; Solicitor General, 1922–3, 1924–8, 1931–2 and Attorney General, 1928–9 and then again in the National Government, 1932–6. He was Minister for Co-ordination of Defence, March 1936 – January 1939; Secretary for Dominions, January – September 1939; and Lord Chancellor in the War Cabinet, 1939–40. In Churchill's government he was briefly Secretary of State for Dominion Affairs in 1940 and then served as Lord Chief Justice of England and Wales, 1940–6.

Wenzel JAKSCH (1896–1966), German politician and journalist in Czechoslovakia. He got trained to be a bricklayer in Vienna where he was involved in the activities of social democratic youth. In 1919 he entered German Social Democratic Party of Workers, became member of its Central Committee, 1921 and of its Presidium, 1924, Deputy Chairman, 1935–8 and Chairman, 1938–9. He was deputy in the National Assembly, 1929–39. In 1938 he stood on pro-Czechoslovak positions and supported defence of territorial integrity of the state. He tried to mediate between the government, Sudeten Germans and British political circles. In 1939–49 he lived in exile in Britain and led opposition of part of Sudeten German democrats against the Czechoslovak government and President Beneš, namely against plans for post-war transfer of German inhabitants from Czechoslovakia. In 1949 he moved to Western Germany where he became a local official and deputy in the Bundestag for SPD. From 1951 he was Chairman of *Seliger-Gemeinde* and from 1959 Chairman of Federal Assembly of Sudeten German Landsmanschafts. He died in a car-accident.

Sir Hubert Miles Gladwyn JEBB, from 1960 1st Baron Gladwyn, known as Gladwyn Jebb, G.C.M.G., G.C.V.O. (1900–1996), British civil servant, diplomat and politician, educated at Eton and Magdalen College, Oxford. He entered the Diplomatic Service in 1924, served in Tehran, Rome and at the Foreign Office – as Private Secretary to Permanent Under-Secretaries of State, 1937–40. He was appointed to the Ministry of Economic Warfare as Chief Executive Officer for SOE in 1940, returned to the Foreign Office in 1942, became head of the Reconstruction Department, and was made a Counsellor in 1943. He attended numerous international conferences, including those in Tehran, Yalta and Potsdam, served as Executive Secretary of the Preparatory Commission of the United Nations in August 1945, being appointed Acting United Nations Secretary-General from October 1945 to February 1946 until the appointment of the first Secretary-General Trygve Lie. Upon his return to London, Jebb served as Deputy to Foreign Secretary Ernest Bevin at the Conference of Foreign Ministers before serving as Foreign Office's United Nations Adviser, 1946–7. He represented the United Kingdom at the Brussels Treaty Permanent Commission and became Deputy Under-Secretary at the Foreign Office, 1949–50. He suceeded Cadogan as Ambassador to the United Nations, 1950–4 and was Ambassador at Paris, 1954–60. He was Deputy Leader of the Liberals in the House of Lords, 1965–1988 and a Member of the European Parliament, 1973–6.

Sir Howard William KENNARD, G.C.M.G., C.V.O. (1878–1955), British diplomat, entered the Foreign Office in 1901, served at Embassies in Rome, 1903, Tehran, 1904 and Washington, 1907; Chargé d'Affaires in Havana, 1911 and Tangier, 1912; member of the FO staff, 1916 and Counsellor, 1919; Minister to Yugoslavia, 1925–9, to Sweden, 1929–31 and to Switzerland, 1931–4; Ambassador to Poland and to the Polish government in exile, 1935–41.

Sir Ivone Augustine KIRKPATRICK, G.C.B., G.C.M.G. (1897–1964), British official and diplomat, educated at Downside and Balliol College, Oxford. He served for four years in the Great War, then entered the Diplomatic Service and served in Rio de Janeiro, at the Foreign Office and in Berlin where he was the First Secretary in 1933–8. He was briefly head of the FO's Central Department, 1940; Director of Foreign Division of the Ministry of Information, 1940; adviser on foreign policy to the BBC until November 1940 and Controller of European Services, 1941–5. He returned to the Foreign Office after the war and was Assistant Under-Secretary of State, 1945; Deputy Under-Secretary, 1948; Permanent Under-Secretary for the German Section, 1949. He was British High Commissioner for Germany, 1950–3 and Permanent Under-Secretary of State at the Foreign Office, 1953–7. He is the author of memoirs *The Inner Circle. The Memoirs of Ivone Kirkpatrick* (1959).

Sir Reginald Wildig Allen LEEPER, K.C.M.G. (1888–1968), British civil servant and diplomat, educated at Trinity College, Melbourne and New College, Oxford. An Australian by birth, he entered the British Foreign Office in 1920, served at Embassies in Poland, 1923–5 and Turkey, 1925–9 and in 1929 joined the News Department. He is recognised as the founder of the British Council: in 1933 he assisted in creating of a Cultural Relations Committee – with the Board of Education and the Department of Overseas Trade, and in 1934 founded the organisation that was to be renamed the British Council. He was head of the newly set-up FO's Political Intelligence Department, 1938–40, and was in charge of SO1 – the propaganda branch of SOE – as Assistant Under-Secretary of State, 1940–41. He was Ambassador to Greece, 1943–5 and to Argentina, 1946–1948. After his retirement he held the honorary position of Vice President of the British Council, 1948–68.

Karel LISICKÝ (1893–1966), Czech diplomat. He fought as a legionnaire in France in World War I, from 1918 served in the Czechoslovak Diplomatic Service, as Legation Counsellor in London, 1934–9; Foreign Ministry official in London, 1939–45; and Minister at the Embassy in London, 1945. From 1948 he lived in exile.

Sir Robert Hamilton Bruce LOCKHART, K.C.M.G. (1887–1970), British journalist, author, secret agent and diplomat, educated at Fettes College. Born to a Scottish family, he joined the Diplomatic Service in 1911 and was Vice-Consul, later Acting British Consul-General in Moscow, 1914–7. He returned to Moscow as head of Special British Mission to the Bolshevik government in January 1918. His task was to counteract German influence and persuade the new Soviet government to allow a Japanese army onto Soviet territory to fight Germany. Instead, he and fellow British agent, Sidney Reilly, were accused of plotting against the Soviet regime, imprisoned in the Kremlin and condemned to death. However, they were exchanged for Maxim Litvinov, who was arrested by the British as a hostage. Lockhart served as Commercial Attaché in Prague, 1919–22, and made numerous friendships there. He worked in private banking, 1923–8 and as a journalist: he was member of the editorial staff of the *Evening Standard*, 1928–37. In September 1939 Rex Leeper invited him to join the Political Intelligence Department of the Foreign Office. He also served as a liaison officer to the Czechoslovak émigrés, and from July 1940 to autumn 1941 as a British Representative to the Czechoslovak provisional government. In 1941–5 he was head of the Political Warfare Executive. After the war he returned to writing, lecturing and broadcasting, and for over 10 years he had weekly BBC broadcasts to Czechoslovakia. He is the author of numerous books about Czechoslovakia, Britain's position in the world as well as several volumes of memoirs – including *Jan Masaryk, a Personal Memoir* (1956).

Ivan Mikhaylovich MAISKY (1884–1975), Soviet diplomat, historian and politician, educated at Historical Faculty of the Moscow University. He was born to a Russified Polish family, joined the Russian Social Democratic Labour Party and later its Menshevik faction. He was frequently arrested and twice exiled to Siberia. From 1908 he lived in Germany and Britain, but returned at the outbreak of the Russian Civil War and joined the local Communist government in Samara, for which he was banished from the Mensheviks. In 1921 he officially joined the All-Russian Communist Party (Bolsheviks) and became President of State Planning Committee of Siberia; Director of Press Department of People's Commissariat for Foreign Affairs, 1922–3; Counsellor at Embassies in London, 1925–7 and in Tokyo, 1927–9; Minister to Finland, 1929–32; and Ambassador to Great Britain, 1932–43. In 1943 he became Deputy Commissar of Foreign Affairs and was a member of Soviet delegations to the conferences in Yalta and Potsdam. In 1945 he retired from active service and devoted himself to the study of history, since 1946 he was a member of the Soviet Academy of Sciences. Shortly before Stalin's death in 1953 he was arrested and sentenced to six years in prison, but was released and fully rehabilitated two years later.

Sir Roger Mellor MAKINS, from 1960 1st Baron Sherfield, G.C.M.G., G.C.B. (1904–1996), British official and diplomat, educated at Winchester and Christ Church, Oxford. He was elected *fellow* at All Souls, Oxford, at the age of 21. He entered the Diplomatic Service in 1928 and served at Embassies in Washington and Oslo and in the FO's Central Department – in 1940–2 as its head. He seconded to the Treasury for service with the Minister Resident in West Africa from July to December 1942 and as Assistant to the Minister Resident at Allied Forces Headquarters, Mediterranean Command from January 1943 to September 1944. He served at the Embassy in Washington, 1945–7, then at the Foreign Office as Assistant Under-Secretary of State, 1947–9 and Deputy Under-Secretary of State, 1949–52. He was British Ambassador to the United States, 1953–6; Joint Permanent Secretary to the Treasury, 1956–60; and Chairman of the Atomic Energy Commission, 1960–4.

Sir Herbert William MALKIN, G.C.M.G., C.B. (1883–1945), British civil servant, educated at Charterhouse and Trinity College, Cambridge. He was called to the Bar at the Inner Temple in 1907, entered the Diplomatic Service in 1911, was Assistant Legal Adviser to the Foreign Office, 1914–25 and member of British delegations to several conferences, including the Paris Peace Conference in 1919 and the Washington Conference in 1920–21. He served as Second Legal Adviser, 1925–9 and Legal Adviser to the Foreign Office, 1929–45.

Sir Geoffrey Le Mesurier MANDER, K.B. (1882–1962), British politician and industrialist, educated at Harrow and Trinity College, Cambridge. He served in the Royal Flying Corps in World War I and was called to the Bar at the Inner Temple in 1921. He became chairman of Mander Brothers Ltd., paint and varnish manufacturers in Wolverhampton and led many progressive initiatives there including the introduction of the 40-hour week – as the first British company in 1931. He was also chairman of Aerostyle Ltd. and deputy chairman of Tung Oil Estates Ltd. He became Liberal M.P. for Wolverhampton East in 1929, actively opposed appeasement and supported the League of Nations in numerous parliamentary debates during the 1930s. He was Parliamentary Private Secretary to Secretary of State for Air Archibald Sinclair, 1942–5 and was expected to become Chief Whip for the Liberals in the House of Commons, but lost his seat at the 1945 general election, in the post-war Labour landslide

Jan MASARYK (1886–1948), Czech diplomat and politician. A son of the first Czechoslovak President, studied at a grammar school in Prague. He lived in the United States, 1906–13 and worked there in ironworks, then served in the Austro-Hungarian Army, 1914–8. From 1919 he was in the Czechoslovak Diplomatic Service – as Chargé d'Affaires in the United States, 1919–20 and Legation Counsellor at the Foreign Ministry in Prague, 1920–4. As Czechoslovak Minister to the United Kingdom in 1925–38 he made numerous friendships amongst British politicians, officials and intellectuals, but failed to anticipate the course of British foreign policy and inform his superiors in Prague accordingly. He became one of the key collaborators of President Edvard Beneš throughout the war as Minister of Foreign Affairs, 1940–5, Deputy Prime Minister, 1942–5 and Acting Minister of National Defence, 1944–5. Yet, his actual influence on Czechoslovak foreign policy was limited. On the other hand, he was generally regarded as a very skillful propagandist – a virtue that he made use of during his repeated long journeys to the United States and as a BBC broadcaster. He remained Minister of Foreign Affairs after the war and refused to resign with the other democratic ministers in February 1948. The circumstances of his death on 10 March 1948 remain a mystery.

Sir Basil Cochrane NEWTON, K.C.M.G. (1899–1965), British diplomat, educated in Wellington and at King's College, Cambridge. He served in the Diplomatic Service from 1912 to 1946, was Counsellor at Embassies in Peking, 1927–9 and in Berlin, 1929–35; Minister to Germany from August 1935 to December 1936 and to Czechoslovakia from December 1936 to March 1939; Ambassador to Iraq, 1939–41.

Sir Philip Bouverie Bowyer NICHOLS, K.C.M.G (1893–1962), British diplomat, educated at Winchester and Balliol College, Oxford. He served in the Great War, 1914–8, entered the Diplomatic Service in 1920, served at Embassies in Vienna, 1920–3, New Zealand, 1928–30 and as 1st Secretary in Rome, 1933–7. He was Acting Counsellor at the Foreign Office, 1937–41, Minister and from 1942 Ambassador to the Czechoslovak government in exile and to Czechoslovakia, 1941–5. He moved to Czechoslovakia and remained Ambassador there until December 1947, then was Ambassador to the Netherlands, 1948–51.

Sir George Arthur Drostan OGILVIE-FORBES, K.C.M.G. (1891–1954), British Army officer and diplomat, educated at New College, Oxford and Bonn University. He was Captain in the Scottish Horse Yeomanry, served in the Great War in Gallipoli, Egypt and Mesopotamia, and became member of General Staff at the War Office in 1918. He entered the Diplomatic Service in 1919, served repeatedly at the Foreign Office and at Legations in Stockholm, Copenhagen and Helsinki; was First Secretary at Legations in Belgrade, 1925 and in Mexico City, 1927–30; Chargé d'Affaires at the Holy See, 1930–2; Acting Counsellor at the Embassy in Baghdad, 1932–5; Counsellor in Madrid, 1935 and in charge of Embassy there, 1936. He was Counsellor at the Embassy in Berlin, 1937–9, and as Chargé d'Affaires there after Munich represented a counterweight to the pro-appeasement Nevile Henderson. He was Minister to Cuba in 1940–4.

Sir Owen St. Clair O'MALLEY, K.C.M.G. (1887–1974), British diplomat, educated at Hillbrow, Rugby, Radley and Magdalen College, Oxford. He entered the Foreign Office in 1911, was Counsellor at the Legation in Peking, 1925–7, at the Foreign Office, 1933–7; Minister to Mexico, 1937–8; in charge of the Embassy in Spain, 1938–9; Minister to Hungary, 1939–41; Ambassador to the Polish government in exile, 1942–5 and to Portugal, 1945–7.

Štefan OSUSKÝ (1889–1973), Slovak lawyer, diplomat and politician. He left Slovakia in 1906 and settled in the United States where he studied theology, philosophy and law. He was co-author of the Cleveland Agreement of 1915 proclaiming co-operation of the Czechs and Slovaks in the struggle for their liberation. From 1916 he was active in the Czechoslovak action in Europe, in 1917–8 as head of the Czechoslovak Press Bureau in Geneva. He was Czechoslovak Minister at Legations in London, 1918–20 and in Paris, 1921–40; Secretary General of the Czechoslovak delegation to the Paris Peace Conference in 1919; Czechoslovak representative at the Reparation Committee of the League of Nations, 1920–30; Chairman of the Control Committee of the League of Nations, 1922–36. He helped to create the Little Entente and supported the orientation of Czechoslovak foreign policy toward France. In March 1939 he refused to hand to the Germans the Czechoslovak Legation in Paris, but later that year he challenged Beneš's leading role in the Czechoslovak action abroad. He was a member of the Czechoslovak National Committee, 1939–40, and in 1940 became State Minister in the Czechoslovak government, but due to constant quarrels with President Beneš, primarily over the future form of Czech-Slovak coexistence, he left all his functions in 1942. After 1945 he lived in the United States where he co-operated with Czechoslovak democratic organisations set-up after 1948. He is an author of numerous political pamphlets, polemical brochures and also biographies of T. G. Masaryk and M. R. Štefánik.

Sir Eric Clare Edmund PHIPPS, G.C.B., G.C.M.G., G.C.V.O. (1875–1945), British diplomat, educated at King's College, Cambridge. He entered the Diplomatic Service in 1899, served at Embassies in Constantinople, Rome, Petrograd, Madrid and Paris. He was British Secretary to the Paris Peace Conference in 1919; Assistant Under-Secretary at the Foreign Office, 1919–20; Counsellor at the Embassy in Brussels, 1919–21; Minister to France, 1922–8 and to Austria, 1928–33; Ambassador to Germany, 1933–7 and to France, 1937–9.

Count Edward Bernard RACZYŃSKI (1891–1993), Polish politician and diplomat, educated in Leipzig, at the London School of Economics and University of Cracow. After a brief service in the Polish Army in 1918 he joined the Polish Diplomatic Service and served in Copenhagen, London and at the Ministry of Foreign Affairs in Warsaw. In 1932 he was appointed as Polish delegate to the League of Nations and represented Poland at the Disarmament Conference. He was Polish Ambassador in London, 1934–45 and also Acting Minister for Foreign Affairs in the Polish government in exile, 1941–3. He remained in Britain after the war, was a member of the Council of Three in 1954 and President of *Rzeczpospolita Polska na Uchodźctwie* [Polish Republic in exile], 1979–86. He published diaries – memoirs *In Allied London* (1962).

Joachim RIBBENTROP (1893–1946), German politician and diplomat. He was a member of the NSDAP from 1932 and was appointed the governmental representative for the disarmament issues. Hitler frequently charged him with various diplomatic tasks. He was Ambassador in London, 1936–8 and Minister of Foreign Affairs, 1938–45. He was found guilty in all four points of charge at the Nuremberg Trial, sentenced to death and executed.

Hubert RIPKA (1895–1958), Czech journalist, politician and historian, educated at the Faculty of Arts, Charles University in Prague. In the interwar period he worked as archivist and later primarily as a journalist specialising in international as well as domestic politics for *Demokratický střed* [Democratic centre], *Národní osvobození* [National liberation] and *Lidové noviny* [People's newspaper]. He was a member of the Czechoslovak National Democracy, and from mid-1930s of the Czechoslovak National Socialist Party. He supported foreign policy of President Beneš, but was a stark opponent of the Czechoslovak acceptance of the Munich Accord. He belonged to the first organisers of the Czechoslovak action in exile, was a member of the Czechoslovak National Committee, 1939–40, State Secretary, 1940–1 and State Minister in the Czechoslovak Foreign Ministry, 1941–5. At the same time he supervised the Czechoslovak BBC broadcasts. In 1945–8 he was a member of the Czechoslovak National Socialist Party Presidium and Minister of Foreign Trade. He resigned on 20 February 1948 and escaped from Czechoslovakia after the Communist take-over. Then he lectured in the United States on international politics and was a member of the Committee of the Council of Free Czechoslovakia. He is the author of numerous books on Central European affairs, modern history of Czechoslovakia and political developments in Yugoslavia and the USSR.

Sir Frank Kenyon ROBERTS, G.C.M.G., G.C.V.O. (1907–1998), British diplomat, educated at Rugby and Trinity College, Cambridge. He entered the Diplomatic Service in 1930, served at Embassies in Paris, 1932–5 and in Cairo, 1937, then in the Central Department – as its acting head in 1942–4. He also acted as Chargé d'Affaires to the Czechoslovak Government in London from 18 July to 6 October 1941. He became Minister Plenipotentiary in Moscow in January 1945 and served repeatedly as Chargé d'Affaires there in 1945–7. Known as 'the pocket Hercules of the Foreign Office' for his small stature and industrious-ness, he played an important role in the early years of the Cold War. In February 1945 he advised Churchill at the Yalta conference, a year later he sent a series of important despatches from Moscow analysing the Communist regime that are often compared to George Kennan's 'long telegram', and in 1948, as Principal Private Secretary of Foreign Secretary Ernest Bevin, he negotiated with Stalin over the Berlin blockade. He served as Assistant Under-Secretary of State, 1949; Deputy UK High Commissioner in India, 1949–51; Deputy Under-Secretary of State in the Foreign Office, 1951; UK Representative on the Brussels Treaty Commission, 1952–4; Ambassador in Belgrade, 1954–7; Permanent UK Representative to NATO, 1957–60; Ambassador in Moscow, 1960–3 and in Bonn, 1963–8. He is the author of rather belated memoirs *Dealing with Dictators* (1991).

Sir Orme Garton SARGENT, G.C.M.G., G.C.B. (1884–1962), British diplomat, nicknamed 'Moley', educated at Radley. He entered the Foreign Office in 1906, served at the Legation in Berne, 1917–9, was member of the British Delegation at the Paris Peace Conference in 1919 and served at the Embassy in Paris in 1920. He was Assistant Under-Secretary of State, 1926–39, then for seven years number 3 at the Foreign Office as Deputy Under-Secretary of State, and replaced Alexander Cadogan as Permanent Under-Secretary of State, 1946–9.

Sir John SIMON, from 1940 Viscount Simon, G.C.S.I., G.C.V.O., K.C. (1873–1954), British politician, educated at Fettes and Wadham College, Oxford, he became *fellow* at All Souls College, Oxford. He went to the Bar and in 1906 also to Parliament as a Liberal M.P. He was Solicitor General and then Attorney General in Asquith's pre-war government and Home Secretary in 1915–6. In 1928 he chaired a governmental commission that was sent to India to study constitutional reform. In 1931 he led a section of the Liberal Party into Ramsay MacDonald's National Government and then was for 14 consecutive years mem-ber of the government – as a fairly unpopular Foreign Secretary (1931–5), more esteemed Home Secretary (1935–7), and highly influential Chancellor of the Exchequer (1937–40). In 1940 Churchill made him Lord Chancellor, but outside the War Cabinet.

Sir Archibald SINCLAIR, from 1952 1st Viscount Thurso, P.C., K.T., C.M.G. (1890–1970), Brit-ish politician, educated at Eton and Sandhurst. He entered the Army in 1910, served under Churchill in the Great War and remained with him as his Personal Secretary at the War Office, 1919–21 and Colonial Office, 1921–2. In 1922 he was elected Liberal M.P. for Caith-ness and Sutherland and became Chief Whip of the Liberal Party, 1930–1. He was briefly Secretary of State for Scotland, but then he left the National Government on the issue of free trade. In 1935 he became Leader of the Opposition Liberals, vigorously opposed Chamberlain, Munich and appeasement, declined to bring his party into the government in September 1939, but was Secretary of State for Air under Churchill, 1940–5.

Jaromír SMUTNÝ (1892–1964), Czech diplomat, educated at Czech University in Prague. He was a legionnaire in Russia and France, 1916–8; entered the Czechoslovak Diplomatic Service in 1919 and served in Lyon and Marseille, 1920–7; Foreign Ministry in Prague, 1927–31; as Legation Counsellor in Warsaw, 1931–7; and at the Foreign Ministry and Presidential Office in 1937. He was head of the Diplomatic Protocol in 1938 and served briefly as Consul-General in Istanbul in early 1939. In March 1939 he offered his services to Edvard Beneš, left for Paris and later for London. He served as head of the Presidential Office in exile, 1940–5; and as Chancellor of the President in Prague, 1945–8. He remained in this office even after accession of Communist President Klement Gottwald in June 1948, but fled the country in July 1949. Later he headed the Edvard Beneš Institute in London. He is the author of documentary memoirs published during the 1950s in exile, as a collection entitled *Svědectví presidentova kancléře* [Testimony of the President's Chancellor] in 1996.

Robert Langford SPEAIGHT, C.M.G. (1906–1976), British civil servant and diplomat, educated at Oundle and Merton College, Oxford. He entered the Diplomatic Service in 1929, served at the Legation in Budapest, 1931–3 and Embassy in Warsaw, 1935–8 – as Charge d'Affaires in 1936, and at the FO's Central Department during World War II. He was transferred to Cairo, 1945–8; was Ambassador at Rangoon, 1950–3; Assistant Under-Secretary of State at the Foreign Office, 1953–6; Minister at Sofia, 1956–8.

Oliver Frederick George STANLEY, M.C., P.C., G.C.S.I. (1896–1950), British politician, educated at Eton. He fought throughout the Great War and reached the rank of Colonel, then went to the Bar and became Conservative M.P. for Westmoreland in 1924. He served as Parliamentary Under-Secretary to the Home Office, 1931–3; Minister of Transport, 1933–4; Minister of Labour, 1934–5; President of the Board of Education, 1935–7; President of the Board of Trade, 1937–40; Secretary for War, 1940. Churchill did not offer him an office he thought acceptable, but he returned to the government as Secretary of State for Colonies, 1942–5. He was also Chancellor of the University of Liverpool after the war.

Robert Jemmett STOPFORD (1895–1978), British civil servant. He served in the Great War and reached the rank of Lieutenant, then worked in various financial institutions and in 1938 also in the Treasury. He led negotiations on the Anglo-German payment agreement of 1938. He was a member of the Runciman mission and from November 1938 to the outbreak of the war he worked as Treasury's liaison officer for financial and refugee questions to the Czecho-Slovak and later Protectorate government. He served at the Ministry of Economic Warfare, 1939–40; as Financial Secretary at the Embassy in Washington, 1940–3 and at the War Office, 1943–5; then in the administration of the City of Trieste, 1946–9. In 1954–68 he was deputy director of the Imperial War Museum.

Sir William STRANG, from 1954 1st Baron Strang of Stonesfield, G.C.M.G., G.C.B. (1893–1978), educated at Palmer's School, University of London and Sorbonne. For his service in the Great War he was awarded M.B.E. He entered the Diplomatic Service in 1919 and served at the British Embassy in Belgrade, 1919–22; at the Foreign Office, 1922–30; and at the Embassy in Moscow, 1930–3. He was head of the League of Nations Section, 1933–7 and of the FO's Central Department, 1937–9. He accompanied Chamberlain to his meetings with Hitler at Berchtesgaden, Godesberg and Munich, and in June 1939 was sent to Moscow to try to negotiate a tripartite Anglo-Franco-Soviet Pact. He was Assistant Under-Secretary of State, 1939–43 and British representative on European Advisory Commission, 1943–5. After the war he was actively involved in the Foreign Office's reform. He served as Political Adviser to Commander-in-Chief of the British Forces in Germany Field Marshal Montgomery, 1945–7; Under-Secretary in the FO's German Section, 1947–9; succeeded Sargent as Permanent Under-Secretary of State at the Foreign Office, 1949–53. After his retirement he was chairman of several institutions including the Council of the Royal Institute of International Affairs, 1958–65, and he also served as Deputy Speaker and Chairman of Committees in the House of Lords. He is the author of several books on British history, the Diplomatic Service as well as memoirs *Home and Abroad* (1956).

Eduard TÁBORSKÝ (1910–1996), Czech lawyer, diplomat and political scientist, educated at the Faculty of Law, Charles University in Prague. He was Personal Secretary of Minister of Foreign Affairs Kamil Krofta, 1937–8. He fled Czechoslovakia in April 1939 and went to Britain via Poland. From July 1939 to May 1945 he was Personal Secretary and legal adviser of President Edvard Beneš. He served as Ambassador in Stockholm after the war, but resigned after the Communist takeover in 1948. He lectured at the University of Stockholm, 1948–9 and University of Texas in Austin from 1949. He is the author of books on modern Czechoslovak history and international communism, as well as documentary memoirs including *President Edvard Beneš between East and West 1938-1948* (1981).

Sir John Monro TROUTBECK, G.B.E., K.C.M.G. (1894–1971), educated at Westminster and Christ Church, Oxford. He entered the Diplomatic Service in 1920, served at Embassies and Legations in Constantinople, Addis Ababa, Rio de Janeiro and from 2 October 1937 until 25 May 1939 in Prague – from 1938 as Chargé d'Affaires. During the war he served at the Foreign Office and Ministry of Economic Warfare, then became Assistant Under-Secretary of State at the Foreign Office, 1946–7; was head of the British Office for the Middle East seated in Cairo, 1947–51; and Ambassador in Baghdad, 1951–5.

Sir Robert Gilbert VANSITTART, from 1941 1st Baron Vansittart, G.C.M.G., G.C.B., M.V.O. (1881–1957), educated at Eton. He entered the Diplomatic Service in 1902, served in Paris, Tehran, Cairo and Stockholm, and was George Curzon's Secretary in 1920–4. He then served as Assistant Under-Secretary of State, Prime Minister's Personal Secretary, 1928–30 and Permanent Under-Secretary of State in the Foreign Office, 1930–7. He was replaced by Alexander Cadogan and became Chief Diplomatic Adviser to the Government, 1938–41 – a newly created position in which he, however, lost his previous influence. Throughout the 1930s he was consequently pointing out the growing German danger and opposing the policy of appeasement. He also became known as a poet and writer.

Sigismund David WALEY, K.C.M.G., M.C. (1887–1962), British civil servant, educated at Rugby and Balliol College, Oxford. Apart from four years in the Army (1916–9), he served from 1910 until 1947 in the Treasury – as Deputy Secretary, 1924–37, Principal Deputy Secretary in the Department of Overseas Trade, 1931–46 and 3rd Secretary, 1946–7.

Sir Horace John WILSON, G.C.B., G.C.M.G., C.B.E. (1882–1972), British civil servant, educated at Kurnella School, Bournemouth, and London School of Economics. He served as a Secretary of the Committee on Production, 1915–8; Assistant Secretary to the Ministry of Labour, 1918–9; Principal Assistant Secretary, 1919–21 and Permanent Secretary,

1921–30; Chief Industrial Adviser to the government, 1930–5; seconded to the Treasury for service with the Prime Minister, 1935–39; Permanent Secretary of the Treasury and Official Head of the Civil Service, 1939–42. He was one of the most influential figures of Neville Chamberlain's era and protagonist of his 'personal diplomacy' before World War II.

Gustav WINTER (1889–1943), Czech journalist and official, educated at the Faculty of Arts, Charles University in Prague. He taught at a Grammar School in Prague before the First World War and then served for three years in the Austro-Hungarian Army. He was a secretary of the Czechoslovak Mission of Supplies at the Paris Peace Conference, 1919–20 and correspondent of the Social-Democratic newspaper *Právo lidu* [People's right] in Paris, 1920–38. He was active in the Czechoslovak action in exile from 1939, was an editor of *Česko-Slovenský boj* [Czecho-Slovak fight] and became an official in the section of information of the Ministry of Foreign Affairs. He is the author of several books about inter-war France.

Helmuth Christian Heinrich WOHLTHAT (1893 – after 1974), German officer and civil servant, educated at Military Academy and Cologne and Columbia Universities. He served in the First World War and reached the rank of 1st Lieutenant in 1917, then was Captain in the Reichswehr, 1919–32. He served in the Reich Ministry of Economics and became Ministerial Director for Special Allocations to Field-Marshal Göring in connection with the Four-Year Plan in 1938. In 1939 he led negotiations about German-Rumanian trade agreement and an economic mission to Spain, in 1940 he became Commissioner for the Dutch banks, and in 1943–4 he chaired German economic mission to Japan.

Abbreviations

C.B. – Companion of the (Order of the) Bath
C.B.E. – Commander of (the Order of) the British Empire
C.H. – Companion of Honour
C.M.G. – Companion of (the Order of) St. Michael and St. George
C.V.O. – Commander of (the Royal) Victorian Order
D.S.O. – Distinguished Service Order
G.B.E. – Knight Grand Cross of (the Order of) the British Empire
G.C.B. – Knight Grand Cross of (the Order of) the Bath
G.C.M.G. – Knight Grand Cross of (the Order of) St. Michael and St. George
G.C.S.I. – Knight Grand Commander of the Order of India
G.C.V.O. – Knight Grand Cross of the (Royal) Victorian Order
K.B. – Knight Bachelor
K.B.E. – Knight Commander of (the Order of) the British Empire
K.C.B. – Knight Commander of (the Order of) the Bath
K.C.M.G. – Knight Commander of (the Order of) St. Michael and St. George
K.C.V.O. – Knight Commander of the Royal Victorian Order
K.G. – Knight of (the Order of) the Garter
K.T. – Knight of the Order of the Thistle
M.B.E. – Member of (the Order of) the British Empire
M.C. – Military Cross
M.V.O. – Member of the Royal Victorian Order
O.B.E. – Officer of (the Order of) the British Empire
O.M. – Member of the Order of Merit
P.C. – Privy Councillor

INDEX*

---

* This index is ordered according to the English alphabet. Therefore the Czech letter "CH" is not re-garded as separate and the same applies to the accented letters such as "Č", "Š" etc.

VÍT SMETANA

IN THE SHADOW OF MUNICH
British Policy towards Czechoslovakia
from the Endorsement to the Renunciation
of the Munich Agreement
(1938–1942)

Published by Charles University in Prague
Karolinum Press
Ovocný trh 3, 116 36 Praha 1
Prague 2008
Vice-Rector-Editor prof. PhDr. Mojmír Horyna
Proof-reading Vladimír Bilčík M.Phil., B.A.
Cover and Layout by Zdeněk Ziegler
Typeset by MU typografické studio
Printed by tiskárna Nakladatelství Karolinum
First Edition
ISBN 978-80-246-1373-4